EVOLUTIONARY MACROECONOMICS

JOHN FOSTER
Department of Political Economy
University of Glasgow

London
ALLEN & UNWIN
Boston Sydney Wellington

Allen & Unwin, the academic imprint of

Unwin Hyman Ltd

PO Box 18, Park Lane, Hemel Hempstead, Herts HP2 4TE, UK
40 Museum Street, London WC1A 1LU, UK
37/39 Queen Elizabeth Street, London SE1 2QB, UK

Allen & Unwin Inc.,
8 Winchester Place, Winchester, Mass. 01890, USA

Allen & Unwin (Australia) Ltd,
8 Napier Street, North Sydney, NSW 2060, Australia

Allen & Unwin (New Zealand) Ltd in association with the Port Nicholson Press Ltd,
60 Cambridge Terrace, Wellington, New Zealand

First published in 1987

To Mishka

British Library Cataloguing in Publication Data

Foster, John, 1947-
Evolutionary macroeconomics.
1. Macroeconomics
I. Title
339 HB172.5
ISBN 0-04-339041-2

Library of Congress Cataloging in Publication Data

Foster, John, 1947-
Evolutionary macroeconomics.
Bibliography: p.
Includes index.
1. Macroeconomics. I. Title.
HB172.5.F67 1987 339 86-22231
ISBN 0-04-339041-2 (alk. paper)

Set in 10 on 11 point Bembo by Columns of Reading
and printed in Great Britain by
Billing and Sons Ltd, London and Worcester

Contents

Preface

This book began, as many do, in dissatisfaction with orthodox modes of thought. It was towards the end of the 1970s when, amidst the computer printouts of an applied macroeconomist, notes began to appear questioning this and that about the nature of the hypotheses that were, purportedly, being put to the test using econometric methods. No notion of a book existed then but, none the less, in retrospect, the beginning of the enterprise was at that time. By 1980, when I visited the University of British Columbia, momentum increased, particularly when I was asked by Keizo Nagatani to read and comment on a draft of his, then forthcoming, book *Macroeconomic Dynamics*. His book made it clear that once the Keynesian model, that we are so familiar with, is set in the Marshallian dynamic context of temporary equilibrium, the prospect of verifying hypotheses, using econometric methods and fixed parameter modelling, is remote indeed. My note writing began to increase and my appetite for computer output began to diminish. There seemed little point in continuing applied research when its methodological basis was so much in question. And there seemed every reason to search for new ways of looking at the macroeconomy.

Thus began several years of foraying into fields beyond economics in an attempt to stand on the outside looking in, to gain a better perspective. It was to prove to be a thoroughly 'unprofessional' strategy, with a *curriculum vitae* in which the flow of published academic papers began to dry up, but an enormously valuable one in terms of learning. Only a small fraction of that learning, and the mounds of notes which accompanied it, is directly reflected in this book, but its indirect influence is everywhere. It was in 1983 that this book could be meaningfully said to have begun its physical existence. Visiting the University of Adelaide in that year I was asked to take a special course called 'Topics in Advanced Economic Theory' which carried the unique privilege that subject matter was unspecified. The course I gave was, loosely speaking, an extended version of Chapters 2, 3 and 4 of this book and the enthusiasm of the students for the material went a long way to persuading me that the notion that macroeconomics should be set in an evolutionary context should be extended into a book. By the end of 1985 the process of distilling my compiled notes had created the remainder of the book.

The result is a book which is devoted to persuading students of economics that there is a case for an evolutionary approach to macroeconomics and that, furthermore, without such an approach, problems such as unemployment and inflation can neither be properly understood nor easily solved. Given the novelty of such a proposition, much of the book is devoted to explaining how evolutionary macroeconomics is different from orthodox macroeconomics, where such ideas come from and whether it is possible to develop a simple analytical framework within which evolutionary tendencies can be discussed. Given that phenomena such as inflation and unemployment are viewed as by-products, or manifestations, of more central evolutionary tendencies in the economic system, less attention is paid to formulating 'testable hypotheses' in the traditional manner and more to policy formulation, with these tendencies in mind. As such, it is very hard to pigeon-hole the book into accepted macroeconomic schools of thought. This is both its strength, providing the basis for a possible new consensus, and a weakness, encouraging rejection by all schools of thought.

The search for a macroeconomic perspective which transcends existing schools of thought really started at the beginning of my academic career at the University of Manchester in the early 1970s. At that time I was exposed to 'monetarist' thought through the sensible critiques of Keynesianism by David Laidler while, at the same time, a vocal post-Keynesian group expounded the advantages of moving Keynesianism in the direction of political economy. It was possible to see great merit in the view of both Milton Friedman and Joan Robinson from their own very different perspectives! Of course, the problem with learning two economic languages instead of one was that it bred an ambivalence which proved uncomfortable for both camps. However, my career took me to the University of Glasgow where such divisions were of no great importance and I was introduced to a third perspective: that of Adam Smith whose writings I read carefully and contemplated for the first time. The seeds of an evolutionary perspective were sown.

Whether or not the evolutionary perspective on macroeconomics, that is no more than a sapling in this book, will grow and survive depends greatly on its wide appeal to readers of all types. It certainly has strong roots, in the form of Keynes's theory of effective demand, and flexibility, which comes from explicit acknowledgement of the validity of the new Classical school's critique of Keynesianism. Furthermore, the book has been written in as non-technical a way as possible to permit readers from widely varying backgrounds to digest its contents. However, that does not mean that the arguments are necessarily straightforward. It is hoped that difficulty in comprehension will draw readers towards the extensive references provided, most of which are not normally encountered in a book on macroeconomics. An undergraduate with a good grounding in intermediate macroeconomics should find no difficulty with the 'commentary' in the first third of the book, after which he or she may be even better placed than a specialized academic economist to cope with the second third of the book. The last third of the book deals with material which relates to topics which a third/fourth year undergraduate or a postgraduate in economics would be dealing with in their coursework in macroeconomics. Indeed, it is hoped that the book will prove attractive to such students as a companion to their more orthodox material and provide the basis for seminar discussion, term papers, etc. Also, students who are fortunate enough to be exposed to Richard Nelson and Sidney Winter's *An Evolutionary Theory of Economic Change* in their advanced microeconomics course will find this book a highly compatible companion. Finally, it is hoped that the penultimate chapter of the book on stagflation policy will be of interest to a wide range of readers interested in economic policy.

I have had many conversations and discussions in the course of writing this book but I would particularly like to thank Bruce Chapman and Keizo Nagatani for allowing me to take up so much of their time discussing ideas that did or did not finish up in this book. I am particularly grateful to Bruce for his encouragement and advice while I was developing the policy proposal in Chapter 12. I would also like to thank my class of '83 at the University of Adelaide for allowing me to test new material on them and for their comments, discussion and general friendliness. Special thanks are reserved for my wife, Mishka Bienkowski, who discussed and debated so many of the ideas in the book as well as providing the necessary encouragement to finish the project. Responsibility for the end result and all its flaws remains, of course, with me.

1 *Introduction*

> The work force is disgusted downs tools and walks,
> innocence is injured experience just talks,
> everyone seeks damages and everyone agrees,
> that these are 'classic symptoms of a monetary squeeze',
> on ITV and BBC they talk about the curse,
> philosophy is useless theology is worse,
> history boils over there's an economics freeze,
> sociologists invent words that mean 'Industrial Disease'.
>
> Mark Knopfler (1982)

It is now commonplace to point out that there is a 'crisis' in economics. As the major economies of the world have been subjected to inflation and rising unemployment over the past decade or so, this view has become widespread. Economists are seen as being unable to agree or to offer clear recommendations to policy-makers. Thus, the crisis is primarily one in macroeconomics, since it is in the area of macroeconomic policy that failure is perceived. Despite protests by economists that there is a great deal more unanimity on issues than would appear, the old adage that 'there is no smoke without fire' seems to hold true. Academic economists have become over-preoccupied with critiques of opposing schools of thought while the old Keynesian consensus in macroeconomics, which prevailed for more than a quarter of a century has been all but extinguished.

Here we shall not be centrally concerned with critiques but, instead, with a search for new directions, beyond the old Keynesian consensus, which can provide analytical guidance to the applied macroeconomist. At the present time, the empirical methodologies available to the applied macroeconomist are guided less by economic theory and more by statistical technique; such is the importance of being able to provide reliable forecasts of key macroeconomic variables. At the same time, the specialization which has taken place in modern economics has ensured that formalism has attained high status in a discipline aspiring to establish itself as a science. However, in mimicking the methods used in, for example, physics, economics now has econometric theorists and mathematical economists who, in their own distinctive ways, have little to offer the applied economist attempting to grapple with real world issues and problems.

Critiques grow easily from such a situation but what is more difficult is the task of attempting to provide something new. Such is the nature of intellectual inertia that this kind of enterprise is likely to be opposed by an unholy alliance of established combatants, leaving the adventurous contributor with no more than the hope that when the defensiveness of such interest groups has passed, that his or her thesis will still be relevant enough to be taken seriously. Good applied economists have never allowed themselves to become swayed by dogmatic arguments. Their understanding of the complexities of the real world places them beyond such debates, seeing different methodologies as simply a collection of tools for different jobs. Only a very limited number of generalizations are accepted as in some sense universal – for example Alfred Marshall's treatment of partial equilibrium of demand and supply in microeconomics or John Maynard Keynes's principle of effective demand in macroeconomics.

There have been many great applied economists in history and, in recent times, the name of Arthur Okun inevitably springs to mind. In his last years he turned his attention away from the diverse economic problems that he tried to design policy to solve, towards the promotion of his overall view of the actual structure of the economy. The vision of the economy that he provided, although presented in the familiar language of orthodox economics, is one that is different to that contained in the principal schools of economic thought. As such, his vision has proved almost indigestible to orthodox economists concerned with providing theories of how the macroeconomy functions.

Our purpose here is, in a sense, to move towards the empirical features of the economy identified by Okun, not by trying to build up from the micro-level, as he did, but rather by arguing that there exist holistic behavioural generalizations at the macro-level that we can work down from. Many of these generalizations were recognized by Okun in his discussions concerning, for example, the role of custom in contractual behaviour. Here, the idea of the existence of holistic, irreducible macro-behaviour will be consolidated and related to macroeconomics as it is commonly understood. By attempting to relate to orthodox macroeconomics on its own ground it is hoped that many of the insights of Okun, as well as many others that we shall discuss, can be seen as specific aspects of more general behaviour.

Once we escape reductionism and the micro–macro

dichotomy, we find ourselves in a world of multilayered behaviour that has dynamic characteristics which can only be conceived of in an evolutionary manner. In orthodox macroeconomics evolutionary behaviour, if considered at all, has usually been relegated to the esoterics of long-run growth processes. The short run has been conceived of as static in evolutionary terms. Much of this book attempts to persuade that macroeconomics must always have an evolutionary perspective, even in the short run. The adoption of such a perspective has already occurred in microeconomics in the many papers and books of Richard Nelson and Sidney Winter. The evolutionary perspective that they espouse has a long history but, in recent times, these authors have perhaps done more than others to attempt to draw together orthodox and evolutionary economic theory.

In this book we are concerned with generalizations suitable for the macroeconomic level of analysis. It is doubtful if this would have been possible without the recent availability of richly developed evolutionary microeconomic models by Nelson and Winter, as well as a number of other authors, to refer the reader to. However, what is being presented here is not merely an aggregation of such models, or a new kind of reductionism. It will be argued that analysis of the macroeconomic system requires an evolutionary approach which is different, in a qualitative sense, to that employed to analyse the 'natural selection' of firms and their products at the microeconomic level. In the economic sphere of behaviour, such selection processes are seen as requiring the pre-existence of certain stability and continuity features of the macroeconomic system which also evolve. 'Complementarity' and 'compatibility' are the words which link micro and macro in evolutionary dynamics.

It is also worth emphasizing, from the outset, that this book is not a development of the new 'socio-biological' approach to evolutionary behaviour, which conceives of individual behaviour as influenced by 'selfish genes'. Although such a genetic approach has obvious uses in explaining sociological behaviour, it will be argued here that, when we are dealing with complex economic behaviour involving imagination and creativity, such an approach is too limited to explain the patterns of behaviour that we observe. However, the general notion that common consciousness exists does constitute an important part of the analysis here and provides the basis for identifying macro–micro links in economic behaviour.

The word evolution tends to conjure up Charles Darwin and 'survival of the fittest' in the popular mind. Social Darwinism has a long history but it is a tradition which has little role to play here. Theories of evolution have moved on in the biological sciences to include harmonious phases in development where 'survival of the fitting', to use Kenneth Boulding's phrase, is more appropriate. Just as social Darwinism is compatible with Adam Smith's 'invisible hand' in the competitive market place, so this new emphasis suits Arthur Okun's 'invisible handshake' in evolving contractual systems. More importantly, this 'new view' of evolution can encapsulate the kind of harmonious economic behaviour that we conceive of in Keynesian macroeconomics.

Throughout the book, great emphasis is laid on the importance of Keynes's ideas because, in evolutionary terms, they stood the test of time and facilitated a phase of evolutionary economic development which has all the characteristics of the new view of evolution. By approaching Keynes in this way, many questions as to whether he was 'right' or 'wrong' become irrelevant. As evolution proceeds, ideas, like organic structures, gradually become obsolete and have to adapt. Failure to do so means that the Darwinian vision of struggle and selection may, indeed, become relevant, with catastrophic effects that are even more violent in human affairs than the theory of natural selection would predict. The Darwinian theory envisages a process of continuous struggle and selection, but as soon as we adopt the new view of long harmonious phases of evolution, we must also accept the related possibility of serious discontinuities.

Evolution is frequently associated with determinism. However, in the discussion and analysis to follow it will be argued that, in the case of a process as sophisticated as economic evolution, development is promoted and catastrophe avoided by the continual application of human imagination and creativity. In as much as these qualitative factors are within human control, then the evolutionary process cannot be deterministic despite the fact that it always contains deterministic features. The forward-looking dimension of economic behaviour, in contrast to the stimulus–response behaviour frequently observed in biological behaviour, counters determinism.

Since our terms of reference are macroeconomic, the kind of forward-looking behaviour that receives most attention in the book is concerned with collective expectations and aspirations and forward-looking actions embodied in social rather than individual contracting. It is in this forward-looking context that the degree of interdependence between macro and micro is emphasized most strongly. Equally, it is in these regions that orthodox macroeconomics has had most difficulty, from Keynes's perceptive acknowledgement of such interdependence through to modern ideas about rational expectations, which try to avoid the implications of this interdependence by making excessively strong and unrealistic assumptions about macro–micro links. Expectations belong in a dynamic setting and, given the manner in which much knowledge is commonly held, the appropriate level of aggregation must be macroeconomic.

One of the main reasons why macroeconomics has remained non-evolutionary for so long is the fact that evolution involves structural change, complicating prediction using comparative–static equilibrium modelling. As the book unfolds the popular vision of the macroeconomist, as someone engaged in administering shocks to such systems in order to examine the effects on target variables, is challenged in a fundamental way. In evolutionary macroeconomics, the macroeconomist is viewed much more as a systems analyst designing policy strategies to facilitate evolution. The nihilist view, that abandonment of the comparative–static equilibrium framework means that empirical methods cannot be used, is countered by the view that evolutionary processes are stable and systematic enough to be verified in empirical terms.

Economists, in their quest for scientific status, have tended to ask too much of the imperfect, secondary source, time-series data that they have been forced to use. Hypothesis testing has become increasingly fashionable, despite the fact that the data frequently support several competing hypotheses, thus breaching the falsifiability criterion so important in other sciences. This obsession with the methodology of the experimental sciences has tended to draw economists away from using their data to its best advantage. Economic time-series data provide a rich picture of the structure of the economic system and how it is evolving. Such a picture provides more than merely descriptive statistics, as any time-series forecaster will attest; it also provides the basis for the isolation of logical propositions concerning the behaviour of the system as a whole. Keynes's depiction of the circular flow of income and the development of the principle of effective demand remains the most spectacular example of this kind of marriage of time-series data and systems logic.

In outlining what this book is about the name Keynes keeps recurring and, indeed, it will be argued that his ideas and their mutation in the Keynesian era provide the starting point for an evolutionary approach to macroeconomics. However, we do not choose to dwell on Keynesian exegesis in this book but, instead, appeal to Keynes's vision repeatedly, whenever it seems appropriate to relate to it, throughout the book. In Chapter 2 we begin, not with Keynes, but with the Keynesian consensus which followed after his death. In true evolutionary spirit, our quest is to discover the origins of decline in the history of this highly successful consensus. We shall also discuss monetarism which is viewed as a manifestation of this decline, rather than a distinctive school of thought in macroeconomics.

In Chapter 3 we examine how the truly distinctive new Classical school developed once the monetarist controversies had weakened the grip of the Keynesian consensus. Adopting a pre-Keynesian view of the nature of the macroeconomy, this new school is viewed as being deliberately strong in the areas where the Keynesian consensus was weak, namely on the 'supply side' and in taking adequate account of expectational processes. In other words, despite the tendency to be theoretically backward, the new Classical school is seen as emphasizing those very areas where Keynesian development must take place. Furthermore, it is the new Classical school which has exposed, through the Lucas critique of policy evaluation, the lack of an evolutionary perspective in Keynesian macroeconomics.

The theme of Keynesian development is the topic of Chapter 4 where the new contractual approach to macroeconomics is evaluated in terms of its ability to take up the new Classical challenge. It is discovered that the modern literature on implicit contracts in the labour market remains so narrowly defined and wedded to orthodox formal modelling that it cannot be generalized to the macroeconomic context in a way that challenges new Classicism. So what began as a promising approach to the explanation of sticky wages is viewed as having foundered because contractual theorists chose merely to extend orthodox micro-foundations rather than replace them. In the second part of the chapter, by way of contrast, a broad-brush sketch of a macroeconomy, which places the contract at the centre of the analysis, is presented. This sketch is designed to raise more questions than it answers and provides the basis for a journey beyond the limits of orthodox economics.

This journey begins in Chapter 5 which enquires as to the nature and validity of the non-economic premisses that lie behind the constructs used in orthodox macroeconomics. These foundations are seen to be derived from philosophy and biology and to operate at two levels. First, scientific materialism is driven on by Darwinist competitive forces and second, *homo economicus* conceptions of individual behaviour ensure a Walrasian competitive outcome. As such, these foundations are viewed as no more than creeds and it is the religious-like aspects of these foundations that are seen as making them so difficult to dislodge. Several of the notable attempts to modify these foundations, through the incorporation of psychological and sociological dimensions, are discussed. However, despite some success in enriching the depiction of microeconomic behaviour, none are seen as having managed to dislodge the simple constructs necessary for macroeconomic analysis.

In Chapter 6 we move beyond economics into the fields of biology and philosophy themselves in order to find out more about the bio-philosophical foundations of macroeconomics. Here we discover that the traditional Darwinian theory of biological evolution has been modified in important ways and that the philosophical construct from which *homo economicus* is derived has come under heavy attack over the past two decades. Instead, the qualitative forces which bind systems together and the creativity necessary for dynamic change are made the centre of attention. This 'systems approach' in both biology and philosophy has obvious parallels in economic systems with implications for the way that we view the macroeconomy and its motion over time.

In Chapter 7 the task of developing these implications begins with a discussion of how the nature of consciousness varies, depending on the level of structural complexity that we study. It is argued that the level of consciousness at which economic behaviour can be classified is not consistent with either the application of simple Darwinian evolutionary dynamics or the *homo economicus* construct. In particular, identification with the consciousness of the individual in the latter is seen as inadequate, particularly in the context of macroeconomic behaviour. Instead, the individual is conceived of as a personality which is composed of a set of consciousnesses ranging from collective ones such as 'the nation' or 'the firm' down to idiosyncratic dimensions of individual personalities. The essence of economic consciousness is seen as being creative, constructive and engaged in coordination, operating at many different levels. We call this consciousness *homo creativus* and identify six postulates which are necessary to capture the essence of its evolutionary dynamics.

In Chapter 8, having created this general construct, we proceed to constrain it by assumptions which enable us to provide a framework suitable for examining behaviour in the short run of evolutionary time. The main purpose of this exercise is to demonstrate the timelessness of the *homo economicus* construct and its aggregation, the Walrasian system, as well as to show how Keynes's principle of effective demand is compatible with an evolutionary approach, provided we remain in the short run. However, Keynes's model is seen as preliminary and incomplete in such a framework, adopting an overly rigid stock/flow dichotomy, suitable for the analysis of system malfunction but unsuitable to deal with evolutionary development.

In Chapter 9 assumptions are relaxed, enabling us to consider the long run of evolutionary time, not for its own sake, but to emphasize how perceptions of the long run are likely to affect behaviour in the short run, which is dominated by outstanding historical commitments. We discuss how it is rational in such circumstances to pursue specific developmental paths for long periods and how inflexibility can result in catastrophic behavioural shifts. It is argued that the inertial quality of economic structure, emphasized by Keynesians, and the forward-looking dimension of economic consciousness, emphasized by rational expectation theorists, can be treated in a unified way in the dynamic framework developed.

In Chapter 10 we return, explicitly, to the macroeconomic level of analysis. The purpose is to argue, not for the augmentation of Keynesian 'demand side' analysis with a suitable 'supply-side', but rather to set the Keynesian model in a short run which is evolutionary in character. To this end, proposals are made whereby the manner in which we analytically divide the macro system is changed to the creativity–production–maintenance delineation that an evolutionary approach demands. It is shown that such an analytical framework is capable of tracing the short-run shifts in economic structure and consciousness upon which long-run economic development depends.

In Chapter 11 this analytical framework is used to discuss the actual evolution of the postwar mixed economy. Propositions are made which would require a rearrangement of macro-data before it could be established whether or not they receive empirical support. However, it is also argued that existing configurations of macro-data shed some light on the process of evolution provided appropriate econometric techniques are adopted. Throughout this empirical discussion it is emphasized that in no sense is a 'hypothesis testing' methodology being proposed. The evolutionary process discussed is in the nature of logical proposition, with empirical methods merely unveiling the historical character of such a process in selected epochs. The purpose of empirical work in this context is to forecast more clearly the process of structural change so that it influences economic consciousness sufficiently to precipitate appropriate structural modifications.

In Chapter 12 we move directly into the zone of economic policy, illustrating the kind of policy required to facilitate evolution in the economic circumstances of the late 1980s. The case selected is the design of an anti-inflation policy as a logical evolutionary development of Keynesian stabilization policy. This new policy attempts to address the perceived weaknesses in Keynesian theory and policy highlighted throughout the book. It does not *replace* Keynesianism but, instead, *augments* it in such a way that evolution can proceed from the configuration of unemployment, low growth and inflation-proneness that characterizes a modern economy such as the UK. However, the proposal remains only an illustrative example designed to precipitate debate and discussion as to how an actual implementable policy could be specified in a way that, in some crude sense, could permit economic evolution to proceed.

2 *The Decline of the Keynesian Consensus*

> The 1930s have been described as the years of high theory, but all the great mass of work that has been done since and the proliferation of academic economic teaching has been very little illuminated by the ideas that emerged at that time, and there are no consistent and accepted answers to the questions that were then raised.
>
> Joan Robinson (1980)

Today, the majority of economists have come to accept that orthodox Keynesian economics can no longer assume the central place in macroeconomic theory and policy that it had done for over a quarter of a century. The Keynesian consensus, within which competing schools of thought could be placed as special cases, has given way under the weight of three bouts of stagflation and external shocks of increasing severity.[1] Traditional Keynesian policy prescriptions have been unable to address simultaneous inflation and unemployment, forcing governments to choose one of these targets at the expense of the other. In the space of a decade, for example, successive Republican and Conservative administrations in the US and UK respectively, switched from emphasis on an expansionary stance to alleviate unemployment to a contractionary stance to reduce the rate of inflation. This change of priorities was accompanied by a preference for monetarist modes of thought concerning the functioning of the macroeconomy even though, in practice, actual policy amounted to Keynesian intervention rather than the strict application of monetarist prescriptions.[2]

In this chapter an attempt will be made to chart the decline of the Keynesian consensus concerning macroeconomic policy, with the focus of attention, not on actual policy decisions, but on the shifts in economic thinking which accompanied macroeconomic change. Consensus involves some degree of unity between economists and policymakers concerning the links between certain basic economic principles and policy actions so that the political pragmatism which surrounds all policy can be anchored to some unquestioned economic beliefs. When such beliefs become untenable, policy-makers are left with only pragmatism, where political priorities tend to dominate economic goals and economists find that they have little pervasive influence on decision-making. We shall begin with an overview of the current crisis in macroeconomic policy then move back in time to the origins of the Keynesian consensus, on to its heyday and, finally, its decline.

The Current Crisis in Anglo–American Macroeconomic Policy

The 1980s have witnessed a pronounced shift away from Keynesian principles in Anglo-American macroeconomic policy. In the United States, the Reagan/Volcker programme of monetary and fiscal curbs had profound repercussions on the world economy. However, political pressures ensured that this new hawkish policy stance would be short lived so that, although monetary control continued to be practised, increases in defence spending reintroduced a strong Keynesian flavour, albeit in an environment of much higher interest rates than had prevailed in the past. In order to observe a much more determined and sustained attempt to apply recessionary policy principles, we must look to the experience of the UK, where Mrs Thatcher pursued, relentlessly, the elimination of inflation while allowing the rate of unemployment to triple. The American observer has much to learn from this British experience given that a central part of the policy was the removal of public deficits. The British problems of today could be the American ones of tomorrow.

The abandonment of unemployment in favour of an inflation target by Mrs Thatcher's government in the UK was met by widespread disapproval amongst economists, particularly when contractionary measures were accompanied by various policy expedients which enhanced the relative position of the better off.[3] However, these latter kinds of political manoeuvres have always been undertaken by Conservative governments in the past; all that happened was that the adoption of contractionary policy brought such redistributive measures into sharper focus. There is nothing uniquely 'Conservative' about the abandonment of Keynesian principles. On the contrary, postwar British history suggests that these principles were espoused at least as strongly by the Conservatives as by the Labour party.[4] In fact, it is Harold Macmillan who always springs to mind as the great Keynesian practitioner and Edward Heath as the prime minister who applied these principles to the bitter end. Support for traditional Keynesian stabilization policy had begun to melt away in Parliament before Mrs Thatcher made her dramatic thrust for power. Monetary control and fiscal stringency were practised under the Callaghan administration, albeit with an IMF threat concentrating the minds of reluctant Labour cabinet ministers.

When Mrs Thatcher pronounced that 'there is no alternative' to her policy, in a fundamental sense she was correct, speaking as a politician requiring pragmatic advice from economists in managing the economy. By the end of the 1970s all schools of macroeconomic thought had come to accept that expansionary macroeconomic policy to alleviate unemployment was accompanied, increasingly, by inflation and balance of payments deficits. The availability of proven methods of controlling prices and incomes was strictly limited and, in any case, the Conservatives had no rapport with the trade unions to aid such an initiative. The horrors of the Heath experiment with controls, which had little trade union support, remained vivid in Mrs Thatcher's memory. Controls were regarded as distorting and inefficient and the works of Milton Friedman and F. A. Hayek were frequently cited to support the view that they were not a feasible option to a government broadly committed to the free market.[5]

Any pragmatic politician will seek an economic theory to provide some kind of logical or empirical rationale which can provide the rhetorical backing for policy actions.[6] Such a theory must be straightforward in its logical structure so that it is communicable, it must be supported by an impressive array of 'scientific' results and it must offer prescriptions which are feasible within the policy transmission channels inherited from the previous government. In the early postwar period Keynesianism fitted the bill but, in 1979, it was monetarism which offered all these things. The quantity theory of money was easy to grasp intuitively, it offered an impressive array of econometric results to the layman and the intermediate objective of monetary control seemed attainable within the framework of monetary policy that existed. The theory reassured that, in as much as monetary control generated unemployment, it would only be a temporary phenomenon.

In retrospect, we know that such a rosy picture did not exist. The quantity theory of money was not as simple as it looked because no one was sure exactly how to define money, the econometric results proved ambiguous and misleading when used for policy purposes and the monetary framework was insufficient to control accurately a chosen monetary target. The budget deficit was perceived as the main cause of monetary control problems, so cuts in government spending were initiated inducing a contractionary fiscal effect which generated much higher unemployment than had been anticipated in the pure monetarist strategy. In turn, the resultant tax losses and increased welfare support caused endogenous pressure to push the budget deficit up again. The hope that higher unemployment was a temporary phenomenon had to be abandoned, particularly when it became clear that the decision to push up the exchange rate as well as interest rates to high levels led to the destruction of industrial capacity which could not be replaced in the near future.[7]

So, interest in monetarist theory was replaced by a pragmatic quest to reduce inflation by 'Keynesian' means, by reducing the budget deficit. However, this did not mean that Mrs Thatcher's rhetoric had readmitted Keynesianism. Instead, there was a reversion to homespun parables about the need to balance the budget, withdrawal of government through privatization and weakening the trade unions, now 'guilty' after their short spell of 'innocence' in her initial phase of monetarism.[8] Monetarism was perceived to have foundered because the economic system was too Keynesian, thus free market principles necessitated intervention to render it less Keynesian and, therefore, more efficient. Mrs Thatcher began to engage in economic restructuring exercises which echoed the prescriptions of the emerging supply-side and new Classical schools of thought which had come to prominence in the United States. However, it would be inaccurate to argue that either of these schools were followed in the manner that monetarism had been in the late 1970s. Mrs Thatcher was merely reverting to the traditional position of the right-wing of the Conservative party which had, in the past, been kept at bay by the Keynesian left. It was political philosophy rather than economic theory that provided the rationale for Mrs Thatcher's new stance.[9]

The Keynesian consensus had long disappeared, leaving a fragmentary collection of schools of thought with confusing overlaps and engaging in complex debates which had little common ground. Most of the discussion was theoretical with no direct policy relevance and, therefore, of little use to any pragmatic politician. From Keynes's *General Theory* onwards macroeconomics had acquired its distinctiveness from the policy issues it attempted to address. It became the arena where economists could apply their logic to policy design and implementation. Today, macroeconomics has evolved into a subject which has a theoretical momentum in its own right, with the original reasons for the micro/macro dichotomy long forgotten. Macroeconomics which is disassociated from policy formulation, is an irrelevancy which is, quite properly, ignored by politicians. The result has been intellectual crisis as the conflictual flavour of political philosophy has replaced the co-operative spirit of economic theory as the basis for policy actions.[10]

In many ways, the blame for the current state of affairs lies with macroeconomists themselves, not with politicians. Inability to depart from familiar orthodoxy amongst Keynesians and the over-selling of old wine in new pseudo-scientific bottles by monetarists have combined to alienate politicians from macroeconomic ideas. The unifying logic of the Keynesian consensus has not been replaced and the economics profession has become discredited in the eyes of the public, caricatured as indulging in endless disagreement to such an extent that it is now forgotten that there was broad consensus within it for over a quarter of a century. Of course, it is inevitable that when such a useful consensus breaks down we should observe, in the first instance, a reversion to older modes of thought long suppressed by the successful consensus. It is also understandable that schools of thought, inevitably with well-defined logical positions, will be particularly ill equipped to cope with the development of new ideas in the ever-changing environment of social and economic development. How often have we all observed a Keynesian or a monetarist draw an IS–LM diagram on a blackboard as the starting point of analysis even though it has been discredited as an adequate representation of the modern economy or useful for 'common ground' communication with other schools? The world is made an approximation of the theoretical model instead of the reverse.[11]

To discover how such an unsatisfactory state of affairs has developed requires some analysis of the development of economic thinking in the Keynesian era. Why was the Keynesian consensus unable to mutate to cope with economic change? Did the breakdown manifest any dynamic characteristics which could assist us in identifying a new set of unifying principles which could provide the basis for a new consensus?

To answer these questions we must go back to the beginnings of the Keynesian consensus in Keynes's *General Theory* and attempt to trace the evolutionary and degenerative patterns of the Keynesian era.

The Origins of the Keynesian Consensus

It is impossible to separate Keynes's *General Theory* from political considerations or from the policy context within which it was to prove so influential. The great achievement of the *General Theory* was not in its clarity as a theoretical contribution – it is so confusing theoretically that it has fuelled endless theoretical debate ever since it was written – but in its ability to relate, in some measure, to a wide range of opinion and expertise. There was something in the *General Theory* for everyone to agree and disagree with, but in each case there was sufficient common ground to enable every reader to come to grips with the central principle of effective demand. In terms of policy, general acceptance of the distinction between effective and potential demand was critical to Keynes. In its time it was a remarkable theoretical advance which could only be deduced from a macroeconomic perspective set in historical time, a perspective thoroughly lacking in the static, microfoundation-based, macroeconomics preferred by the Classical economists.

The magnitude of this breakthrough was emphasized in the following thirty years when, despite the debates which raged in macroeconomics, the principle of effective demand was accepted by Keynesians, post-Keynesians and monetarists alike. It formed a solid base upon which consensus could exist with all the other issues concerning monetary versus fiscal policy, liquidity preference versus loanable funds, risk versus uncertainty, etc., relegated to secondary status despite their seeming importance to academic economists. So long as the principle of effective demand was accepted, all schools would continue to recognize the need for the government to intervene in some way to stabilize the economy.

Unlike the issues which divided, for example, monetarists and Keynesians, the principle of effective demand was an outcome of logic rather than empirical observation. This logic was applied to a system of income-expenditure-output flows which was assumed to contain asymmetries. When a contractionary shock affected this system, downward rigidities were confronted which resulted in under-utilized capacity. Although we now know from systems theory that such an asymmetry is predictable in an evolving, interdependent system, to Keynes the insight was largely intuitive and confined mainly to an example in the labour market. It is hard to assess, in retrospect, whether Keynes fully grasped the systems point and merely used the labour market as a parable in order to communicate with those who could not grasp such an unfamiliar point, or whether Keynes's perception of asymmetry extended no further than the labour market.

Narrowing down the asymmetry point to the labour market had the drawback that it permitted not only those who could not grasp what Keynes was saying to see what the effect would be if, indeed, wages were rigid, but it also allowed Classical economists to argue that Keynes was only raising an issue as to the degree of perfection of the labour market. Keynes's eagerness to go along with anyone who managed to fit what he was saying into their frame of reference, provided they took on board the principle of effective demand, was ultimately to undermine the policy which he promoted.[12] Two sharply differing interpretations of what he said, one as a special case of the Classical system and the other as a convenient adjunct to state interventionism, co-existed so long as stabilization policy continued to prevent significant unemployment and promote economic growth. Keynes's new way of looking at the economic system remained locked within the pages of his book except for a few perceptive, but largely ignored, reiterations and extensions by, for example, George Shackle and Joan Robinson.[13]

Related directly to his conception of the economic system as one of interdependent flows, where income effects, or complementarities, were seen as much more important than price effects, or substitutions, Keynes also provided a new perspective on the role of money. A flow system where there are uncertainties and asymmetries, by necessity, requires that stocks are held. Given that in a monetized economy money stocks are held by everyone, whether individually or as part of organizations, Keynes promoted money from its lowly status in the Classical system as merely a 'veil', where fluctuations in its amount altered prices, to a position of fundamental importance. Money represented a central social convention that was the great co-ordinator of economic activity. As such it had real value so that expansions in its quantity could generate real output increases, provided potential for additional activity existed. The converse was also perceived to be true; if speculators preferred idle balances to financial assets, then higher interest rates and liquidity shortages could exercise a brake on activity. Although it was these same speculators, along with businessmen with erratic expectations, who led Keynes to prefer fiscal policy to monetary policy for stabilization purposes, nonetheless, he succeeded in emphasizing the importance of money stocks in facilitating real activity.[14]

Although this was the case in theory, in practice postwar Keynesian policy-makers were to care little about money, preferring merely to accommodate fiscal policy and achieve preferred interest rate and exchange rate targets.[15] This would hardly have mattered had stabilization policy not been more than that. In practice, the postwar period witnessed the expansion of the mixed economy.[16] Typically, fiscal expansion involved cumulative expansions in public spending as a proportion of total spending rather than an oscillating policy around a constant proportional mean. Allowing monetary accommodation to permit expansions in social services on an upward trend was not what Keynes had in mind in advocating monetary accommodation. Rather, he was advocating that such accommodation could stabilize interest rates and thus render speculation unprofitable as a natural concomitant to anti-cyclical policy.[17]

Although Keynes did, indeed, discuss extension of social ownership of the means of production at the end of the *General Theory* he did so in a polemical fashion which was disassociated from the main body of the short-run theory in the book. The difficulty that he perceived with investment behaviour in the private sector in the 1930s was seen as a problem that would continue to exist and lead to an increasing role for government in providing the stimulus and motivation for investment. It would be easy to dismiss these general remarks as an attempt to forge links with the Cambridge radicals who surrounded Keynes. However, if we view Keynes as thinking in terms of system evolution, then his remarks constituted no more than the position that further evolution of the economic system was likely to result in increased interdependence between productive organizations where mutual or social decision-making would become increasingly important. Indeed, some post-Keynesian economists have clung to those remarks, attributing to them a theoretical status that Keynes clearly did not intend them to have.[18] Keynes, in sharp contrast to Marxists, had no deterministic view as to the evolution of the economic system, insisting that useful theory and policy advice could only be provided in a short-run context. Such was the strength of this conviction that he was prepared to disagree publicly with his old friend and colleague Dennis Robertson when the latter insisted in raising medium-run questions concerning the dynamics of investment and medium-run monetary behaviour beyond the narrow confines of liquidity preference.[19]

To Keynes, what was important beyond the short run lay in the political arena. He was quite aware, writing in the 1930s, that the Labour party had formed a successful alliance, between Cambridge-dominated intellectuals and the trade union movement, which would ultimately come to power. He was also aware that such a government would wish to have an industrial policy which would involve intervention in the process of investment. As a Liberal, Keynes was clearly apprehensive about such a political development, but in terms of social evolution he seemed to have come to terms with it. After his death, the hasty nationalizations of the first Labour government quickly gave 'industrial policy' a tarnished reputation.[20] From then on, Britain was not to have such a policy as understood in, for example, France and Germany, but, instead, stabilization policy, overseen by Conservative governments for most of the period. Public investment was not the central concern but rather the development of the Welfare State, very much along the lines suggested by the Liberal party in Keynes's own time.

The implementation of stabilization policy, within a Keynesian consensus, provided conditions extremely favourable to business growth for nearly two decades. Furthermore, what was vital to the development of the world economy was that the Keynesian message was taken up strongly by its most important member, the United States. However, in order that a country, where the free market was held up with almost religious faith, could accept the Keynesian message, it was necessary to modify it in a way which would preserve those ideological foundations. The United States, which had pioneered stabilization policy in the 'New Deal' experiment, seized upon Keynes's insight and integrated it into its economic traditions to provide what was to become the theoretical basis for an international consensus. The emerging Keynesian orthodoxy was very much an American orthodoxy and it was one which Keynes's old colleagues in Cambridge, such as Joan Robinson, regarded as fundamentally non-progressive, despite its advocacy of stabilization policy. Keynes had achieved his political goal of providing a consensus for macroeconomic policy, but economics was not set for drastic change. Mrs Robinson and her colleagues had quickly to abandon their drive to reconstruct economics, building on Keynes's insights, in the early 1950s. Instead, an academic battle began, which lasted the rest of Mrs Robinson's life, to defend the insights of Keynes from a creeping revisionism which threatened to return economics to the old Classical world.[21] It was always a futile battle for, as time passed, it was inevitable that evolution of the economic system would render his old insights increasingly incomplete and, thus, more susceptible to attack.

Keynes offered intellectual credibility to a fundamental policy innovation. Once the difficult hurdle of policy acceptance is jumped, it is likely that any policy will be used continually until it proves ineffectual. Acrimonious academic squabbles, like those instigated in Cambridge, were, in the end, self-defeating for academic writing in economics seems often more concerned with providing a supportive mythology than with scientific advance. As such, the emerging Keynesian orthodoxy, which was so hotly criticized by the post-Keynesians, was converting millions of Americans to an otherwise alien policy position.[22] Keynes himself seemed to be much more aware than his Cambridge supporters that 'academic scribblers' are feted or ignored depending on whether their ideas are compatible with some contemporary political or administrative purpose. He was more than willing to trade long-term theoretical consistency and obscurity for short-term adaptability and policy influence. As an evolutionary thinker, Keynes was disinterested in the unknowable long run, preferring to attempt to guide evolution itself by influencing the short run. This could only happen if his insight could be given continuity with prevailing modes of thought. Regression to these older ways would only occur if the economic system evolved to a position where Keynes's insight became incomplete or redundant – conditions which Keynes could not foresee and which were not addressed in the *General Theory* in any case.

The Keynesian Consensus

The *General Theory* was a controversial book from the day it was published and it is not surprising to find so many subsequent papers, books and reviews which attempted to interpret its contents.[23] Understandably, much of this interpretation consists of attempts to fit Keynes's ideas into existing frames of reference. By the mid 1950s it became clear that the interpretations of Hicks (1937) and Hansen (1953) were to become the ones favoured in the new macroeconomic textbooks.

Today we are all familiar with the IS–LM model's structure, shortcomings and advantages. However, it is often forgotten that it was only in the 1960s that macroeconomics was taught in an IS–LM framework by macroeconomists who were keen to include explicitly the possibility of active monetary policy. In the 1950s, macroeconomics was, more often than not, taught using the *General Theory* along with Hansen's *A Guide to Keynes*. The early consensus was that fiscal policy, accompanied by accommodating monetary policy, was the appropriate measure to stabilize the economy. A full IS–LM model was unnecessary to demonstrate the transmission of such a policy into unemployment, inflation and the balance of payments. By the end of the 1950s the Radcliffe Committee Report had added its weight to this position.

In the early days of the Keynesian consensus a much more fundamental development was the application of econometric methods to aggregate data. Despite Keynes's scepticism concerning the usefulness of econometric methods, the *General Theory* presented a case for intervention which necessitated some kind of empirical knowledge of the behaviour of key aggregates over time.[24] First, in order to establish the nature, size and timing of fiscal intervention, some knowledge of the marginal propensity to consume and the determinants of fixed investment was necessary. Second, an ability to forecast ahead for at least a year could enable policy-makers to prepare discretionary actions in anticipation of predictable developments. A macroeconometric model which described as fully as the availability of data permitted the behaviour of aggregate variables was highly desirable if 'fine-tuning' was to become a reality.

In the United States the Cowles Foundation and the National Bureau of Economic Research pioneered econometric modelling, not only in terms of generating short-term forecasts, but also in developing dynamic models of business cycles. The latter development was more in the spirit of Robertson than Keynes but, in practice, was founded on a more pragmatic view that, in as much as the economy did exhibit cyclical regularities, these would have to be taken into account by the macro-policy-makers. Today, we are accustomed to thinking of econometric methods as being applied to test hypotheses, but this was not so in the early Keynesian days. Business cycle models could not really discriminate one theory from another and short-term forecasting models contained systems of estimating equations which were extremely difficult to match up to theoretical counterparts.

These econometric exercises led to significant advances in the range and quality of economic information available to government. New data series were created to meet modelling needs and remarkably accurate short-term forecasts were produced to aid policy-making in general. However, it would be unreasonable to suppose that all decision-making was based on this new economic information. Policy-making continued to be a somewhat pragmatic exercise with political priorities such as the proximity of elections, total numbers of public sector houses built per annum, etc., exercising a significant influence on the stance of fiscal policy. Despite this political reality, governments were anxious to project an image of controlling the economy in a scientific manner and, thus, supported econometric modelling activities, elevating considerably the status of economists, both within the civil service and outside, in the universities and research institutes.

In addition to providing policy-makers with better information, econometric methods were also used, particularly in the United States, to test hypotheses concerning the key aggregate relationships highlighted in the *General Theory*: the consumption function, the investment function and the demand for money function. From the outset, this empirical approach to macroeconomics was dismissed in Cambridge by post-Keynesians, who reiterated Keynes's doubts as to the validity of econometric tests which used aggregate data replete with measurement errors, proxies for unobservable variables and arbitrary assumptions concerning information and adjustment lags.[25] Indeed, early experiments to test hypotheses concerning consumption and investment yielded contradictory results and evidence of unexplained instabilities in observed associations. However, attempts to use econometric methods for hypothesis testing were not abandoned but, instead, they were extended with the help of a quite different methodological approach.

In the 1950s, Milton Friedman was regarded as a rather eccentric economist, who subscribed to the Keynesian view that stabilization policy was necessary, but disagreed with Keynes's policy preferences and dismissed much of the empirical evidence presented in support of Keynes's hypotheses. In that decade Friedman's views on the role of money had little impact; what was more influential was his empirical methodology. Friedman revived an approach which was popular in the natural sciences in the inter-war period which can be labelled as 'positivism'.[26]

The criteria upon which to judge theories was seen in terms of their predictiveness rather than their realism, given that it would be impossible to encapsulate reality in available data. Furthermore, the simpler the theory which predicts best, the more useful that theory is perceived to be. For the policy-maker, such a methodology had obvious attractions. Friedman went on to argue that the empirical estimation conducted by Keynesians was not founded on a well-specified theory of economic behaviour and, as such, could not be said to have supported any hypothesis. In order to provide a focus for his view, Friedman mounted a critique of James Duesenberry's study of consumption behaviour which attempted to reconcile the conflicting evidence of long-run, short-run and cross-section studies in terms of interdependence of tastes.[27] He argued that, once utility functions are assumed to be interdependent, no clear hypothesis is being tested and Duesenberry's statistical results are rendered meaningless and, in particular, of little help in forecasting. Instead, Friedman propounded his own 'permanent income' hypothesis which was based on the orthodox Hicksian theory of consumer choice. This theory was used to guide the selection of variables for inclusion in an aggregate specification which Friedman claimed was superior within his methodological frame of reference.

Despite the objections of Keynesians, such as Paul Samuelson, it became clear that Friedman was advocating what many American Keynesians were already practising.[28] Furthermore, Friedman's insistence that macro-hypotheses should be well founded in the optimizing behaviour of individuals was well received in the United States for, although there had been a revolution in thought concerning macroeconomic policy, there had been no revolution in microeconomics. Despite the work of Edward Chamberlin on imperfect competition, orthodox competitive microeconomics continued to be taught as a major adjunct to the mythology of the 'free enterprise' economy. Many economists felt that there should be formal links between this orthodox microeconomics and Keynesian macroeconomics. The idea of applying 'positivism' was also compelling in a different sense for it raised economics to the status of a 'science'. Indeed, by the beginning of the 1960s the methodology of positive economics had reached the level of Richard Lipsey's first-year undergraduate text. Even though Friedman's anti-Keynesian results were hotly debated and disputed, American Keynesians, such as Tobin and Modigliani, subscribed to a diluted version of Friedman's views. They tested hypotheses using econometric methods based on orthodox microeconomic behaviour. What they refused to do was to abandon completely realism for predictiveness. They wanted to be scientists in the formal sense of uncovering the 'true' structure of economic behaviour rather than being merely aggregate predictors. Methodologically, they wanted to have their cake and eat it too.[29]

Although the Hicks–Hansen interpretation of the *General Theory* was of little consequence for practical policy-making, it gradually became the major vehicle for the massive development of an academic mythology which was taught and debated within. As a general equilibrium approach, it contained the necessary orthodox microeconomic foundations and was capable of rendering various competing views as special cases. Thus, it provided an academic consensus which was a necessary adjunct to the prevalent policy consensus, sharing the common root of the principle of effective demand. Despite a number of nagging theoretical problems, such as justifying money in a general equilibrium framework, the IS–LM consensus thrived just as long as it simulated correctly the links between exogenous shocks and ultimate changes in inflation and unemployment. For pedagogical purposes, it did not matter that the IS and LM curves were unobservable, for, in the dynamic macroeconometric models, they formed the long-run equilibria upon which short-run disequilibria could be modelled. There was genuine optimism that the growth of econometric testing would finally resolve the empirical debates as to the magnitude of critical parameters and that resultant increases in the sophistication of econometric forecasting would lead to 'fine-tuning' to a high degree of precision.[30]

Although the 1950s and the early 1960s were not characterized by any significant rates of inflation, some inflation did manifest itself on the cyclical upswings of the healthy growth path of that era. Although, in a general sense, the Keynesian model could explain inflation in terms of aggregate demand, the static equilibrium framework of the Hicks–Hansen model was inappropriate to capture the price dynamics which are presumed to be induced by excess demand when the economy is expanded towards full employment. The discovery of the Phillips curve provided the missing link between inflation and unemployment. Although economists heralded the Phillips curve as a scientific advance which confronted policy-makers with a quantifiable choice of combinations of inflation and unemployment, in practice, policy-makers had always been aware of the cyclical inverse association between these target macro-variables. Econometric verification of this regularity did not have much impact on policy-making. Stabilization policy continued to be practised as before with decisions about how to counter inflation having less to do with maintaining higher unemployment levels and more to do with the need to introduce prices and incomes controls to curb any undesired inflation.

The Phillips curve represented further consolidation of the Keynesian consensus and its attendant mythology. Econometric methods were, again, hailed as a successful scientific development of economics. The subsequent 'Phillips curve industry', which examined the relationship from a bewildering number of directions, not only provided macroeconomics with a disequilibrium dimension but also welded closer links between macroeconomics and the microeconomics of the labour market. The importance Keynes had assigned to the labour market was increased in the Keynesian consensus. The Lipsey-inspired view that the Phillips curve could be construed as a manifestation of a disequilibrium response to excess demand did, however, modify Keynes's view considerably. Keynes focused on downward rigidities of wage rates, the Keynesians contemplated situations where the rate of increase of wages varied in response to excess demand. In other words, the competitive market view of the labour market was held to be predictive in a growing context but not in a stagnation context. These competitive forces were slow but disequilibrium would ultimately give way to a new equilibrium. Once the door had been re-opened to competitive equilibrium in the labour market another link between orthodox neo-classical microeconomics and macroeconomics was re-forged. Edmund Phelps and his associates began to argue that unemployment was a product of job-searching behaviour in the face of deficient information and adjustment costs.[31] Keynes's view of the functioning of the labour market was portrayed as an oversimplification which could not provide any prediction as to the course of wages.

In the 1960s the full implications of treating the labour

market as a competitive market in disequilibrium were not fully appreciated by orthodox Keynesians, only a decade later would they realize that such an approach ushered in the end of the Keynesian consensus and a re-affirmation of the Classical view. Of course, the post-Keynesians had consistently dismissed this development of the Keynesian consensus, from the Phillips curve on, insisting that wage inflation was not merely a manifestation of excess demand in a slowly clearing competitive labour market but the outcome of 'income share' competition in imperfectly competitive markets. However, not being at the centre of the academic consensus, their views carried little influence. Just as the work of Keynesians such as James Tobin on the speculative demand for money had been more Classical than of Keynes, so the Keynesian proponents of Phillips curve disequilibrium obscured Keynes's insight into the importance of relativities in wage determination and replaced it with a Classical vision of the labour market.

By the mid 1960s it was becoming increasingly apparent to many Keynesians that the Lipsey-Phillips curve was incompatible with the IS–LM depiction of the labour market. It was not simultaneously possible to argue for stabilization policy because of rigidity of money wages in the labour market while at the same time asserting that it was a competitive market which would eventually clear. Given the apparent empirical verification of the Lipsey-Phillips curve at that time, Keynesians were being forced to reconsider the validity of the Hicks–Hansen interpretation of the *General Theory*. The phenomenon of inflation, not of central concern in the *General Theory*, was gradually bringing about new conditions which would induce a reversion to Classical thinking out of the synthesis of macroeconomics and neo-classical microeconomics. In the mid 1960s the structural shift in the macroeconomy towards inflation and, ultimately, stagflation had only started but, already, the Keynesian consensus had begun to disintegrate.

The Beginning of the End

The inconsistency between the static equilibrium Hicks–Hansen model and the dynamic disequilibrium Phillips curve relationship provided an impetus in the 1960s to attempts to reappraise the message of the *General Theory*. The first major dissenter to the orthodox Hicks–Hansen view was Don Patinkin who argued that it was incorrect to cast the *General*

Theory in terms of general equilibrium for two reasons. First, a model with a stock/flow structure could not be meaningfully viewed as a general equilibrium model. Second, as a matter of logic, the existence of involuntary unemployment was inconsistent with equilibrium in a general equilibrium model with fully flexible prices. Thus, the Hicks–Hansen 'equilibrium-with-rigidities' interpretation was seen as evading the important theoretical issues raised by Keynes concerning the existence of market disequilibrium.[32]

Patinkin went on to argue, with great conviction, that the Hicks–Hansen model was no more than a trivial special case of the Classical model which not only undervalued the importance of Keynes's message but also gave no clue as to the longer-run dynamics of the Keynesian system. To Patinkin, the fundamental insight provided by Keynes was that, in a short-run context, the macroeconomy was in continual disequilibrium tending only in the long run towards general equilibrium. Thus, the Classical model was a special case (equilibrium) within general disequilibrium. Patinkin then went on to extend Keynes's insight by providing arguments that disequilibrium was generated by rational economic agents in the face of information and adjustment costs. Furthermore, in a world of disequilibrium, the holding of stocks of money becomes a natural dimension of economic behaviour and the key to long-run adjustment towards market equilibrium. However, because Patinkin saw 'real balance' effects as slow to operate, he confirmed the view that short-run stabilization policy, with the emphasis on monetary policy, would often be necessary to aid the restoration of macroeconomic equilibrium.

Patinkin's contribution did not, however, result in the abandonment of the IS-LM model as the core construct of the Keynesian consensus. Instead it became a kind of 'short-run impact of policy' model which was subject to a bewildering array of possible shifts of the curves as the economy proceeded into the long run.[33] If anything, its pedagogic potential was enhanced rather than reduced. More significantly, this new perception of the IS–LM model had changed the Keynesian consensus in one fundamental respect. It now allowed money to play a much more important role than previously: the status of LM relative to IS had increased sharply, enabling Friedman and others who subscribed to the quantity theory of money to be embraced within the Keynesian consensus. Patinkin had paved the way for the monetarist 'counter-revolution' to come.

In the late 1960s, shortly after Patinkin's ideas had become well known, the conversion of those remaining Keynesians who had resisted his theoretical attack on the Hicks–Hansen model was achieved by the co-operative efforts of Robert Clower and Axel Leijonhufvud. They were prepared to go much further and claim that Keynes was arguing, not just that markets manifested disequilibrium, but that many markets, including the labour market, did not have a Walrasian auctioneer. Thus they had no market clearing mechanism except the interactive expectations of market participants. Configurations of expectations could emerge where a market became 'stuck' in disequilibrium. Clower demonstrated the link between inconsistent expectations and deficient demand and Leijonhufvud undertook the exegesis necessary to establish that it was the market-clearing problem that was Keynes's central concern. What was particularly appealing about this work to Keynesians was that it highlighted the importance of expectations.

It had always been felt that the Hicks–Hansen comparative statics were deficient in this respect, even as a short-run policy impact model. Also, unlike Patinkin, Clower and Leijonhufvud did not offer only a new framework for the re-integration of Keynesian and Classical thought, but, instead, a set of loose ends which offered the exciting promise of a new macroeconomics built on expectational foundations. Their reinterpretation of Keynes seemed open-ended, relating just as easily to the work of George Shackle on Keynesian expectations as to that of Fisherian expectations in the quantity theory tradition. Post-Keynesian views on the role of money could be discussed as comfortably as those of Friedman and non-market clearing could form the basis of a Robinson-style argument for non-equilibrium just as well as a Patinkin-style one for long-run general equilibrium. In essence, Clower and Leijonhufvud seemed to reinstate and extend the forward-looking dimension of macroeconomics which was so central to Keynes's thought. Thus, in retrospect, it is not surprising that their work was hailed as, simultaneously, providing a new unifying emphasis and the appropriate standpoint for the further development of Keynesian thought. Formation of expectations out of uncertainty and their impact on prices and quantities seemed to offer the possibility of a new consensus set within the dynamics of historical time.

Indeed, they provided the basis, along with Patinkin, for the development of a new disequilibrium dynamic approach to macroeconomics, most frequently associated with the work of

Robert Barro and Herschel Grossman, which attempted to formalize a model where market clearing could be inhibited because of deficient information accompanied by slow adjustment.[34] However, a decade of analysis of this type has yielded models which are complex theoretically and untestable, using econometric methods.[35] In terms of the previously stated requirements of pragmatic politicians, the approach has proved unilluminating in a policy context. Meanwhile, Barro (1979), upon discovering that the imposition of rational expectations about future market clearing rendered the model an equilibrium one, even in the short run, joined the ranks of the new Classical school.

The optimism that the Clower–Leijonhufvud work would lead to a new Keynesian consensus was unfounded. Instead, their work contributed to ending that consensus, not in any intentional way, but because the insistent reversion of the neoclassical synthesis back to pre-Keynesian modes of thinking led to their work being used to argue, once again, that the Keynesian consensus was invalid. They narrowed the pedagogic role of IS–LM even further than Patinkin, arguing that there was no guarantee that general equilibrium, in the Walrasian sense, would prevail, therefore IS–LM was neither reliable as a starting point for *ceteris paribus* exercises concerning policy impact, starting at equilibrium, nor as a long-run equilibrium target on which short-run analysis could be hung. The configuration and shifts of the curves were entirely subject to expectations and existed in their conventional form only as a special case. It was no longer illuminating to depict Keynesianism and monetarism in terms of the relative slopes of IS and LM curves. Communication was no longer possible within the Keynesian consensus and IS–LM was no longer any qualitative guide to policy-makers because the missing amalgam of expectations and adjustment lags rendered the outcome of a policy intractable, even in the short run. The presumed association between simple IS–LM and complex macroeconometric forecasting models was removed and the latter, while remaining an indispensable adjunct to macroeconomic policy up to the present day, began to be more about statistical time-series models and less about identifiable economic models.[36]

It has been observed that the momentum behind the decline of the Keynesian consensus came from the emergence of inflation and the resultant dilemma which faced policy-makers, armed only with the instruments of stabilization policy. Inflation is a dynamic phenomenon which fits badly into a comparative static IS-LM model even though, with suitable mental gymnastics, it is still possible to reconcile IS–LM and the Phillips curve through the medium of excess demand. The coincidence of inflation and unemployment not only contradicted the logic of IS–LM but also incapacitated stabilization policy which could not lower both together. Prices and incomes policies, which had no theoretical foundation in the Keynesian consensus, had to be introduced by politicians to buttress expansionary stabilization policy.

So, by the beginning of the 1970s, the onset of serious stagflation had precipitated the demise of the Keynesian consensus. Its central construct, within which competing schools could communicate, had been destroyed by the Patinkin/Clower/Leijonhufvud contributions. The link between economic theory and practice had been broken by the breakdown of the Phillips curve. Of course, there is no sudden death or birth of economic thought and Keynesian economics continued to be taught and remained embedded in the framework of macroeconomic policy long after the early 1970s. The death throes of the Keynesian consensus were protracted and can only be appreciated indirectly through study of the emergence of monetarism and its subsequent mutation into the new Classical/supply-side doctrine of the present day. The decline of one doctrine and the rise of another can be difficult to separate. Although the word 'monetarism' came into being at the beginning of the 1970s we have to trace its birth to much earlier times as we shall see in the next chapter.

Conclusion

In the 1980s we have witnessed a distinct shift away from Keynesian policy, directed at the minimization of unemployment. 'Inflation first' strategies have come to dominate in both the US and the UK, although it is in the latter that we have observed the more strident efforts to precipitate recession and reduce budget deficits, running directly counter to Keynesian principles. The Reagan administration was slower in abandoning such principles due to a political commitment to increased defence spending and also due to the stronger influence of the economics profession on the process of policy formation. However, in the late 1980s we are now witnessing the enactment of the Gramm/Rudmann balanced budget proposals, ensuring that, in the US too, the residual influence of the old Keynesian consensus is being extinguished.

The Keynesian consensus was always stronger in the US, thus it is not surprising that it lingered longer there than in the UK, where political priorities have been more influential in the framing of macroeconomic policy. Thus it follows that, although it is sensible to look towards the UK for the best example of the retreat of Keynesian policy-making, it is to the US that we look to trace the decline in the Keynesian consensus in macroeconomic analysis. We have seen how, although Keynes's theory of effective demand can be viewed as emanating from a primitive 'systems' perspective, the Keynesian consensus in the US took as its core construct the IS-LM model. This model contains no systems perspective and represented a compromise model within which the theory of effective demand is permitted to reside along with pre-Keynesian notions of general equilibrium in markets.

With the primitive systems perspective removed, Keynes's concern with the evolution of capitalist economics could no longer be expressed clearly. Keynes's insistence in analysing the short run and only the preconditions for long-run change, rather than attempting to analyse the long-run process itself, became locked up in the pages of the *General Theory*. Furthermore, just as Keynes had based his whole analysis on explicit recognition that the structure of the 1930s economy was quite different to that of the late nineteenth century, so structural change rendered his model obsolete with regard to the late twentieth century. A model directed towards involuntary unemployment could not deal with simultaneous inflation.

The Keynesian consensus was built around a model which had no evolutionary flexibility and, so, the fragile consensus ended in macroeconomic theory and policy, pushing ideas back towards the Classical elements of the consensus. As in the 1930s, the rise of non-interventionism pushed economic policy-making towards pragmatism, dominated by political interest and political philosophy. However, the fragmentation which occurred did not happen quickly for the Keynesian consensus contained a profound vision of the economic system. As we shall see, new Classical modes of thought could not eject Keynesianism easily and pragmatic policy-makers found it difficult to escape from the well-worn institutional channels of Keynesian policy-making.

Notes

1 See Dean (1981) and Sidelsky (1977) for discussion of the decline of the Keynesian consensus from a US and UK perspective, respectively. Nordhaus (1983) vividly describes the confusion in macroeconomics which resulted.
2 See Artis *et al*. (1984) for discussion and empirical analysis of the non-monetarist aspects of Mrs Thatcher's economic strategy from a Keynesian perspective. Friedman (1980) offers theoretical observations as to why the strategy did not accord with monetarist principles as he saw them and Foster (1981) speculates as to the political influences which led to this deviation of policy practice from stated theoretical principles.
3 Perhaps the most striking illustration of the extent of this disapproval is the 'letter of protest' signed by the 364 British economists in 1982.
4 See Mosley (1984) and Bleaney (1985) for a more detailed discussion of the history of Keynesian policy in practice under successive governments in the postwar period.
5 This position was been clearly articulated in Brittan (1983).
6 The much quoted view of Keynes still holds true in this regard: '. . . the ideas of economists and political philosophers, both when they are right and when they are wrong, are more powerful than is commonly understood. Indeed the world is ruled by little else. Practical men, who believe themselves to be quite exempt from any intellectual influences, are usually slaves of some defunct economist. Madmen in authority, who hear voices in the air, are distilling their frenzy from some academic scribbler of a few years back.' (Keynes, quoted in Breit and Ransom (1971), p. v.)
7 By 1982, even the London Business School macroeconometric modellers, who had provided empirical support for the 'high exchange rate' policy that had been pursued, began to record with concern the high rate of capacity loss induced by contractionary policy.
8 A central plank in the monetarist view throughout the 1970s was that trade unions do not cause inflation, except as a by-product of monetary accommodation by 'weak' government. See Laidler (1981) for a retrospective assessment of this position.
9 What this meant in practice was the opportunistic selection of fragments of supply–side or new Classical thought whenever deemed necessary to bolster a political argument. In this sense, there was a sharp contrast with Ronald Reagan's economic policy in the US which evolved coherently from a well-developed system of linkages between economic advice and policy implementation. Milton Friedman's uneasiness when giving evidence to the UK Treasury in 1980 was well founded. The 'New-Right' freely admitted that they did not like having policy guided by economists but, nonetheless, did not hesitate to use economic

evidence if it seemed to concur with their philosophical views.

10 Words like 'irrelevance' and 'crisis' have appeared with increasing frequency in economic book titles of the 1980s. Most scathing are, of course, those of economists who have been close to politics such as Lord Balogh (1982) and Lord Kaldor (1972, 1982). However, the perception of crisis has permeated a much broader class of observers even beyond the discipline of economics itself (see, for example, Bell and Kristol, 1981).

11 'Paradigm resistance' as an intellectual phenomenon has been recognized since T. Kuhn's (1962, 1970) path-breaking analysis of scientific revolutions. However it has been increasingly argued that Kuhn's hypothesis does not fit economics (see Ward, 1972) and explanations have turned to 'protective belts' (Lakatos, 1970) and related concepts (see Cross, 1982, for a good discussion) which focus on interest groups and ideologies as much as scientific method.

12 The most striking example of this is contained in Keynes's correspondence with Hicks (Hicks, 1973) on the adequacy of the Hicksian interpretation of his macroeconomic theory.

13 Both of these 'unorthodox' interpreters wrote on Keynes's thought. Perhaps the best representations are Shackle (1973) and Robinson (1965). Both authors followed these papers with their own particular developments of the dynamic perspective they saw in the *General Theory*. In Chapter 5 we will consider their respective approaches to macro-dynamics.

14 Macroeconomic textbooks are noticeably weak in discussing adequately Keynes's views on money, monetary behaviour and monetary policy. Attention tends to be devoted instead to the ideas which stem from Tobin (1958) and Friedman (1956). However, Keynes's monetary ideas are clearly exposited and skilfully interpreted by Chick (1983) and Davidson (1972, 1978).

15 This uncaring attitude about money is popularly associated with the report of Lord Radcliffe (1959), yet it seems to be a popular misconception for the message of the report was that the totality of credit was important in addition to money which was an important constituent. (See the Wilson Report, 1980, for an exposition of this view.)

16 Addison (1977) describes how there existed great enthusiasm for the policy proposals contained in the Beveridge Report after 1942. The tangible promise of a new Welfare State was much more real to the ordinary person than the complexities of Keynes's stabilization policy proposals.

17 In the wake of Tobin's (1958) development of a portfolio model of the demand for money, Keynes's view of the role of speculation was de-emphasized. Fortunately, it was revived by Minsky (1976) and complemented the renewed emphasis amongst post-Keynesians in 'The State of Long-Term Expectation' (see Loasby, 1976).

18 See Eatwell and Milgate (1983) for a good example.

19 See Presley (1979) and Wilson (1980) for some discussion of the Keynes–Robertson controversy. However, Robertson (1940) provides the best insight into the strength of disagreement that existed on these issues.

20 See Cairncross (1985) for a good account of the process of policy formation in the early years of the postwar period.

21 See the preface to Robinson's (1980) reprint of her book of essays published in 1952 for her view of how American Keynesianism took a 'wrong turn'.

22 Boland (1985) argues that post-Keynesians were wrong from the outset in seeing the *General Theory* as an alternative to neoclassical economics because Keynes continued to use 'psychologistic individualism' at the core of his theory in the same manner as before. However, such a view is only valid from a strict methodological perspective and, as we shall see, such a perspective is too narrow to deal with the role and impact of ideas.

23 Chick (1983) offers the most insightful recent attempt to disentangle this literature on Keynesian exegesis and interpretation.

24 See Lawson (1985) for discussion of Keynes's view of econometric methods and Pesaran and Smith (1985) for an historical analysis of why the econometric practice advocated by Tinbergen (1939) still became an essential adjunct to Keynesian policy.

25 This critique did not result in an econometric vacuum in Cambridge. On the contrary, a strong econometric tradition, centred around the inspiration and commitment of Richard Stone, grew up. Testing individual hypotheses was not the objective but rather the development of a multi-sector dynamic macroeconometric model to explain the process of economic growth.

26 Despite the use of the word 'positive' in the title of Friedman (1953), Boland (1982), in his excellent assessment of Friedman's methodology, prefers to label it 'instrumentalism', in contrast to the 'conventionalism' adopted by Keynesians. See, also, Dow (1985) for detailed discussion of these methodological distinctions.

27 See Duesenberry (1949) and Friedman (1957).

28 Wong (1973, 1978) shows that Samuelson's (1963) attempts to counter Friedman's instrumentalism is no more than a conventionalist expressing a dislike for an unorthodox convention.

29 Some measure of just how far Keynesians have wandered into ambiguous territory between the methodology of Keynes and Friedman can be gauged by the following statement by Hendry (1980, p. 396): 'Taken literally, Keynes comes close to asserting that no economic theory is ever testable, in which case, of course, economics itself ceases to be scientific – I doubt if Keynes intended this implication.'

30 Such a progressive view of macroeconomics can be found most

strongly in the writings of Harry Johnson. See, for example, Johnson (1971).

31 See the Phelps (1970) volume which, ostensibly, attempts to provide micro-foundations for the Phillips curve yet, in retrospect, can be seen as rejecting it in favour of different, neoclassical, relationships.

32 Patinkin has written extensively on these issues – Patinkin (1965) remains the classic and best exposition of his ideas.

33 This is really only possible if 'slow adjustment' rather than 'informational deficiency' aspects of disequilibrium are emphasized. Patinkin did, indeed, emphasize the former with the latter being depicted in terms of the technical and economic constraints of information gathering which is, again, really about 'slow adjustment'. Expectation formation in the face of 'informational deficiency' is not developed as it is by Clower (1965) so IS–LM can still be used as an analytical departure point.

34 It is not altogether clear whether the Barro–Grossman (1971) approach does follow from Leijonhufvud (1968) as directly as from Clower (1965). It has become clearer from Leijonhufvud's later work (see, particularly, 1981) that his conception of long-run equilibrium is the 'Austrian' one of 'co-ordination of opportunities' rather than the Walrasian one. Some of the more confusing parts of his 1968 classic become much more comprehensible in this light. Thus, it could be argued that much of Leijonhufvud's insight remains underdeveloped – a defect that we attempt to remedy later in this book.

35 See Casson (1981) for a non-technical exposition of the disequilibrium approach to macroeconomics.

36 This 'measurement without theory' (Courakis, 1978) crisis in Keynesian macroeconomics, at all levels of aggregation, has stemmed from the 'dynamization' of hypotheses by positing some form of disequilibrium adjustment. In this sense the disequilibrium approach has pushed macroeconomists and econometricians into reconsidering some of the fundamental issues raised in the old Keynes/Tinbergen debate. Remedies tend to differ (see Hendry, 1980, and Leamer, 1983).

3 *The Rise of New Classical Macroeconomics*

> Actions based on inaccurate anticipations will not long survive experiences of a contrary character, so that the facts will soon override anticipation except where they agree.
>
> John Maynard Keynes (1930)

In his 1971 survey of 'The Keynesian revolution and the monetarist counter-revolution', Harry Johnson, himself a leading monetarist, predicted that monetarism would peter out as a challenge to the prevailing Keynesian orthodoxy. Also in 1971, another monetarist, David Laidler argued that monetarism stood or fell on the empirical observation of a stable demand for money function. Events since then have shown that both were wrong, monetarism ousted Keynesianism as the conventional wisdom and, furthermore, did so over a period where the demand for money proved to be an unstable and troublesome function for monetarists.

To Laidler and Johnson, monetarism was never a doctrine designed to wind the clock back to the Classical era but rather an attempt to try to provide money with a much more prominent role in macroeconomics than it had been given in the postwar period. Neither was interested in denying the relevance of the principle of effective demand which formed the core of the Keynesian orthodoxy, but wished to explore the ways in which changes in the money stock interacted with it to yield price and output changes. Friedman's (1971) essay, once again, emphasized the complementary links between monetarism and Keynesianism rather than the substitution of one doctrine for another.

None of these leading proponents of monetarism seemed to appreciate fully the extent of the shift back to Classical thinking within which they were key actors. Today their writings seem somewhat bemused as they survey the state of macroeconomic theory and the stance of economic policy in the 1980s. In this chapter the purpose is to trace, once again in an evolutionary way, how and why the new Classical doctrine rose to prominence with a force that surprised even the monetarists who had laid its foundations.

The Origins of Monetarism

The term 'monetarist' only came into popular usage in macroeconomics in the early 1970s.[1] However, the intellectual tradition that Milton Friedman and his disciples belong to has a very long history, dating back to the eighteenth century. In those pre-industrial days, philosophers such as David Hume perceived that an increase in the amount of currency in the economy provided a stimulus to demand and to price inflation in economies without the industrial capacity to provide more goods.[2] Hume also noted the tendency for currency growth to cause balance of payments deficits and consequent surpluses in other countries, thus providing the fundamentals of the monetary theory of the balance of payments which now forms the theoretical core of international monetarism.[3]

Even in those early days there was a rudimentary version of the monetarist–Keynesian debate which centred on whether or not the economic system should be centrally controlled through a semi-feudal hierarchy with the state at the centre or through decentralized and uncontrolled markets. The prevailing conservative view was that only the former was viable and that without an authoritarian system the economy would degenerate into Hobbesian chaos. Such a view was challenged by radicals such as David Hume and Adam Smith who argued that rational, self-interested individuals would eagerly engage in trade within a framework of laws and ethics if they were only given the opportunity to do so.[4] It was a position which could only be held safely in eighteenth century Scotland because of the unique conjunction of a tolerant Protestant religion and a government so distant, both geographically and culturally, that it could not curb this rise of radical thought. The Scottish Enlightenment challenged the authoritarian alliance of church and state on all fronts. For example, Hume laid the foundations of a scientific methodology which was based on empiricism rather than theology and, even in the relatively tolerant atmosphere of Edinburgh, was labelled a heretic for his position.[5]

Once again if we look at the modern monetarist–Keynesian debate we can observe this same methodological divide. Friedman adopts a position very similar to that of Hume arguing for 'positive' economics, i.e. evaluating theories in terms of their predictive content in an attempt to make economics less 'theoretical' and more 'scientific'.[6] The more we delve into the philosophical foundations of monetarism the more we discover that the position held is that of the eighteenth century Scottish Enlightenment with the modern day equivalent of semi-feudalism being the interventionism of Keynesian governments. It is now a conservative rather than a radical position for two reasons. First, Smith and Hume were radical because they advocated a new development – the extension of the market system. Friedman is conservative because he wishes to 'unwind' mixed economies to return to some past competitive golden age. Second, Friedman is regarded as a conservative because he is confronted, not with oppressive feudalism, but with social democracies which have introduced radical welfare changes beyond the wildest dreams of Smith. Only by following James Buchanan and inventing theories of corrupt bureaucracies, penal regulations and the squandering of resources in the public sector can we reconstitute a modern version of the eighteenth century semi-feudal state.[7] Modern monetarists have tended to try to turn back the evolutionary clock, their eighteenth-century ancestors were trying to wind it up.

During the nineteenth century, Smith's advocacy of the free market and Hume's empirical methodology provided the philosophical basis for industrial development. Gradually, classical political economy, which concentrated on the distributional flows between groups such as capitalists, workers and *rentiers*, gave way to neo-classical economics which focused attention on rational individuals who interacted gainfully through markets. The emergence of Marxism, operating in the old classical political economy mode, reinforced this tendency while encouraging significant social reforms to curb the exploitative excesses of some capitalists. Again there was a rudimentary form of the monetarist–Keynesian debate, this time much closer to its modern descendant. Welfare for the poor and unemployed was opposed by many who felt that support would make such people lazy and unwilling to work. Safety regulations would result in the closure of productive enterprises. This view held that, although it might not appear so, there really was a competitive market in operation, that it was efficient and any social intervention would ultimately make people worse off rather than better off. The social reformers did not see such perfection in the operation of the market and argued for legislative intervention.

This debate, although still one concerning beliefs about the operation of market forces, was quite different to that in the eighteenth century. To Smith, the world was imperfect and the goal was more competitive markets, which could be achieved if government intervened to liberalize markets. To modern neo-classical microeconomists, the world was already competitive and intervention to correct for 'excesses' within a market context inhibited market forces. The switch from market radicalism to market conservatism had begun to take place. The illusion of the free market, in as much as it prevented social intervention, perpetuated the exploitative gains of the large corporations and became more propagandist than ideological.

By the early twentieth century, neo-classical micro-economics had evolved to a central orthodoxy which became increasingly formalized as a static system of interactive markets yielding full employment of resources through the operation of the relative price system. Macroeconomics had hardly any meaning except in terms of the quantity theory of money which had been inherited as part of the tradition. Monetary policy, as it always had been, was a policy at the disposal of the government to stimulate demand, but the Classical model, with its fully employed resources, meant that the only possible outcome of such a policy would be on prices, not output.

The quantity theory of money was derived from the simple identity $MV \equiv PY$, where M is the stock of money in circulation; V is the velocity of circulation per period; P is the price level; Y is real income or output per period. As it stands, this identity hardly seems to offer much of an explanation of anything and only becomes a theory if certain assumptions are made. *If* the money stock is definable, e.g. currency in a non-bank economy under the control of the authorities, and *if* the velocity of circulation is stable ($V = \bar{V}$), *then* changes in M will result in changes in PY. *If* output is at its full employment level ($Y = \bar{Y}$) *then* there will be a proportional relationship between monetary growth and inflation ($\Delta P = \Delta M$). Two justifications for $\bar{V}$ were offered. First, Irvine Fisher argued that V was determined institutionally by the receipt and disbursement habits in the economic system. Second, Alfred Marshall argued that V was determined behaviourally by individuals' desires to hold money.[8] The demand for money was dependent on PY, i.e. money income, and if the money stock was increased individuals would have excess balances to spend, thus driving up prices.

Now, in theory, this was fine but the reality of the nineteenth and early twentieth centuries was one of business cycle fluctuations. In other words the assumption of $Y = \bar{Y}$ was not always met and a debate developed as to whether monetary changes should be induced to attempt to stabilize these fluctuations. Classical economics offered a firm 'no' but pragmatic politics often dictated 'yes'. These experiments in stabilization were conducted in the dark for, as yet, there was no economic theory of how such monetary changes affected the economy below full employment. By the 1920s and 1930s, and the oscillating crises of severe inflation followed by deep depression, it became urgent that some understanding of the below full employment economy be produced. Classical economics, plus the quantity theory, had little to offer for it was cast in static equilibrium terms. All inflation was attributable to over-expansion of the money supply, all unemployment was voluntary and due to lazy workers being unwilling to work at the prevailing wage rate determined by the labour market. Free market conservatism had now taken on a frightening 'head in the sand' stance as the forces of totalitarianism of both the political right and left began to threaten the very existence of the free market economies in Europe.[9]

As demands grew for 'public works' to reduce unemployment the Classical orthodoxy began to crumble from within. Knut Wicksell offered an analysis of the disequilibrium dynamics of the quantity theory in a world where money was predominantly bank deposits, not currency.[10] An increase in the money supply, he argued, increased loanable funds available, thus drove down the real rate of interest below its natural rate as determined by productivity and thrift. This increased demand for funds for investment in plant and equipment creating overall excess demand in the economy, thus driving up prices, lowering the real value of the money stock until the interest rate rose again to its 'natural' rate. So, in a modern economy with a banking system it was theoretically possible to meander out of equilibrium. The next crucial contribution was Keynes's *Treatise on Money*, which also dealt with the theoretical consequences of disequilibrium in the market for loanable funds. Soon it became clear that, once out of equilibrium, the quantity theory became much less predictable in terms of its short-term dynamics even if it did prevail in the long run. Disequilibrium in the market system in general was even more difficult to grasp and the inter-war period gradually became characterized by confusion. Some economists argued in equilibrium, some in disequilibrium and, to complicate matters more, Joan Robinson and Edward Chamberlin developed their theories of imperfect competition which called into question the validity of the underlying assumption of competition. If we define a debate as an interaction which proceeds upon the premise of certain agreed conventions, there was little constructive debate, only the presentation of different basic assumptions upon which meaningful dialogue was almost impossible. The fundamental dispute, as always, was about the existence and extent of competitive markets, but this time it was about neither the attainment of an ideal, nor the maintenance of an ideology, but the survival of liberal democracy itself. Keynes, who has been classified as both Keynesian and monetarist in retrospective studies, provided the necessary consensus and, in so doing, pushed the quantity theory with its preoccupation with monetary control into the background.

The Monetarist Takeover

In the era of the Keynesian consensus, those who insisted that the quantity theory of money continued to be relevant to macroeconomic analysis became a small minority in the United States. They were known collectively as the 'Chicago School' which carried on in the traditions of Alfred Marshall and Irvine Fisher, insisting on there being a role for monetary policy and issuing warnings as to the inflationary consequences of monetary laxity.

It has already been pointed out that Friedman's main influence during the 1950s and most of the 1960s was at an empirical rather than a theoretical level in macroeconomics. However, by the end of the 1960s conditions were ripe for a push into the centre of the macroeconomic arena. The second half of that decade witnessed the emergence of an inflationary problem that soon seemed to be inexplicable within the analytics of the Phillips curve. In other words, the transmission mechanism between demand management and prices and quantities was proving to be much more obscure than Keynesian economics had suggested. As has already been observed, it was this empirical reality which helped to generate such widespread interest in the reappraisals of Keynes and pushed macroeconomics into such a state of flux. Friedman had prepared himself over many years for the onset of this economic condition and when it arrived he had at his disposal an integrated structure of ideas and evidence of overwhelming power.

Friedman's 'positive' methodology took empirical shape in his work on two structural equations of the Keynesian system: the consumption function and the demand for money function.[11] His strategic objectives in each case were different. His work on consumption was designed to establish that the evidence argued for a much longer run and expectational treatment than that provided by Keynes. On the other hand, his demand for money studies were designed to establish that the demand for money relationship was much more stable than Keynes implied with an interest elasticity much lower than Keynesians believed. Thus, the consumption studies were designed to force the policy debate out of the short-run context and the demand for money studies were designed to persuade policy-makers that monetary policy could be a predictable instrument of stabilization policy. If we look at the debates Friedman had with key American Keynesians, such as James Tobin and Franco Modigliani, we see that he was fairly successful on both counts, even though neither of these Keynesians departed from an essentially eclectic position concerning macroeconomic policy.[12]

Much stronger objections were made concerning the evidence, presented in Friedman and Schwartz (1963) and Friedman and Meiselman (1963), which attempted to establish a causal link between monetary growth and nominal income growth through long-run reduced form studies of the United States. Although the validity of these tests was successfully refuted, they were an important part of Friedman's strategy for they established money's importance, irrespective of its endogeneity or exogeneity, and also enabled Friedman to reach a much wider audience with his message concerning empirical methodology. He was no longer regarded as an eccentric throwback to the pre-Keynesian era, but rather a Keynesian who wished to see empirical economics used most effectively in the service of policy and who argued that the available evidence suggested that monetary policy should have a more central role in stabilization policy. By the late 1960s, therefore, Friedman was extremely well prepared for the inflation crisis which developed.

Inflation was developing because of the widespread practice

of allowing monetary policy to accommodate fiscal policy, Friedman argued. By 1967, when Friedman gave his famous presidential address to the American Economic Association, such a statement was not very controversial and could have been made by many other Keynesians at that time. What was new was his statement that there is a direct link between monetary growth and inflation through the medium of inflation expectations in the labour market. This statement was so distinct from Keynesianism that it became necessary to invent a new label for such an idea. In 1968, Karl Brunner called it 'monetarism' and the name stuck.

Wicksell's (1936) model linking inflation expectations and nominal interest rates had been taken by Friedman from its quantity theory context and used to link inflation expectations and the rate of change of money wages. It provided an explanation of why the Phillips curve was breaking down, using an expectations hypothesis precisely at the time when the Keynesian reappraisers where calling for a more forward-looking approach founded in a disequilibrium framework. Instead of Wicksell's natural rate of interest, Friedman used Phelps's natural rate of unemployment around which to pivot the Phillips curve as a short-run disequilibrium relationship. Monetarism may have been conceived in studies of money's relation to nominal income and inflation but it was born, not in the macroeconomic arena, but in the labour market, at the core of the Keynesian consensus. Irrespective of whether money wages were rigid downwards in specific circumstances, such as the Great Depression, rational labour suppliers would generally attempt to adjust their real wages upwards to take account of expected inflation.[13]

Friedman offered Keynesians a new transmission mechanism of inflation which they could use without any commitment to monetary growth as the cause of excess demand and without any need to abandon the notion that there was a negatively sloped Phillips curve, provided the coefficient on inflation expectations was less than one. The latter was seen as an empirical question. However, in order to answer it Keynesians had to adopt Friedman's 'positive' empirical testing procedure in an unqualified manner. Although American Keynesians had shown unwillingness to do this in the context of reduced forms of macro-models, the labour market was a familiar Keynesian empirical testing ground where there was, already, a general anxiety to re-establish some kind of respecified Phillips curve to guide policy. And so the empirical battle, which was already being fought with regard to the relative interest elasticities of IS and LM curves, was extended to the size of the estimated coefficient on expected inflation in wage equations. Friedman had shifted the ground of the debate from the Keynesian consensus to his own.

The early 1970s saw the full development of monetarism and the retreat of Keynesians who did not prosper in this new empirical context. Inflation worsened, the Phillips curve became more distant and the body of evidence linking monetary growth and inflation became ever more voluminous. Despite Keynesian protests about the validity of most of this evidence, political inability to cope with inflation and a distinct lack of Keynesian alternatives was leading politicians to become sympathetic towards the monetarist position. The disastrous period of the Heath–Barber administration in the UK seemed to provide an even more immediate monetarist lesson than econometric results. Also, the monetarist explanation of international inflation, through excessive US dollar expansion, offered an explanation which was not part of the Keynesian explanations on offer.

As the 1970s unfolded and successive bouts of stagflation came and went, unemployment became a less and less important variable in explaining wage inflation and estimates of the coefficient on inflation expectations, variously defined, rose up towards unity.[14] The extent to which acceptance of this coefficient as the focus of debate was a Faustian bargain became increasingly apparent to Keynesians. There was no route back to debates concerning interest elasticities because the key structural equations in the Keynesian macro-model had all become unstable in the 1970s. The 'dynamization' necessary to re-establish enough stability for forecasting purposes tended to extinguish any kind of useful results for making elasticity judgements in a comparative static model, which had, in any case, been theoretically discredited in the Keynesian re-appraisal.

The failure of the new Keynesian disequilibrium approach to provide a consensus which could have dislodged the monetarist consensus which began to form during the 1970s reflects the priorities which macroeconomics has to meet. In general, economic hypotheses are difficult to test while, in contrast, it is possible to take a large number of time series, integrate them through some kind of dynamic modelling procedure and obtain excellent forecasts over short-run periods. In other words, we can find out a great deal about the future of the economic system without having much of an understanding of economic behaviour. Policy-makers use macroeconomic theories to guide them in introducing new policies while, at the same time, use forecasting models to gauge what the short-run impact of policy changes will be. They prefer their theories to be extremely simple and *logically consistent*. Providing a piece of supportive evidence is helpful but only in a subsidiary way compared to arguments that a new idea will be consistent with other goals. Retrospective evidence is of limited help in introducing a policy innovation which will alter the behavioural structure of the economic system.

Monetarism succeeded by keeping its prescriptions simple and consistent within a particular world view, only using empirical evidence either to discuss the claims of the opposition or to help promote their own position. Provided prescriptions work for policy-makers, little else will be asked and no attention will be paid to academic debates. The new Keynesian disequilibrium approach did not founder on lack of evidence but through failing to provide a policy logic which could be applied. In contrast, the old Keynesian logic had survived on very little evidence for a long time. It, too, required forecasting models which were built around the policy instruments and targets that the overriding logic of effective demand required. Monetarism evolved with a clear understanding of such priorities, the new Keynesian disequilibrium approach failed because these priorities had been long forgotten.

Paradoxically, the monetarist tradition that we identify with Friedman did not consolidate itself after its rise to pre-eminence. Instead, it rapidly evolved into what Tobin (1980) calls Mark II monetarism, or new Classical macroeconomics.[15] Mark I monetarism was inextricably bound up with Keynesianism, sharing many common premisses and, in many respects, reviving Keynes's own views as contained in the *Treatise on Money* and the *Tract for Monetary Reform*. It is quite mistaken to look on monetarism as a substitute for Keynesianism. It was, rather, a complementary development of orthodox Keynesianism designed to enhance its ability to cope with a world of inflation. Monetarism did not reject the central insight of the *General Theory*, namely, the principle of effective demand, and sought to offer a policy framework on the demand side to enable stabilization policy to be more effective. Monetarists did not return to the old quantity theory world where prices were determined by money with real wages determined in the labour market. Their analysis of the short run allowed for disequilibrium in the former and price expectational effects in the latter and, as such, offered an analysis which was heavily influenced by the Keynesian era.

As Modigliani and other American Keynesians appreciated, Friedman was not seeking to reinstate Classical economics but merely attempting to offer some important qualifications derivable from the Classical tradition.[16] The simultaneous existence of disequilibrium and expectational factors in the short run pointed to a shift away from complicated discretionary policy towards simple policy rules and automatic stabilizers. However, as time passed, it became clear that empirical evidence would not provide the level of predictiveness necessary to translate monetarism into actual policy. Key equations such as the demand for money function were found to be unstable and policy sensitive, leaving monetarism no better founded than Keynesianism to offer policy guidance in the short run. Continued reliance was placed on macroeconometric models and these were all essentially Keynesian in construction. Clearly, if simple, direct, policy advice was to be provided, then all remnants of Keynesianism would have to be ejected, with less dependence on empirical evidence and more on offering a body of logic which was internally consistent. If this was achieved then there would be no danger of policy advice degenerating into pseudo-Keynesianism – the logic would dictate adherence to certain policy principles through thick and thin.

The New Classical Counter-revolution

It has been argued that the critical feature of Friedman's analysis which won over orthodox Keynesians to monetarism either directly or indirectly through acceptance of the monetarist framework was the introduction of forward-looking expectations into macroeconomics at its Keynesian heart – the labour market. These expectations were not introduced only in a theoretical way but with empirical content. Expectations were supposed to be adaptive, constructed on exponential smoothing principles long used in marketing departments to forecast sales.

The whole foundation of the monetarist transmission mechanism lies in the proposition that real rather than money wages are negotiated for in the labour market and that there exists a process of market clearing which pushes unemployment inexorably towards its 'natural' rate. For all this to happen, economic agents must be 'rational', not suffering from money illusion. Almost as soon as the label 'monetarism' came into common usage there were those who pointed out that the rational agent would also search for an 'optimal' expectation, adaptive expectations being an optimal forecast only in special circumstances.[17] A forecast was regarded as 'optimal' provided it was an unbiased predictor, indicating the absence of any further useful information, not only of a statistical type, but also of any economic relationships that might exist. And so were born 'rational expectations', cast in terms of the econometrics of errors in the style of John Muth's work in financial markets a decade earlier.[18]

In the late 1970s when, in many ways, monetarism was in its period of ascendancy in the academic domain, if not the political arena, the rational expectations hypothesis was not taken at all seriously by most macroeconomists, including many monetarists who found the idea appealing but were not prepared to adopt its logic for policy at high levels of aggregation under strong Walrasian market-clearing assumptions.[19] It was generally viewed as a theoretical exercise in exploring the full implications of various monetarist assumptions concerning information availability and use. Furthermore, there is little doubt that its best known practitioners, such as Robert Lucas, regarded the approach as a theoretical exercise which could not provide any guidance to practical policy-making.[20] As such, it was an undoubted success because it made clear the implications of assumptions often vague and implicit in monetarist analysis.

In particular, the monetarist contention that there would be no long-run trade-off between inflation and unemployment was derived more rigorously.[21] The proposition that economic agents formed rational expectations which embodied beliefs in market clearing and quantity theory links between monetary growth and inflation led to the conclusion that the hypothesis maintained by Keynesians, that the estimated coefficient on inflation expectations should be less than one, is irrational. In other words the empirical debate concerning this coefficient which had exercised monetarists and Keynesians for a large part of the 1970s was irrelevant.

The problem with tests of expectation augmented wage inflation models had always been the measurement of expectations. Translating the qualitative and immeasurable into the quantitative and testable inevitably meant the presence of measurement error and consequent estimated coefficient bias.[22] Furthermore, a proxy for expectations could well be picking up some entirely different hypothesis. It is not surprising, in the circumstances, that using assumptions about logic would seem to be more useful and that whether or not an expectation was an unbiased predictor would be attractive in the domain of forecasting. The new Classicals argued that, as a *logical necessity*, no long-run Phillips trade-off could exist and, furthermore, any short-run trade-off would be merely a product of temporary expectational errors. In the *short run*, the economic system was in equilibrium with regard to whatever expectations were formed. It followed directly that neither fiscal nor monetary policy was predictable in the short run or effective in the long run. Provided the rationality and market clearing assumptions made by monetarists, as well as many Keynesians, were maintained, the new Classical logic must prevail. Only some new underlying assumptions concerning rationality and the nature of equilibrium could yield any other result.

Once this had been established, there was no need to cling to the old Keynesian disequilibrium framework of the Phillips curve at all. New Classicals returned to the aggregate supply/demand framework of the pre-Keynesian era arguing for a vertical aggregate supply curve which could only become non-vertical in the face of 'surprises'. With the aid of 'rational expectations' the new Classicals had purged all residual Keynesian elements from monetarist analysis and the Keynesian consensus was truly at an end. The principle of effective demand was removed and Say's Law reinstated. The new Classical analysis provided no consensus within which a Keynesian position could be expressed. The nearest to a Keynesian position related to the 'degree of strength' of rationality assumptions, but this was no more than an explicit attempt to extend optimization into a world of adjustment costs, complicating the optimal equilibrium path to new Classical long-run equilibrium. These modifications were only remotely 'Keynesian' and more to do with generalizing the 'new Classical' approach so that it could be set more explicitly within an inter-temporal context. For Keynesians there was no return except through a fundamental revision of the basic behavioural postulates contained in the micro-foundations of macroeconomics. This was recognized with most clarity by Joan Robinson until the end of her life, but sadly misunderstood by American Keynesians who could not challenge their orthodox foundations as laid down by Samuelson (1947).[23]

The development of new Classical logic forced monetarists into a dilemma position for, suddenly, a convenient way of explaining the breakdown of the Phillips curve and drawing the focus of the Keynesian–monetarist debate into their framework had sharpened into a non-interventionist logic which excluded Keynesianism. Instead of facilitating policy debate as to gradualist versus sharp-shock monetary control and its effects on price/quantity dynamics, monetarists found themselves having to defend their new found consensus position.[24] Friedman had won the day by bringing monetarism into the labour market only to find that the 'new' macroeconomics that followed destroyed the position of all but a small minority of monetarists. Gradualist monetarists, typified by Laidler, were driven ultimately to consider the incorporation of models of imperfect competition into their analysis in order to preserve a meaningful discussion of the effects of monetary policy. In other words, propositions concerning rational expectations were not challenged but those concerning the nature of the market clearing process were.[25]

Although the introduction of imperfect competition represents a kind of 'fundamental assumption' response, it presents particular difficulties for monetarists. From the outset, Friedman has argued consistently that imperfectly competitive micro-foundations involve a loss of predictiveness for the sake of greater realism. This has demonstrably been the case in recent Keynesian literature and is no less so in monetarist developments even though the intent is different, i.e. it is no longer a question of arguing for the most effective policy prediction but for any policy at all. This shift in monetarist thinking has not only been forced by the new Classical challenge but also because of the failure of their own positive methodology in the 1970s. It was a decade where monetarists observed breakdowns in key structural equations such as the demand for money function, and where econometric forecasting equations depended much more on autoregressive processes and less on economic theories set rigorously in micro-foundations.[26] Friedman's early optimism about the use of positivist/instrumentalist methodology had foundered in empirical difficulties, leaving strong statements about rigour, simplicity and predictiveness looking rather meaningless. A new generation of econometric model-builders had grown up building large macroeconometric models which provided the foundation for macroeconomic policy debate, while the monetarist preoccupation with expectations had moved them in the opposite direction and spawned the new Classical school. Preoccupation with reduced-form studies of the association between money, money income and prices continued, however, narrowing the focus on old quantity theory of money issues in a manner which was compatible with the new Classical approach. Evidence which supported the contention that inflation was caused, or even associated with, monetary growth became a major component of models of rational expectations concerning inflation.

The uneasy role of monetarism as the intermediary between the non-communicating new Classical and Keynesian schools of thought led to the development of a non-progressive eclecticism in monetarist ranks. Although international monetarism continues to provide original analysis and commands increasing respect, at the domestic level, monetarism is no longer a distinctive school with a clear macroeconomic policy thrust. In recent times, strong policy statements have come from the new Classical school and its polar opposite, the post-Keynesian school. Despite their fundamental differences, both these schools are distinct from monetarism and Keynesianism in one fundamental sense. They say something explicit about the supply side of the economy.

The decline of monetarism can be traced directly to the fact that it was wedded to a demand side model, drawing in old Classical propositions concerning the supply side. New Classicals, in turn, demonstrated that these supply side assumptions, when conjoined with demand, implied a set of logical conclusions about the ineffectiveness of demand management. The rise of new Classical thought is founded on a re-emphasis of the importance of the supply side. Monetarism had always restricted its use of Classical supply side assumptions to mounting critiques of demand side Keynesianism. For example, beliefs that the private sector was inherently stable and capable of self-generating growth, that crowding out of fiscal policy would ultimately prevail, that there was a 'natural' rate of unemployment, all constituted critiques. In contrast, the new Classicals pulled these together into a supply side approach where the demand side was regarded as a peripheral rather than a central concern which could be dealt with simply in terms of money growth and inflation expectations.

The Keynesian consensus failed because it could not cope with inflation; the monetarist consensus failed because it couldn't deal with the supply side and governments' concern with rising unemployment and falling rates of productivity growth. Furthermore, experiments with monetarism quickly demonstrated that a policy founded on market-clearing principles could not work in an imperfect world. Only by adopting new Classical proposals, that changes on the supply side could increase efficiency in this regard, could the logic of monetarism survive. New Classical macro-policy ineffectiveness propositions are accompanied by a broad range of disaggregated studies on the effects of cartels, unemployment benefits, subsidies, etc., all cast within a neo-classical framework. From the controversial work of Laffer (1983) through to the more academic contributions of, for example, Martin Feldstein, there exists a range of studies which are a natural complement to the new Classical macroeconomics.[27]

There is a tendency, particularly on the Keynesian side, to equate the rise of new Classical macroeconomics with conservative politics. New Classical macroeconomics is portrayed as no more than the old Classical economics dressed up in new expectational clothes. To take such a view is to oversimplify and to underestimate the serious neglect of the supply side in the Keynesian consensus which, in turn, provided the favourable conditions in which this new approach could prosper. Although there are parallels with the old Classical economics, the focus of attention is quite different. For example, the range and diversity of analysis and evidence presented in new Classical economics had no parallel in the inter-war years. This new work attempts to forge a basis for the introduction of supply-side incentives which are entirely new in historical experience. Issues are being tackled which cannot fit into the Keynesian framework and even the policy ineffectiveness thesis is grounded in an expectational framework which offers potential as the launching pad for new forward-looking ways of dealing with the economic system.[28]

The rise of new Classical economics grew out of dissatisfaction with the Keynesian consensus which had grown inflexible and blinkered to evolution of the economic system. It was inevitable that the first response would be reactionary, with old ideas, suppressed for so long, rising to prominence. The same process occurred in the inter-war years when the Classical orthodoxy could not deal with economic events and there was a regression to old totalitarian ideas, of both right and left, inherited from earlier eras. Furthermore, it is not surprising to find that the promotion of such ideas is undertaken by interest groups who suffer most from the orthodoxy's flaws.

In the early 1970s, monetarism was promoted most strongly by participants in financial markets who were experiencing negative real rates of return on financial assets due to inflation. It was in their interest to promote monetary control which could simultaneously raise nominal interest rates and lower inflation. The adoption of monetarist policies, in turn, freed governments from Keynesian commitments to unemployment and enabled Conservatives to pursue strategies of a more political nature which had been demoted to secondary importance in the Keynesian era. Again, the interest groups who advocated a return to freer markets formed a 'right–left' spectrum. The 'right' promoted market principles backed by more law and order as providing the relative inequality necessary for prosperity and the 'left' argued that freer markets would lead to a more libertarian society.

The resultant alliance between interest and ideology provided a formidable base for the development of the new Classical/supply side economics which, in turn, could be used to provide a basis for policy-making and receive widespread support. The approach has many of the attractions isolated earlier: it is simple to understand, appealing to man-in-the-street intuition; it is backed by complex logic at the macro level and a wide range of empirical studies at the micro level; the policies proposed (such as tax cuts) are implementable. On the political side, Keynesianism can be equated with socialism with some effect, particularly in the United States, building on the innate distrust of government which has persisted through the postwar period.[29]

Although it is inevitable that political interest and economic policy become more intimate in periods of crisis, it would seem to be incorrect to view the rise of new Classical thinking as solely political. We have witnessed only a reactionary response to the failure of the Keynesian consensus. This response identified correctly the Keynesian weakness on the supply side and has offered proposals that require innovative supply side alternatives. It is entirely appropriate that supply side issues should have come to dominate the policy debate; what is inappropriate is the restrictive market clearing model within which such important considerations have been placed.

Macroeconomics, as we have understood it in the past, has been dispensed with through the logical development of the Walrasian elements of the Keynesian consensus. The concept of rational expectations is an entirely appropriate demand side development but one which is limited in its potential applicability through the underlying narrow presumption of market clearing.[30] There is no doubt that the Lucas critique of policy simulation is widely accepted as a quite general problem for policy study, providing a fundamental challenge which requires a fundamental response.[31] Monetarism asked key questions concerning the generality of Keynesian macroeconomics. The new Classical school is asking key questions as to the adequacy of underlying behavioural assumptions concerning economic agents and their interaction that provide the foundation of macroeconomic analysis.

Some post-Keynesians protest that they have already provided the political economy upon which alternative approaches can be developed, but the test of time has shown that they have had little influence on the Keynesian orthodoxy.[32] There has been a long and healthy suspicion of approaches based on political theories of group conflict which lack, in any economic sense, predictiveness or a logic which transcends the elementary struggle for survival.[33]

An essential precondition of any new approach is to offer a logically consistent economic alternative to the Walrasian basis for macroeconomics. Imperfectly competitive models have not managed to offer such an alternative – they have existed from the seminal contributions of Edward Chamberlin and Joan Robinson in the 1930s to the complex model, for example, of Negishi in the late 1970s, and have yet to prove a viable basis for macroeconomic thought. Like the post-Keynesian analysis, there is a lack of a simple unifying theme or myth of economic harmony, so well articulated in the Walrasian model.[34] 'Imperfection' implies an inefficient mess, generating an analytical blur at the macro-level without any long-run tendency towards a harmonious state of affairs. The new Classical response to the presumed existence of imperfect competition is to argue, logically, that a Pareto improvement could be gained by attempting to reduce its incidence, rather than to worry about attempting to develop a new macroeconomics from such an insecure basis.[35] Given the microfoundations that exist, this position would seem to be correct.[36]

No matter how esoteric and divorced from reality the perfect market might seem to be, pragmatic politicians who try to implement policies to move closer to this ideal have a philosophical notion that it represents the 'common good'.[37] Until economists can offer another conception of the common good which coincides more properly with the current evolutionary state of the macroeconomy, we can expect to observe the continuation of political pragmatism without consensus, the destructive imposition of hardship on the underprivileged in the name of efficiency and the continued decline in the status of macroeconomists within society.[38]

Conclusion

It has been pointed out that the origins of monetarism are far from conservative, beginning as radicalism in the eighteenth century and evolving towards the quantity theory tradition of the early twentieth century, which provided the first analytical context for the contemplation of stabilization through monetary means. The monetarist 'counter-revolution' was viewed as more of an attempt to take over the Keynesian consensus rather than replace it with the old Classical doctrines. For methodological reasons, monetarism was built firmly on neo-classical micro-foundations and only mutated into the new Classical macroeconomics when the 'positivist' methodology adopted proved to be inadequate. Once the bond with empirical evidence had been broken, the expectational approach pioneered by monetarists became dominated by logic alone, fuelled by the observation of an economy where inflation and monetary growth moved closely together.

The new Classical approach can be viewed as the culmination of a process which began in the early adoption of a Walrasian framework in the Keynesian consensus. As the empirical basis of Keynesianism, then its variant, monetarism, faded away, so the force of Walrasian logic grew in strength. By the early 1980s, the divorce between macroeconomic theory and the interrelated subjects of macroeconomic forecasting and management of the economy was complete. The logic of political philosophy could be applied with the full backing of new Classical economic logic. Untrammelled with any need to understand any technical economic arguments, the administrations of Reagan and Thatcher proceeded to attempt, pragmatically and in their different ways, to move towards their philosophical goals, despite the economic chaos that might ensue in the short run.

It has been argued that this political dimension of the new Classical approach has served to diminish the importance of its development. Although dressed in reactionary clothing, this new school has highlighted two fundamental deficiencies in the

Keynesian consensus. First, the degree to which expectations are important in a highly interdependent system can no longer be avoided. Second, the insight that such expectations are formed endogenously has emphasized, particularly through the Lucas critique of policy evaluation, that economic behaviour will adapt or evolve to take account of changes in the structure of economic policy. Third, the importance of understanding and developing new policies which take explicit account of the supply side has challenged the demand-side bias of much of Keynesian thought. As yet, these challenges have not been adequately countered by Keynesian economists, so there is no reason for politicians to abandon their new school in favour of one which history has rendered obsolete.

Many commentators have warned of the dangers that recourse to myth and philosophy, as the basis for policy-making, hold for the modern macroeconomy. To others the development of more sophisticated econometric forecasting seems to delude them into thinking that the reverse is the case, confusing the management of the economy, as it exists, with the setting of new policy priorities to alter economic structure. There seems no case for hoping that it is possible to 'econometrically model' our way out of the crisis. Only by meeting the central ideas and inspirations of the new Classical school head on can there be any prospect of change. As we shall see in later chapters, this involves travelling into non-economic territory, often an unpalatable journey for the economist. However, in the meantime, in the next chapter, the route will be charted from familiar landmarks which seem to point in the correct direction.

Notes

1 See Laidler (1981) for a comprehensive analysis of monetarism with discussion by Tobin, Meade and Matthews. Also, Mayer (1978) offers an assessment from a different perspective.

2 See Hume (1752) reprinted in Rotwein (1955).

3 See Dornbush (1980) for a full exposition of international monetarism and Keynesianism.

4 To appreciate this point fully it is necessary to consider Smith's *Wealth of Nations* in conjunction with his *Theory of Moral Sentiments* (see Smith, 1749; 1976).

5 Scottish scepticism has a very long history. Duns Scotus (1265–1308), born and educated on North Uist in the Outer Hebrides and who later taught at Oxford, Paris and Cologne,

argued against the philosophy of his contemporary Aquinas, maintaining that religion and theology were beyond reason and rested on faith. The schoolroom term 'dunce' perpetuates his memory and emphasizes the disgust of the religious establishment towards the enlightened views of philosophers such as Hume (1939) many centuries later. See Macfie (1955) for a history of the Scottish tradition in economic thought.

6 See Friedman (1953).

7 For a good example of this position see Brennan and Buchanan (1981), and Buchanan and Wagner (1977, 1978).

8 See Fisher (1911) and Marshall (1923).

9 See Robbins (1934) for a good example of such a position on government intervention.

10 See Wicksell (1936), and Strom and Thalberg (1979) for various appraisals of Wicksell's contributions.

11 See Friedman (1956, 1957). His methodology was also, of course, exposited by his students. See, for example, Cagan (1956).

12 Both Tobin (1958) and Modigliani (1954, 1963) share Friedman's general vision of micro-foundations to a large degree. Thus, today, modern macroeconomic textbooks can distinguish their models in a common analytical framework (or paradigm).

13 See Laidler and Parkin (1975) for a good exposition of this model and its development.

14 See Santomero and Seater (1978) for a survey of this evidence.

15 See Kevin Hoover (1984) for a comparison of monetarism and new Classical economics. He emphasizes the fact that the former comes from the Marshallian tradition and the latter the Walrasian tradition.

16 See Modigliani (1977) for a clear statement that he regarded Freidman's views as essentially similar to his own looked at from a slightly different perspective.

17 See Laidler and Parkin (1975) for extended discussion of the shift away from 'adaptive expectations' to 'optimal predictors' in monetarist thought.

18 See Muth (1961) for his seminal contribution. For general surveys and evaluations Begg (1982), Sheffrin (1983) and Carter/Maddock (1984) offer a range of views on the subject.

19 See Laidler (1982) for a clear monetarist statement along these lines.

20 See Lucas and Sargent (1981) for a statement of this position.

21 To quote Thomas Sargent: 'The natural rate hypothesis is taken to assert that only the *current* unexpected part of inflation (or of any other variable) affects unemployment. Neither the expected part of inflation nor any lagged unexpected rate of inflation is permitted to affect unemployment. Now this seems to be a much too stringent interpretation of the natural rate hypothesis, in the sense that one can produce a model which would deliver all the "neutrality" results associated with the natural rate hypothesis but

which at the same time is rejected by the tests. . . Such models are arrived at by considering the implication of permitting *lagged* unexpected parts of inflation (or any other variable) to affect unemployment' (Sargent 1976, p. 73). As Carter and Maddock (1984) point out, this quote illustrates the manner in which the natural rate hypothesis was refined to take it further away from the monetarist version and its associated inability to provide empirical support for strong versions of the rational expectations hypothesis.

22 A point made, of course, by Friedman (1957) in his 'econometrics of errors' study of the consumption function.

23 See Robinson (1971, 1973) and contrast with Tobin (1980) who continues to use orthodox micro-foundations beneath the Keynesian pseudo-natural rate: the 'non-accelerating inflation rate of unemployment' (NAIRU).

24 The best example of such a defence is in Stein (1982).

25 See Laidler (1982a) for the explicit introduction of imperfect competition into monetarist analysis and Laidler (1982) for support of the concept of rational expectations but with much broader discussion of market structure including a juxtaposition of the 'Austrian' and Walrasian concepts of equilibrium.

26 We have already discussed this shift and Courakis's (1978) protestations. In many ways it was a problem that weighed much more heavily on monetarists than Keynesians, given their more clearly specified empirical methodology and their commitment to empiricism which new Classicals had shed. It was no longer possible to argue support for a hypothesis without a high standard of dynamic modelling accompanied by good diagnostics. When Friedman and Schwartz (1982) published their UK study they were subject to the kind of attack from Hendry and Ericsson (1983) that would have been unimaginable a decade earlier.

27 There was nothing new about these studies. They came from a long neo-classical microeconomic tradition in the US which previously didn't connect with a compatible macroeconomics.

28 As Kevin Hoover argues, in his excellent comparison of monetarism and new Classical economics: '. . . the Lucas critique . . . follows from the insistence on general interdependence and not from the rational expectations hypothesis itself' (Hoover, 1984, p. 68). It is this emphasis on interdependence in a forward-looking context that offers potential for the future.

29 The Institute of Economic Affairs was at the forefront, in the postwar period, in promulgating anti-government propaganda. Their Hobart Papers series focused on short, journalistic monographs written by economists with the free market close to their hearts. Complex theoretical and empirical analysis was simplified and linked to outspoken policy recommendation with little or no attempt to offer balance in terms of allowing other points of view to be expressed.

30 This was perceived as early as 1976 by William Poole and has recently been argued, more formally, by John Taylor. (See, for example, Taylor, 1983.)

31 The Lucas (1976) critique of policy simulation argues, quite straightforwardly, that the Keynesian macroeconometric modellers' habit of 'rerunning history', by introducing policy impulses into their estimated models, is invalid because these impulses would result in a change in the structure of the model as expectations of policy impact are formed.

32 See Eichner (1979) and Crotty (1980) for general appraisals of the post-Keynesian approach. See also Tobin (1959) for a typical response by the Keynesian orthodoxy. More recently, the tendency has been to move away from Keynes towards the dynamic analysis of Michael Kalecki (see, for example, Sawyer, 1982).

33 The spirit of pessimism which permeates some of the post-Keynesian writings comes, of course, from strong historical connections with Marxist or neo-Marxist thought. It was something which Joan Robinson continually tried to combat (see, for example, Robinson, 1980), but remains to this day (see, for example, Rowthorn, 1977, 1980).

34 The need for such a unifying myth was well understood in the inter-war years and constituted a more important source of resistance to Keynes's thought than mere reality. To quote Boris Ischboldin (Sharpe, 1974, reviews his writings), who was many years ahead of his time in his grasp of the dynamics of the economic system but acutely aware of its dependence on human ideas: 'We are firmly convinced that in the present Epoch of the rising self-consciousness of the man in the street and of the continuous deepening of the second great technological revolution our system of private property and individual initiative needs a powerful myth in Sorel's or Pareto's sense if it has to ward off successfully the increasing blows delivered by pure collectivism' (Ischboldin, p. 506).

35 See Minford (1983) for a good statement of this position.

36 See Weintraub (1979) for a comprehensive survey of the micro-foundations on offer.

37 To appreciate fully this position it is necessary to depart into political philosophy and the contemporary work of, for example, Rawls (1971) and Nozick (1970). Such political analysis has been influential on the economic policy stance of, for example, James Buchanan and his colleagues at Virginia Polytechnic Institute.

38 See Boland (1982) and Caldwell (1982) for assessments of the consequences of persisting with neo-classical/reductionist ways of thinking. For a less methodological approach, see Akerloff (1979).

4 *New Directions in Keynesian Economics*

> It seems to me that equilibrium theorists are saying: the world must be like the Walrasian model because that is the model we have. Those who are in touch with reality seem to say: the world is not like the Walrasian model, but perhaps the resemblance could be made closer. That is real progress. I would like to argue for even a little more imagination: the world may have its reasons for being non-Walrasian.
>
> Robert Solow (1983)

The rise in new Classical economics to the level of influencing policy in the US and the UK has been founded solidly on market clearing principles. Its success has been based on confronting both monetarists and, to a lesser extent, orthodox Keynesians with the logical implications of maintaining that market clearing equilibrium exists in the long run. It has been pointed out, with impeccable clarity, that the existence of rational expectations in conjunction with this widely held view of equilibrium renders the supply side the critical area of attention. In turn, analysis of the supply side has been in terms of changing the structure of incentives and disincentives faced by the rational economic agents who make supply side decisions in order to maximize utility.

The denial of slow market adjustment in favour of expectational errors to justify temporary deviations from full information equilibrium provides a logic which is so sharp as to be out of tune with empirical reality.[1] Serial correlation in critical magnitudes has been difficult to deny and has lain uncomfortably with the concept of rational expectations. One solution has been to weaken the axioms of rationality by raising information barriers and thus extending the length of time over which short-run expectational errors could have a distorting effect. However, such an approach proves extremely uncomfortable for new Classicals because it seems to permit interventionist cases to be made in certain circumstances, even though they are so seriously qualified that they cease to be very Keynesian in spirit.[2]

This defect has been largely remedied by the explicit acknowledgement of the existence of contractual arrangements which are viewed as rational devices in certain market conditions.[3] Theorists such as John Taylor have demonstrated that the existence of optimal contracts permits serial correlation to exist even with strong rational expectations and continuous equilibrium.[4] Thus, with the help of the optimal contract, new Classical economics can continue to argue that rational expectations disqualify all demand management policy. The rigidity imposed by the existence of unexpired contracts can enable Keynesian policy to have short-run effects, but at the expense of inflation which leads to shortening of contract periods and a tendency for the economic system to move towards the non-contractual new Classical story.[5]

On the face of it, explicit acknowledgement of the fact that economic agents form contractual arrangements into the future seems to have strengthened the new Classical ability to make theory consistent with economic reality. As such, the contractual approach has taken on an unappealing, almost trivial guise, despite the high hopes expressed in the second half of the 1970s that a new basis for macroeconomics had been discovered. Now, although it is perfectly understandable that the contractual approach could never be more than a means to an end in new Classical economics, why has it failed to bear fruit in Keynesian analysis, which has always been concerned with 'rigidities', particularly in the labour market? The purpose of this chapter is to attempt to answer this question. First, an overview and evaluation of the development of the contractual approach is presented. It is argued that Keynesian development has been stultified by its supply side and, in the second part of the chapter, an attempt is made to clarify the nature of this supply side problem in Keynesian thought. In the third part of the chapter an attempt is made to demonstrate the manner in which Keynesian thought might evolve once it is freed of its supply side problem. This demonstration is presented in the form of a 'scenario', designed to raise more questions than it answers, and, in the chapter that follows, the task of attempting to convert assertions into something with more theoretical substance will begin.

The Development of the Modern Contractual Approach

In Chapter 2 it was observed that the work of Patinkin (1956) and Clower (1965) spawned the disequilibrium approach which has at its core the idea of quantity constrained equilibrium. The approach was intended to offer an explanation of short-run wage and price rigidities as an alternative to the discredited IS–LM model. However, it has been pointed out that it did not prove to be successful in reconstituting the Keynesian consensus, despite its compatibility with orthodox microeconomics. While, in the mid 1970s, this approach was being developed further by, for example, Benassy (1975), Dreze (1975), Younes (1975) and Malinvaud (1977), there emerged a quite different approach to explaining wage and price rigidities, again purporting to have its roots in the *General Theory* but cast more formally in modern human capital theory. The approach began with the view, emphasized by Keynes, that workers resisted cuts in money wages for fear of losing their relative position but would tolerate price induced real wage cuts because they left relativities untouched. The general hypothesis seemed to be that 'fairness' was a force which was a criterion in labour supply decisions in addition to real wage levels. Keynes never attempted to operationalize the notion of 'fairness' and, as such, the idea remained in the background in the Keynesian era.[6]

In the 1960s the development of the human capital approach to the labour market decision led to the conclusion that the existence of job-specific skills and training meant that the relationship between wage and the marginal product of labour might not prevail except over a whole career and that firms would retain skilled labour in recessions. Thus, the incidence of lay-offs could be explained through the acknowledgement of the qualitative diversity of skills and the consequent existence of different degrees of bonding between workers and firms. Although this approach did not explain much in terms of macroeconomics it did establish the notion of some kind of 'contract' between workers and firms which could provide a rationale for inflexibilities in the short run.

The idea became fairly general and, thus, applicable to macroeconomic issues in the wake of the work of Azariadis (1975) and Baily (1974) who argued that even with homogeneous labour and zero transaction costs a case could be made for the existence of implicit contracts between two parties. They argued that the labour market had both a spot and a forward dimension where labour services could be traded for insurance cover. The net effect of such behaviour was to stabilize the purchasing power of wages and fluctuations in employment.[7]

This 'implicit contracts' approach then became the subject of much research in the labour market context in an attempt to establish, theoretically, whether or not voluntary or involuntary unemployment would be generated in recessions. The role of unemployment benefits as a source of external insurance was also discussed in some detail, including considerations of the 'moral hazard' involved in such arrangements. Throughout this literature there is a general tendency to continue to retain the homogeneous labour assumption, although explicit account of information and adjustment costs is taken in modelling optimal contracts. Even so, the underlying core of the analysis is the Walras-Arrow-Debreu model and the central question asked is whether or not the existence of risk-reducing implicit contracts can generate involuntary unemployment solutions. In other words, the contractual approach has not been developed in its own right but rather as a forward-market extension of the spot-market model in an attempt to generate Keynes-Hicks style results. Characterization of the macro-system is strictly from neoclassical micro-foundations with contractual modifications floating up from the labour market. Thus, the approach is in the job-search tradition of attempting to provide better micro-foundations for macroeconomics.[8]

More recently, one fundamental departure from the Walrasian paradigm has been to argue that information is asymmetric as between workers and employers.[9] In particular, cases where the marginal revenue product of labour is known only to the entrepreneur have been developed. The upshot of this work is, unsurprisingly, that private information is sufficient to explain departures of employment from its Pareto optimal level, but does not offer any prediction as to whether this inefficiency will take the form of involuntary unemployment. Much depends on the nature of the asymmetry. This ambiguous result means that we are not much further forward for we knew already that the Walrasian system was only Pareto optimal with symmetric/public information.

Thus, the contractual literature comes as something of a disappointment to macroeconomists. A promising idea after being subject to rigorous mathematical logic turns out to be unhelpful. To quote Azariadis and Stiglitz (1984):

> Whatever progress we have made towards understanding fluctuations in employment has not dispelled the dense fog that still shrouds the issue of wage rigidity.

They go on to add that:

> Macroeconomic applications require the imbedding of contracts in some aggregative model of general equilibrium that contains at least one paper asset.

These quotes make quite explicit that the contractual approach has been considered in a strictly limited context: explaining wage rigidities in a competitive market context. Thus, as such, the approach involves no revolution in thinking, merely the extension of neo-classical optimizing behaviour into an intertemporal framework, or, to put it another way, the extension of the human capital approach from microeconomics into macroeconomics. Many authors, as we have seen, regard this as a stringent context within which to deal with contracts, i.e. if a rigid wage/price result can be generated in such a context it is likely to be generally valid in cases of heterogeneous labour and imperfect competition. However, at the same time, there is a danger that the contractual approach may be undersold when it is set in a context which contains notions of equilibria and expectations which render time a theoretical construct and contracts a trivial extension of powerful statics. Indeed, if we look at the impact of the contractual approach on macroeconomic modelling we see that it is used only to justify lags because of the existence of outstanding contracts. The approach is regarded as fundamentally suspect because it predicts that contracts should allow full indexation yet such a prediction is not borne out in reality, particularly in labour markets.[10] This inability of the contractual approach to 'explain the evidence' has resulted in macroeconomists sticking with the disequilibrium or rational expectations approach.

Okun (1981) argued that if we are to appreciate fully the fundamental role of contracting in the economic system we must operate within an imperfectly competitive framework and accept that a wide diversity of contractual arrangements coexist. It is well known that it is difficult to aggregate from conventional treatments of imperfect competition to the macroeconomic level in any tractable way that can be simply specified. Also, it is well known that heterogeneous contracts cannot be dealt with in any formal way. This unquantifiable dimension of the contractual approach is reflected strongly in Okun's book and this is so much so that some see his contribution as one in microeconomics rather than macroeconomics.[11] So, once again, the contractual approach is not permitted to enter macroeconomics in any formal way, facing the ancient blockage that all imperfectly competitive microeconomics has confronted throughout the Keynesian era.

Prices and Quantities is Okun's statement of how he viewed the economic system. It was a book written in the light of a career which was concerned with the provision of useful advice to policy-makers rather than the culmination of some grand theoretical synthesis. Okun was widely acknowledged as having a remarkable understanding of the economic system and how it had changed over the postwar period. In his book he attempted, in an informal way, to present his world view. Although he emphasizes, like many other Keynesians, the fact that the economic system is characterized by imperfect competition, his analysis goes much further in innovative directions. He perceives that the key feature of this type of economy is not the degree to which it deviates from some notion of perfect competition but that such a system is characterized by a system of contracts, both implicit and explicit, which constitute the core basis upon which economic activity can proceed. To Okun, the existence of contractual bonding is the central feature of the economic system upon which, for example, anti-inflation policy should be built. Contracting was not something which was a by-product of market activity, or the basis for exercises in game theory, but a phenomenon which had a life of its own. The contract, and the productive co-ordination which it yielded, was something more than the mere outcome of price differentials and competitive forces. Although the latter were always important at the margin and in crises, where they could be of brief, but potentially catastrophic importance, they were secondary to the relentless tendency toward contractual activity.

Okun's book does not spell out this message in a direct sense – it was not his style to become preoccupied with extended discussion of fundamentals. Rather his book is a collection of a large number of analyses of particular situations which are of policy relevance, but in each one the same point keeps coming through. The overlap between Okun's treatment of many of these issues and conventional treatments of the same questions is large – Okun was always more than eager to integrate his views with those of others, wherever possible. In terms of presenting a theoretical innovation, the trouble with such an approach is that the message is confused and ambiguous to those who attempt to fit what he has to say into their own analytical frameworks. The essays in Tobin (1983) serve to emphasize the extent to which Okun's central message was not taken on board and the manner in which his ideas have been filed back into old ways of looking at the modern economy. It is clear that Okun's ideas require restatement and development in the evolutionary context which permeates his book.

It is a truism that discussion of forward-looking contracts which attempt to account for, explicitly, the characteristics of historical time will not prosper within an auction market framework set in abstract time. Only with a compatible behavioural framework can the contractual approach be useful at the macroeconomic level. But what is the force which keeps pushing macroeconomics back towards the auction market? Certainly not the good intentions of Keynesians for they would dearly like to revitalize their flagging school. No, it is the inherent dichotomization of the macroeconomy into aggregate demand and supply that is the problem.

The difficulty with imperfectly competitive microfoundations on the supply side has always been the inability to generate an unambiguous aggregate production function through which to link output and employment. In order to render aggregate supply meaningful in its interaction with aggregate demand it has always been necessary to make simplifying assumptions concerning the productive structure and, from Keynes on, these assumptions have been neoclassical.[12] Thus, Keynesian macroeconomics, although demand side in emphasis, becomes extremely vulnerable on the supply side, as new Classicals have forcibly demonstrated. The contractual approach has suffered from the same malaise, strait-jacketed by the demand/supply dichotomy upon which it is built. So long as this dichotomy is preserved, attempts such as Okun's to provide a realistic depiction of the supply side are futile. Orthodox macroeconomics will always demand severe simplification, homogeneity and aggregative compatibility on the supply side. But is it really necessary to insist on an aggregate supply/demand dichotomy in Keynesian economics?

The Keynesian Supply Side

Any discussion of the supply side of the Keynesian model must, of course, begin in Keynes's *General Theory*. It was there that Say's Law was reversed and aggregate demand became the prime mover in macroeconomic analysis. As has been repeatedly emphasized, the degree of interdependence of supply and demand at the aggregate level is so high that it is difficult to conceive of their independence even in an abstract way.[13] If, indeed, interdependence is their key characteristic and we retain the auction market vision of the economy, then Say's Law would seem to be affirmed and the Walrasian depiction of the system is an appropriate vehicle for explaining how interdependence 'works'. What Keynes did was to split the macroeconomy up into consumers and producers, both demanding and supplying in two markets: the product and the labour markets. This division makes it no easier to disentangle aggregate demand from aggregate supply than before, but what it does do is to show that *effective* demand can be below the notional equilibrium of the two.

Effective demand was a magnitude which was observable in historical time, unlike its theoretical aggregate supply and demand parents. Thus, when Keynes discusses aggregate supply he does so in a theoretical manner which is necessarily static in nature. It is not the objective here to offer an intensive account of how Keynes envisaged aggregate supply, for that has already been done with great thoroughness, particularly by Victoria Chick. We need not do so for Keynes did not give it too much attention: 'Keynes seems to have assumed that the supply-side was easily understood. (How wrong he was!)' Chick (1983), p. 82. Essentially, Keynes followed the Marshallian method when dealing with the supply side, getting into the 'short run' by fixing a factor (capital) and assuming diminishing returns to labour along a production function.

Now, although Keynes went to great lengths on the demand side to get his analysis into historical time, his Marshallian supply side analysis remains in abstract time – a contrived short run created by taking capital out of the picture and having producers wholly concerned with their derived labour demand, remaining in equilibrium through their profit maximizing urges. Meanwhile, on the demand side, these same producers roll up their sleeves and participate in the dynamics of historical time, altering their flows of expenditure on capital in ways so powerful that the stability of the whole economy is affected. This schizophrenia among producers, on the one hand obsessively concerned with changing their capital stock and, on the other, calmly maintaining static equilibrium in factor markets as if capital was fixed, is entirely the product of pushing together a historical time short run with an abstract time short run. It was a very necessary division for Keynes's model because it enabled him to track demand side instability reliably to employment.

The fire of historical time dynamics was not allowed to burn into the Marshallian theory of the firm and its demand for labour but, instead, it ignited the other side of the labour market: labour supply. Actual earnings in any period were associated with aggregate income and, in turn, expenditure. Thus, there was no guarantee that wage cuts would stimulate employment, but, perhaps more significantly, Keynes introduced historical time behaviour in labour supply whereby money wages are fixed because of a very real world concern for relativities. In abstract time this looked irrational in comparison with the neat marginalist principles being continuously practised on the other side of the labour market. The historical time vision of labour supply was further developed by Keynes in his view that real wages could be cut by raising prices, again suggesting abstract time irrationality. Of course, there was nothing irrational about ignoring prices in the Great Depression compared with, say, the 1970s.[14] However, irrespective of the historical time antics of labour supply, whatever labour was supplied, at whatever wage, would be fed into the timeless productive structure to compute an output. Thus, an aggregate supply curve could be envisaged which intersects with an aggregate demand curve at effective demand which could be below full employment. This 'supply curve' constitutes more of a 'capacity-utilization' curve prevailing in conditions where the assumptions underlying neo-classical production theory are breached. This inconsistency has left many an able student of macroeconomics struggling to comprehend the slick analysis of his intermediate textbook!

It was argued in Chapter 2 that the resultant model was extremely successful in achieving Keynes's primary objectives. The fact that an abstract time production sector meshed uneasily with a historical time analysis of effective demand was not an immediate problem for Keynes. In fact it may have been something of an advantage in the eclectic mixture that it produced. Although the revolutionary aspects of his model all lay in the macroeconomic, or holistic characterizations of behaviour set in historical time, the very essence of historical time is that the world changes and characterizations become dated. Although the central theory of effective demand did not date because its logic applies to any monetary economy, Keynes's holistic characterizations of investor optimism/pessimism, labour supply responses and speculator behaviour in financial markets all gradually become obsolete or heavily qualified. This was not the case with the supply side analysis of the productive sector in abstract time. The principles involved were immune to historical obsolescence.

Keynes had not gone far enough in his historical time analysis and the points of interface between history and abstraction remained blurred. For example, the interaction between producers' behaviour with regard to capital formation and the direct implications for patterns of demand in the labour market were not tied together even though both involved profit. The role of flows of credit in capital formation, emphasized in the *Treatise on Money*, were underplayed in favour of liquidity considerations necessary to maintain current production. In the labour market the implicit contractual arrangements which lay behind sluggish wage change were not developed by Keynes. It is clear why; admission that contractual commitments existed into the future would vastly complicate and even destroy the marginal productivity theory of labour demand, and Roy Harrod had warned Keynes of the consequences of that.[15]

Keynes was able to clothe his macroeconomic analysis with historical time expectations and anticipations but could not provide anything more than comparative statics to analyse macro-dynamics. The temporal fabric of contract, custom and commitment, within which expectations and anticipations naturally reside, was missing.[16] The debate as to whether Keynes was a special case of the Classics or vice versa is in this sense irrelevant. Keynes could never be a special case of the Classics for the Classical system cannot admit historical time and, equally, it is trivial to argue that Classical analysis can be a special case in historical time. Keynes's analysis was a special case of a more general, and yet to be discovered, historical time analysis.[17]

We saw in Chapters 2 and 3 how Keynesians and monetarists chiselled away at the historical time dimensions of the *General Theory*, gradually exposing its Achilles' heel on the supply side. Earnest attempts to reconstruct Keynes's system to extend rather than reduce its historical time content were rare. There were a few post-Keynesians, most notably Jan Kregel, who made rather isolated efforts to place Keynes in the correct perspective and attempted to develop his ideas.[18] However, many post-Keynesians seemed to be more interested in the discontinuity features of historical time rather than the continuity aspects, tending to discredit historical time analysis in the eyes of orthodox Keynesians. There is a clear trade-off between history and analysis. The latter must have enough of the former to be 'relevant', but not too much, otherwise it is no longer of value beyond a very short period of history. In general, the dynamics of conflict tend to be very history specific whereas the features of continuity tend to have a long analytical life. The principle of effective demand falls into the latter category.

There has been an increasing tendency in post-Keynesian economics to favour Michael Kalecki's analysis over that of Keynes because it is more realistic.[19] In turn, the institutionalists tend to argue that Keynes was too 'psychologistic' in his treatment of economic behaviour, leaving his analysis open to the kind of neo-classical revisionism that we have discussed in previous chapters.[20] The institutionalists argue, quite correctly, that the abstract time conceptions of the productive structure in Keynes's thought should be replaced by a more explicit institutional approach couched in historical time. However, it does not necessarily follow that the 'psychologism' of Keynes need be abandoned. If that is done all that we have is history and no analysis. There is no 'black and white' division of institutions and social psychology. Customs, contracts and conventions reside as much in the latter as the former. As Keynes perceived correctly, these are social phenomena which relate to the analysis of the future and form an indissoluble relativistic link with the institutional constraints of the past.[21]

It is not possible to determine the institutional structure of the future from the institutions of the past, yet, as Keynes perceived, the evolution of that structure can be facilitated by appropriate socio-psychological conditions. The institutionalists seem to misunderstand the nature of Keynes's 'psychologism' which they tend to equate with neo-classical visions of rationality. Although it is true that Keynes presented a schizophrenic vision in this regard, he clearly saw the importance of group identities. Of course, it is easy for an institutionalist to criticize the group psychologies that Keynes identified because they shift over time more quickly than institutions do. Nonetheless, these psychologies remain vitally important for any short-run macroeconomic analysis. Keynes was correct in his view that it was necessary to hold productive structure 'constant' in some sense, in order to focus on the flow characteristics of the macroeconomy; the problems arose from his Marshallian method of achieving such constancy.[22] In the chapters that follow we shall present some justification for this view as well as caution against the over-zealous use of psychologism by, for example, George Shackle and the 'Austrians'.

The Keynesian supply side can be divided into two camps: the orthodox Keynesians who continue to keep the supply side in abstract time, and the institutionalist post-Keynesians who operate in historical time but prefer a mixture of historical inertia and indeterminate conflict dynamics. The latter deny the validity of the aggregate demand/supply dichotomy as well as the notion of Walrasian equilibrium only to leave us with a characterization of the macroeconomy which is profoundly pessimistic. The curbing of power and 'enlightened' social planning are the routes to economic development. We are left wondering just how those modern economies, which have had little of either, did so well over the past forty years. Why were social democracies not immobilized by the bitter group struggles that have characterized the supposedly planned economies such as Poland? Something is missing in post-Keynesian historical time analysis, rendering it unsuitable as a complement to Keynesian theory or as an adequate explanation of the historical experience of Keynesian policy.

In the ensuing chapters an attempt will be made to offer a vision of the macroeconomy which develops directly from Keynes's insight. However, in the first instance, it will be necessary to depart from macroeconomics into other branches of economics as well as other disciplines. In order to give the reader some feeling for where we are going, a sketch, or scenario, of the modern macroeconomy in historical time will be presented. This sketch focuses on the contract, but from an entirely different standpoint to that taken in most of the 'contractual approach' literature, raising questions that it is hoped will be answered adequately in the remainder of the book.

The Evolution of the Contractual System

Today, if we look at the modern economic system, what we observe is a vast structure of contracts both implicit and explicit. The auction market is no longer the typical institutional arrangement for price setting except in the case of durable stocks: antiques, commodities, financial assets, etc. Trade, i.e. flows of goods and services and flows of labour services, is no longer approximated by an auction. As Okun

(1981) emphasized, both types of trade are subject to contractual arrangements between buyers and sellers. Firms advertise to weld an implicit contract with loyal customers, and they negotiate explicit and implicit contracts with labour to ensure continuity in sophisticated production processes. As the economic system has evolved towards greater complexity of production, requiring more specialized skills, the contract has proved to be the rational device to foster co-operation in production and consumption which is stable and where innovations can be developed within a system of contractual security.[23]

The auction market is inefficient in a heterogeneous economy and has all but disappeared. We teach about the interaction of flow demand and supply to determine an equilibrium price but where do we observe such a phenomenon in its pure form? The aforementioned markets for stocks are essentially speculative, reflecting expectational effects concerning the dynamics of the vast contractual economy. Even in agriculture, that much quoted example of a competitive market, producers need to have their income guarantees so that they can operate on a contractual basis the same as the rest of the system.

The auction market becomes a special case in a contractual system. It operates only in circumstances where there is a primitive implicit contract, i.e. that buyers and sellers agree to have an auction where trade occurs, obeying the market clearing rules laid down by the auctioneer. It is a system which can cope with expectations which generate, for example, cobweb disequilibrium paths as producers struggle to alter their output in line with expected prices. It is very unsuited to any form of production which requires guarantees to enable a producer to produce a novel product. He will not do so unless, first, he enters an explicit contract with the buyer or, second, he is able to inform buyers ahead of time, through communication such as advertising, of the novel features of his product, i.e. unless he can attempt to weld some kind of implicit contract.

So the auction market model is truly static in the sense that the productive flows that generate the stocks for sale on auction day cannot develop quantitatively or qualitatively. For that to happen, aspirations, ideas and innovations require contracts. Then there is no open market as such, only a web of contracts. Marketeers will protest that everything is traded ultimately at some price in a contractual system so that the principles of market clearing remain. However, in a system which is contractual, what is critical for clearing is that income and credit availability is sufficient to produce expenditure to purchase output produced. Demand and supply, as Keynes taught us, are not independent in a contractual system. The price set on a contract is the sum of input prices plus a mark-up and what matters is that buyers have sufficient spending power and information of the product to purchase the output. If this is not the case then some contracts will yield insufficient income which, in turn, causes chain reactions to other contracts.

Price in a contractual situation is the outcome of forward-looking negotiation between interested parties, not an auction market. The criterion which is fundamental is the notion of fairness, for an onerous or dishonest contract is unlikely to yield very much useful co-operation. It is this principle of fairness which has led to the modern explosion of the contractual system. Adam Smith praised the market because it fostered constructive self-interest and saw beneath it the importance of a system of values. Even Smith's baker probably had an order book which provided an implicit contract that depended on promises being fulfilled. Smith's view was radical because much thought in his time still held that only systems of command, i.e. implicit and explicit contracts of a one-sided type, could ensure prosperity. Smith's anti-authoritarianism and his trust in fairness anticipated a far reaching revolution in thought. His perception of the productivity advantages of the division of labour, as the specialized, interdependent market economy evolved, was borne out by history. His tendency to underestimate the ability of authoritarian practices that he criticized to survive in the new capitalist organizations was more a product of his enthusiastic idealism than naivety. It was not until the later stages of capitalist development that conditions became favourable for the rise of the Marxist view that there had, indeed, been the kind of evolution that Smith had predicted, but the new social contract – between workers and capitalists – was essentially exploitative.

The development of Marxist thought, following Smith, led to a constructive reaction that generally reduced the unequal nature of the capitalist–worker contract and brought the state into the structure of the economy, overseeing controls on working conditions and restrictive practices. Essentially, the state accepted an implicit social contract to prevent, simultaneously, the excesses of monopoly capitalism and to encourage competition. Within such an environment, emphasis on the importance of the contract, already inherent in the *Wealth of*

Nations, did not increase but declined. Ricardian visions of a contractual economy, where prices were determined by contractual negotiation, had acquired a conflictual flavour which posed a threat to the free market. Consequently, neo-classical economists preferred to expand the auction market model toward Walrasian generality, a structure which was perceived as Pareto optimal in terms of social welfare. Economics began to part company with reality, going into a static abstraction which was ideologically useful but quite irrelevant to understanding the evolution of the economic system.[24] Meanwhile, the economic system was developing through forward-looking contracts backed by loans from a risk-bearing financial system. By the time Joseph Schumpeter attempted to place competition in a dynamic perspective his model had become non-absorbable into the orthodox auction market economics that had developed.

By the 1930s, the contractual economy had become so integrated that exogenous contractionary shocks tended to induce severe short-run utilization problems. So it was necessary for the state to extend further its social contract. Forward-looking contracting in the complex industrial structure required a guarantee that income–expenditure flows would be maintained to ensure that growing capacity would be utilized. Although Keynes challenged the validity of the auction market model, he did so in an eclectic way which allowed the neo-classical vision of the economic system to perpetuate, modified by a 'special case' in the labour market.

Keynesian stabilization policy provided a social contract which encouraged contractual confidence like never before, yielding the most dramatic and sustained rates of economic growth in recorded history. The economic system became so concentrated and integrated contractually that the income–expenditure problem that Keynes had observed became an expenditure–income problem of inflation. Expansionary shocks to expenditure began to transmit quickly to income through the closely bound contracts of an expanding system, generating inflationary spirals. The auction market, far from being a place for clearing flow demands and supplies, became an arena where suppliers of vital inputs into a dependent system could increase their income by collusion and where speculators could capitalize on a general tendency for prices to rise.

Thus, the very success of the contractual system had created an environment where forming contracts became less attractive. The contractual system, being forward-looking, had always required some degree of stability in the value of money. Removal of this stability meant that existing contracts could result in unanticipated gains and losses to either side and future contracts became subject to a new form of uncertainty.[25] Once again, we had a situation where contractual adventure, outside of inflation related activities such as property development, was diminishing with the inevitable result that the economic system could not develop fast enough to absorb increased labour supply. In the end, government, still with a predominantly auction market view of the economic system, tackled the problem of inflation using the instruments bequeathed to it from the days of Keynesian demand management, pulling the levers in the opposite direction, hoping that the mechanism which used to be so effective in expanding output would now reduce inflation, just as auction market analysis suggested it would. And it did, but not for the reasons suggested.

It is well known in systems theory that a system which evolves smoothly into a complex, specialized and interdependent structure is asymmetric in its parameters.[26] In decline it does not reverse smoothly, it fragments. Fragmentation of the contractual system is not likely to improve it but merely ensure that its problems will become more intense. Conservative governments, because they have the wrong paradigm, have been imposing policies which are reinforcing the underlying break-up of the contractual system which had begun to manifest itself in simultaneous inflation and unemployment. A contractual system which is breaking up because the unit of account is no longer sufficiently independent to be relied upon requires a policy which restores this reliability. Monetary control was supposed to do this but the problem with monetary control is that it conflicts with the fundamental social contract to provide sufficient liquidity to guarantee capacity utilization. Growth needs monetary expansion. Reduction of that expansion, although it may help to lower inflation, does not provide a good environment for contractual adventure, it simply withdraws the basis of the social contract upon which the system has come to depend. In conjunction with fiscal contraction it operates on a highly sensitive system in a devastating manner.

Instead of moving the economic system towards a socially optimal position, deflationary policies act in the opposite direction. Once we view the economic system as an evolving structure of interlocking and interdependent contractual obligations, optimality relates to a situation where there is a maximum amount of contractual confidence translating itself into high rates of productivity growth. Thus, policy in an evolutionary setting should be designed to provide incentives for the formation and completion of contractual obligations. Keynesian expansionism provided a crude strategy to do this by guaranteeing that increased production would be met by buoyant demand. Despite the introduction of prices and incomes policies, such attempts to rely on demand management to stimulate supply ultimately proved too crude for the sophisticated system that came into being, with its sensitive expectational and aspirational feedback loops. The tendency for workers to make relative comparisons of wages with those in other firms, industries and occupations observed by Keynes, the tendency of consumers to make relative consumption comparisons observed by Duesenberry (1949), and the tendency of firms to normal cost price in contestable markets observed by Andrews (1964), all increased in strength as economic evolution proceeded. In other words, the matrix of implicit and explicit contracts expanded with great rapidity.

As this process proceeded, an increasing proportion of income constituted economic rent rather than returns for productive effort. Quite naturally, if the dominant social contract involves indiscriminate support of all activities, then, to an increasing extent, income will disassociate itself from productive effort. The new Classicals tend to see this process as inefficient, yet in many ways it was essential to distribute the fruits of progress, a point clearly grasped by politicians such as Macmillan. Removal of the Keynesian social contract merely emphasizes, more brutally than before, that economic rents will accrue to those with tangible property rights or contracts enforceable by the law. Further progress should not require that the spread of economic rents be narrowed but, instead, that new, highly productive ventures are rewarded so that they, in turn, can further contribute to the provision of more economic rent in the economic system, spread through the private and public sectors.

The new Classicals argue along similar lines concerning incentives, but their analysis ignores both the contractual system and the related existence of economic rent. General tax cuts increase the disposable income of individuals earning economic rents as much as those who depend on their productive effort. Policies which cut welfare benefits and deregulate safety standards alienate the underprivileged, reducing their capacity to form creative contractual bonds and forcing them to submit to exploitative employment. Although deflationary policy eradicates inflation, the resultant withdrawal of the Keynesian social contract means the suspension of many contracts based upon it. This, in turn, has adverse 'supply side' effects that cannot be detected in the new Classical model.

Our sketch of the evolution of the contractual economy is now complete. We are in the 1980s and approaching an evolutionary crisis of unpredictable extent or timing. In some economies the onset of catastrophic conditions are more likely than in others, depending very much on the unique evolutionary paths of different countries and the kind of macroeconomic policies that they have chosen to pursue. History tells us clearly that the economic and political fortunes of different countries have been of a widely varying character at a point in time and in the same place over time. However, history also tells us that the development of social innovations at appropriate times has minimized the seriousness of crises and facilitated subsequent periods of evolutionary development. It is, of course, the existence of the latter possibility that is of interest to the macroeconomist.

Conclusion

It has been argued that the absence of a contractual perspective of the economic system has led to the application of economic policies which have damaged the evolutionary potential of that system. Indeed, the lack of such a perspective has prevented macroeconomic analysis from recognizing, explicitly, the evolutionary character of the macro-system. In the first part of the chapter it was shown how narrow and confining contracts have been dealt with from the orthodox market clearing perspective. This theoretically precise but empty development has been deliberately juxtaposed with a sweeping set of generalizations concerning the evolutionary nature of the contractual system. A theorist would be inclined to dismiss the latter as a set of assertions lacking logical development. However, any broad-brush sketch is designed, not to provide answers but, rather, to stimulate questions.

Clearly, the perceptive macro-theorist would be particularly interested in two questions. First, much is made of contractual interdependence, but the macro-interdependence theory that we have is the Walrasian one set in a system of clearing markets. How can a macro-model which emphasizes the kind of contractual interdependence discussed, be specified in a way that provides a paradigm within which macro-analysis can be set? Second, once we depart from a system of markets, will rational economic man still be rational in the manner of orthodox *homo economicus* or will we require an alternative simplification?

These are important and difficult questions to answer since they take us behind the formal theoretical manipulations with which we are familiar and have, almost instinctively, been applied in the recent contractual literature. The theoretical constructs which form paradigms, such as the Walrasian system and the *homo economicus* abstraction, are not quantifiable in any sense but rather *qualitative*, forming no more than an intellectual basis for the quantifiable in formal theoretical and empirical analysis. As such, these constructs reside in an area variously labelled as subjective, normative, ideological, etc. Consequently, it is necessary to look beyond what we would normally view as economics to discover alternative constructs. We saw, in our assessment of Keynesian attempts to develop the 'supply side', that some post-Keynesians have tried to develop an institutional alternative which draws on inter-disciplinary material. However, in doing so they have tended to throw out Keynes's preliminary, but profound insights into socio-psychological factors and their role in the macro-economy. On the other hand, post-Keynesians such as George Shackle recognize explicitly the importance of Keynes's socio-psychological factors and have proceeded to attempt to develop them into suitable theoretical constructs. Institutionalists see these constructs as so different to their own that they choose to classify them as 'neo-Austrian' and closer to Hayek than to our orthodox vision of Keynes.

As soon as we tamper with core constructs in economics, the way in which we normally partition schools of thought tends to break down. Thus, there exists an inbuilt resistance amongst orthodox economists to playing with core constructs and the chaotic character of the post-Keynesian 'school' is frequently pointed to as the inevitable outcome of meddling with fundamentals. In the next two chapters we shall take care to move cautiously into these sensitive areas, being careful not to alienate the sceptical economist along the way. By the end of this journey we shall be a long way from territory familiar to the macroeconomist, but well-placed to attempt to provide answers to the two aforementioned questions we would expect a theorist to ask.

Notes

1 In particular, see Grossman and Stiglitz (1980) who argue that an informationally efficient market, never out of equilibrium, is a *logical* impossibility in historical time. Hahn (1980) launches a similar attack against the monetarist tendency to assume the existence of some kind of long-run Walrasian equilibrium.
2 See Carter and Maddock (1984) for detailed discussion of this dilemma which confronts new Classical economists.
3 See Poole (1976) for one of the first attempts to utilize contracts in this manner in macroeconomics.
4 See Taylor (1980, 1983) and Sargent (1984).
5 See Parkin (1986) for a transitional model along these lines.
6 The most strenuous modern attempts to operationalize the concept of 'fairness' and the related notion that 'custom' has important economic effects have been made by George Akerlof. See, in particular, Akerlof (1984), for a 'retrospective' on his efforts.
7 See Azariadis and Stiglitz (1983) and Rosen (1985) for good expositions of this approach and surveys of the various theoretical contributions which have appeared in this tradition.
8 See Weintraub (1979) for extended discussion of how the neo-classical tradition has restricted the manner in which micro-foundations have been linked to macroeconomics.
9 See Azariadis and Stiglitz (1983) and Hart (1983) for good expositions of this approach.
10 See Dornbush and Simonsen (1983) for discussion of the factors which lead to indexation of money-valued contracts.
11 See Bosworth in Tobin (1982), p. 121.
12 See Chick (1983) for a full discussion of the manner in which the Keynesian supply side is constructed.
13 See Patinkin (1976) for an expression of this view.
14 See Trevithick (1975) for some discussion of this dimension of Keynes's thought.
15 To requote from Chick (1983): 'The effectiveness of your work . . . is diminished if you try to eradicate very deep-rooted habits of thought *unnecessarily*. One of these is the supply and demand analysis. I am not merely thinking of the aged and fossilised, but of the younger generation who have been thinking perhaps only for a few years but very hard about these topics. It is doing great violence to their fundamental groundwork of thought, if you tell them that two independent demand and supply functions won't jointly determine price and quantity. Tell them that there may be more than one solution. Tell them that we don't know the supply function. Tell them that the *ceteris paribus* clause is inadmissible and that we can discover more important functional relationships governing price and quantity in this case which render the s. and

d. analysis nugatory. But don't impugn that analysis itself.' (p. 132)

16 See Hodgson (1985) for extended discussion of this incompleteness in Keynes's thought.

17 Joan Robinson saw this more clearly than most post-war Keynesians (see Robinson, 1978a).

18 See Kregel (1973, 1976, 1980) and Eichner and Kregel (1975).

19 See Sawyer (1982) who argues that Kalecki's analysis is superior to Keynes's in this regard on four counts. See Taylor (1983) for an example of the use of Kaleckian analysis in the context of the macroeconomics of developing countries.

20 See Hodgson (1985) for a clear statement of this position.

21 Again, Kregel seems to appreciate this relativity more than most post-Keynesians: 'The system reacts to the absence of the information the market cannot provide by creating uncertainty-reducing institutions: wage contracts, debt contracts, supply agreements, administered prices, trading agreements' (Kregel, 1980, p. 46).

22 See Nagatani (1981) for an excellent attempt to develop the Marshallian method further than Keynes did in order to highlight the key questions that Keynesian macroeconomists have to answer. In particular, once the Marshallian treatment of logical time is exposited more fully, Nagatani shows that many of the tenets of monetarism and rational expectations do not stand up well, once denied the Walrasian framework. Hicks (1977, 1979), from a slightly different perspective, does the same thing.

23 In political science the past decade has also witnessed the rise of the implicit contract approach inspired by Rawls (1971). Olson (1982) has provided a link between the two disciplines in presenting his long-run political economy of social evolution.

24 Even though the neo-classical abstraction was unhelpful in interpreting the evolution of the economic system, this does not mean that such an abstraction did not have a constructive role in promoting that evolution. Ischboldin's work has already been mentioned in this regard.

25 See Foster (1976) for discussion of the redistributive potential of inflation.

26 For an introduction to systems theory see Emery (1969, 1981).

5 *The Bio-philosophical Foundations of Macroeconomics*

> If we object that . . . historicizing, psychologizing and sociologizing are not the business of economics, then we must conclude that the objector thinks that long-term growth theory is not the business of economics.
>
> Herbert Simon (1984)

In the last chapter it was argued that the contractual approach has not succeeded in gaining the central place in macroeconomics that any casual inspection of the structure and evolution of the macro-system would suggest. The problem was seen as being one that stems from the continued use of neo-classical behavioural foundations, where economic agents are presumed to be rational utility maximizers interacting in markets which tend toward equilibrium solutions. A continuing theme of previous chapters has been the view that the rise and fall of the Keynesian consensus can be attributed to the continued existence and ultimate strengthening of these foundations, forcing new developments in macroeconomics to fit into a behavioural context to which they are ill suited. It is no longer possible for the theory of effective demand, concerning the functioning of an interdependent flow system, to co-exist with a Walrasian theory concerning the interaction of a system of auction markets which abstracts from time.

It is essential to take up Robert Solow's challenge and attempt to provide foundations for macroeconomics which can admit the theory of effective demand, as well as any other properties of systems which might appear relevant to the behaviour of the macroeconomy. It would be misleading to suggest that we are to undertake a search for 'micro-foundations' simply because the separation of microeconomics from macroeconomics is an artificial distinction. It should not be possible to have foundations of macroeconomics which can be detached from the macroeconomic perspective. Indeed, in the Walrasian system a separate market cannot be looked on independently because of its interdependence with other markets. It is this unity which has given the Walrasian system so much intellectual authority.[1] By the same token, it is a lack of micro–macro unity that has been the weakness of imperfectly competitive foundations. Because they are classified as deviations from market perfection it is true, by definition, that they cannot form into an integrated micro–macro structure which is manageable. Although such models are extremely useful when we are enquiring into the behavioural implications of different market structures, as a basis for macroeconomics they form no more than a critique of the Walrasian system.[2]

The purpose of what follows is not to challenge the usefulness of orthodox or unorthodox microeconomics in its myriad of applications in disaggregated sectors of the economic system, however defined. Rather, the objective is to develop behavioural constructs which are suited, explicitly, to the macroeconomic level of analysis. It is a 'top-down' rather than a 'bottom-up' perspective. In order to avoid any confusion in this regard, we call them 'bio-philosophical' foundations. The Walrasian system is built entirely on notions of competition which are biological in origin combined with a system of social rules and logical propositions which are philosophical in nature.[3] The Walrasian model does not have microeconomic foundations which are separable but it does have bio-philosophical foundations which can be isolated. In this chapter, the adequacy of these bio-philosophical foundations will be looked at, then attempts by economists to construct new foundations, beyond the realm of macroeconomics, will be considered.

The Creed of Scientific Materialism

It is striking just how resistant the Walrasian system with its *homo economicus* basis has been to attacks from dissenting economists. A cursory glance at recent academic journals demonstrates that the competitive vision of the economic system is as strong as ever. Since it is out of the question actually to test empirically the validity of this system of thought, therefore, in a scientific sense, there has been no reason why it should have been abandoned. It is a world view which provides a 'research programme' or a paradigm within which specific hypotheses can be generated and tested.[4]

The strength of this common vision within the economics profession is remarkable in the sense that it arises not simply from the paradigm resistance, identified by Kuhn (1970) within the physical sciences, but more from attempts to hold on to the distinctiveness and identity of the subject itself.[5] Any economist who meanders too far into sociology, psychology, philosophy or politics constantly runs the risk of ridicule by his peers for 'soft' analysis or even banishment to the limbo land of 'normative', 'unscientific' or 'value-laden' analysis.[6] Those who do take such a path tend to offer lengthy apologies and/or complex justifications for their deviation and, even then, will not be included within the orthodoxy unless ingenious translation into conventional terminology is undertaken.[7] Not surprisingly, this ensures that the conventional framework is kept largely intact with the contribution added as a 'special case', thus consolidating the orthodoxy by seemingly extending its versatility.[8]

Given the depth of the crisis that now exists in economics, so vividly depicted in, for example, Bell and Kristol (1982), it is surprising that such a situation should persist. Kuhnian and Lakatosian explanations are inadequate, as Archibald (1979) has emphasized. It seems that economics is not a science in the conventional sense of the word but rather a specialized fragment of philosophy. As such, a system of logic can persist because it serves to define and delineate a philosophical specialism. In this sense, economics is analogous to a branch of metaphysics or a religious creed. To challenge fundamentals is to commit heresy.[9]

Looking on economics in this way in no way diminishes its importance.[10] As Ischboldin (1958) emphasized, myths are utterly fundamental to the proper functioning of any socio-economic system. When myths have become useless or counterproductive they will tend to change for, as Fromm (1956) emphasized, to function in the reality of experience one must construct imaginary, but consistent, visions of the unknown. However, such change is a much more serious business than Kuhnian paradigm shifts in scientific methodology. In the past, religious reformations have been accompanied by social upheaval of varying severity. Since the time of Adam Smith, the founding father of the capitalist belief system, we have had, of course, the upheaval caused by the widespread adoption of Marxism as a creed in support of the practice of communism. As religious splits go in history, this one was not particularly fundamental – rather analogous to Protestantism versus Catholicism under the common banner of Christianity, or perhaps less disturbing than even that division.

As Fromm (1956) pointed out, capitalism and communism share the same 'religious' roots, i.e. a belief in scientific materialism combined with an acceptance of the evolutionary principle of natural selection. The two creeds differ only in the degree to which they accept these two bio-philosophical foundations. Capitalism, following Smith, became an extension of Christianity, which provided its value structure. In turn, this value structure permitted a competitive process analogous to natural selection to occur in the market place. On the other hand, Marxists saw the process of natural selection as a social struggle between classes, analogous to species, with an ongoing dialectic promoting constructive social development. Christianity was viewed as merely a device used by vested interests to permit exploitation and inhibit progress. The inevitability and desirability of material progress promoted by scientific advance is a foundation of both capitalist and communist creed.

When we examine attempts to replace the Walrasian conception of the macro-system we discover that this prior philosophical commitment to materialism and progress presents resistance at two levels. First, we face the belief that a critique of the Walrasian system must also be a critique of capitalism. Thus, the position must be 'sociological' and, therefore, in the eyes of the free market economist, in the same category as the communist creed. Second, if we challenge the psychological notion of economic agents as utility maximizers attempting to expand the production and consumption of quantities of material goods, we are labelled as 'anti-progressive', breaching the vision of man as rational and scientific.[11] The latter, of course, has a much longer history, dating back to Aristotle, who laid down the philosophic roots upon which scientific materialism is based.[12]

Although the creed of scientific materialism has been challenged in other disciplines, such a challenge is met in economics by objections from both capitalist and socialist proponents.[13] This is understandable given that, of all the specialist offshoots of philosophy, economics espouses, more than any other, the scientific materialist principle. Correspondingly, debate of this principle is permitted to a much lesser degree than in other disciplines. Also, even when empirical evidence is presented in another discipline, it is with great difficulty that results are accepted in economics. In subjects where quantification is difficult at the best of times, agreement concerning the interpretation of results between subjects is even more difficult. In any case, the logical position that the bio-philosophical core of economics is above and beyond empirical questioning can be used as a last resort.

This logical core resides in the imaginary world of ideals to which real world behaviour is seen as tending towards and therefore approximating. Only logical argument that such idealism is misleading can carry any conviction and any counter-argument will, in turn, have to hinge on macro-evidence that the world has altered in such a way that obsolescence has occurred. Great difficulty lies here, for such macro-evidence is not of the type that we would normally present as a test of a hypothesis but rather a sweep of historical description within which the conventional system of logic looks uncomfortable. No test of a hypothesis is presented but merely a flow of experience with which bio-philosophical logic must correspond before it can, in turn, provide the basis for more specialized analysis. Both Darwin and Marx presented such evidence in support of bio-philosophical logic in order to demonstrate that their logic, irrespective of its ultimate 'truth', was in some minimal sense compatible with history.[14]

Such attempts to establish the inconsistency of orthodox bio-philosophical logic with history and the superiority of a new logic are both essential and difficult. Visions of history are themselves conditioned by the prevailing orthodoxy, as well as the subjective experience of particular individuals and groups. Unfortunately, the orthodox mixture of bio-philosophical logic and history, the conservative ideology, tends to be held by the successful and powerful who find that it concurs well with their own subjective experience. The wider discrepancies between ideals and reality in macro-experience tend to be overlooked or ignored. Smith presented a vision which corresponded well with the subjective experience of the emerging capitalist group of his time that felt oppressed by the prevailing merchantilist and semi-feudal orthodoxy. His vision linked the aspirations of this capitalist group to the bio-philosophical logic of competition and the macro-experience of economic development. Marx, also, managed to produce an ideology which married the subjective experience of exploitation amongst the underprivileged to his mixture of bio-philosophical logic and macro-experience.

Perhaps the clinching aspect of a bio-philosophical logic is the importance of some continuity links with the existing orthodoxy, which lead ultimately to vital concessions by enlightened members of the conservative group. Marx did not deny the importance of capitalism in scientific material progress; Smith did not deny that the system of custom, ethics and law inherited from the semi-feudal era was vital to capitalism. Keynes, as we have seen, was the great reconciler of radical reform with the interests of his own class, permitting an evolutionary alternative to the right-wing and left-wing variants of totalitarianism which threatened to crush capitalism in his time. In recent times, the orthodoxy has been a Keynesian one which believes in managed capitalism to promote maximum rates of economic growth. Although the group that is most likely to promote new bio-philosophical foundations is the diffuse one suffering from 'relative deprivation', however defined, in the end the approach will have to be thoroughly integrated into the macroeconomics of the Keynesian orthodoxy. The interdisciplinary modifications will have to be 'filtered' through this perspective.

Resistance to interdisciplinary work in mainstream economics is much stronger today than a century ago, for understandable reasons. First, in an era where material growth has been assigned such a high priority by society it has been inevitable that economics has been elevated to the highest status amongst the social sciences. Secondly, whereas other social sciences seem to focus on disorders and conflict, economics deals with the business of human co-ordination to produce and distribute. Rational, optimizing behaviour is converted into productivity through the operation of self-interest and competition, the same forces which yield destruction in other social sciences. Thirdly, as we have seen, economics developed a quantitative dimension, where it seemed possible to test hypotheses, thus elevating its status to a 'young science'. Given these three factors, it is not surprising that confident, successful economics has been unwilling to be influenced by other disciplines. In fact, it has been so successful that it has, instead, begun to influence other disciplines. The Beckerian school has extended *homo economicus* to the modelling of sociological phenomena such as marriage, divorce, etc.[15] Buchanan has used 'rational economic man' to explore political behaviour.[16] The formal rigour of neo-classical economic logic has proved increasingly attractive in disciplines which lack a strong analytical core.[17] However, the majority of social scientists continue to reject the *homo economicus* representation as a useful way of depicting any more than a very narrow dimension of human behaviour.

The interdisciplinary approach seems to offer little prospect of providing a better basis for macroeconomics. The mixture of vested interests and different behavioural premisses has resulted in past failures, except where co-participants have been allied under some political banner. 'Development studies' offer, perhaps, the best example of the interdisciplinary problem. In addition, we have already discussed the way that incorporation of fragments of analysis, gleaned from other social sciences on a piecemeal basis, tends merely to extend the versatility of the orthodox paradigm. Instead of trying to develop some ambiguous amalgam of incompatible modern specialisms, it is necessary to get to the core of the existing bio-philosophical foundations to examine, in the most basic sense, where they come from.

Competition and Natural Selection

The bio-philosophical foundations of economics were laid down long before social science had emerged as a branch of applied philosophy concerned with human behaviour and then fragmented into specialized disciplines. The distinctive disciplines in those days which were pertinent to economic analysis were natural science and biology. The power of the Newtonian revolution in physics was considerable and it was understandable that economists should consider the extent to which Newtonian laws could be applied to the motion of the economic system. To keep economics within the bounds of quantitative science was thoroughly Aristotelian. Hume's scientific materialist methodology became the application of physical analogies to economics. Later, this became formalized into theories where definable entities, individuals with independent utility functions, interacted through the law of supply and demand. Such physical analogies could also take advantage of mathematical formalization and, in turn, offer the prospect of empirical testing.

However, Newtonian physics is static in the sense that it explores laws of motion which determine the way that a disturbance sets in motion matter which comes to rest at equilibrium. Demand and supply are viewed as flows which are 'equilibriated' by price movement. Now at first glance it seems inappropriate to mimic Newtonian laws within such a context and, indeed, some recent critics of neo-classical economics argue that we should think in terms of 'market balance' rather than equilibrium. These critics tend to miss the point by focusing too narrowly on the perception of flows. Newtonian physics analyses the behaviour of solid structures, abstracting from any consideration as to whether inflows of energy or outflows of characteristics, including entropic degeneration, are taking place. The market is a structure, a social structure which, clearly, is likely to be much more unstable than a physical structure. None the less, analytically, it can be viewed as 'solid' and, thus, no different to a physical structure. Just as a flow disturbance such as Newton's falling apple experiences velocity and acceleration before equilibrium is regained, so a flow shock to demand or supply will set in motion price changes which lead to structural modification before the system settles down again. The apple has moved to a lower level through the law of gravity. The equilibrium quantity traded has changed through the operation of the law of supply and demand. The market structure will tend to equilibrium just as surely as the apple falls to the ground and produces a new spatial configuration of the environment.

So it is, indeed, permissible in logic to regard the social structure that we call a market, or a market system, to be in 'equilibrium'. The difference is that, because physics deals with solids which exhibit motions that can be monitored in experiments, the law of gravity could be empirically defined in terms of the mathematics of velocity and acceleration. Not so in economics – the market is a *qualitative* structure, an institutional arrangement or, more fundamentally, a social idea. We can witness its alteration in structure through observing price changes and quantities traded and we can say that, given the behavioural assumptions concerning suppliers and demanders, *ceteris paribus*, these price changes are predictable. Prices assume higher and lower levels in market structures just like Newton's apples.

This notion that it is not demand and supply that are in equilibrium, but the market structure, translates the analysis directly into a macroeconomic proposition. It is 'static' in the sense that Newtonian physics is, i.e. the *structure* of the matter, which is subject to motion in space and time, is given. Matter will not mutate or alter its energy bonding beyond the Newtonian rules of the game. The latter would be chemistry and *not* subject to Newtonian laws. Thus 'static' Newtonian physics is perfectly capable of modelling the dynamics of matter over time – indeed, that is the goal. By the same token, a Walrasian competitive system need not be as 'out of time' as some critics have implied. Provided it is a system of 'solid' market structures subject to external shocks, as in a physics experiment, then, given time, structural rearrangement will take place through the forces proposed.

The problem for economics is not that a Walrasian model is incapable of being simulated in real time but that the structure it is trying to analyse is not tightly bonded; it is organic, as in biology. Furthermore, it remains only a social idea. In order to retain the physical analogy, human beings have to be rendered somewhat schizophrenic, being part economic part non-economic. In the former, they behave according to impeccable Newtonian laws, in the latter, they are busy devising economic institutions to that end. The inseparability of human behaviour into such categories, both at the individual and social level, ensures that the division cannot be quantified empirically and, at the same time, maintains the strict division of economics from the other social sciences that we have discussed.

The spatial problem that the Walrasian system as a structure might be diluted seriously by the overlap of other social structures is well accepted by economists, not in the model's formal structure, but in the discussion which surrounds it concerning laws, institutions, customs, etc.[18] In this respect it is no different from physics – in the real world physical laws become lost in bio-chemical complexity. The market structure is a social idea – it is observable in institutional form and the Walrasian system involves a logic which demonstrates the social benefits of such an idea. Just as Newtonian physics helps build structures such as bridges, so Walrasian economics stimulates the development of new market structures from the social imagination.

The difficulty lies, not in the spatial restrictiveness of the Walrasian model, but in its inter-temporal characteristics. Newtonian laws of the universe always 'fit' despite the fact that the increased sophistication of science, as the construction of more complex structure proceeds, requires new sets of laws. Thus the advent of the Einsteinian revolution in thinking about physics. The laws of the universe are there to be discovered but, over time, the 'laws' of economics will depend on the development of economic institutions and new social ideas. The acceptance of the Walrasian idea could give rise to behaviour which renders the economic system quite different to the Walrasian model. Physicists do not have to deal with the fact that upon the discovery of Newtonian laws, matter begins to alter in response to the laws it conforms to. The market structure is an institution which is not static. So long as social evolution proceeds then the institutional basis of market structure will alter. Although the Walrasian concept may have proved to be an innovative social idea when capitalism was developing, the extensive development of markets may well point to some other social innovation as superior.

The paradox that the widespread acceptance of the competitive market structure leads to less of a role for the competitive model is only a paradox if we confine ourselves to a narrow economic perspective. Economic success inevitably means social change, which, in turn, will alter the economic priorities and needs of people. The process of discovery in sciences such as physics is, indeed, mirrored in economics. However, what is being discovered are social ideas, not universal facts. It may be that the discovery of useful social structures does constitute such a parallel in the sense that at each stage in evolution there is an optimal set of structures which can permit further evolution. Whether such evolution is predetermined or the outcome of unique circumstances is immaterial. All that is important here is that evolution is taking place. The optimal social idea, thus, can change over time.

Of course, in an evolutionary context, old ideas are never abandoned but incorporated. The competitive model could never have become transcendent without the legal and ethical structure that had provided the innovative basis of the pre-capitalist era. The Keynesian vision could never have worked except within the context of considerable belief in the capitalist system. Furthermore, it takes a long time to dispense with an old and valuable idea. For example, capitalist thought went through a 'throwback' crisis in the second half of the late nineteenth century when Ricardian economics gave way to Marxism and conflict theories, which rejected the competitive mode of thought and redeveloped 'political' ideas of the pre-Smith era. However, this led to the mutation rather than the collapse of the competitive belief system. In more recent times we have seen Keynes, like Smith, laying the foundations of a new bio-philosophic framework. Once again, this new vision of the economic system had eventually to confront 'throwback' theories promoting the old competitive ideal, once again providing a spur for the mutation of orthodox ideas.

Social ideas change as part of the general evolutionary

tendency, therefore, any static structure cannot offer social benefit indefinitely. There is little doubt that the evolutionary nature of the economic system was well appreciated by the early proponents of the competitive ideal such as Adam Smith, although this was not so in the later Walrasian formulations of the competitive system where, for example, the evolutionary model of competition developed by Schumpeter was non-absorbable into orthodox economics. Yet, in a sense, the Walrasian system takes due cognizance of evolutionary principles.

The writings of Charles Darwin had a profound influence in the late nineteenth century. His theory of biological evolution through natural selection provided an ideal complement to the scientific materialism of the natural sciences. Darwin provided fragments of evidence to support his case but, like Walras, he provided a world view within which ideas could be developed without recourse to religious principles. As such, the prospect of incorporation into the dynamics of human behaviour were considerable. The market system in the long run could be characterized as a structure which became increasingly complex through survival of the fittest. In other words, not only did the market system offer the most efficient way of producing a fixed basket of goods, as captured by the static Walrasian model, but also the development of more complex products could also be rationalized. Competition between selfish economic agents and natural selection had a great deal in common.

The vision of a Walrasian system where there is a continuous replacement of new products for old over time could not be specified formally, in strict Newtonian terms, but it was intuitively appealing. The difficulty with formal incorporation was that the malleability of product structures presented an ever present opportunity for selfish economic agents to attain monopoly advantage and secure economic rents, causing the analogy with the Newtonian law to break down. Furthermore, the introduction of natural selection principles over time introduced the possibility that the non-economic behavioural system might also be subject to such principles. After all, it was a biological theory.

Karl Marx ensured that evolutionary principles of natural selection would be kept at some distance from the competitive model in its period of formalization. He treated the social system as an evolutionary one with groups struggling for social power. Social classes were like species with conflict leading to new social relations. Economic exploitation formed the central materialist core of his system, with capitalism reduced to no more than another variant of the imperialism of the past. Social competition paved the way for socialism, where domination of the natural world and social harmony over the distribution of economic product would ultimately prevail. Marx used the theory of natural selection to provide a powerful alternative to the Walrasian system. Again, a world view, but one set in a biological rather than physical analogy and firmly rooted in historical time. As Karl Popper has emphasized, it was a world view which was ultimately political rather than economic.[19] The shock waves of Marxism were enough to squash any discussion of evolutionary principles in economic orthodoxy. Despite the protests raised by Thorstein Veblen and, later, Joseph Schumpeter, the temptation to qualify the bio-philosophical basis was firmly resisted, despite the wholly unsatisfactory attempts to deal with long-run phenomena such as economies of scale and technological progress within the competitive model.

This inability to cope with the full implications of natural selection came to a head in the inter-war years when difficulties in capitalist countries led to the rejection of competitive market principles and a preference for *social* theories of natural selection. The transition from a belief system which emphasized market competition was not difficult. If converts subscribed to group selection, they became communists; if individual selection was favoured, they became fascists. *Mein Kampf*, like *Das Kapital*, laid great emphasis on the contribution of Darwin's theory of natural selection. Although totalitarianism looked backwards to the pre-competitive era, both variants shared a ruthless commitment to progress in the scientific materialist sense. In practice, both were the antithesis of the competitive economy, relying on hierarchical structures of command to generate production. Both rejected the Christian traditions espoused by capitalism and, with them, the ethical and moral codes which were so essential to market success. The Walrasian economics had espoused scientific materialism but it had not implied that such an approach should be extended to all human behaviour. It was a refinement of the Protestant ethic to provide a useful social innovation, not an attempt to replace Christianity by a new materialist religion.

Although these difficulties in dealing with natural selection resulted in dark days for the competitive principle in the 1930s, it is undoubtedly the case that the Keynesian modification could only have grown out of the moral and ethical background to capitalist thought. Furthermore, the forces of totalitarianism on both right and left served to highlight the urgent nature of the Keynesian modification. Scientific materialism remained, of course, alive and well in the explosive growth of the Keynesian era when welfarism tended to fulfil many of the functions of the old morality and ethics contained in religious principles. However, as religious principles withered away and scientific materialism took their place, it became clear that the *homo economicus* model could not stand by itself nor could self-interest, in a competitive market context, either depict the real context of economic interaction or generate market solutions in the absence of some kind of ethical structure. The Walrasian model had become obsolete in its prime function of providing the necessary bio-philosophical belief system which yields maximum social benefit. The economic and non-economic could no longer be separated in the highly interdependent system which had developed. The schizophrenic approach could no longer be upheld because *homo economicus*, believing in scientific materialism, had become, in Herbert Marcuse's terminology, a 'one-dimensional-man'. Economic beliefs had to become multi-dimensional again in order to prevent unbalanced economic development of the individual and society.

The Ghost in the Machine

The link between the Walrasian system and *homo economicus* is market demand and supply, a dichotomy or idealized construct which provided the intellectual foundation of economics in modern times. As Alfred Marshall demonstrated in his *Principles of Economics*, demand and supply could be extremely useful in the partial analysis of market price determination in the short run. *Homo economicus* was created in order to argue, logically, for downward-sloping demand curves. This 'rational economic man' was part and parcel of all the *ceteris paribus* assumptions necessary for partial analysis, assumptions which would be relaxed as demand theory was applied in the empirical domain. However, in order to aggregate to the Walrasian level it is necessary to insist on *homo economicus* and market clearing *as a condition of aggregation*. It follows that the kind of relaxation of *ceteris paribus* permissible at the micro-market level cannot be undertaken at the macro level. The useful demand/supply dichotomy at the micro level becomes a useless one at the macro level.

Of course, this was recognized by Keynes who replaced it with a macro-dichotomy between income and expenditure which had no micro-foundation but was clearly of great empirical value. In terms of demand, Keynes emphasized a force which was of secondary importance in the study of micro-markets – the income effect – and ignored what was of primary importance – the substitution effect. Micro-market equilibrium, determined by price, was replaced by macro-equilibrium, which was determined by the multiplier process. The latter was not necessarily coincident with the former, in Walrasian guise, *either* because *homo economicus* did not exist *or* because market clearing was not universal. Most of the debate has centred on the latter, the former being either retained or completely rejected along with the whole Walrasian conception.

There is a widespread black and white presumption about *homo economicus*. If you remove him then macroeconomics is plunged into the non-economic and the hopeless. Rarely is the point ever made that our rational friend is inappropriate in any case for macroeconomics and that, perhaps, he might, as Robert Solow implies, have a cousin better suited to the job of providing macroeconomic foundations. *Homo economicus* was an abstraction of human behaviour for a particular purpose. It is quite conceivable that we can make another kind of abstraction for an entirely different purpose, i.e. to understand economic behaviour which extends far beyond market behaviour into the kinds of stable flow characteristics that we perceive in a macroeconomy, irrespective of price dynamics. It is well known that a Walrasian macro-model has no formal way of 'developing' and conventional models have to rely on investment behaviour to generate growth in some vague manner.[20]

Keynes saw, quite clearly, that investment behaviour must be beyond conventional analysis: he attributed it to 'animal spirits' which were defined as a preference for action rather than inaction.[21] The macroeconomy developed, not through *homo economicus*, but through a seemingly irrational sense of adventure. The fundamental source of economic development is, thus, beyond the compass of *homo economicus*. The uncertainty that this state of affairs caused convinced Keynes that stabilization policy should be restricted to the short run and longer run developments should be ignored as intractable.

Although Keynes was quite aware that the impact of net investment on the size of the capital stock left his model incomplete, he insisted to his colleague, Dennis Robertson, that tracking disequilibrium paths and modelling wealth effects into the long run was a fruitless exercise.

If we compare the disagreement between Keynes and Robertson as to long-run adjustment to the agreement between Keynes and Hicks on the Walrasian interpretation of the *General Theory*, we gain the impression that Keynes had a degree of ambivalence about *homo economicus*. As we have already argued, he could envisage entrepreneurs operating in such a way in the short run, but in the long run he could not see the neo-classical depiction of entrepreneurial behaviour as valid. Marshallian belief concerning the usefulness of *homo economicus* in micro-market applications was mixed with an intuitive feeling of the centrality of expectational interdependence, evidenced in bouts of optimism and pessimism, at the macroeconomic level. In the short run we could hold such expectations steady and apply *homo economicus* and market principles, tempered by the existence of spatial interdependences or 'rigidities' in the labour market, but inter-temporal expectational interdependence ruled out the use of either in the long run.

Clearly, Keynes viewed the short run as something of a special case of a general long-run behavioural process which he could grasp intuitively but found difficult to formalize within the economic analysis that he had learned from Marshall. After his death, the gap was filled by the post-Keynesians who built on Keynes's 'parable of the widow's cruse' to generate a distributional model of the long run which owes more to the Ricardian/Marxist tradition which Keynes distanced himself from.[22] The latter was based on class analysis, linking investment to profits, and containing little in the way of 'animal spirits', as understood in the *General Theory*.

If we argue that this post-Keynesian development is not of Keynes but more of Kalecki and Sraffa, linking back to Ricardo and Marx, then we can agree with Joan Robinson that Keynes's short-run model was only a beginning. By the end of her life, Joan Robinson recognized that the only way that a proper context for Keynesian economics could be developed was to go right back to the bio-philosophical foundations. She asked primitive questions like: 'What are the questions?' 'What is time?'[23] George Shackle, similarly, endeavoured to redefine the forward-looking dimensions of behaviour to attempt to place Keynes within a better context than Walras.

Although both Robinson and Shackle attempt to bury *homo economicus* and market clearing as any basis for considering the macroeconomy, there remains a reluctance to depart entirely from the scientific materialist frame of reference. Robinson tends to retain the view that the pre-eminent priority is economic progress which is reducible to material growth. In her view, the primary goal of workers is to maximize the size of wages, with little sympathy for social or ecological issues. The scientific materialist conception is not in question, only the distribution of the resultant output. Semantics about freedom and liberty are not discussed – the prior freedom is material share. Such an economic outlook, married to a simplistic conception of social relations where people form class solidarity and engage in struggle, was unlikely to permit the kind of bio-philosophic development necessary to develop Keynesian 'beginnings'.

Shackle does not concentrate on economic action for material gain but, instead, attempts to develop Keynes's perception of the interdependence of expectations.[24] *Homo economicus* is not riven from the market and enmeshed in class struggle, Robinson-style, but rather he retains the vision of individual maximization of material satisfactions in a world of optimism and pessimism. Shackle recognizes perceptual interdependence but in a way that suits the analysis of oligopolistic behaviour rather than analysis of the macro-system.[25] The 'social binding', overplayed in Robinson, is underplayed in Shackle leaving a sophisticated model of economic behaviour which contains lexicographic preferences instead of indifference curves and expectations which emphasize interdependence but little in the way of a structure that could provide a foundation for macroeconomic analysis. Shackle sees Keynes's 'animal spirits' as driven by the human imagination, yet the links between the psyche of the entrepreneur and the macroeconomy are not formalized. Shackle emphasizes the individual's perception as he operates within an economic framework, whereas Robinson emphasizes the interaction of individuals to form alliances which engage in struggle. Shackle views Keynes as offering a 'kaleidic' method, by which he means the interaction of reasoned or rational action and the imagination which generates optimistic or pessimistic outcomes. Although Shackle argues that Keynes's insight with regard to this dual dimension of perception forms the beginning of a new approach, he was not able to develop it into something which could provide a better foundation for macroeconomics.[26]

There is little doubt that, although he could not quite escape the grip of scientific materialism and build new bio-philosophical foundations drawing on other disciplines, Shackle grasps, better than any other writer, the essence of the new foundations that lay in Keynes's intuition. The *General Theory* dealt with only a short-run dimension of this new thought, for profoundly practical and sensible reasons. Had Keynes lived longer, he may have been able to formalize his intuition for he was a rare breed of economist with a diverse store of knowledge and experience, who could think as easily in the qualitative world of aesthetics as the quantitative world of economics.

Today, it is unusual to find economists with such breadth, so specialized has the discipline become. Correspondingly, it is more difficult to escape the confines of the prevailing orthodoxy, not simply because of the sheer difficulty in spanning other disciplines which have also become specialized and jargon-bound, but also because of the need to perform translations into orthodox terms. Joan Robinson argued that most of the disputes in economics centre on the basic premisses that are held by both sides.[27] In interdisciplinary communication this problem is amplified and has prevented even radicals such as Shackle and Robinson from throwing off completely the bio-philosophical foundations of orthodox macroeconomics.

In order to provide a basis for the isolation of new bio-philosophical foundations, an attempt will now be made to review briefly recent contributions by economists who have offered new perspectives outside the confines of macroeconomics. The objective is not to offer a comprehensive review of what constitutes a fragmentary literature but to select important representatives of different approaches in an attempt to highlight influences that seem relevant to any new bio-philosophical foundations of macroeconomics. With their help we can begin to throw off the strait-jacket that Shackle and Robinson struggled to escape from in the Keynesian era.

Economic Radicalism

Since the mid 1960s there has been an explosion of research which attempts to extend the horizons of economic behaviour.

Little of this new material has dented the orthodoxy which underlies macroeconomics, although inroads have been made in other areas. The new studies tend to be classified into special 'lower order' boxes: political economy and social economics. This apartheid ensures that little damage will be caused to orthodox ideas, particularly in macroeconomics, while toleration of these areas ensures that economists cannot be charged with narrowness of view. Tokenism, the legacy of the 1960s, takes on many dimensions. New journals have sprung up such as the *Journal of Radical Political Economy*, the *International Journal of Social Economics*, the *Journal of Post-Keynesian Economics* and the *Cambridge Journal of Economics*, to select a few which are representative of the different emphases taken. None have been taken very seriously by orthodox economists who frequently seem to regard a publication in such journals more as a stigma than a contribution to academic merit. By their very nature, of course, these journals are open to criticism for they lack the very thing that the orthodoxy has: a commonly agreed set of bio-philosophical foundations. Instead, they tend to be a rag-bag of unorthodox insights and unconventional ideas loosely held together by the relevant editorial board's own collective view.[28] Thus is created the distinctiveness of the various journals but nothing which could be construed as a simple, clearly-defined set of new bio-philosophical foundations.

Although there is considerable overlap, the new approaches can be divided into two broad categories: the socio-psychological and the socio-political approach. In practice, elements of both approaches can be present with only a variation of emphasis. Also, in order to communicate effectively, the approaches tend to be set either as a development of, or in juxtaposition to, old orthodoxies.

The Socio-political Approach It is best to deal with the socio-political approach first since it is related to long-standing schools such as, for example, the post-Keynesian school in America and the Cambridge school in England. There is nothing new in the basic idea that political factors are inseparable from economic analysis.[29] To develop such an analysis, all that is necessary is to assume that individuals form alliances to enter into political conflict of some degree, from mere trade union/employer negotiation, through to all-out warfare between social classes or other defined groups. The basic rationale that lies behind such a framework is simple. The individual is weak and exploitable by himself, therefore it may be rational to sacrifice individual freedom for the advantage of enhanced security and power. The processes whereby such bonds evolve are not usually the centre of attention but, instead, attention is focused on the conflictual interactions between interest groups. Strategic alliances are generally viewed as being formed under the pressure of exploitation – for example, Kenneth Galbraith calls it 'countervailing power', and Marx called it the politicization of the proletariat. Once groups are defined, the analysis is strictly political with game theory often applied in well defined situations such as industrial relations where there is a substantial contractual interdependence, to strategic considerations in poorly defined situations of conflict.

Advocates of this approach, such as Marxists, often tend to get back towards a more economic type of analysis by abstracting from this conflict, labelling it as a 'dialectical' process which resolves itself into a set of economic arrangements that are in some way superior in an evolutionary sense. Thus, it becomes a 'systems approach' to provide a completely integrated dynamic story. However, the bulk of the socio-political analyses do not culminate in grand theories of the development of systems. They merely conceive of the individual differently to *homo economicus*. The latter cannot exist in an exploitative environment because, by himself, he would become a slave without any economic freedom. Thus, he must become a component member of a social group which, in turn, will exert political power to extract economic gains. In other words, to be economically free requires prior socio-political responses.

Not only does this analysis completely destroy *homo economicus* but it also removes the market as a general economic instrument. Large groups engaged in political confrontation cannot be perceived as independent, like atomistic demanders and suppliers. Their interdependence is often the basis of their political power and, not surprisingly, economists using these foundations have preferred the Ricardian analysis of economic rents to determine prices.[30] The notion of competition can be preserved, but rather in terms of the search for innovations in order to gain economic rents, Schumpeterian-style.

Clearly, the socio-political approach differs radically from the *homo economicus* approach in a fundamental bio-philosophical way. The individual *never* behaves in such a rational economic way; economic behaviour is something which is the concern of his group, however defined. Modern developments of this approach are, thus, completely non-absorbable into orthodox traditions except in as much as the social group may attempt to achieve the same kind of scientific materialist goals in total production and consumption. Such isolation would seem to disqualify the socio-political approach as being 'economic', not in the sense that it rejects *homo economicus*, but rather that it fails to capture the constructive, co-operative spirit of economic behaviour so well integrated into neo-classical economics.

The implied loss of individual economic freedom and the unconstructive dimension of the socio-political approach has served to heighten the orthodoxy's rejection of any kind of socio-political considerations, except in the rather narrowly defined industrial relations context where game theoretic models of negotiation are permissible because they can be subject to conventional probabilistic and 'expected costs' forms of analysis. Although the socio-political school is alive and well in modern social science it can be regarded as a generalization of political science rather than a branch of economics for, in the end, it is political interactions that determine economic outcomes which, in turn, rely on some kind of obscure social interaction. Not surprisingly, this social interaction, in practice, is seen as no more than a kind of totalitarianism to promote scientific materialism, in the eyes of neo-classical economists.

It would be true to say that political events over the past twenty years have led to a general rejection of the socio-political approach amongst economists except those with overriding left-wing political views. *Homo economicus* is an idealistic construct which captures the creative spirit of economic behaviour. The socio-political construct is also idealistic but cannot capture economic behaviour without the superimposition of some kind of social Darwinism. It is analogous to arguing that marriage is an arrangement that emerges from the dialectics of divorce. Although such a perspective may shed some light on the evolution of the institution of marriage, it does not explain the existence of the institution of marriage in the first place, except as an entirely exploitative arrangement. The truth or otherwise of such an evolutionary view is impossible to verify in any empirical sense and, therefore, exists only as a form of dynamic logic. As such, it is inappropriate for generating the kind of philosophical basis from which economic co-operation can develop, and is therefore a dubious bio-philosophical basis for examining a stable structure such as the macroeconomy. This will become more apparent in the analytical framework to be developed in subsequent chapters.

Concern with the inadequacy of *homo economicus* in recent times has not led to a wholesale shift to the pessimistic socio-political approach but rather to a view which emphasizes the psychology of the individual and the importance of his interaction with his society and his environment. The rigid social interactive assumptions of the socio-political approach have not been taken on board but, instead, a much more flexible view of social interaction has developed, as we shall see below. Perhaps, more critically, the scientific materialist foundations, adhered to by both the orthodox and socio-political approaches, have been questioned. Relationships between individuals are viewed beyond their material relations and the identification of progress with material growth is called into question, particularly by the ecologically minded. As we shall see in the next chapter, this view, which became significant in the late 1960s, has developed more fully in other social sciences. However, a number of economists have attempted to say the same things with very limited success. There are enough of them now to consider them a school of thought, although they have not integrated their ideas into any kind of framework which could challenge the orthodoxy or even the socio-political approach.

The Socio-psychological Approach There are, undoubtedly, considerable advantages to thinking within a system of formal logic and that is one of the main reasons why people discard old orthodoxies so reluctantly. For someone tutored in a system of formal logic, a reading of new 'social economics' journals which have sprung up over the past twenty years can be an irritating experience. The papers which appear tend to be very informal, repetitive and unsystematic. The only real unity that seems to exist is a condemnation of orthodox modes of thought and the same criticisms recur over and over again. As such it is not a literature which deserves careful reviewing, at least not by someone who is preoccupied with the specific task of searching for some foundations for macroeconomics. The landmarks which have stood out in this literature have tended to be in book form, offering sufficient length to permit ideas to be well founded in extended historical and interdisciplinary discussion.

Despite the growth of the socio-psychological approach to

economic thinking from the mid 1960s onwards, it was not until the mid 1970s that sufficiently powerful statements were made which could penetrate the armour of orthodox economics.[31] Two books, Tibor Scitovsky's *Joyless Economy* (1976) and Fred Hirsch's *Social Limits to Growth* (1977), in the United States and Great Britain respectively, managed to reach a wide cross-section of the economics profession. Both were highly respected economists who mounted attacks on the scientific materialist philosophical underpinnings of economics, stimulated by the perceived inability of orthodox economics to explain the problems of affluence which had begun to manifest themselves in the Keynesian era of rapid growth. The thrust of the two books is different, with Scitovsky drawing primarily on psychological studies and Hirsch on sociological literature, although the overlap is considerable.

Scitovsky argues that to set up a model of economic behaviour in terms of material satisfaction is to miss out a factor of rapidly growing importance: novelty. He provides extensive empirical support from psychology for this view. His view of human satisfaction is relativistic, juxtaposing habitual behaviour and the search for novelty as the proper context for economic behaviour. The introduction of a qualitative notion such as novelty, of course, is a fatal blow for the *homo economicus* vision since choice does not hang on material quantity but rather the *composition* of a basket of goods and services. Scitovsky attempts to offer a psychological frame of reference within which relative deprivation, the modern malady, can have some meaning.

Hirsch tends to take the sociological route, emphasizing the interdependence of tastes and the growing demands for goods merely in a positional sense. The centrality of social status and the relativity of consumption experience again points to predictions that quantitative material growth need not result in greater happiness. Whereas Scitovsky concentrates on the psychological processes that override the *homo economicus* construct and alter the meaning of individual rationality, Hirsch emphasizes the importance of social norms and ethics as rational devices, in a socio-psychological sense, in a society which has a tendency towards positional competition based on material goods. Where Scitovsky offers a psychological basis for the analysis of relative deprivation, Hirsch provides a sociological context within which the causes and cures of that condition can be dealt with.

Despite the fact that both books are full of insights which

seem to ring true in an intuitive sense, it would be fair to say that both have been passed by. Scitovsky comments in his preface as to how an unholy alliance between the orthodoxy and radicals tended to form to reject his approach despite its extensive use of empirical evidence from psychology. As has been emphasized, scientific materialism is bigger than mere empirical evidence. It is clear that neither author succeeded in producing a *system of logic* which could confront the orthodoxy, despite the utter reasonableness of what was being said. Both works now enter the orthodoxy as 'cautionary tales', rather than catalysts for fundamental revision.

Understandably, most impact has tended to occur in the area of public goods. The question of altruism has always been of importance in this area and, thus, the issues raised by Hirsch are particularly important. Paradoxically, the theory of public goods has tended to adopt *homo economicus* more eagerly than macroeconomics and it has been only very recently that attempts have been made to extend the notion of rationality.[32] For example, Margolis (1982) translates the evolutionary behavioural models of Downs (1957) and Olson (1965) into individual behaviour terms. The striking feature of Margolis's analysis is the degree to which he must set it within the established welfare economics that exists. Altruism, as a word, implies something separate (like 'externality') from the normal state of things and Margolis does not achieve the logical power which could dislodge this dichotomy.[33]

Another area where it has been traditional to emphasize the limitations of *homo economicus* is in the theory of the firm. Ever since Simon's (1955, 1976) arguments that rationality is 'bounded' there has been an ongoing tradition of operating beyond such a narrow behavioural construct. Recently, Earl (1983) has attempted to pull the bounded rationality idea into the centre of economic analysis. Building on Shackle's emphasis of the importance of 'imagination' in economic decision-making and resultant 'potential supply curves', Earl tries to argue for a relativistic theory of choice which is 'lexicographic' rather than 'compensatory' and which can be developed empirically using the motivational testing developed by Kelly (1963). In contrast to the narrow focus of Margolis, Earl's approach is broad and similar in spirit to Scitovsky in that it leans more heavily on psychology than on sociology, understandably in a book which is addressed more towards microeconomic than macroeconomic issues. Earl offers a compelling way of looking at economic behaviour which relates sympathetically towards orthodox analysis and offers the promise of empirical applicability.

Earl's conceptual framework represents an extremely original combination of approaches drawn from economics and psychology yet, in a sense, it does not present the kind of simple logical base from which macroeconomic analysis could be constructed. It was not the objective to do so as compared with, for example, the work of Tylecote (1981) which was an explicit attempt to modify the behavioural foundations of macroeconomics in order to understand macro-phenomena better. None the less, Earl's book is replete with ideas that would seem to be highly relevant to macroeconomic analysis and the foundations discussed in subsequent chapters echo many of his perceptions of economic behaviour.

A recurring theme in many of the socio-psychological approaches is the question of behavioural dynamics. It is inevitable, if writers manage to escape the grip of static *homo economicus*, that they should begin to consider interactions beyond the narrow utility maximizing context. We have already seen that the socio-political school set behavioural dynamics in a dialectical context which yields evolutionary changes. In fact, given the simplicity of the bio-philosophical foundations in the socio-political approach, the literature is able to deal with the nature of the resultant macro-dynamic processes in historical time without difficulty. The socio-psychological school tends, on the other hand, to be pre-occupied with ways in which *homo economicus* can be modified to generate 'compromise' foundations. Thus, the simplicity of *homo economicus* is lost and his usefulness for providing foundations for macroeconomics is diminished. The system dynamics which occur at the macroeconomic level become unclear and are discussed in an intuitive and speculative way by many socio-psychological writers. Those interested in explaining the dynamics of the macroeconomy have, like the socio-politicals, been forced to keep their bio-philosophical foundations simple.

Conclusion

This chapter began with a discussion of the non-economic premisses which lay behind the orthodox foundations of modern macroeconomics. The foundations were found to exist on two levels: the first emphasizing *homo economicus* operating in clearing markets, and the second emphasizing scientific materialism driven on by competitive forces. It has been argued that these foundations have nothing to do with empirical reality but are ideals which constitute creeds, akin to religions, which permit economic development to proceed. Although the first dimension of the orthodox creed has come under constant challenge from Marxism for over a hundred years, it is only in the past twenty years that the second part, the core, has been challenged extensively.

Religious reformations are difficult and the second part of the chapter considered the various attempts to challenge the orthodoxy. The socio-psychological (analogous to microeconomic) and the socio-political (analogous to macroeconomic) approaches were evaluated in terms of offering different bio-philosophical foundations. The lack of success of these innovations was attributed to the inability of any writer to produce a simple analytical competitor to *homo economicus* which could take over as the basis of macroeconomics. Each writer has made considerable efforts to incorporate logic derived from other disciplines, yet none have stripped their modifications down to analytical essentials which could perform the pedagogic function so important to any creed, ideology or idealism, while at the same time keeping the distinctiveness of economics intact. The evolution of ideas is not about substitution but rather about the addition of innovations which allow old ideas to continue to have their place in the structure of thought. The immensely successful ideals of orthodox economic logic must survive as a special case of any new logic which enables economics to deal with substantial areas of economic activity beyond the compass of existing analysis. The macroeconomy cannot be analysed if only part of that economy is captured, either in terms of its structure or in terms of the completeness of general behavioural postulates.

It has been argued that in order to maintain the *homo economicus* construct, a schizophrenic view of the human psyche has to be taken. Thus, the Walrasian macroeconomics, which is built on such a construct, must also be schizophrenic or, rather, incomplete as a representation of behaviour. We have seen how economists have endeavoured to qualify the *homo economicus* vision in various ways, by appealing for the explicit inclusion of constructs drawn from subjects such as politics, psychology, sociology and management. Although there is an implicit bio-philosophical coherence running throughout these endeavours they are continually directed towards the concerns of particular economic specialisms and never quite get to offering an alternative to the scientific materialist dimension of economic foundations which could be utilized in macroeconomics. In order to obtain a clear view of the bio-philosophical essence that we wish to distil it is now necessary to move more directly into the disciplines of biology and philosophy.

Notes

1 See Hahn (1977) for a discussion of the conceptual usefulness of the interdependence which characterizes the Walrasian system.

2 See Weintraub (1979) for a survey of attempts to develop imperfectly competitive foundations for macroeconomics, and Friedman (1953) for early development of this view of imperfectly competitive foundations.

3 Hahn has pointed out that the only competitor is the Marxist system which is also built on biological foundations involving the competition of groups rather than atomistic economic agents: 'Despite the descriptive and predictive inadequacies, general equilibrium theory provides a basic framework for comprehending economic activity, one whose only real rival at present is Marxism.' Ascribed to F. Hahn (1979) in a lecture at M.I.T. by McMahon (1981).

4 See Boland (1982) for an excellent discussion of this paradigm.

5 See Kuhn (1977) for a more developed statement of his position. See Ward (1972) and Cross (1982) for discussion of the non-Kuhnian aspects of this resistance. Also, Hutchinson (1978) provides a much broader approach.

6 To pick two extreme examples from many cases, see Lipsey's first-year textbook for a very basic statement of this view, and Laidler and Parkin's (1975) survey of inflation where cost inflation theorists are labelled as 'sociological'.

7 Akerlof (1984), Lancaster (1966), Leibenstein (1950, 1976), Margolis (1982), Marshak (1968), all provide examples of the ingenuity required to translate unorthodox ideas into a formalization acceptable to the orthodoxy. See Taylor (1984) for a critique of Sen's (1982) work along these lines.

8 McCloskey (1983) shows how economists who take a formal, mathematical approach in academic articles adopt a quite different stance when dealing with policy issues in popular literature. Paul Samuelson's polemical pieces in *Newsweek* are a clear example, as are James Tobin's frequent appeals for Keynesian policies.

9 Proponents of particular doctrines often refer to their opponents' doctrines as merely creeds or dogma but fail to perceive the same characteristic of their own position. See Friedman (1953) and

Kaldor (1982) for good examples. See Katouzian (1980) for an analysis of the interplay between ideology and economics.

10 Dow argues that it *enhances* its importance: 'From the Kuhnian standpoint the greater problems facing economists in interpreting observations place even more weight on the conceptualization process, and thus on the metaphysical, linguistic and metaphorical content of a paradigm' (Dow, 1985, p. 38). Weisskopf (1979) has attempted to offer a 'Heisenbergian' alternative which takes more explicit account of such factors, particularly in ideological form.

11 See Boland (1982) for a discussion of neo-classical 'psychologism'.

12 See Pirsig (1974) for a discussion of this Aristotelian inheritance in modern philosophy and scientific methodology.

13 See Scitovsky's (1976) preface for a somewhat bewildered acknowledgement of this 'unholy alliance'.

14 It is quite common for the 'historical sweep' type of evidence to be presented as broad support for a very precise shift in bio-philosophical foundations. Perhaps the best recent successful example in macroeconomics was the Friedman and Schwartz (1963) historical study.

15 See Becker (1976) for an exposition of his 'economic' approach to non-economic behaviour. Hollis and Nell (1975) offer a strong rebuttal of this approach. Schneider (1974) explains the origins of *homo economicus*.

16 See Buchanan and Tulloch (1962) for an example of this in the politico-economic area of 'public choice'. Downs (1957) started a trend amongst political scientists where an economic approach is adopted.

17 See Blondel (1981) for a commentary on the manner in which the 'economic' approach has developed in political science.

18 See Sen (1970, 1977) for discussion of such interactions and their economic implications in terms of economic efficiency and welfare.

19 See Popper (1944, 1961) for an evaluation of the Marxist world view.

20 Neo-classical growth models, so popular in the 1960s and early 1970s, created an illusion that investment was the prime mover in the growth process. In fact the source of growth in those models came from population growth and technical progress, with capital investment, perhaps, providing a 'vehicle' for the latter and also ensuring that the 'warranted' rate of growth kept pace with the 'natural' rate. Neo-classical growth models did not tell us much about economic growth, merely the formal conditions that would ensure that competitive forces would always keep the economic system in a kind of dynamic version of the Walrasian system. See Solow (1970) for what still constitutes a lucid perspective on growth theory and how it does not help us to unravel the empirical picture provided by, for example, Denison (1962).

21 See Dow and Dow (1985) for an extended discussion of Keynes's vision of 'animal spirits'.

22 The seminal contribution was by Kaldor (1955) with important development by Pasinetti (1974).

23 See Robinson (1977, 1980a) for evidence of increased preoccupation with such questions towards the end of her life.

24 See Shackle (1974) for his interpretation and suggestions for development of Keynes's thought on expectations.

25 See Earl (1983, 1984) for the application of Shackle's expectational scheme at the microeconomic level of analysis.

26 Shackle's treatment of expectations has much in common with the Austrian view dating back to Mises (1949). As a highly individualistic approach the macroeconomic level of analysis is generally rejected by this school as particularly meaningful or insightful. See Lachmann (1976).

27 See Robinson (1977).

28 In the preface to Arestis and Skouras (1985), which is a collection of the radical *Thames Papers in Political Economy*, Eichner states in a Foreword: 'Some of the papers are the result of an invitation to a well-known post-Keynesian or other critic of conventional economics . . . others are papers which Skouras and Arestis have either heard given . . . or have heard about from others . . . In this way, the editors can determine the content of the *Papers* rather than depend on chance submission: indeed, articles are not normally submitted for publication' (Arestis and Skouras, 1985, p. x).

29 In the political economy which preceded Irvine Fisher and Alfred Marshall, it was regarded as unnatural and misleading to separate the two. See Schumpeter (1974) for emphasis of this point.

30 See Robinson and Eatwell (1977) for a gentle introduction to this approach, and Eatwell and Milgate (1983) for attempts to extend and develop it in Keynesian macroeconomics.

31 See Katona (1975) for a comprehensive discussion of the relationship between economics and psychology and a review of how approaches used in the latter can be applied in the former. Furnam and Lewis (1986) provide an appraisal of economic theories of behaviour from the perspective of social psychology.

32 See Collard (1978) for a good review of the ways in which altruism has been reconciled with orthodox theory.

33 Another interesting attempt to provide a post-Hirschian analysis is that of Jones (1984) who develops a behavioural model in which 'conformism' is rational, thus providing behavioural support for the kinds of macroeconomic propositions made by Duesenberry (1949). However, like Margolis (1982), Jones is concerned with adapting rather than replacing *homo economicus*.

6 *General Behavioural Dynamics: from Structure to Consciousness*

> Quality is the continuing stimulus which our environment puts upon us to create the world in which we live. All of it. Every last bit of it.
>
> Robert Pirsig (1974)

We have discussed how economists have challenged the orthodox model of *homo economicus* through the integration of both psychological and sociological perspectives with economics. It has been observed that such initiatives have had little impact on macroeconomics which has retained the Walrasian conception of competitive markets, strengthened with new developments, such as rational expectations. In a sense, this strengthening of orthodox macroeconomics has recognized the key area of development, namely the question of how adjustment behaviour actually takes place in historical time and how forward-looking perception influences such adjustments. Modern macroeconomics asks the right questions but provides answers within a framework which is ill suited to the tasks at hand.

In this chapter an excursion will be made into contemporary biology and philosophy to demonstrate that the existing foundations of macroeconomics have become inappropriate to capture the functioning of the modern economy in a useful way. It will be shown that radical critiques of established biological and philosophical ideas are directed at a general bio-philosophical view of human behaviour which is upheld more strongly in orthodox economic thought than any other discipline. Correspondingly, the irrationality perceived in this bio-philosophical core also constitutes irrationality in the economic sphere. The corrections suggested to provide a more rational basis for the analysis of human behaviour, therefore, are applicable to economics, particularly macroeconomics with its preoccupation with the essence of a whole system which, in turn, has developed to become the core of the social system. However, let us begin with an appraisal of what is sometimes called the 'systems approach' in economics. This approach is holistic and evolutionary, tending to cut across all schools of economic thought and involving writers that we have already mentioned in the previous chapter. By its very nature, the approach does not probe the bio-philosophical foundations of macroeconomics but, none the less, the way in which behavioural dynamics are depicted raises fundamental questions about such foundations that are worth dwelling on in subsequent parts of this chapter.

The Systems Approach

All schools of economic thought provide analysis of the behaviour of the economic system. However, the distinctive feature of the systems approach is in the explicit incorporation of a developmental dimension, whereby the system evolves in a non-random manner in historical time.[1] Attempts to dynamize the Walrasian model in neo-classical growth models do not qualify as part of the systems approach because they do not involve structural change, only changes in input–output flows. Equally, macro-models which are translated from abstract to historical time through the auxiliary hypotheses of expectational and adjustment lags are not part of the systems approach. They, too, involve no structural change. The latter approach is common in Keynesian 'short-run' macro-modelling, on the grounds that structural change is a long-run phenomenon.

This Keynesian distinction between the short run and the long run is mediated by the medium run, which has been the focus of business cycle studies.[2] Now, although such studies commonly do not have any notion of structural equilibrium built into them, they hardly qualify as part of the systems approach because they are usually 'data-specific' containing little in the way of a strong connection between theory and evidence. In other words, the observed cycles are consistent with a wide range of different kinds of dynamic hypotheses. Attempts at simulating such cycles and growth paths, using even quite simple expectational and adjustment hypotheses, have been notorious for their capacity to develop serious and unobserved instability.[3] Keynes's scepticism about extending his historical time model beyond the short run has been amply vindicated in the postwar era.

The systems approach is evolutionary in character with a lineage dating back to the nineteenth century and, particularly, Thorstein Veblen (1898).[4] Technological innovation, the structure altering quality of the macroeconomy, is not relegated to 'residual' status, as in neo-classical growth theory, but promoted to the very centre of macro-dynamics. Like the socio-political Marxists, early proponents of the systems approach, such as Schumpeter (1934), argued that Darwin-inspired dialectical processes provided the vehicle for historical time analysis. However, Schumpeter took a much less rigid view of the economic interest groups involved in struggle, preferring to emphasize competition between firms which itself changed in character in the course of history.

We have already discussed how this evolutionary approach could not find favour either with neo-classical economists, who found the closeness to Marx uncomfortable, or with Keynesians, who were preoccupied with the short run and stabilization. However, in the postwar period, Georgescu-Roegen (1971) and Boulding (1981) continued to be insistent proponents of the systems approach and the evolutionary perspective. Both attempted to get away from the 'red in claw and tooth' image of evolution, emphasizing the co-operative characteristics of evolution, citing Kropotkin (1902), and pointing out that economic principles such as 'comparative advantage' were about symbiosis rather than conflict. Also, Boulding, in particular, argued that Keynes's theory of effective demand qualified as a systems approach which was compatible with an evolutionary approach to the macroeconomy.

By the 1970s the systems approach was beginning to lose its Darwinian flavour almost completely.[5] Writers such as Schumacher (1977) even abandoned Darwinian evolution entirely as relevant to the analysis of economic behaviour. He viewed human consciousness at a different level to that in other organisms and, therefore, saw sophisticated behaviour in the economic arena as above biological analogies.[6] Social and economic evolution to Schumacher was more about the qualitative aspects of consciousness that lay behind evolving structure than structure itself. Schumacher's view was opposed to scientific materialism, reinstating Hegel for Marx, seeing evolution as a spiritual thing, a triumph of human imagination and creativity over harsh reality. Today, after his death, this approach has come to be associated with 'Buddhist' economics, which relates the economic system directly to the system of thought in Buddhist religious principles. Schumacher didn't waste time trawling the empirical findings of psychology and sociology for support but, instead, attempted to discover alternative bio-philosophical premisses in philosophy and religion.

Schumacher was an idealist and little concerned with macroeconomics and its problems. However, what is interesting from the macro-perspective is the vision of the unity of consciousness, encapsulated in religious and ethical principles, that lies behind the economic system. He is not guilty of 'psychologism' because he is not concerned with the individual's consciousness, but rather with the harmony between individuals. Making similar points to Hirsch and Scitovsky, he does not attempt to 'justify' them in a socio-psychological way but rather conceives of group consciousness as a fundamental human condition. However, neither does he confine group consciousness only to interest groups, in the style of the socio-political school.

Schumacher emphasizes the importance of commonly held systems of thought, creeds, or Hirsch's 'rational ethics'. Boulding and Georgescu-Roegen subscribe to the less philosophical position that evolution is about 'bonding' processes and the formation of cumulative systems or structures. This new evolutionary approach is dramatically different to the old one. Perpetual revolution, or dialectics, is replaced by symbiotic development as the primary engine of evolution. Revolution may be necessary to crack ossified socioeconomic structures but the question being asked is what facilitates the long periods of co-operative activity in between crises? The answers come in terms of ethics, creeds or even communist ideology. The Walrasians conceived of the economic system in terms of Newtonian physics, the Marxists placed social Darwinism at the centre of the stage and the new systems approach is more analogous to the science of chemistry, enquiring as to the socioeconomic bonding processes which permit symbiotic mutation. Chemistry is subject to chemical rules; socioeconomic bonding is subject to conventions and beliefs which permit organic development.

Chemistry enquires into structure, taking as given the bonding rules that exist. So too, in economics, do we have an interest in structure. The institutionalists tend to overemphasize the chemistry analogy without enough appreciation of the consciousness 'bonding' that Schumacher 'preached' about. Without a balanced appreciation of both, system dynamics are incomplete. If we look beyond economics into management science and organization theory, where the systems approach has been more fully developed, we see the way in which this balance is understood and how shifts in this balance lead to variations in evolutionary dynamics. Earl (1984) examines these shifts in the context of the 'product cycle' while Simon (1984) emphasizes the importance of hierarchical structure in organizational development.[7] In turn, the evolution of firms viewed as 'systems' has been taken up strongly by Nelson and Winter (1982) and Kay (1982).

The 'consciousness' dimension in structural change emphasized by Nelson/Winter and Kay remains the same as that emphasized by Veblen and Schumpeter: the creativity embodied in invention and innovation. It follows that in searching for bio-philosophical foundations for macroeconomics, such a creative process will be important, but not the only important form of creativity. The 'social creativity' of ethics, custom and convention emphasized by Hirsch and Schumacher will also have an important, and even prior role to play in the evolution of the macro-system. It is these very general aspects of consciousness and structure which we need to distil at the macro-level. In order to do this we must leave the rather fragmentary treatment of consciousness in the 'systems approach' of economics and look elsewhere for a more coherent approach.

Dichotomies

A great deal of constructive logic has centred on the development of analytical dichotomies in order to gain an understanding of real world phenomena. Economics has been no exception in this regard.[8] The analytical separation of demand and supply to explain observed price and quantity provided economics with an extraordinarily powerful dichotomy upon which the Walrasian model is built. Keynes propounded an equally powerful dichotomy, tied much more closely to the behaviour of a macro-system: the division of aggregate income and aggregate expenditure. Neither of these illuminating dichotomies isolated behaviour that was necessarily exclusive to different individuals – an economic agent could be, simultaneously, demander and supplier or spender and earner.

Although both these dichotomies deal with flows over time they are both essentially static in the sense that the economic structure through which flows occur is fixed. In other words, the flows in question are set within a predefined spatial structure. In the first case, it is 'market structure' with *homo economicus* providing a highly structured spatial representation of component behaviour. In the second case, it is the 'structure of the economy' which is divided spatially into consumers, investors, etc. Dynamics enter through another analytical dichotomy, that of *ex ante* and *ex post*, which permits the analysis of how a given structure copes with flow shocks and regains equilibrium.

The fact that there are separate dichotomies to deal with statics and dynamics reflects a fundamental separation of space and time. The spatial rearrangement caused by flow shocks of various kinds can be captured with mathematical precision, but to model dynamics, *ceteris paribus* assumptions have to be made to permit the use of calculus in the Newtonian style. Although it is possible to consider successive shocks and subsequent dynamics in a way that seems to match real experience it is in fact a mirage – space and time are kept entirely separate from each other because each shock sets in motion a unique tendency towards a new equilibrium which is unaffected by any subsequent shock. In other words, each spatial shock is accompanied by an abstract time dimension. A proper integration of space and time would involve successive shocks revising the dynamics precipitated by previous shocks and subsequent shocks being affected by the dynamics which are precipitated from previous shocks. Clearly, to permit such an integration of space and time involves the abandonment of the cause–effect or stimulus–response methodology of science along with all the purpose-built rules of mathematics which constitute its formalization.

The separation of the perceived motion of matter into a time dimension and a space dimension was an extremely useful dichotomy in the history of science. Measurement of distance and the passing of time permitted motional dynamics to be expressed in speed, for example, provided matter adhered to physical rules. Such knowledge aided the design of physical systems with complex interconnections, including feedback mechanisms. The machine is a structure which is *built up* from scientific principles, plus human imagination. Science developed for this purpose – to aid creativity and predict the performance of a created structure, not to predict the interactive complexity of the natural world. The space–time dichotomy, in the end, is of use in an analytical structuring sense.

In reality, neither space nor time have any absolute and separate existence; they are relativities which look at the structure of motional dynamics from different directions. The spatial perspective acknowledges that there exist bonded structures of energy, in the form of various types of matter, which have dimensions. Thus, space derives its meaning from motional regularity which is so closely bonded as to constitute 'solidity'. The time dimension also deals with motional regularity but from *inside* rather than *outside* structure. Time acknowledges the regularity of movement of matter within spatial structure. Both abstractions give rise to constructs such as maps and clocks which aid constructive behaviour. How useful are these abstractions of motional relativity in the context of economics?

Undoubtedly they are useful for the design and construction of efficient factories, but that is only the scientific application writ larger. As constructs which aid the understanding of underlying economic behaviour in the economic system, they are not particularly helpful. The spatial equivalent to structure of matter is economic structure which is much more susceptible to the law of entropy and structural mutation than anything in physical science. By the same token, the linear concept of time is not particularly enlightening when we are dealing with intra-structural regularities which are constantly altering.[9] As Keynes recognized, conventional abstractions of space and time are only useful in an analytical sense in 'short-run' study where the evolutionary progress of the system and the creative dimension of human imagination are held constant.[10]

In attempting to analyse the perceived structures of the economic system, it is quite admissible to pretend that we are dealing with some kind of machine, for the economic system is not the natural order of things, but an evolved structure emanating from the creative capacity of human minds. Constructs such as time and space are fundamental organizational conventions in this structure and, as such, have an extremely important role to play. Also, space and time are two of many constructs which underlie the motional regularity of economic structure. The 'chemistry' of the interaction of all behavioural constructs is constantly subject to change so that 'physical' laws of economic motion, which presume that space and time are exogenous, cannot be discovered. Thus, any strict analogy between economic structure and a machine will always be misleading, not only in terms of its ability to cope with structural change, but also in terms of narrowing the focus of attention to phenomena which are quantifiable in terms of space and time. If we are dealing with system malfunction the analogy is useful, as Keynes demonstrated, in helping to cope with the situation. However, it is not helpful to explore the mutative implications of Keynesian system correction or to isolate what past tendencies gave rise to the malfunction.[11]

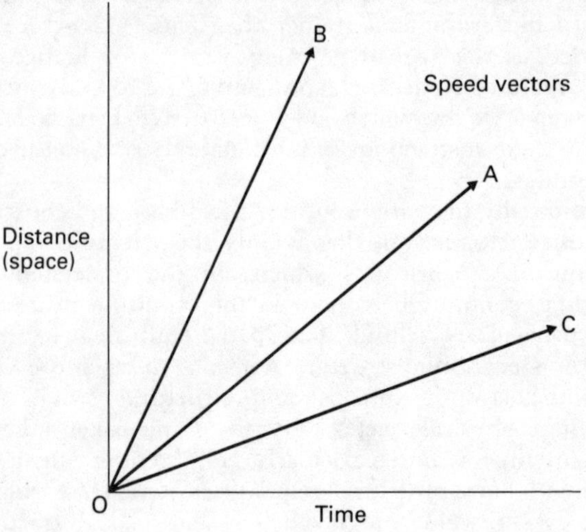

Figure 6.1 Time-space method of characterizing motion

In Figure 6.1 we have the physical time–space method of characterizing motion in terms of velocities, with accelerations and decelerations permitting movement from one velocity to another. Economics has contrived to generalize this approach to the motion of structure, where efficiency is analogous to velocity. For such an approach to be valid, the subjects, like 'road' and 'car' must be structurally 'distant' and not subsets of some greater structure. For example, velocity measures cannot be measures of efficiency when roads grow wider to accommodate traffic and cars are designed to go faster on wider roads.

Evolutionary macroeconomics cannot be captured by positing independent space and time constructs. They must be interdependent, with spatial characteristics of structure constantly changing and notions of time inseparable from the evolution of structure which is taking place.[12] The universal adoption of space and time conventions render both extremely important in the structure that we perceive, but not independent axes from which we can plot the motion of structure. The convention of time is a co-ordinator just as the convention of money is. Just as money can become valueless in its co-ordinating function in certain circumstances, so time can become of little help when the scope for planning and co-ordination is limited.

The dichotomy of space and time performs three functions: first, it *enables description* of structural motion to take place; second, it can be used to *aid the design* of new structure; and third, it can be *used analytically* in controlled experiments. In economics, it remains invaluable in its first application, as a descriptive device. At the macroeconomic level, in its second application, it has been superseded by the dichotomy of time and money. Aggregation over space is achieved by monetary valuation, money being a much more relevant convention than distance in the economic system. Efficiency is measured in terms of monetary flows per unit of time. The dichotomy has no place in economics in terms of its third application since the possibility of controlled economic experiments makes no sense when the subjects have non-mechanical forward-looking capabilities which interfere with monetary (spatial) behaviour rendering money and time non-independent.

The Biological Analogy

The abandonment of space and time abstractions and the notions of 'equilibrium' that go along with them is often regarded as the end of any kind of analytical content in economics and Friedman's dictum is often heard: in as much as the space–time analogy is useful, even in an imperfect sense, then it should be retained. But it does not necessarily follow. The space–time abstraction is useful in physics because it aids the discovery of invariant natural laws of motion. The mutation of matter can be conveniently separated into chemistry where, again, the qualitative interactions of matter are repeatable. In human behaviour the 'physics' and the 'chemistry' are mixed up, but not necessarily in an intractable way. Once we depart from the world of chemical matter and move to the organic world we perceive physical/chemical changes occurring simultaneously in well defined and repeatable ways. In studying the growth and development of an organism we would never dream of looking at it in terms of a mere chemical reaction or as matter which 'just moves'. The organism changes, simultaneously in quantitative and qualitative ways. We tend to study the organism, not as a structure moving in and out of equilibrium due to a succession of shocks but rather as a motional phenomenon.[13] We record how its motional complexity develops and how it interacts motionally with its environment. No mathematical formalization is necessary, yet biologists can predict with a high degree of accuracy, using time and space in their descriptive role alone, the developmental pattern of the organism. The patterning of structure alters in a way that can be tracked using *qualitative* analysis.

Of course, the biologist finds it much more difficult to macro-model ecosystems since observation is difficult over relevant time periods and because they tend to be heterogeneous in their composition. However, theories of evolution do exist which, generally, are extensions of micro-studies of the behaviour of organisms. Even the macro-behaviour of the ecosystem can be founded on behavioural foundations quite different to those found in economics. Since economic behaviour would seem closer to biological behaviour, why then, isn't the method of biologists used? It is not the case that if we abandon Newtonian methods that 'there is no alternative'. The problem in the past, as we have seen, was the over-literal translation of biological analogy, on the one hand, in Marxist economics, and its implicit acknowledgement, on the other hand, in the Walrasian story. If adoption of the Newtonian method leads to an overly restrictive short-run model, the biological analogies have tended to adapt extremely long-run processes into the much shorter run context of economic evolution. To find an evolutionary basis for macroeconomics, it is necessary to look much more carefully at aspects of behaviour that are not simply biological, but uniquely human.

At present, we have biological studies of animal behaviour which are aggregated in a qualitative way to the ecological level. In modelling evolution, a division of opinion has grown up between the traditional Darwinists with their 'survival of the fittest' natural selection model and the Kropotkin revivalists who see evolution as much more to do with symbiotic relationships. The former emphasizes struggle and power whereas the latter co-operation and compromise. It is not a debate which can be resolved from empirical evidence, for examples of both processes can be shown to exist. It is more than likely that both processes exist in evolution with the question centring on which is primary and secondary in the evolutionary experience.

We saw in the last chapter how the biological analogy has been translated into social Darwinism in the past, particularly in the case of Marx who 'solved' the problem of integrating the individual and the group by setting the analogy in a macro-framework where individuals were subsumed into classes which behaved like species. We have also seen how social Darwinism was used in the 'philosophy' of fascism to depict the individual struggle for power translating itself into totalitarian hierarchies. As we have observed, these unfortunate attempts at biological analysis led orthodox economists to push the mechanics of evolution firmly into the background of Walrasian conceptions of the economic system so that today attempts at reviving social Darwinism are rare.[14]

Modern attempts to place economic behaviour in an evolutionary framework by, for example, Boulding (1981) have tended to be built on the Kropotkin vision. The emphasis is not on struggle but on the adaptability of species so that they do not become obsolete in the sense of being unable to take new opportunities or occupy new 'niches' in the structure of things. Struggle is thus the death throe of a species which has become over-specialized, neglecting the adaptability that forward planning necessitates. Boulding calls it 'survival of the fitting'.[15] This vision of evolution accords very well with economic development both in terms of what economics, as a distinctive discipline, ought to be interested in, and in terms of the way in which, for example, firms grow and decline in the real world.

Social Darwinism is essentially the province of political science rather than economics, if we define economics as being about co-ordinated productive behaviour. We discussed in the last chapter how economists such as Schumacher have gone further and argued that the social Darwinist concept of evolution is particularly inappropriate in the economic sphere because human behaviour involves creativity by individuals who have a degree of 'self-awareness' not possessed by lower forms of life. The ideas which contribute to the evolution of the economic system involve an interaction of social philosophy and individual behaviour which has no useful parallel in the very long-run perspective of ecological evolution. Economic evolution can thus be an extremely rapid process with potential for periods of sustained harmony and abrupt catastrophes. Keynes perceived this with great clarity in his discussion of 'animal spirits' prevailing beyond the short run and was given to calling economics a 'moral science' because of his belief in the prior importance of the qualitative over the quantitative.

In the context of economic behaviour and the existence of forward planning not found in species evolution, conflictual struggles appear as a manifestation of system inefficiency if we translate the Kropotkin vision into economics. Erich Fromm, whose work is to be discussed below, makes much of the point that to attempt to see evolution as the outcome of permanent political power struggles is irrational in the context of socioeconomic behaviour. The importance of philosophy in economic evolution is undeniable if we view economic structure as the outcome of human imagination. This is a philosophical position which has been growing in importance and one to which we now turn.

The Popular Philosophers

The issue as to what foundations we choose to discuss human behaviour has become a major issue in social philosophy over the past two decades. Although some of the issues raised have been translated into economics by the authors cited in the last chapter, they have done so in a necessarily fragmentary manner. The construction of macroeconomic theories is not based on attempting to extend the versatility of economics to cope with various psychological and social interactions, but rather with isolating some 'universals' which can shine through the complexity of the economic system. The logical constructs which can aid macroeconomic thought reside in the generalities of social philosophy rather than their more empirical offshoots, psychology and sociology. Of course, social philosophy is a large subject which will not be surveyed here. The objective of a mere economist is more modest: to introduce the reader to the work of three representative writers, all of them in different segments of social philosophy, with virtually no cross-referencing to each other's work. Each has attempted to communicate, not with fellow academics, but with a radically inclined 'thinking' public and, in doing so, each has, in his time, become the focus of a popular movement. Although none of them have written about the subject of economics, they all present a common thesis which attacks the very foundations upon which orthodox economics is based both in its capitalist and socialist manifestations.

Herbert Marcuse In the 1960s, Herbert Marcuse, influenced by the 'structuralism' of the Levi-Strauss school in Paris, launched a profound attack on what he called 'scientific rationality'. Tracing the history of such rationality back to Aristotle, he argues that it constitutes an ideology which results in, what he calls, 'false consciousness' in modern society. In conjunction with the pervasive influence of modern mass-media, which are seen as having replaced the informal channels of ideology within old social structures such as family and community, he traces the ascendancy of 'one-dimensional man'. This character holds an ideology which includes the belief that the natural world must be dominated, that material progress must be pursued as a primary goal using the fruits of scientific advance to that end. Although Marcuse takes as his starting point a Marxist vision of alienation and exploitation within a capitalist society, one-dimensionality is identified, equally, within communist societies. It is not surprising to find that his thesis was subsequently dismissed by Marxists given its tendency to view dialectics from the standpoint of Hegel rather than Marx, with qualities such as ideology interfering with the 'materialist interpretation of history'.

Much of the debate concerning Marcuse's work has been in terms of evaluating it in the context of revolutionary sociology and, as such, it is rejected by Marxists and non-Marxists alike.[16] Yet there is little doubt that it caught the imagination of a generation who could not quite identify the source of their unrest, but saw in Marcuse's writing some truth. It was a thoroughly un-Marxist generation who were, quite clearly, attracted by the philosophical rather than the political content of his book. The powerful images of human imagination, formed over centuries of cultural development in language, art, literature and ideology, was a vision that everyone could identify with. Economic theory, in this context, is merely an intellectual extreme of formalization of constructs which perpetrate a whole culture.

Marcuse was interested in 'universals' such as church, state, etc., arguing that although they cannot be quantified, they have a meaning which is perfectly well understood by everyone. They are 'wholes' which are irreducible into sums of parts in the 'scientific rational' mode of thinking. To Marcuse, qualities such as ideology are not normative asides but the vital engine of the whole socioeconomic system. Change, to him, did not come from 'Kuhnian' paradigm shift but rather through radical art which he saw as effectively partitioned and silenced in the modern media. We have already discussed the role of economic myths and Marcuse links them through ideology to every individual in society. The 'qualitative' is reinstated as a valid philosophical dimension of human behaviour, describing the structural bonding created and unified by the human imagination. Through these qualitative visions, co-ordination and unification of, for example, nature and individuals is possible.

Macroeconomics is preoccupied by universals in Marcuse's sense: the economy, consumers, trade unions, markets, etc. In other words, qualities which acquire the solidity of economic institutions. These qualities, or structures, cannot be analysed using the quantitative techniques of 'positivist' science in terms of the comparative behaviour of matter in space and time. Such a reductionist approach would remove the structural essence which determines the nature of the motional experience. Marcuse argues that such a position does not constitute a retreat from reality, since the qualities involved have clear empirical meaning and are frequently measurable in an empirical setting. In economics, this is particularly true, given that quantitative output emanates from structures, measurable within the convention of monetary value. Although it may be appropriate to model the microeconomics of project appraisal in quantitative terms, the macroeconomic perspective is thoroughly qualitative, held together by a unifying structure of conventions, ethics and ideologies. Perhaps, more importantly, Marcuse emphasizes that the existence of such qualities reflects rational social behaviour, in contrast to conventional economic analysis that argues that the 'one dimensionality' of *homo economicus* offers a rational basis for analysis. Of course, Marcuse did not develop an adequate basis for extending our notion of rational economic behaviour in this direction – that is a theme we shall take up in the next chapter.

Robert Pirsig Marcuse's book is complex, it is controversial and heavily clothed in the terminology of sociology. A decade later, long after the campus 'revolutions' had died down in the United States, there appeared a much more simply constructed book entitled *Zen and the Art of Motorcycle Maintenance* by Robert Pirsig. It was far from an exhortation to revolution but rather a book that was compatible with the 'cult of the individual' of the 1970s. Written in the style of a novel interspersed by rhetorical discourse, it was a remarkable attempt to communicate philosophical ideas to a broad range of readers. Although in an entirely different context, the theme of the book is similar to Marcuse. Pirsig is also concerned with the historical ascendancy of Aristotelian rationality, the decline in the role of 'quality', the resultant incapacity of individuals to think in logical ways and the unappealing aesthetic characteristics of a materialist world.

Pirsig's primary interest is scientific methodology and here the parallels with economic methodology are extremely close. The development of the idea that scientific discovery, following Poincaré (1905), is about the quality of imagination is extended into the everyday concern with human behaviour and the difficulties caused by operating with an inappropriate philosophy of reason. Marcuse was concerned with the implications for society, Pirsig for the individual's psychological disposition. Like Marcuse, the power of myths, religions and ideologies constitute the prior basis for behaviour. Not just social behaviour, but the internal 'balance' of the individual. For Pirsig, the ultimate horrors of scientific materialism reside in the communist cultures, in contrast to Marcuse who addressed himself mainly to capitalism. Given Pirsig's focus on the individual, this different emphasis is understandable and echoed a general popular shift in the 1970s. However, there is little doubt that both writers look at the same issue from different directions. They both argue that the central conception of human behaviour excludes a fundamental dimension of reality and, as such, distorts that reality, given the prior importance of the quality of human imagination. Furthermore, to both, quality is very real for, although it cannot be measured directly, it is well understood throughout society. Quality forms the structure which holds the macroeconomy together.

Pirsig sees the conjunction of interactions such as mind and matter as constituting a qualitative event and, furthermore, argues that quality can vary on a hierarchy of usefulness. He divides this hierarchy into two segments, which he labels 'romantic' and 'classical', which are not dissimilar to the economist's division between invention and innovation in the context of technical progress. Romantic quality is beyond 'rational' consciousness – inspirational processes are below the level of awareness.[17] Classical quality deals with the application of intuition within well defined empirical contexts of the problem solving variety. Structuring can occur at various levels of informality or formality, yielding different types of creativity. In the abstraction of the former lies both fundamental scientific breakthrough and the 'hip' world of fashion and other subtle relativities. Conventional scientific logic, as well as the development of skills, resides in the latter. Or to put it another way, the former deals with perceptual structuring and the latter with the development of activity to a high level of co-ordination.

Whereas Marcuse attempted to analyse the qualitative dimension of socio-economic relations and the manner in which individuals are conditioned into commonly held qualitative perceptions which prevent them from pursuing their best interests, Pirsig was concerned with the nature of the perception–action relationship in general and the manner in which it is determined by qualitative considerations. Just as the former was pessimistic about the ability of individuals to break out of qualitative social structuring in the form of ideology, so Pirsig was pessimistic about the ability of an individual, with essentially the same malaise, from finding any new ideology which did not reject the scientific materialist mode of thought. What we learn from Pirsig in our quest for macroeconomic foundations is that there is a division, analytically, between a subject's perception of the environment and a subject's attempts to interact with the environment. This is distinct from Marcuse's point yet important, as we shall see, in any attempt to develop suitable foundations of macroeconomic analysis.

Erich Fromm Erich Fromm attempted, throughout his career, to use the discipline of social psychology as the foundation of a 'humanistic' social philosophy. His books are written for a broad audience, the best known being *The Sane Society* (1955) and his last book *To Have or to Be?* (1980) which became one of the inspirational texts of the 'Greens' in Europe in the 1980s. Fromm, like Marcuse and Pirsig, examines the prevailing scientific materialist ideology and argues that it has induced a form of socio-psychological 'insanity' in modern society.[18] He uses his earlier work on the role of religions and myths to deal with the materialist myth which propels economic progress and argues that it is a myth which has outlived its usefulness to society.[19] He argues from his socio-psychological standpoint that structured myths about the unknown are vital for the psychological security of people to such an extent that they will be retained even when they run counter to the interests of the individual.

Whereas Marcuse sees ideology as a repressive force emanating from vested interests, Fromm observes it from the standpoint of the recipient's need for a validating mythology. Although Pirsig also recognizes this need in a general sense, Fromm emphasizes, to a much greater degree, the social dimension of such a need. Marcuse was pessimistic about society being stuck with an inappropriate ideology which no individual could challenge effectively. Pirsig was pessimistic about the individual being stuck with an inappropriate ideology which, if replaced, forced the individual into isolation. Fromm integrates the individual and society in such a way that ideology need not be as static as these other authors imply. For him it is not necessary for deprived minorities to initiate revolution, Marcuse-style, or for individuals to retreat into Zen Buddhism, Pirsig-style. In fact he viewed both as counter-productive by themselves, unless accompanied by a broadly-based shift in ideology. Furthermore, he saw no reason why such a shift could not take place provided that vested interests were made to see that they are as much prisoners of inappropriate ideology as the exploited.

In order to explain the dynamics of ideology between individuals and society, Fromm uses an analytical distinction between two types of strategic responses in motional situations. An individual can either react in a predative way to possess or consume, or in a co-operative way to initiate co-ordinated motions. He argues that there is a significant range of situations where a choice between each strategy can be made. Which choice is actually made will depend, critically, on ideology, ethics, values, etc. Robinson Crusoe's decision not to eat Man Friday but to attempt to coax him into a co-operative situation was determined by cultural values. Fromm devotes a great deal of his writing to examining the cumulative interactions between alienating experience and propaganda which generates adherence to, for example, fascist thought.[20] In contrast, he demonstrates the extent to which adherence to many religious principles opens up co-operative possibilities between individuals which initiate virtuous circles in the interplay between experience and ethics. He emphasizes the rapidity with which the ideological perception of an individual can change from allegiance to a totalitarian dictator through to 'born-again' Christianity.

The strategy suggested by the prevailing orthodox ideology is seen as having profound implications for social harmony and creative development. Possessive or 'having' strategies result in a stagnant, conflict ridden society, whereas co-operative or 'being' strategies lead to a developing, secure society. Scientific materialism is seen as a 'having' ideology, once old ethical principles embodied in religion have faded away, opening the door to totalitarian solutions to social problems. Fromm provides an extensive range of historical examples which suggest that such situations have existed in the past and he sees their resolution as one of persuading the purveyors of conventional ideology that there is a more rational alternative. Clearly, economists, as the central custodians of the prevailing ideology, are one of the main targets in any attempt at such a conversion. However, as we have already argued, being at the intellectual core of ideology is the most resistant point in any structure of thought.

What Fromm offers the macroeconomic perspective is a simple dichotomy between two types of general strategy, one which involves constructive economic development and another which does not. Thus any evolutionary approach to macroeconomics should be able to reflect the nature of strategy choice dictated by the prevailing ideology. The existing Walrasian conception of the macroeconomy has no evolutionary dimension and only an idealized notion of the world in which *homo economicus* securely operates. Thus, it cannot encapsulate the strategic dimension that Fromm presents nor can it capture the notions of security and freedom which ideology conveys. To extend macroeconomics to incorporate these Frommian dimensions would go a long way to freeing ideology from the 'fix' identified by Marcuse and Pirsig.

Conclusion

In this chapter we have tried to depart from economics into the general areas of biology and philosophy in search of more appropriate bio-philosophical foundations of macroeconomics. In the biological area we have pointed to the fact that the qualitative methods of analysing organic development seem more appropriate than Newtonian analogies with their space–time abstractions. Motional development is not well described in the latter framework because space and time cannot be regarded as exogenous constructs. Evolutionary development demands that they be endogenous.

Traditional views of evolution as a process of natural selection are regarded as inadequate to encapsulate economic development, which is at a sophisticated level in the hierarchy of behaviour and concerned with symbiosis and attainment of high levels of economic co-operation. Following modern developments in evolutionary theory, the 'survival of the fitting' analysis of Kropotkin is seen as more appropriate to economics. Evolution is seen less in terms of struggle and more in terms of taking opportunities that present themselves to produce innovative, creative activity. The 'struggle' dimension of evolution in the sphere of human affairs is the concern of political scientists, not economists. Only by concentrating on the distinctive phenomenon of constructive economic development can economics hope to retain its identity in an evolutionary context. Once we have accepted the idea that, as economic development accelerates, it is no longer possible to cast our vision in terms of fixed structures of thought, then we have to allow for the influence of the qualitative. The philosophical or imaginative dimension of behaviour must be incorporated at the root of macroeconomics as the foundation of evolutionary change.

In order to explore the manner in which the philosophical dimension of behaviour could be included in the foundations of macroeconomics, the work of three 'popular philosophers' was considered. In the first, the work of Marcuse supported the view that macroeconomics as the study of the structure of the economy must necessarily deal with qualitative structures which have meaning but are difficult to define in quantitative terms. Macroeconomics cannot be reduced to microfoundations without losing essential meaning. Marcuse taught us that the macroeconomy has two dimensions, the qualitative which is the structure of human imagination and the quantitative, which is the total amount of activity recorded over time. This is a social dichotomy which implies that quantitative assessments are only valid if, in some sense, the qualitative, e.g. ideology, is held constant. Marcuse is concerned with the extent to which the intensity of an ideology is increased in circumstances where it is becoming more inappropriate to the evolutionary stage of society. The control of ideology by vested interests provides the impetus behind his pessimistic macro-scenario.

Pirsig is also interested in philosophical universals which influence economic creativity, but from the perspective of the individual. He is interested in the motional development of the individual in a general sense and he, too, draws out a dichotomy between the qualitative and the quantitative. The qualitative perceptions of the individual are held to be analytically distinct from activity observed. The individual is not seen to be in the pitiless grip of social conditioning but able to choose different philosophical positions at the cost of different degrees of social acceptance. Pirsig is clearly on the other side of the coin to Marcuse. The former emphasizes the possibilities of choosing alternative philosophical positions in the perceptual zone, at the risk of social exclusion. The latter emphasizes the overwhelming force of social conditioning on perception, thus inhibiting the scope of activity. Like society, the individual's motional structure is determined by the philosophical dimension of perception. For both there is a rigidity in the social ideology, in Pirsig's case deriving from the historical development of philosophy and in Marcuse's case deriving from the existence of individual vested interests, i.e. from political considerations. Both perceive a discontinuity between the prevailing social ideology and individual interest.

Fromm argues that such a discontinuity is ephemeral and, ultimately, the appropriate ideology will evolve. In answer to Pirsig, philosophy and metaphysics have demonstrated an historical ability to change. In answer to Marcuse, vested interests cannot perpetuate an inappropriate ideology indefinitely because it is not in their interests any more than the exploited. Fromm accepts the analytical dichotomy between perception and action and how ideology in the former dictates the nature of the latter. But he goes on to argue that this interaction can, in turn, be classified as to whether it is predative or co-operative in nature. Motional interaction can, thus, be divided into perception and action constructs within a given strategic framework which can be separated into two qualitatively different zones. Fromm thus links together the individual and society, the micro and the macro, with social ideology facilitating a pattern of structured motions amongst individuals which can result in development, on the one hand, or repression and conflict on the other. Marcuse and Pirsig's alienated individuals cannot correct the situation and are more likely to take up the predatory ideologies. Progress for Fromm resides firmly in enlightenment of the majority.

In constructing foundations for macroeconomics it is

essential, first, to cast all behaviour in an evolutionary framework where the focus of attention is the motional interaction of subject with the environment. Second, the features of interest to the economist are those evolutionary situations where co-operative structures evolve to advance economic development. Although the political problems which arise in the course of evolution are recognized it is beyond the compass of economics to analyse these except to say that in a limited, macroeconomic, evolutionary sense they constitute periods of 'irrationality'. Third, rationality requires redefinition by casting it explicitly within the dynamics of structured motion, utilizing the qualitative/quantitative distinctions raised by our popular philosophers. Fourth, the unity of 'macro' and 'micro' through the hierarchies of thought and action require explicit development.

Approaching the subject of macroeconomics through the inclusion of qualitative forces, embedded in the human imagination, might still seem somewhat implausible to many economists. However, it does not take long to discover that all conventional economic logic reduces to the same thing and that modern developments such as rational expectations are symptomatic of a need to move in the direction suggested here. The next three chapters will demonstrate that such a development is extremely practical and sensible, in contrast to the approach of, for example, Schumacher who correctly rejects social Darwinism but unrealistically attempts to argue that scientific materialism can be replaced by a new ideology or set of religious values. His approach is echoed not only in 'Buddhist' economics but also 'Islamic' economics and the various Christian economic philosophies that have risen to prominence over the past decade. The approach here is more modest.

Like that of the popular philosophers discussed in this chapter, the objective is to emphasize the powerful and inertial quality of ideology which has served society well in the past. The purpose is not to suggest any alternative set of ethics or ideology but simply to provide a framework which permits the incorporation of new additions to the cumulation of human ideas that we have. Thus, the analysis will not be 'normative' but 'positive', in terms of current terminology, building on rational postulates concerning human behaviour. The central focus of attention will be the structure of motion, a quality which absorbs energy and yields outputs or characteristics and can be depicted equally, at the level of the economy or the individual. As we shall see in the following chapters, both can be dealt with within the same motional model of a structure or a system and both can be integrated through the hierarchical bonding that characterizes all organizational structures.

Notes

1 See Sachs (1976) and Jordan (1981) for particularly clear definitions of what is meant by the general systems approach from which we can derive particular cases in economics.
2 See Matthews (1959) for a good survey of the development of business cycle studies in the early postwar Keynesian literature, and Zarnowitz (1985) for a survey of the changes in business cycle theory since then.
3 See Harrod's (1939) classic article showing how a plausible view of businessmen's expectations generates a 'knife-edge' growth path in a Keynesian model. See, also, Blatt (1983) for an exposition of the instability of neo-classical and other popular types of dynamic models.
4 See Seckler (1975) for an appraisal of Veblen's contributions and the 'institutionalist' school which followed. See also Commons (1961) for a key statement of the institutionalist position. See Gordon (1980) and Williamson (1985) for an overview of modern developments.
5 It had done so much earlier in management science and industrial sociology. By the mid 1960s Katz and Kahn (1966) had provided a systematic treatment of the organization as a socio-psychological entity, providing the basis for much of the 'strategy and structure' analysis to follow.
6 A parallel development was taking place in management science within which the systems approach lay much more comfortably than in economics. See, in particular, the pioneering efforts of Ackoff and Emery (1972).
7 See Handy (1981) for a comprehensive exposition of the organizational theorist's approach to development. Chandler (1962, 1977) was a prominent pioneer in bringing together consciousness and structure to analyse the dynamics of managerial systems. See also Williamson (1985) for a good selection of papers using this approach.
8 See Chick (1973) for some discussion of the role of dichotomies in economics. Klein (1983) discusses the relevance of the supply/demand dichotomy in Keynesian macroeconomics.
9 See Boulding (1981) for further discussion of linear time versus 'evolutionary' time.
10 This has rarely been appreciated in orthodox macroeconomics. However, see Allais's (1966) analysis of the demand for money for a heroic attempt to cope with this problem.

11 See Cencini (1984) for an example of the problems which arise if the space–time analogy is taken literally in Keynesian historical time analysis.

12 See Averitt (1975) and Bausor (1982–83) for variations on this theme.

13 Systems theorists tend to distinguish this motional dynamic by referring to it as *homeostasis* (see Cannon, 1963 for the classic development of this concept) rather than equilibrium, in other words, as a system which is controlled by feedback loops as it continually absorbs energy. See Ashby (1967) for some formalization of this concept as a dynamic 'steady-state'.

14 A particularly insightful attempt to marry together Darwinian style competition between firms and information gathering in the face of market uncertainty was undertaken by Alchian (1950). See also Haavelmo (1954) for an original attempt to take an evolutionary approach to economic development and Penrose (1952) for a biological approach to the theory of the firm.

15 This 'new view' of evolution has now become widely accepted in biological circles, given that it is able to accommodate the Darwinian mechanism in particular conditions. See Eldredge (1985) for an exposition of what is now called the theory of punctuated equilibria.

16 See MacIntyre (1970) for a particularly scathing rebuke.

17 Polanyi (1967) has written extensively on the importance of this kind of pre-intellectual awareness or what he calls 'tacit knowledge'. Scientific rationality has been haunted by this throughout history and it was given great prominence at the turn of the century by Poincaré (1905). Koestler (1964, 1975) is the modern populariser.

18 See also Koestler (1978) for a similar conclusion from a different psychological perspective.

19 See Fromm (1941).

20 See Fromm (1941). and also Arendt (1951) for analysis along similar lines.

7 The Foundations of an Evolutionary Approach to Economic Behaviour

> . . . it is especially needful to remember that economic problems are imperfectly presented when they are treated as problems of statical equilibrium and not organic growth.
>
> Alfred Marshall (1890)

In order to offer an alternative to *homo economicus* which can provide a better foundation for the analysis of macroeconomic behaviour, it is necessary to distil the essence of the bio-philosophical developments discussed in Chapter 6. The objective is to provide an abstraction which is at a comparable level of generality to *homo economicus*, first, to enable the reader, familiar with this conventional abstraction, to see how it differs from the one proposed and, second, to enable us to classify *homo economicus* as a special case.

As we saw in previous chapters, the main thrust of macroeconomic debate in modern times has centred on the degree to which we can use the abstraction of the auction market as a useful guide to macroeconomic analysis. Thus, we find it straightforward to classify the various schools of macroeconomic thought in terms of the degree to which they accept the market abstraction. We saw, too, in Chapter 4 how the new contractual approach has, in the main, continued to espouse *homo economicus* as the centre-piece of the models developed. In this chapter it will be argued that it is the appropriateness of *homo economicus* for macroeconomics, rather than the degree to which markets clear, which is crucial. *Homo economicus* was developed to explain why demand curves slope downwards in microeconomics and, as such, he is inseparable from the market context in which he is seen to operate. What we shall attempt to do is to offer *homo creativus* as an alternative, an abstraction better suited to macroeconomic analysis, irrespective of the precise nature of the market process which is presumed to exist.

To some it may be rather puzzling to attempt to search for macroeconomic foundations beyond markets, those great co-ordinating institutions in the macroeconomy. Thus, it is necessary to devote some time to developing the general behavioural characteristics of *homo creativus*. To achieve this, we shall present a set of postulates which dissolves the macro/micro distinction and admits behavioural dynamics from the outset.[1] That is the objective of this chapter.

Structured Motion

As Georgescu-Roegen (1971) emphasized, any attempt to model the dynamics of structured motion should begin with the second law of thermodynamics. All structures that exist consist of energy bondings which contain potential energy. Any motional interaction between the structure and the environment will lower that potential energy. In turn, absorption of new energy permits the structure to replenish its potential energy and continue to interact. Boulding (1981) has emphasized that when we move from the traditional experiments in the physics classroom to the evolutionary context, so familiar to biologists, the second law must be modified to deal with the mutative capabilities of living organisms. These organisms transform primary energy, e.g. sunlight, into an energy potential which is *qualitatively* complex. In other words, these organisms will use primary energy to transform non-organic materials into a set of embodied qualities or characteristics which are highly complex and subtle. For example, a plant will invest much primary energy in creating a brightly coloured, ingeniously shaped flower to attract the bee. So much energy is devoted to organization of structure that the primary energy potential of the plant is only a tiny fraction of the total energy absorbed. Thus, primary energy inputs are used up in generating qualitative outputs such as shape and colour.[2] However, sharply defined organic structures, such as flowers, cannot be sustained. Colour fades and physical degeneration accelerates.

The law of entropy is irresistible in the presence of all structured motion.[3] Commitment to distinctive structure is, in some degree, irreversible so that, despite maintenance through the infusion of more primary energy, the organism will be subject to degeneration. The law of entropy is, in turn, defied by the process of reproduction. Individuals live and die but the species carries on. Individual mortality is the price paid for specialized motional characteristics which necessarily involve a commitment to decentralized sub-structuring. We observe that species which have no strong specialist characteristics tend to have no distinctive individualism and are able to mutate much more easily.

In the highly specialized case of the human being, individualism is a distinctive characteristic, not so much in terms of biological motion but in the creation of material and organizational 'externalized' structure. These external structures, produced by the imagination, which is a dimension of self-awareness, are subject to a high degree of entropy since they have no independent means of maintenance.[4] Also, being peripheral, they can be detached from the core, i.e. the individual or the group, without fatal damage, like a plant losing a branch.

Perception and action combine to release highly sophisticated forms of energy: perceptual knowledge and volitional skill. Such energy constitutes the basis of power since its application can initiate massive entropic energy releases or great cumulations of potential energy in creating structure. The second law of thermodynamics must always prevail, but in the case of human creativity, the energy of imagination can co-ordinate energy concentration or entropy release in a 'multiplier' or 'chain reactive' manner yielding effects much greater than the net energy input into the human organism itself. Thus the second law of thermodynamics operates in a qualitatively different way as we move from mineral to human structure. Figure 7.1 provides a schematic classification of the four distinct but overlapping levels of qualitative structure through which the law operates.

Mineral structure is created by the external application of

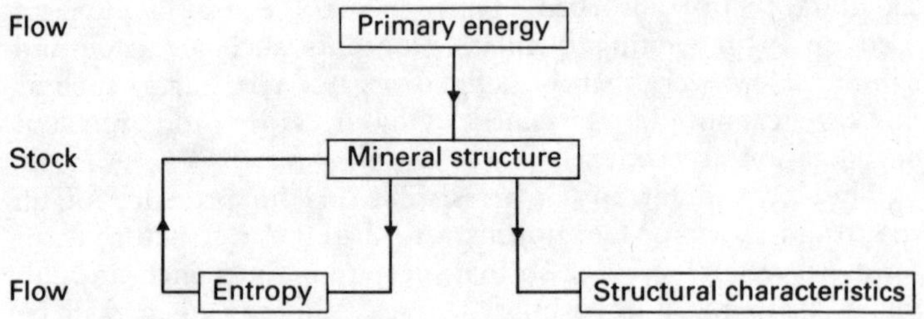

Figure 7.1 Level 1: mineral structure

energy. It has no self-maintenance ability so, as entropy proceeds through interaction with the environment, structural characteristics weaken in the direction of randomness. The rate at which entropic decay occurs might be very slow in durable tightly bonded cases and fast in others. In general, the more sophisticated the mineral structure, the faster is the rate of decay. Motor cars are mineral structures which decay quickly because, despite maintenance (i.e. the input of further energy) their motional complexity renders them very fast decayers. A piece of rock, on the other hand, is so tightly bonded that its rate of decay is extremely slow. With mineral structure, the rate of decay towards randomness is predictable using stochastic methods.

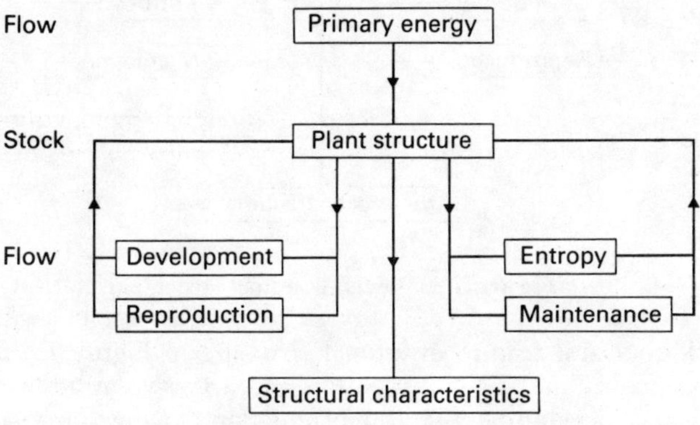

Figure 7.2 Level 2: plant structure

Plant structure contains a quality lacking in mineral structure which we call 'life'. This necessitates an additional dimension to motional flow. Plants inherit a capacity to absorb primary energy which they combine with minerals to enable development of the plant. The existence of entropy in individual plants also necessitates reproduction to maintain the continuity of the species. The individual is indistinct from the species in any qualitative sense – plant cuttings can live independently, such is the lack of specialization of function. If we look at Figure 7.2 as a depiction of the species, then development would constitute evolution and entropy would be resisted in the absence of a major environmental catastrophe. If Figure 7.2 is restricted to a unit, say a tree, then entropy would finally overwhelm development and end its life. Once again, plants vary in their rate of decay depending on the durability of their structure. Trees can live for hundreds of years, micro-organisms for only minutes. In general, the more durable are structural units, the slower evolution will proceed. Short-lived organisms are observed to mutate with great rapidity.

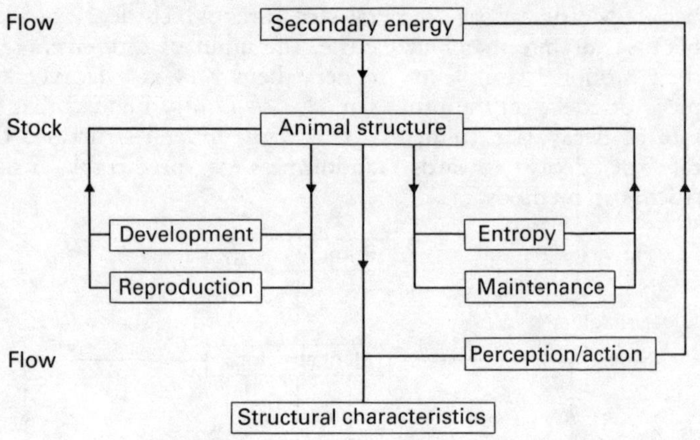

Figure 7.3 Level 3: animal structure

The critical feature of animal structure in Figure 7.3 is the existence of mobility. Perception and activity, in addition to assisting development and reproduction, enables animals to secure energy from secondary sources which they can assimilate rapidly enough to permit volition. Animals, being more complex and specialized are more 'individual' than plants with well defined development (or maturation) periods as well as more selective reproductive systems. Complexity of structure ensures that entropy leads to short lives and abrupt death while, at the same time, the mobility of the species enables it to evolve rapidly into new niches in the ecosystem. Once again, individual mortality can facilitate species flexibility, not in terms of rapid physiological mutation, but rather in terms of rearrangement of the interface between the animal and the environment. The sheer specialized complexity of the highly developed animals renders physiological rearrangement very difficult and something which only occurs in catastrophic conditions. Structuring is arranged on a core–peripheral hierarchical basis which does not permit significant rearrangement, so that interface flexibility is the main adaptive strategy.[5]

Any proper consideration of evolution should not be restricted to the physiological. Instead, the totality of animal structure, including environmental bondings that it creates, has to be considered.

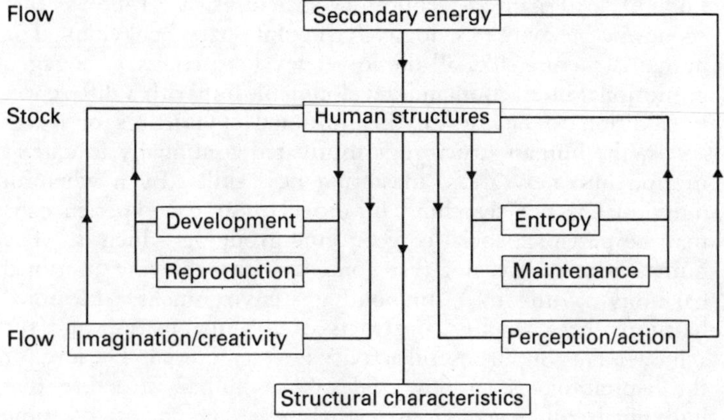

Figure 7.4 Level 4: human structure

The best example of an animal which is highly specialized and individualistic but mutates physiologically at very low rates is the human species. Evolution is almost completely concerned with environmental interface. However, human beings go beyond the flexible responsiveness of animals into the creation of new structures in the surrounding environment. These new structures emanate from imagination and creativity utilizing stocks of perceptual knowledge and acquired skill. Thus, in Figure 7.4, a fourth flow feedback into structure is added. The human being has the capacity to conceptualize and store concepts in the brain to such an extent that individual consciousness has the quality of translating ideas into actual structure. This quality, although not unknown in the individual consciousness of other animal species, is much less developed and likely to be confined to the creation of social structures and the development of innovative hunting techniques. Furthermore, human groups have the capacity to store and pass on concepts to descendants in order that they too can order and reorder the environment. Just as the individualism of animals enables the species to be flexible, so the individual ability to conceptualize provides the human species, or the relevant community, with an ability to be flexible in the application of useful concepts, which are passed on to ensure continuity of the externalized structure and further evolution of new structure.

Since the bulk of human evolution consists of the construction of externalized economic structures, it follows that economic behaviour is, logically, evolutionary behaviour. The human structure, like all the lower level structures, is engaged in motional interaction and development, but with a difference. In addition to having all the motional experiences of lower levels, the human structure is motivated continually to extend motion into new areas, mastering new skills. Even when an individual is not searching for novel motional experience he may be part of a social or economic grouping which is.[6] The human structure is not just content with achieving motional harmony with the surrounding environment. Motional harmony between the constructs of the imagination and the achievements of purposeful activity is also required. The idea, or the aspiration, is so powerful in the human structure that individuals will even sacrifice themselves in pursuit of some esoteric social ideal.

Homo economicus has no ability to do such things – altruistic acts are generally irrational, although proponents are quite happy to witness altruism in animals as the outcome of 'instinct'. Neither does he have imagination, despite possessing perfect knowledge, or a need to acquire new skills, despite his ability to optimize in matching his tastes with his purchases. He is 'motionless man' who finds motion between those moments of hedonistic delight uncomfortable and vacuous. Irrespective of his appropriateness to explain why demand curves slope downwards, he is of little use in the explicitly motional context pioneered by Keynes at the macroeconomic level. There is no place in the *homo economicus* model for motional activity to convert aspiration into actuality through the marriage of imagination and creativity in human consciousness. It cannot encapsulate the enjoyment of conceptualization for its own sake any more than it reflects the love of motion for its own sake so obvious in animal behaviour.

The conceptual dimension of human motion overlays the other types of motion discussed. Although animal needs to engage in the simpler perception/action nexus of predatory and social behaviour and the more primitive plant needs merely to 'vegetate' are important, they assume a lower priority as the human being develops the conceptual/creative dimension of motion.[7] To give these up is to suffer a sense of relative deprivation as Scitovsky and Fromm have emphasized. In affluent societies where people have experienced a sense of aspiration it is essential that an explicitly motional context is adopted to capture behaviour.

In order to offer an alternative to *homo economicus* suitable for the task at hand it is necessary to develop a set of postulates which provide the bio-philosophical basis for behavioural dynamics. At this stage we will not stray too far from *homo economicus* in the sense that we shall remain in the 'evolutionary short run' and that we shall treat the economic agent as having a fixed conceptual structure which is comparable to a state of 'perfect knowledge'. We will also provide a setting similar to that embodied in the assumption of a reliable set of institutions such as legally protected markets.

Homo Creativus

We have tried to set economic behaviour in its proper context – as a dimension of the human tendency to create structured interactions with the external environment of an innovative character. Primary and secondary energy inputs are translated into stores of qualitative potential energy in the form of perceptual understanding and acquired skills. The authors of *homo economicus* dealt with an individual, an independent structure, with independent tastes and independent skills, free to choose. *Homo creativus* is different, seeking new ways of becoming *part* of new structured interactions with the environment.[8] As this is achieved, consciousness is no longer independent but welded to greater consciousnesses. Thus, individual personalities evolve as unique configurations of greater consciousnesses rather than as idiosyncratic, independent entities.[9] For the self-aware, 'alienation' from greater consciousnesses is an undesired condition. Furthermore, as Scitovsky emphasizes, *homo creativus* finds boredom a distressing condition, i.e. when events run so smoothly that interaction requires no demands on available intellectual energy. Thus, we have a broad vision of *homo creativus* as a restless composite consciousness, constantly desiring integration into broader consciousness while, at the same time, not wishing to be so integrated that all independent volition is removed. There exists a relativity of security needs and freedom needs which forms a trade-off for *homo creativus* and conditions his perception of risks in an uncertain world.

In formalizing this vision into a simple model of dynamic behaviour we need to state some basic behavioural postulates accompanied by a set of simplifying assumptions which we can relax later.[10] In selecting the latter we shall try to make *homo creativus* operate in comparable conditions to *homo economicus*. In other words, we shall attempt to generate a set of assumptions which can accommodate the notion of static equilibrium.

P1: The Consciousness Postulate

There exists a flow of motional events that a self-aware agent perceives and a flow of actions initiated by the agent. The potential to comprehend external events and the potential to interact represents consciousness. As economists we are accustomed to identifying the *unit of consciousness* (*U*) with the individual. However, any survey of other behavioural sciences suggests that *U* can be viewed usefully at many levels; for example, sociologists frequently postulate group consciousness. Psychologists, on the other hand, often use an analytical distinction between the conscious and the unconscious when dealing with the individual. In other words, the latter is a source of behaviour which belongs to a non-individual consciousness, for example, the species in instinctual behaviour. Furthermore, social psychologists will break down this dichotomy and view the individual as operating within several overlapping consciousness units.[11] Personality, or individuality, becomes a question of the unique pattern and weighting of a set of consciousness units ranging from the macro, e.g. the nation, down to the micro, e.g. the truly idiosyncratic consciousness of the individual.[12]

The *homo economicus* abstraction pretends that there is a unique consciousness which is economic and co-exists in a non-overlapping way with non-economic consciousness. Furthermore, this unit is individual specific i.e. *socio-economicus* is not permitted to exist. Although the implications of these partitions will be explored later, for now we can side-step them by postulating that we are simply dealing with a unity of consciousness which could be part individual or group. Thus, *U* is not fixed at any level of aggregation but is seen as existing in an empirical sense if purposeful, non-random, motional activity can be observed. Since the nature and extent of *U*s are likely to shift over time, the configuration of *U*s for any individual or the number of individuals that any *U* encompasses can only be defined at a point in time, i.e. in static or spatial terms. Any *U*, thus defined, is, in effect, a relativity. It has internal motional structure which is at a higher level of 'bondedness' than the co-ordination that it actively pursues in the external environment. *U* is probably better defined, in a topological sense, as a concentration centre of motional co-ordination which weakens and merges with others as we move in a peripheral direction. The essence of consciousness is the ability to draw a line on this continuum which divides 'internal' structure from 'external' consciousness. If external bonding rises to levels consistent with those on the periphery of internal *U*, then consciousness will 'solidify' into structure which will then contain a more extensive and complex range of co-ordinated motion.

The topological character of consciousness is very important even though the internal/external dichotomy exists. For example, a stone has a very tightly bound motional structure but no interactive capacity to co-ordinate with the external environment. Randomness dominates external 'behaviour'. This sharp physical dichotomy has no topological character, thus, no *U* exists. Consciousness can only exist when there exists co-ordinating potential beyond internal motional structure.

Let us now state the 'consciousness' postulate P1:

> A unit of consciousness (*U*) can be said to exist when we observe a motional structure displaying co-ordinated interactions with the external environment. Thus *U* constitutes a set which ranges from interactions having near random outcomes through to interactions at a level of co-ordination which almost makes them part of 'internal' motional structure itself.

P2: The Co-ordination Postulate

In our taxonomy of structured motion, *U*s are viewed as engaged in motional activity to trap energy in order to maintain the output of structural characteristics. Related activity involved the development of structure in line with 'blueprints' contained in the conscious or unconscious and the execution of maintenance procedures to counter entropy inducing forces from the external environment. In all these three activities there exists a dominating bio-philosophical motivation: the maximization of co-ordination between *U* and the environment. Maintenance is defensive, attempting to push *U* away from the randomness generated by entropy, development involves the extension of structured motion towards a more co-ordinated ideal and, of course, energy processing itself fuels the motional structure that exists at any point in time.

Homo economicus is envisioned as maximizing utility from consumption subject to a budget constraint and subject to a given set of tastes. The budget constraint denotes the limit placed on energy input and the set of tastes indicates the configuration of output characteristics preferred. Neither maintenance nor development enter the picture because *homo economicus* is set in a frictionless world in which he is a developed, static structure. It is not necessary to maximize co-ordination for it is maximized *by assumption*. P1 suggests that he is so co-ordinated that it is unlikely that he is conscious at all! And, if we look on his structural equilibrium merely as an ideal, then we are confronted with the logical conclusion that he must be less happy when he is in 'disequilibrium'. The restriction of utility maximization to acts of consumption means that acts of non-consumption have no utility and, therefore, have to be justified by the promise of future consumption. In orthodox neo-classical economics, saving and 'altruism' are justified in this manner.

This narrowness of conception of co-ordination in the sphere of economics has also led to artificial visions of risk and uncertainty as they appear in our consciousness. They enter as contrived special cases where a probabilistic game is added on to conventional utility maximization, i.e. the gambling truism that higher return is obtained by assuming more risk can generate new utility maximization outcomes provided risk aversion or risk loving is built into the set of tastes. Uncertainty is trivialized into probabilistic games and 'rates of time preference', in order that *homo economicus* can keep his eye firmly fixed on the utility-maximization-from-consumption solution. The concepts invoked, however, betray the true maximization problem that exists. For example, Tobin has to introduce 'risk aversion' to explain the observed demand for money relation, but does not rule out the quirky 'risk lover' as irrational.[13] Shadowy 'psychological' behaviour determines the rational economic outcome. Time preference is fundamental in any *homo economicus* model which tries to deal with the future – thus uncertainty is brought in through the back door to deal with real time situations.

Economic analysis has been hampered persistently by the

fact that only a special case of the maximization problem faced by an economic agent has been confronted.[14] This has been particularly true in macroeconomics, with its explicit dynamic nature.

Let us state the 'co-ordination' postulate P2 before moving on to demonstrate this special case status:

> Any consciousness unit (*U*) continuously attempts to maximize the degree of motional co-ordination experienced both within internal motional structure and external consciousness.

P3: The Inertia Postulate

The vision conveyed by P2 is one where a *U* simultaneously attempts to promote stability of structure while also attempting to extend structure towards the aspirations contained in consciousness. János Kornai, in his pioneering work, gave high status to aspiration in analysing dynamic behaviour while emphasizing the power of inertia.[15] The image he conveys is one where motional behaviour is critically dependent on existing internal structure at any point in time and limited by the constraints imposed by this structure on the possibilities contained in consciousness. Behaviour tends to be 'directional' in a cumulative sense – Boulding calls it 'time's arrow'. Choice is influenced by history and imagination and, in turn, one affects the other. We may homogenize structure inherited from history by a budget constraint and narrow imagination down to a set of consumption tastes, but, as Keynes showed, once we put these elements of *homo economicus* into historical time we can see that they are inadequate to capture macro-behaviour where limits on income-flow, because of lack of imagination, will limit consumption and elicit a feedback process which alters history.

Thus, when we state in P2 that co-ordination is to be maximized in the *flow* of motion we must also consider the *stock* of structure. Motional structure is a qualitative concept. The idle machine is no more than a heap of metal – it is structure because the parts are ordered to provide the potential to generate output. Internal structure is no more than a qualitative phenomenon which can be *unconsciously* relied upon to function. Consciousness is concerned with external structure which is unreliable and demands attention.

The distinction between stocks and flows has always provided great insights in economics but has also been the subject of much confusion. Sometimes flows have been identified as something between 'stock equilibria' and sometimes general equilibrium of flows has been envisaged without any stock in existence. Often, these distinctions have been no more than semantic or the outcome of necessary assumptions. In the case of *homo economicus* we have a conception that contains a stock of tastes which interacts with a flow of income to yield a flow of consumption. In turn, the flow of income derives from a stock of productive skills. In order to examine the flows, the stocks must be held constant. In the 'long run', in some mystifying way, tastes and skills can change through the operation of 'relative prices'. Should these relative prices change there would be no inertia, only adjustment lags of a smooth variety and, in the absence of relative price changes, there would be no change in the structure of skills and tastes because there would be no aspirations, no consciousness in the P1 sense. In order to analyse real world motional behaviour, the stocks used in mobilizing motional behaviour must be extended to include a stock of external consciousness, which contains potential skills, tastes, etc., which lack certainty. These are operationally constrained by existing internal structure, either because they are inconsistent in some sense or because maintenance and energy absorption (i.e. survival) precludes their consideration in the maximization decision.

Let us state the 'inertia' postulate P3:

> Any consciousness unit (*U*) which pursues the goal of co-ordination maximization will be constrained by the existence of a given stock of internal structure and a stock of external consciousness. The former diverts motional resources towards maintenance needs and the latter confines the range of structural development. At any point in time there will exist a trade-off between freedom and security. Over time, freedom will be required to enhance security and, also, security will be necessary in order to have freedom.

P4: The Sequential Postulate

In P3 we have what Neil Kay refers to as a 'strange loop' between the pursuit of freedom and security.[16] It is a 'Catch 22' situation explicitly avoided by *homo economicus*, but one that *homo creativus* is constantly trying to overcome. We know, of course, that the latter is doomed to failure in this endeavour, for the law of entropy will have its way with all structures. If *homo economicus* was to have his immortality shield dissolved he would discover that he was confronted with the dual terrors of structural degeneration and uncertainty in his consciousness interfering with his carefully calculated consumption plans. *Homo creativus* is much better adjusted to this reality because he is equipped to enjoy *any* motional activity which contains a relativity of tension and aspiration. What he dislikes are states of *homo economicus* equilibrium where all motion is boringly predictable making no creative demands on his consciousness. The prospect of indefinite equilibrium soon leads to a preference for artificially generated randomness such as games and gambling. However, his superb adaptability ensures that even in degenerative crises he will resort to tactics which ensure continued enjoyment. One device is to adapt consciousness. For example, the old will frequently 'identify' with the family experiences rather than their own or they will develop a religious consciousness of universal dimension.

In less terminal circumstances *homo creativus* will subvert the inevitable logic of the 'strange loop' by suddenly abandoning 'internal structure' and starting again. For the present we will not be concerned with these strategic questions of a longer run nature. What is of more pressing interest is the question of 'risk' raised by the freedom/security trade-off in P3. Clearly, spending time involved with creativity in the zone of external consciousness will increase the risk of damage to internal structure because of lack of attention. The degree of vulnerability of the latter will depend on how extensive its defensiveness is. The old economic postulate holds – portfolio diversification lowers risk. But, again, let us hold on to the short run where we are dealing with a given fixed structure and decisions have to be made as to how much risk to assume.

First of all, departure into the uncertain zone of external consciousness will be motivated by the existence of an aspiration which seems attainable, given the configuration of internal structure. As *U* proceeds into this imperfectly understood zone, risk will be incurred. There is the risk of failure and also the risk that existing structure will be damaged either from the failure itself or merely from neglect. Here we can apply the old rules of marginal utility. Motionally, *U* will engage in speculative activity up to the point where the expected marginal utility from motional achievement equals the expected utility from engaging in maintenance activity. The former will involve an assessment of the rate of improvement of co-ordination towards the target and the latter will involve an assessment of expected increase in losses from no maintenance, as time elapses. Switches will occur in time as rises in 'fear' result in maintenance checks to dissipate expected marginal loss before returning to creative activity again. The critical difference between this kind of marginalism and the orthodox type is that it is set in historical time. Time dictates an endogenous rise in the assessment of loss per additional time unit while time also permits cumulations in utility from achievement. Thus, periods of concentrated behaviour emerge. If structure is held to be gravely under threat then all time will be spent on defensive measures because the expected reductions in losses will exceed the expected gains from even one moment of creative activity.

Needless to say history will not always work out as expected. Disappointments will arise in the case of aspirations which lead to their abandonment and structural damage will occur leading to periods of repair and lowered confidence in creative potential. Cumulations of accidents over time, as well as the increase of potential losses from more developed structure, are normal in the process of evolution leading to the onset of conservatism and caution.

Let us state the 'sequential' postulate P4:

> Any consciousness unit (*U*) will attempt to maximize co-ordination by setting aspirations and generating utility from achievement of them while, at the same time, there will be a perceived threat to existing structure with expected losses cumulating over time as maintenance is neglected. Interactive sequences will be dictated by the highest expected motional utility amongst available activities.

P5: The Intensity Postulate

In P4 it has been postulated that *U* will rationally choose periods of activity which maximize motional utility subject to the constraints imposed by existing structure and available aspiration in the external consciousness. Now we must introduce the notion of the *intensity* of actual and potential structure, for it has a bearing on the maximizing decision chosen. Existing structure is very intense if it is fragile in the sense that a peripheral threat could damage the core of structure. High intensity can exist for many reasons. Perhaps existing structure is very specialized and lacking in an extensive defence mechanism, or perhaps a dimension of existing structure is the presence of an oppressive force which could destroy the core of structure in the event of even a small error of judgement. Clearly, such a *U* will embark on strictly limited and unambitious sorties into the external consciousness zone.

If we turn to the external consciousness zone itself, the intensity associated with different aspirations will vary considerably. Very intense projects will involve the sinking of time and money without tangible return until the project is complete. Clearly, these will not tend to be embarked upon without a highly secure existing structure and well defined plans as to how the aspiration can be achieved. Low intensity aspirations, on the other hand, will involve immediate achievement. For example, golfers can improve their scores from the beginning with little commitment. In contrast, professional golfers are involved in the high intensity activity of winning money. Also, not only does high intensity of structure reduce the scope to pursue alternative highly intense aspirations, but any aspiration that is pursued intensely will be constrained to be close to the area of specialism. For example, if structure is highly intense because of an oppressive force, the aspiration pursued will be that dictated by the force. If high intensity of existing structure is because of the development of a specialism, then the aspiration is likely to be development consistent with that specialism, despite the need for balance.

The logic of P3, which binds development and existing structure, applies with even greater force in the presence of high intensities. Once again, what we tend to observe in the case of high intensities is the extension of the unit of consciousness to a wider set of individuals. Specialists are bonded into groups, those under an oppressive force become subsumed into that force. On the consciousness side, highly intense projects tend to have risk shared widely through binding arrangements such as legal contracts. Again, these are '*U* mutation' issues to be considered later.

Let us now state the 'intensity' postulate P5:

> Any consciousness unit's decision with regard to the pattern of motional activity over time will be influenced by the intensity of existing structure and the intensity associated with different aspirations.

P6: The Power Postulate

In P5, the concept of intensity of existing structure led logically to consideration of situations where P3 constraints are of the 'threat' variety. This threat can arise either because of the existence of an external *U*, which could precipitate undesired conflict if not accommodated, or because existing structure has become so inflexible and specialized that it is subject to high rates of entropy and, consequently, requires excessive maintenance activity. *U* can become a slave of its own 'inappropriate' structure as much as an external force.

The fear of conflict and its consequent release of energy from existing structure is well embedded in the maximization postulates P2 and P4. It emphasizes the point that existing structure is a *power-base*. P5 emphasizes that creative development may or may not increase the relative power characteristic of existing structure, depending on intensity. The existence of power is vital even for the most co-operative and creative *U*, for power is the source of energy input essential for the continuity of structure. However, power need not be gained only from creative development, it can also be gained from threat and conflict situations. Just as power is used to obtain energy input, so extension of structure can be gained from the oppressive use of force. By its very nature, such structure tends to be very intense, demanding extensive defence and maintenance to hold it together. Thus, such a structure tends to be static in an evolutionary sense. In other words, accumulation of power by force leads to the consolidation of U^A, increasing the output of U^A-characteristics rather than the expansion of the set of *U*-characteristics through creative development. By threat, other *U*s are forced to co-ordinate as quantitative extensions of the greater *U*.

The coerced, on the other hand, co-ordinate as directed simply because they perceive their power as inferior to that of the greater *U*. Provided the resultant disutility, generated from spending periods in activity which does not involve a chosen aspiration, is compensated by a power reward in the form of energy input to existing structure, then co-operation will exist. Non-co-operation will involve expected conflict losses in excess of the aspirational sacrifice. *U* will be 'alienated' but will continue to follow the dictates of P3 and maximize the degree of co-ordination within the perceived constraints. Only when the aspirational sacrifice exceeds the expected conflict losses will *U* willingly engage in attempts to 'break out'. The alternative course of action, perhaps encouraged by the greater *U*, is for the lesser *U* to 'merge' through 'loyalty' and share in the aspirational achievements of the greater *U*.[17]

These power relations are clearly very important in

economic co-ordination and much of complex creativity involves organizational hierarchies which operate along power lines through contractual agreement between individual *U*s. Greater *U*s which wish to be creative have to operate through organizational hierarchies not dissimilar to those used by greater *U*s which are authoritarian in nature. Unfortunately, much of socio-political analysis has focused on the latter type of situation which is regarded as 'distributionally unfair'. For example, the removal of labour surplus by capitalists in Marxist economics, and the expropriation of economic rent in Ricardian analysis are both about the operation of force. Marxist dynamics stem from the proposition that capitalists reinvest, i.e. the greater *U* is socially creative, in contrast to, say, pyramid builders in ancient Egypt. The dynamic circle is closed by supposing that this power and exploitation lead to the formation of working class consciousness in order to break the grip of the greater *U*. The existence of power relations is the province of political scientists yet we cannot abstract from them completely and retain a dynamic economic framework. We must be aware that the economic outcome will be influenced by power relations as an *integral part* of economic co-ordination and creativity, not something which is separable.[18]

Our task as economists is to allow a political dimension within which, for example, Bienkowski's 'process of petrification' can be analysed.[19] When power relations come to dominate co-ordination then the rate of economic creativity will decline. *Homo economicus* is blissfully removed from this dynamic reality, despite the fact that one of the heroes of his creators, Adam Smith, stated precisely the same evolutionary point against the Hobbesians of his day. His prescription was a 'macro-innovation' by the greater *U*: the liberalization of markets and the strengthening of legal support to such institutions. For now, all that is necessary is to formally recognize the power dimension in *homo creativus* as set out in the 'power' postulate P6:

> Any consciousness unit (*U*) will have a power-base in existing structure which can be employed for the purposes of acquiring inputs to generate output of characteristics while, at the same time, will be confronted with other power-bases which will require the sacrifice of motional effort. Discontinuities in the balance of power will result in conflict situations which are rational responses in historical time.

Conclusion

In this chapter an attempt has been made to provide a framework within which the bio-philosophical foundations discussed in Chapter 6 can be dealt with in a systematic way. In the first part of the chapter, four levels of motional structure and consciousness were isolated. As we moved from the first level up to the fourth level, emphasis shifted from structure to consciousness, and it was at the fourth level, which is concerned with structure creating activity, that we placed the economic dimension of human behaviour. Given the high degree of potential flexibility of behaviour at the fourth level, it was identified as more philosophical than biological in nature. It follows, of course that attempts to analyse fourth-level economic behaviour using only biological analogies are unlikely to be very enlightening.

In particular, it was argued that once we depart from the biological definition of the individual into broader zones of human consciousness, there is no necessity for a one-for-one identification of consciousness and individual, as has been the norm in *homo economicus* conceptions of human consciousness. It was argued that consciousness can be extended beyond one individual and, furthermore, any individual can 'identify' with many different consciousnesses, creating the uniqueness of individual personality. Thus, in analysing economic behaviour, the relevant units are not likely to be individuals but collective entities varying in their coverage of all individuals. In other words, units of consciousness can be as much 'macro' as 'micro' in nature.

The idea that there is common consciousness or, rather, common unconsciousness, between individuals has already been developed by the socio-biological school in terms of 'genetic selfishness'. However, such a model would appear to best explain behaviour which is strongly connected to biological considerations rather than fourth-level behaviour, with its substantial philosophical content. The variety and extent of collective consciousness in the economic sphere is too complex to be reducible to genetic considerations alone, although there is little doubt that, in times of serious crisis, such biological priorities should become more relevant to the explanation of the alliances that form. However, here our notion of collective consciousness is more expansive, being viewed as something which is desired as a goal in itself and not just as a means to an end.

Building on this view of consciousness, the second part of the chapter isolates six postulates which encapsulate the behaviour of any given unit of consciousness. These are intended to be general, making the assumption that any consciousness unit is a rational maximizing entity which seeks maximum co-ordination as its goal, subject to the dynamic constraints that it faces. The vision of existing structure and external consciousness is topological, with 'identity' being very much a matter of subjective judgement as to whether a higher aspiration is to be achieved or not. Thus, identity clearly becomes a very slippery concept indeed in the course of historical time as aspirations change, structure deteriorates and consciousnesses merge together. Throughout the discussion an attempt was made to discuss behaviour as if the consciousness unit was fixed. In other words, in evolutionary time an attempt was made to remain in the short run.

This is in no sense a deficiency because, in evolutionary time, the long run is critically dictated by action in the short run. Aspirations, which guide long-run evolution, are formed from past knowledge already 'in structure', current experience and past commitments. The long run is not characterized by equilibrium but rather 'idealizations', as Kornai emphasizes. The long run unfolds successes and failures, creative expansions and conflictual crises. It is the logic of history and the irreversibility of structural development that dictates the long run and, in turn, the new conditions for short-run behaviour.

The long-run/short-run division is a useful dichotomy used to great effect in all of economics. The short run is emphasized here, much in the spirit of Keynes, because the long-run outcome of aspiration configurations (Keynes's 'animal spirits') are difficult to fathom and the conflict that can arise is beyond the province of economic analysis. We are in the short run, we are interested in fostering economic creativity and avoiding long-run paths which will lead to conflict. Keynes called economics a 'moral science' and, indeed, one of the prime tasks of the economist is to 'invent' laws and rules which facilitate the smooth transition from the short run that exists to a long run characterized by creative evolution.

Our six postulates have introduced *homo creativus* who, unlike his cousin *homo economicus*, is firmly embedded in historical time. He seeks motional co-ordination, he has aspirations in terms of creative achievements, he is faced by inertial and power constraints and, sometimes, has to fight for survival. Our next task is to explore the possibility of translating these general postulates into an appropriate analytical framework for dealing with quantifiable economic behaviour. This is necessary, despite the fact that many of the qualitative aspects of economic behaviour are unquantifiable. However, many *are* quantifiable in the economic sphere. Thus, it is necessary to be able to demonstrate quantifiability in particular cases and relate them to more familiar propositions in economics. We must be well prepared for re-entry into the highly aggregated and quantified world of macroeconomics.

Notes

1 See Heiner (1983) for an excellent exposition of behavioural analysis, in an evolutionary framework, which shares many of the features contained in these chapters. The perspective is different but the spirit is the same. See also Kaldor (1986) for a more informal plea for an evolutionary perspective.

2 See Worster (1977), particularly in Part 5, for a discussion of how the scientific materialist vision of 'agricultural efficiency' ignored qualitative output with serious ecological repercussions. See also, Harris (1975) for a compelling account of how the 'economic' approach can lead to serious misunderstandings of costs and benefits in an ecologically complex setting.

3 See Rifkin (1980) for an example of how the law of entropy is gaining increasing recognition in economics.

4 Boulding (1981) goes as far as to label machines as dependent 'species'.

5 See Worster (1977) for historical discussions of how poorly the carniverous animals have managed to mutate when they have been ousted from their ecological niches by humans. The successful have been those which have managed to adapt their interface in a way compatible with human society.

6 See Scitovsky (1976) for many examples.

7 The new socio-biological school of thought, which we associate with Dawkins (1976), Maynard-Smith (1976) and Wilson (1975), argues that common behavioural links between individuals is because of shared genes. This common consciousness theory is one which tends to be most useful in the case of animal structure. With human structure the links are more 'cultural' than genetic. However, there is, undoubtedly, a role for socio-biology in economics. See Hirshleifer (1977) for some views as to what this role might be in economics and Masters (1981) for a sceptical view of its general applicability in the social sciences.

8 This notion that aggregation should be replaced by holistic views of common consciousness across many individuals was pioneered by Angyal (1969, 1981). In economics, Laffont (1975) has labelled

this proposition as 'Kantian'. See Green (1977) for discussion of the aggregation problems in trying to go from individual to macro-behaviour in the orthodox manner.

9 This 'Gestalt' notion of the individual is emphasized by Allport (1955) and is central to the approach of Penrose (1959) and to the development of 'meta-rules' in Nelson and Winter (1982).

10 See Emery (1981a) for a general introduction to the kind of simplified behavioural construct that will be developed here.

11 In order to build predictive models, psychologists have attempted to provide structuring hypotheses as to how these consciousnesses interact with each other. Since Maslow (1954) there has been much work in psychology in terms of the 'hierarchy of needs' which comes from personality structure. As Earl (1982) has argued, the sophisticated human-structure level that we analyse in economics is, perhaps, better understood using the construct-theory approach pioneered by Kelly (1963), since perceptual constructs would seem to be vital in the generation of innovation and creativity.

12 If we look at Trivers's (1971) classic treatment of altruism between individuals we see that he argues that it is more likely the smaller and more intimate the group of individuals studied. Clearly, there is some implicit appeal to some definable group consciousness in such an argument. Thus in order to 'justify' altruism it becomes inescapable that the identification of individual and consciousness must be qualified.

13 See Tobin's (1958) classic demand for money paper.

14 See Day (1967) for discussion of the way in which marginalism can be used in more general conceptions of behaviour than those contained in *homo economicus*.

15 See Kornai (1971) for views on the relativity of inertia and aspiration.

16 See Kay (1984) for a discussion of strange loops.

17 Arendt (1951) and Fromm (1956) analyse the process whereby the alienated turn to hero worship and, for example, participation in right-wing political hierarchies for no more economic gain but a strong sense of identification with the achievements of power. Fromm, in particular, argues that this can constitute a sado-masochistic interaction, even in an economic context.

18 See Guha (1981) for a depiction of evolutionary development which is dictated almost entirely by power relations and, as such, almost impossible to model in any general way.

19 See Bienkowski (1981) for an analysis of how power relations evolve from, and ultimately constrain, successful economic co-operation.

8 *Economic Behaviour in the Short Run of Evolutionary Time*

> The first heroic step is to divide actuality into two parts – one representing the partial process in point; the other, its environment (so to speak) separated by a boundary consisting of an anthropomorphic void.
>
> Nicholas Georgescu-Roegen (1970)

The general postulates in Chapter 7 were developed for any consciousness unit that can be identified. The particular type of consciousness unit that we are interested in we can call 'macro-consciousness'. This kind of unit is shared by many individuals in a collective sense. Marcuse gave us many examples: the nation, the community, the corporation, etc., all qualitative and invisible, yet very concrete and well understood. The need to identify with macro-consciousness is so strong that individuals will voluntarily create identifications for enjoyment, e.g. 'supporting' a football club. The macro-consciousness unit that we are interested in can be loosely described as the economy. Like all consciousness units, it exhibits internal motional structure and external consciousness.

Macro-structure manifests itself in terms of laws, customs, conventions, ethics, etc., on the qualitative side, and infrastructure, public goods, administrative bureaucracies, etc., on the quantitative side. The custodian of macro-structure is the government which is the focus of external macro-consciousness. Because macro-structure must be very stable and reliable in order that the rest of the economic system can function and develop in security, macro-consciousness tends to be very conservative and preoccupied with maintenance rather than creative and innovative activity. Although we all tend to identify with macro-structure as it exists, we have no individual way of influencing the collective external consciousness dimension except through the political process. The purpose of the political process is to enable innovative social activity to occur in external macro-consciousness so that, for example, laws are changed and macro-structure can mutate to meet the changing needs of an evolving economic system.

Of course, we know from history that the macro-structure at the 'core' of the economic system has often tended to remain very inert and inconsistent with the development of structure and consciousness on the 'periphery' of the economic system. This obsolescence of macro-structure and fragmentation of macro-consciousness has led, in the past, to revolution, civil war and other serious social upheaval. For macro-economists, the slowness with which macro-structure mutates is both an advantage and a disadvantage. On the one hand, it enables us to operate in an 'evolutionary short run' and examine how the government can ensure that a given macro-structure yields the maximum amount of benefit to society. On the other hand, success in this endeavour tends to lead to non-evolutionary ways of thinking, so that the development of crises can neither be averted nor predicted. Keynes understood better than most that the real world policy context is the evolutionary short run but that the long run is fluid in evolutionary terms. This theoretical insight has often been mistaken as mere pragmatism.[1] Furthermore, it was Keynes who grasped that government was not only the custodian of macro-structure, but an integral part of it so that, in truly Einsteinian fashion, it is part of the experiments that it conducts.

The identification of government with the core of macro-structure rather than, say, the market core so favoured by libertarians, is based on historical reality. We have argued that markets are only tenable with a prior legal framework and, in times of national emergency, the system of markets has often had to give way to 'national priorities'. Government has always been at the core of the macro-system in its unrivalled co-ordinating position. In evolution what has happened is that *the nature of its co-ordinating function has altered in critical ways.* Olson, for example, has argued that the turbulence of war is a prerequisite of social innovation at the governmental level and, indeed, he cites many illustrations from history.[2] However, as the character of government has changed from semi-feudal to democratic, so has the nature of governmental flexibility. Government has become more capable of reform, a key feature of modern democratic governments being their active endeavours to avoid crises.[3] In other words, as stabilization has itself become a goal of government, so the incidence of crisis has been reduced. This has been reflected in the political arena as well where the pursuit of economic stabilization in a world of growing economic interdependence has reduced the probability of 'hot' wars occurring. Only on the economically unstable periphery of the world economy, in the developing countries, have we witnessed serious political upheaval over the past four decades.

The macro-consciousness unit, at the level of the economy, has been depicted as more concerned with internal structure rather than external consciousness. In turn, sub-macro consciousnesses are more concerned with external consciousness and engaging in creativity and innovation as we move to the periphery of the economic system. The stability of macro-structure provides the security necessary to engage in adventure and the degree to which this symbiotic relationship works between internal macro-structure and external micro-consciousness will depend on a hierarchy of consistency extending from the core of the economic system. However, the micro-consciousness is not liberated completely from concerns about the maintenance of internal structure because a 'parental' macro-structure exists. The *homo creativus* postulates will operate at all levels whether it be 'macro' or 'micro'; only the nature of the internal structure/external consciousness relativity varies in ways to be discussed.[4]

However, our objective is not to allow our analysis to become too clogged up with real world complexity if we are to end up with an abstraction suitable for macroeconomic analysis. Models have already been developed in industrial economics which are evolutionary, providing behavioural theories of the firm with a truly dynamic character. The path-breaking works of Nelson and Winter in the US and Kay in the UK have already been mentioned.[5] In a sense, our purpose here is to provide a skeletal model which offers general features which are compatible with the 'microeconomics' that these authors provide as well as the post-Shacklian treatment of consciousness in, for example, Earl's work. *Homo economicus* was purpose-built to offer a general characterization for use in short-run aggregate market analysis, leaving the diverse discussion of actual market behaviour to microeconomists. Similarly, *homo creativus* offers a skeletal representation to be given meat at the sub-aggregate by evolutionary studies of actual firms, industries, consumer groups, etc.

A Dynamic Dichotomy

Our purpose in proposing *homo creativus* was to offer a behavioural characterization which is seen as compatible with the dynamic nature of Keynesian macroeconomics, yet our ultimate objective is to supersede that macroeconomics with something more insightful and relevant to the 1980s. However, we must be able to walk before we can run so, in the first instance, it is necessary to restrict the generality of our evolutionary framework, embodied in the *homo creativus* postulates. We must stay in the evolutionary short run so that we can identify clearly both the Keynesian and *homo economicus* cases. Let us begin this task by making two simplifying assumptions.

A1: The Immortality Assumption Internal structure is not subject to entropic decay. In other words, no events occur which internal structure cannot deal with given its structure of peripheral defence.

A2: The Static Consciousness Assumption External consciousness is fixed in the sense that the consciousness unit does not mutate by merging with other consciousnesses or suddenly disappear as a new consciousness is created.

A1 and A2 permit us to deal with motional behaviour in real time in a way analogous to Newtonian physics. The latter takes mass, which is a point in motional space, as fixed and then deals with motional relativities through time in terms of velocities which are fixed in terms of, for example, the law of gravity. Thus, masses track out velocity paths through time when a force is exerted upon them. At the end of the experiment the mass is the same and the laws of motion to which it adheres remain the same. However, we have argued that this sharpness of division between stock and flow does not exist in the case of the motion of a consciousness structure, even if we make restrictive assumptions A1 and A2.

As consciousness postulate P1 makes clear, the division of internal structure and external consciousness is really one of degree. Unlike mass in physics, the consciousness unit is a *flexible* form of structure which can initiate various degrees of motional interaction with the external environment. As we observed in Chapter 5, the velocity measure in physics is strictly a space–time relation without any 'structural' connotation.

On the other hand, the consciousness unit is interested in efficiency, i.e. the degree to which measured motion is 'on target'. Thus, motion is 'structured' by aspiration, becoming internal structure when motional achievement is equal to aspiration. Although, in many cases, it may be possible to measure precisely motional achievement in terms of, say, velocities, the degree of structuring that takes place cannot be captured by the space–time dichotomy. In particular, the cause–effect mechanics implied by the space–time dichotomy, whereby there is an information-then-adjustment sequence, is inadmissible and leads, in the case of forward-looking purposeful behaviour, to situations of infinite regress. In such circumstances, as we discussed in Chapter 6, perception and action are *simultaneous* generators of an event. It is necessary to recognize, explicitly, that fourth-level motional behaviour is more than simple stimulus–response.

With A1 and A2 we have 'insulated' our consciousness unit (U) from external disturbances in a similar fashion to the controlled conditions necessary for a physics experiment. In order to analyse the 'chemistry' of motional activity it is necessary to divide conceptually any motional event, potential or actual, into a perceptual and an active dimension. Consciousness U represents a *stock* of *perceptual imagery* of the surrounding world and *accumulated skill* in dealing with situations in this world. A motional event constitutes a *flow* of *effective perception* and *effective action* which yields an actual motional event which is quantifiable in terms of space and time. This analytical division of perception and action is an *ex ante* dichotomy which can capture the gap between aspiration and achievement. The *ex post* outcome cannot be divided in this way; it is merely an event consigned to history, but which augments the stock of knowledge and experience for future occasions. When an *ex post* outcome coincides regularly with an *ex ante* goal then that event moves from external consciousness to the unconsciousness of internal structure. Thus, that event becomes dimensionless in terms of our consciousness dichotomy.[6] Let us state this more formally:

$U^\star$: the consciousness set;
$P^\star$: the perceptual imagery set;
$A^\star$: the skill potential set.

$P^\star$ and $A^\star$ both contain elements which have no motional potential either because a perceptual image has no skill potential counterpart or vice versa. Typically, this is the 'outer zone' of metaphysical belief and, also, dominating constraints which serve to *define* the feasible range of motional possibilities. These tend to be qualitative in nature, dictating the direction rather than the extent of the feasible range:

U: the feasible consciousness set;
P: the relevant knowledge set;
A: the relevant skill set.

U is a defined matrix of Ps and As which relate to identified motional events that are feasible:

$$P = \{P_1 \ldots P_i \ldots P_n\} \qquad A = \{A_1 \ldots A_i \ldots A_n\}$$

If we select any potential motional event:

$$U_i = \{P_i, A_i\}$$

we can say that U_i represents a goal or aspiration which requires a knowledge level P_i and a skill A_i to be achieved. We can dichotomize U because $\{P_i, A_i\}$ elements will contain a gap between aspiration and potential achievement. In other words, each element will contain 'efficiency' parameters:

$$P_i^e = kP_i$$

and

$$A_i^e = sA_i$$

Thus, P_i^e represents the level of perceptual knowledge relative to aspiration P_i assuming $A_i^e = A_i$. On the other hand, A_i^e represents the level of skill relative to the necessary skill level, assuming $P_i^e = P_i$. The interaction of P_i^e and A_i^e will yield a mean expected motional outcome. In U there will exist a finite number of U_i with P_i^e and A_i^e which we can order in terms of the size of k and s in the range 0 to 1 and, given that k and s are quantitative, we can arrange them in diagrammatic form as in Figure 8.1.

In Figure 8.1 we can chart any U_i in terms of its aspiration/efficiency characteristics, ranging from $k = 0$, $s = 0$ which is *pure randomness* through to $k = 1$, $s = 1$ which is 100% success or 'goal perfection'. Thus we have represented U as a

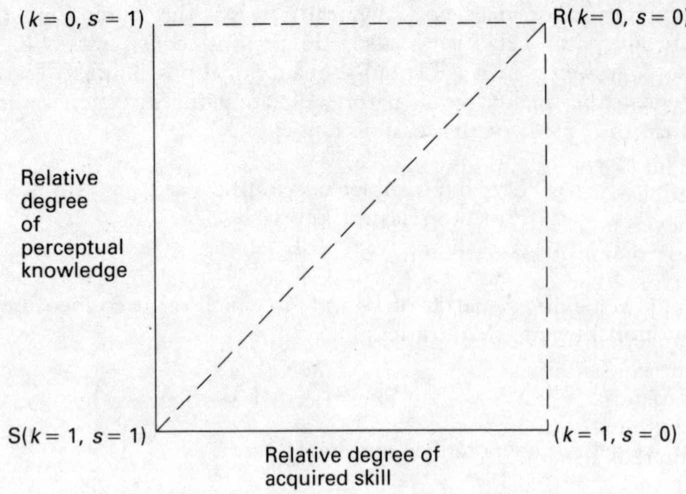

Figure 8.1 The external consciousness box

'box' in perception/action space. To the north and east of the box lies ($U^\star - U$), i.e. the myths, power centres, etc. which hold the box together. And ($k = 1$, $s = 1$) is the dimensionless point of structure (analogous to mass). The core of U lies near this point whereas the periphery of U lies towards ($k = 0$, $s = 0$). All *ex post* outcomes, at least as long as we maintain A1 and A2, will be on the SR diagonal. Furthermore, A1 and A2 give the consciousness box 'firm' edges when, in reality, these edges will be extremely 'fuzzy' and of vital importance in the evolutionary long run.

The co-ordination postulate P2 tells us that consciousness units will attempt to maximize utility from motional interaction by improving co-ordination. The inertia postulate P3 tells us that 'stock' constraints will be faced and the sequential postulate P4 depicts $U^\star$ as pulling k and s towards unity to match achievement with aspiration. In other words, there will be a systematic drive to reduce the uncertainty contained in U in order to minimize the incidence of randomized outcomes. Improving co-ordination and reducing uncertainty are different sides of the same motional coin.

P4 emphasizes that operating in the U zone of uncertainty will involve *risk* of some degree. Again let us, temporarily, simplify the nature of risk by reinforcing A1 and A2 with a third assumption.

A3: The No Damage Assumption Whatever the motional interaction attempted in the *U*-box, there is no risk to internal structure if an interaction fails, only the time invested and the incremental motional output foregone.

Thus P4 is 'fixed' and we have a 'cotton wool' world where novice skiers never break legs and inexperienced motorists never injure themselves or damage their car. Safety nets and parental protection abound – we are never punished for making errors. The corollary is that consciousness units never gamble with existing structure. Thus A1 and A2 ensure that external 'unanticipated' shocks are not encountered and A3 ensures that the consciousness unit does not actively seek 'zero-sum game' situations. Clearly, for this scenario to be realistic there must be continual activity in the provision of *systems of defence* to keep internal structure maintained and shock-proof.

A4: The Preventative Maintenance Assumption Over time a certain proportion of historical time will be devoted to the maintenance of systems of defence in order that full anticipation of all external shocks can exist. This is a preventative form of maintenance rather than an *ex post* repair form.

This assumption confines risk to our consciousness box in Figure 8.1 by enabling the consciousness unit to know the exact amount of maintenance dictated by P4 to keep existing structure perfectly safe. We can now envisage a situation where the consciousness unit seeks to increase co-ordination by pulling all k_i and s_i towards unity and, as structure increases, the proportion of time devoted to preventative maintenance, or simply management, will increase. When we confront the choice implied by P4, we must acknowledge that operating in the uncertain *U* zone induces *tension* and, as *achievement* proceeds, this tension tends to zero. The manner in which utility derives from this relativity of tension and achievement will depend on the nature of the co-ordination attempted. In terms of the intensity postulate (P5), we can divide interactions into two basic types.

The Discrete Event In this case the outcome is a binary one of success or failure where k and s will pertain to the *probability* of success. The product of k and s will yield the probability of success along the SR diagonal in Figure 8.1. We would expect outcomes to have the normal kind of probability distributions around such expected values. It is clear from Figure 8.2 that there exists a non-linear relationship between increments in k and s and increases in expected values. This non-linear 'productivity improvement' is a well known feature of learning processes.[7]

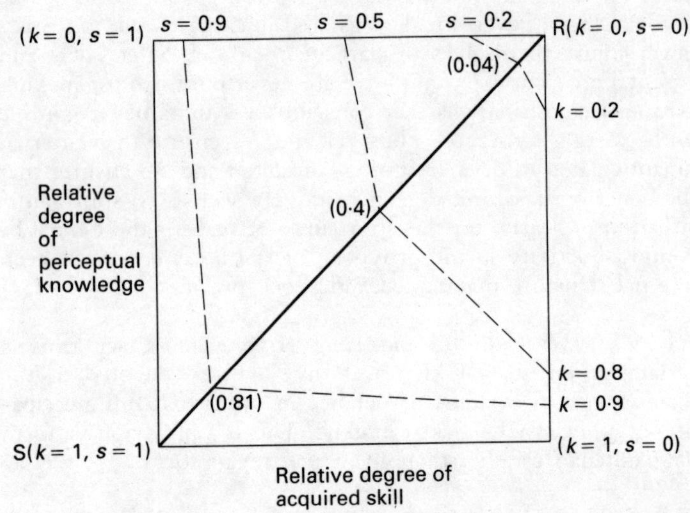

Figure 8.2 Practice makes perfect: non-hierarchical learning

The Continuous Event These events involve situations where the outcome is incremental, i.e. where partial success is possible. It is efficiency rather than probability that k and s measure in this case. Whereas a discrete event might be hitting a bull's-eye on a target, a continuous event would involve a scoring system say from 100 to 0 directly proportional to distance from the bull's-eye.

The multiplicative solution of k and s used in both the discrete probabilistic outcome and the continuous efficiency outcome apply to motions which are non-hierarchical, i.e. there are a range of solutions to be understood and a range of skills to apply. However, it is frequently the case that co-ordination has a core and a periphery, i.e. there are basic skills and basic knowledge which will provide a basic outcome. Learning consists of adding on peripheral belts to structure. Thus the most likely probability or efficiency will not be the multiplicative combination of k and s but rather their weighted

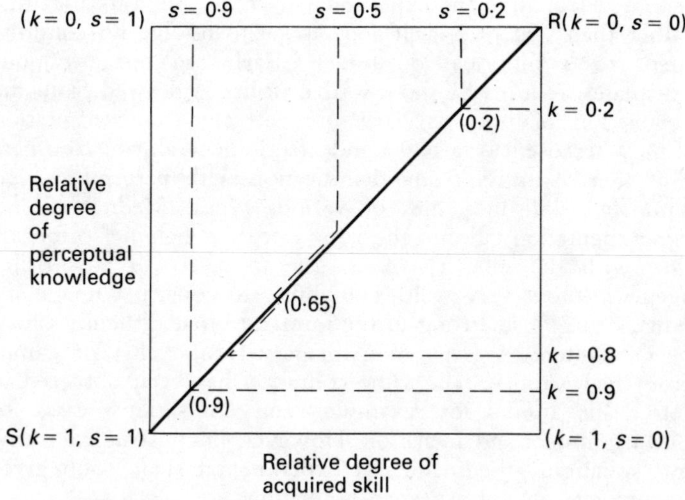

Figure 8.3 Gaining gumption: hierarchical learning

average $(k + s)/2$. Figure 8.3 takes the same k and s values as Figure 8.2 and shows the higher efficiencies and probabilities that result from structure being hierarchical.

Most learning consists of the 'building up' type rather than the 'widening' type. Indeed, hierarchical patterning is often adopted to achieve the latter. Furthermore, learning may well contain different phases, e.g. unstructured to begin with, becoming structured at a more advanced stage, or vice versa.[8]

The most extreme example of structuring is the aspiration which requires explicit core–peripheral planning and the outcome does not materialize until completion. Development is both hierarchical and discrete at the same time. Therefore, Figure 8.3 would not contain efficiencies or probabilities but rather, say, 0.2 of a bridge, 0.65, 0.9, etc. Each phase of such a highly intense project would be construed as an interim aspiration in itself.

Thus, all types of co-ordination activity can be reflected in our external consciousness box with mean outcomes depending on the quality of perceptual knowledge and accumulated skill. Now, although a great deal of learning can be gained 'on the job', it is frequently preferable for a $U^\star$ merely to observe or, on the skill side, only experiment. Thus k and s can be lifted out of the peripheral zone of randomness before real interaction begins. Meditative and experimental activity build up potential rather than structure itself and, as such, involve no commitment to a motional outcome. Clearly, in terms of our postulates, it must be the case that utility is derived from the acquisition of potential structure relevant to an aspiration simply because it is raising *k* and/or *s*. In general, consciousness units derive utility from identification with perceptions and simulated skill in games of various types. Meditation and experimentation fall into the same category, helping to forge a link with the imagery of an aspiration, as all advertising agencies know very well. The ability to construct imaginary worlds can be so strong in the immature that difficulties may be encountered in separating imagery from reality or games from real activity. The same condition has been observed in intoxicant users, for example, and in serious cases of disillusionment and alienation. However, in constructive learning situations, the meditative/experimental stage soon gives way to attempts at actual co-ordination.

In Figure 8.2, given certain simplifying assumptions, we have developed a short-run static taxonomy within which dynamic behaviour can be analysed. The SR line contains average efficiencies, probabilities and degrees of progress for all possible motional events in *U*. Actual outcomes will also fall on SR. P4 ensures that consciousness units will attempt to move each motional event to the desired level of co-ordination at S(*k*1*s*1). A4 ensures that, as *U* 'empties' of motional potential, activity will be taken up, increasingly, by managerial activity, as dictated by P3, and we can conceive of a position of 'structural equilibrium' where all activity has become 'managerial'. The *U* box is effectively empty and we have a stable internal structure.

As such, this structural equilibrium is a very short-run special case generated by assumptions A1 to A4. However, it is also similar to the abstract time *long-run* micro-equilibrium of *homo economicus* or the macro-equilibrium of the Walrasian system.[9] It is a state of perfect foresight, full adjustment and fixed structure in terms of 'tastes' and institutions. Provided we construe maintenance activity as just another necessary input to generate output characteristics, then both these micro- and macro-equilibria can be described. The former is co-ordinated through rational optimization and the latter through perfectly clearing markets. And, of course, each depends on the other to operate perfectly. It has been frequently pointed out that such aggregate links require all individuals to be identical.[10] Thus, we have a special case of our evolutionary special case. First, because in our scheme there is no requirement that all 'consciousness units' are identical and, indeed, what differentiates individuals is the combination of consciousnesses that they hold. Second, there is no need and, indeed, it would not be possible, for a perfect market to do the co-ordination job at the macro-level. Macro-consciousness exists in our analysis as a 'core' consciousness that is universally upheld and is 'prior' in the hierarchy of consciousness over more peripheral consciousness. As such, co-ordination at the macro-level can take any convenient form. If we argue for the existence of a periphery of co-ordinated auction markets then the argument will depend critically on the existence of the Walrasian auctioneer as part of macro-consciousness.

As we have noted, *homo economicus* operates under optimizing rules which ensure that motional analysis is qualitatively rigid. In other words, it has no dimension in Figure 8.2, it is only a point.[11] Once we relax our assumptions A1 to A4, this 'homogeneous consciousness' special case of our evolutionary special case deserves hardly a mention. The consciousness box has permitted us to conceive of individuals as engaging primarily, in structure altering activity, or creativity. However, the box has not specified actual dynamic paths in historical time – it is 'comparative static' in the sense that it relates actuality to aspirations without any historical time dynamics 'in between'. However, it remains historical time analysis in the same sense as Keynes's theory of effective demand.

In a sense, the observable dynamics in moving away from R towards S through time are quite specific in character. In microeconomics the nature of these dynamics will be much influenced by the nature of the aspiration and the institutional structure involved. Some aspirations will be driven by necessity to maintain structure, while some will be borne out of 'spare temporal capacity' where extension into *U* can proceed. Some aspirations will be passive, i.e. aspirations to form aspirations through meditation and experimentation. Just as structure 'locks in' behaviour, so will choice in *U* be directed by commitments and plans. From the macroeconomic perspective we need not concern ourselves about the many cases and switches, etc., involved at the sub-aggregate level.

The 'core' macro-consciousness is concerned with holding economic structure together by laws, conventions and guarantees.[12] Unlike individuals, with their many consciousnesses and inability to deal with a wide range of co-ordinations simultaneously, macro-consciousness can embrace a vast range of activities simultaneously to the extent that it is necessary to abstract from them. The macro-consciousness is very conservative about the logical structure that lies at its heart. Progress into U is permitted by a process of precedent so that new macro-structure is permitted to develop very slowly indeed and only when there is obvious social utility from doing so.[13] Furthermore, we shall see later that situations can arise where there may be no U box available for government manoeuvres because of the power postulate (P6) type of restrictions placed by strong vested interests.

However, there is little doubt that societies have macro-aspirations of some type which the macro-system evolves towards. Improvements yield social 'utility' in terms of national well-being. The consensus may be that, for example, productivity growth is a 'good thing' and, thus, we can characterize this in our consciousness box. An aspiration can be stated in terms of some target rate of growth and each year we can measure the rate of progress towards that goal as social imagination and social skills interact. Typically, a government which oversees such progress will receive the vote of the public in some way.[14]

Government, like any $U^{\star}$, will be faced with the general problem that it is not enough merely to facilitate efficiency gains within macroeconomic structure by providing maintenance cover. Contractualized planning of new social possibilities may be necessary to ensure social cohesiveness and to permit development. Without these, the consistency between macro-structure and micro-consciousness may break up, paradoxically, through an excessive concern for maintenance of existing structure at the expense of new initiatives. Most critics of government point to the support of 'lame ducks' and excessive protection through social welfare programmes as undermining innovatory activity. Adopting, as they almost always do, some approximation to the *homo economicus* special case in our 'cotton-wool' world, it is not surprising that they underestimate seriously the importance of maintenance activity in macro-structure.

We are not, as yet, well placed to deal with threat to structure given our four assumptions. What we have is an over-idealized world where co-ordination choice can take place in safety with regard to external threat and internal unity. Such a simplification is of some limited usefulness given that we can pick out historical periods where it provided a good approximation of the truth before consistency of macro-structure and micro-consciousness began to blur as the benefits of some social advance began to disappear. For a while, historical dynamics can be approximated by quantitative mathematic description, but not for ever. The smooth calculus of experience curves contrasts sharply with the non-parametric suddenness of catastrophe.

It has been argued that *homo economicus* conceptions of micro-consciousness and Walrasian conceptions of macro-consciousness are idealizations which exclude any analysis of even short-run behaviour. Orthodox proponents of these idealizations, on the other hand, have argued that a timeless theory is essential as a basis for economic analysis.[15] Here we have argued that it is not the timelessness which is at issue but the unmeasurable assumptions about motion which insulate these idealizations from real world applicability and, thus, undermine their usefulness as the basis of research programmes. Our *homo creativus* also remains an idealization, insulated from the conflictual real world through our strong assumptions about defined sets of knowledge and ability and defined 'stock' of structure. However, by interpreting *homo creativus* positions as aspirational in nature and identifying utility as being yielded by the tension reduction associated with achievement, we have a new idealization which is capable of dealing with actual dynamics in the real world. Furthermore, reductionism is avoided by appealing to the view that individuals are multi-conscious.

However, it remains an idealization of a rather happy world of economic co-operation, creativity and positive-sum games. The consciousness box offers a creative opportunity to develop structure and become a contented manager of a sophisticated motional structure. The commonplace idealization of economic progress fits nicely into the *homo creativus* conceptualization. Each multi-conscious individual or group will pursue unique developmental paths depending on the 'personality' yielded by particular consciousness configurations. We know, of course, that the world is not like that but *homo creativus* still captures the essence of constructive aspiration, which is a vitally important part of macro-consciousness, at the core of economic structure. Supporters of the more restrictive *homo economicus* concept are likely to protest that the motional conception of *homo creativus* looks more like a Pandora's Box of forces which are not *economic* idealizations. Indeed it would make little sense to specify behavioural dynamics in historical time without incorporating the forces of power and threat and the mortality cycle that characterize all organic life.

However, such claims are misplaced for *homo creativus* remains only a comparative static idealization, but one better connected to the empirical world of historical dynamics than *homo economicus* with his 'information and adjustment lag' dynamics. *Homo creativus* has been deliberately controlled by assumptions A1 to A4 to demonstrate the exact nature of *homo economicus* and Walrasian macroeconomics. However, in order to show the relevance of the *homo creativus* in a more dynamic world, it is necessary to relax those assumptions. In doing so we shall be able to discuss Keynes's method of capturing dynamic behaviour in a comparative static framework.

Stock-Flow Relativity

The world that Keynes was concerned with was not the cosy one that we have described, but one which had been plagued by instability – hyperinflation in the 1920s and depression in the 1930s – a period delineated in the history books by the major European wars before and after. *Homo creativus*, as depicted and at whatever level of consciousness we set him, had little relevance to much of the conflictual and destructive behaviour of that time. Of course *homo economicus* was not very relevant either, a point made forcefully by Keynes, as we saw in Chapter 2. However, Keynes did not offer a general attack on *homo economicus* microeconomics but preferred to be selective, reserving his primary insights for macroeconomic analysis. It is in the latter that the method which Keynes adopted can be encapsulated within our *homo creativus* dichotomy, provided that we suitably extend it to cover the kind of historical situation that Keynes was concerned with.

In order to enter Keynes's world we must abandon assumptions A1 to A4. Structure is now permitted to suffer from entropy and, despite the time devoted to maintenance in A4, the non-linear nature of entropy processes will always render a static structure's life finite. A2 is retained simply to remain in the evolutionary short run and the domain of Keynes's analysis. Keynes refused to address directly the question of mutating and radically shifting consciousnesses in his depiction of 'animal spirits'.[16] He did, however, acknowledge their existence and their importance, but preferred to look 'into structure' rather than out into external consciousness. So, to examine the short-run structural problem, A2 can be kept in place.

Homo creativus now has a two dimensional problem to solve. Pursuit of new structure is constrained not only by a need to maintain existing structure but also 'fire-fighting' as unanticipated damage has to be repaired.

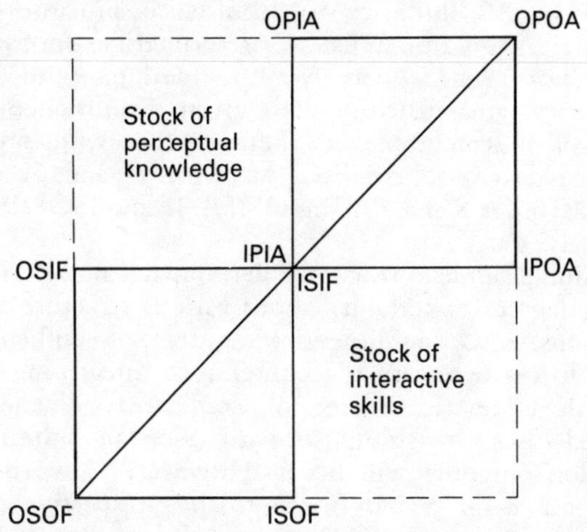

Figure 8.4 The external consciousness box: introducing conflict

In Figure 8.4 we can make this explicit by extending Figure 8.2 so that we have a zone of effective conflict in addition to our zone of effective co-ordination. Once again we can divide conflict outcomes *ex ante* into perceptual (strategic *S*) and action (force *F*) components. Existing structure at any point in time is given and, as such, it constitutes a source of power definable in terms of *S* and *F*. Structure can be viewed from two perspectives, first in terms of IPIA (short for our previous S (k = 1, s = 1) point), and, second, in terms of ISIF, as an absorber or exploiter which transforms input flows into output flows. Furthermore, we have already discussed in the power postulate P6 how an ISIF will also be subject to more powerful forces which direct and mould structure. Thus, if we hold time constant, we perceive IPIA/ISIF as being in a power hierarchy. The nature of this hierarchy will have a critical influence on structural development potential. In our idealized *homo creativus* case we supposed the existence of some benign 'parental authority' permitting directed development. However, we could, equally, have the case of a slave-owner wielding power which closed the creative development box and established fixed arrangements of motional servitude.

Thus any structure will be vulnerable to external force and, in turn, will be able to exert a certain degree of force on the external environment. Clearly, such pressures will mould consciousness and structure over historical time. However, our retention of A2 distances us from such processes in our evolutionary short run. What we are primarily concerned with in the short run, where we are dealing with a *given* consciousness and structure with given maintenance systems built into that structure, is its ability to cope with imperfectly anticipated force or conflict. As with *P* and *A* we can motionally order *S* and *F* along OSIF/ISIF and ISOF/ISIF axes, respectively.

The dimensionless stock of perceptual knowledge yields different degrees of certainty about various structure threatening motions. Also, the dimensionless stock of conflictual skills contains forces necessary to counter such threatening motion, held with a certain degree of confidence. The ISIF, or structured cases, are straightforward; a certain submission or domination outcome will occur. However, as we deal with motions down the *S* and *F* axes to their respective zeros we encounter increasing uncertainty as to the outcome. Near ISIF the risks can be reasonably well calculated.[17] For example, when part of existing structure is being gambled on horse races, the odds set reflect quite accurately the probability of win/lose outcomes. However, in the case of true uncertainty, which exists in undesired conflictual events such as 'accidents', *S* and *F* are very distinct, *ex ante*. The outcome is not amenable to probability calculation but will be a unique 'situation-specific' outcome from *S* and *F* characteristics. As in the creative case, we could define qualitatively different outcomes. In discrete situations we could infer probability of destruction or survival of structure while in other continuous situations it would be the 'degree of damage' that we could infer. Furthermore, the motion may well be 'chain reactive' with structural alteration leading on to new conflictual events involving different aspects of structure. Because conflict *alters structure* through energy release and absorption, no notion of structural equilibrium is relevant and conflict can assume a historical dynamic of its own involving the ongoing *rational* calculation of altering consciousness.[18]

Since conflict dynamics involve destruction and structural

change it is hardly worth pursuing examples of *S/F* combinations except to say that the 'discreteness' of structure will be important. Much of the non-linear catastrophic nature of entropy comes from the fact that once the defences of a discrete structure have been breached then the *S/F* combination of the defender are likely to be near OSOF given lack of planning or experience in defending the core structure. Continuous or flexible structure, being decentralized and less hierarchical is, thus, less susceptible to entropic decline. Such distinctions are, of course, well known to military strategists and will not be dwelt on here. Of much greater interest to the economist is the design of systems or macro-consciousness which enable the discrete structures vitally necessary to economic development to evolve in security.

Conflict between structures is undesired in itself and also because it debilitates evolutionary development since time and resources are devoted to increased maintenance (defence) of structure as well as conflict. Creativity diminishes and, paradoxically, cumbersomely defended structures are even more prone to entropic decay than before.

In terms of our diagrammatic exposition, Figure 8.5 illustrates the nature of balanced evolution, where structure develops from $(IPIA)_0$ to $(IPIA)_1$ while old structure, of highly uncertain vulnerability, is discarded. At the same time, new possibilities open up in consciousness as OPOA shifts. All evolutionary development which involves discrete entropic structures is subject to this developmental pattern where old structure 'dies' and new structure is 'born'. Petrification and the resultant process of fragmentation is a constant threat to evolutionary processes. More will be said about the historical nature of these evolutionary processes in the next chapter. For present purposes, in the evolutionary short run, with A2 in place, we have established that a stagnating motional situation will naturally begin to exhibit a short-run tendency towards structural rigidity, increased use of force and a non-linear increase in conflict.

It was precisely this short-run evolutionary situation of structural fragmentation that Keynes was preoccupied with in his macroeconomic analysis. He was concerned with macroeconomic structure and the problem that existed in macroconsciousness which resulted in stagnation. Keynes did not disaggregate in order to isolate one 'problem' group that, in some causal sense, was the source of the prevailing malaise, but rather engaged in a particular disaggregation to demonstrate

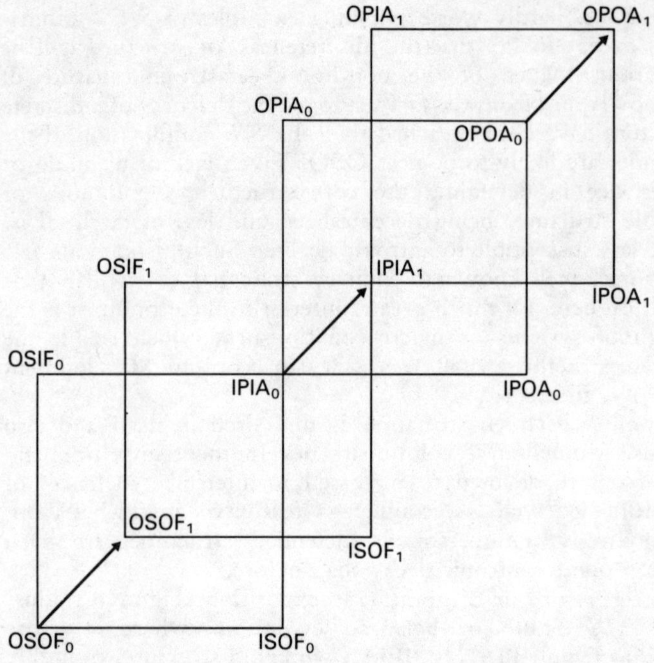

Figure 8.5 Escaping entropy and promoting development

the *interdependency* contained in macro-structure. Or, at a more basic level, through the principle of effective demand he established that macro-structure had a holistic identity that was not reducible into microeconomic parts. Keynes did identify the cause of stagnation of macro-structure in the interplay of investor pessimism and speculator liquidity preference. The effect was unemployment of resources. Although Keynes tended to have sympathy with the plight of nervous investors and antagonism towards speculators who earned predative gains from structural decline, he clearly saw the situation as a crisis of macro-consciousness that government was capable of rectifying.

In terms of Figure 8.5, Keynes's dynamic vision involved the depiction of simultaneous slowing of structural development in the co-ordination box, through cuts in investment expenditure and an increase in structural decline, accompanied by increased activity in the conflict box as resistance to entropy increased in labour groups and protective strategies were adopted by firms and financiers. Once the entropy rate exceeded the creativity rate then structure declined and, along with it, output. For Keynes, the key to this structural problem lay in the interaction of stocks and flows in macro-structure. Investors, already committed to discrete capital stocks, feared shortages of liquidity when flows of income were disturbed, while at the same time, part of the stock of liquidity was demanded by speculators wishing to capitalize on the chain reactions between nervous investment cuts and income–expenditure flows. The authorities' attempts to engage in monetary control created inconsistencies between sub-macro-consciousness, with creative 'animal spirits', on the one hand, and the conflictual speculative urge on the other. This schizophrenia had, in the nineteenth century, led to business cycles but, after the experiences of the 1920s, it had given way to a dull and protracted pessimism on all sides, in the banking system, in investment, among speculators and in government itself. Keynes suggested that conditions were so bleak that even if the authorities tried to release extra liquidity they might find themselves in an expectational trap.

However, even though Keynes made much of the state of confidence as a key factor, he chose, as we have seen, Marshallian characteristics of macro-structure which were more mechanical than socio-psychological and were easily translated into a Walrasian conception of the macro-system. In Chapter 2 we concluded that there was indeed some merit in taking such an approach at the time even though there would be costs further up the evolutionary path. He chose a method which focused on flow equilibrium in its notional and effective forms, showing how expenditure shocks divided the two and altered structure. As we know, the elements of this approach became stylized in the IS-LM model of orthodox macroeconomics.

Orthodox macroeconomics deals with flows, measured in monetary units, over time. The macro-system, thus depicted, is analysed in terms of flow equilibrium. Flow shocks disturb this equilibrium, setting off disequilibrium adjustment processes which culminate in the restoration of new flow equilibria. This is the method of 'comparative statics' as practised in orthodox macroeconomics. We have already argued in Chapter 7 that even though macro-structure is 'looser' than physical structure, there is still a role for this kind of method over short historical periods. In order to engage in 'comparative statics' the structure, through which motion flows, must be held constant, otherwise the equilibrium method cannot be used. This is the truly static nature of the model in evolutionary terms. This fixed structure consists of a set of institutional arrangements, socially determined, plus a set of behavioural assumptions concerning individuals or groups. In this respect orthodox Keynesian macroeconomics adopts the same method as neo-classical market analysis. The static premisses concerning economic structure tend to be pushed into the background as the 'short run' is modelled using disequilibrium dynamics and the 'long run' by growth models which capture the expansion of economic activity. Furthermore, the latter need not be restricted to quantitative expansion if technical progress is allowed to arrive like 'manna from heaven'.

The difficulties involved in assuming fixed economic structure have been alluded to frequently in the history of economic thought. For example, Keynes saw difficulties in using the equilibrium method beyond the short run because of the inherent structure-altering effects of capital investment which, in turn, was not viewed as determinable in terms of quantifiable behavioural rules. Although Keynes had essentially saved the equilibrium method by taking it from its redundant Walrasian market context and applying it to short-run income–expenditure flows, he remained cautious as to its usefulness. The long run was the province of evolution and economic structure was not exempt from evolutionary tendencies.

Keynes's use of the equilibrium method for studying the short-run characteristics of the macro-structure was wholly appropriate for his task at hand. The economic structure upon which he employed such a method was portrayed as having evolved from the Classical conception in two ways. First, 'credit money' had come to be vitally important in facilitating the circular flow of income and expenditure. Second, the degree of contractual commitment and interdependence which had come to exist in an economy, which could no longer be characterized by a system of markets, meant that the system responded asymetrically to expansionary and contractionary shocks. A monetary shock of a deflationary nature could result not simply in a disequilibrium process to re-establish a new flow equilibrium at a new set of prices but a *temporary collapse of structure itself*. Equilibrium of flows in this revised structure – 'underemployment equilibrium' – was perfectly possible in the absence of an income–expenditure 'stabilizer'. The structural breakdown described by Keynes was not analysable using 'comparative statics', since the two equilibria in question related to *different structures*. Keynes solved this problem by suggesting a stabilizing structural change, i.e. the introduction of a government with a stabilization policy, which would then make the underemployment equilibrium a point of disequilibrium, in the new scheme of things, and permit equilibrium analysis to be used. With this social innovation, the equilibrium method could then be used to discuss the equilibrating policy responses to macroeconomic shocks.

That Keynes was referring to disequilibrium only after structural fragmentation had been avoided by a structural development is not a point which is made particularly explicit in the Keynesian exegesis literature. In particular, the new 'disequilibrium approach' seems to be founded on an association of market disequilibrium with a very special case of structural fragmentation, i.e. temporary market failure. Not surprisingly, neo-classical economists have made short work of such a contention with the introduction of an expectational dimension to markets. While, at the same time, those wedded to structural change, more than even Keynes, reject the disequilibrium approach on the opposite grounds. Whether or not Keynes was correct in his continued use of the equilibrium method in one structure in preference to another is not something that can easily be evaluated. In an evolutionary context, adherence to any fixed economic structure will ultimately become an obsolete position yet may yield great benefits for a long time. It is these very benefits which permit the evolution which leads to obsolescence. Although such an interaction is of great interest and will receive more attention in the next chapter, the relevant feature of Keynes's macroeconomics, for immediate purposes, is the manner in which he took a structuralist view of the economic system. As such, his depiction of the temporal and spatial dimensions of behaviour is different to the Classical economists.

The motional flows which interested the Classical economists were flows of quantities, regulated by price fluctuations and accompanied by a faith that the latter would ensure flow equilibrium in economic (Walrasian) structure. The behaviour of economic agents in such a model consists of sets of optimization rules which render microeconomics and macroeconomics indistinguishable. The spatial dimension of motional behaviour is removed by assumptions concerning the qualitative homogeneity of different individuals, firms, etc., and the temporal dimension by assumptions of perfect knowledge, full adjustment, etc. Keynes, on the other hand, introduced the motional behaviour of economic agents directly into his model. The consumption and production aspects of economic agents' behaviour were given explicit dimension over time in expenditure and income. Determination of output flows is not the outcome of some esoteric price interaction but is ground out of the historical dynamics of income and expenditure interactions. The multiplier is a thoroughly dynamic equilibrator which captures the temporal dimension of motion. In a spatial sense, Keynes also extended the motional picture of behaviour. Consumers, investors and money holders, even though an economic agent could be all three at once, were separated by Keynes as key interactors in analysing behaviour from a macroeconomic perspective. Individuals were not so much independent entities whose behaviour could be aggregated to the macro-level. Rather, individuals were divided into distinctive macro-consciousnesses. Keynes had prised apart the old division between individualism and class collectivism by presenting individuals who were members of several relevant groups at once.

The picture that Keynes presents in his model is extremely well tailored to investigating the short-run behaviour of an interdependent system in historical time. 'Equilibrium' is not something which is left to the 'magic' of the market, but involves certain motional decisions by government over time. *Ex ante* forward-planning decisions by firms and consumers are reconciled by government from its vantage point over the whole system. With nervousness concerning structural failure removed, aspirations and activity could be brought together in contractual union. Equilibrium is thus translated into the historical context of observable motional behaviour. Disequilibrium relates, not to whether everything which has been produced is sold, but rather whether or not income is sufficient to ensure that the aspirations of consumers and producers coincide. The latter is not the same as the former because the latter also relates to making plans in the security that they will be realized.

This forward-looking dimension of Keynes's conception of macro-equilibrium has not been done justice to in orthodox Keynesianism, as Shackle has emphasized, essentially because it is qualitative. The 'animal spirits' which dictate fluctuations in investment expenditure in turn affect income. This precipitates appropriate stabilization action which can be viewed as the enactment of a particular forward-looking commitment by the authorities at the core of macro-consciousness. The disappearance of Keynes's forward-looking perspective in the Keynesian orthodoxy can be attributed to a lack of identification of Keynes's stock–flow dichotomy with the core–peripheral or structuralist perspective discussed here. Relativistic tension between core and periphery does not appear explicitly in Keynesian stock–flow analysis.

There are two key stocks in the Keynesian orthodoxy; money and real capital, but they are approached in a quantitative rather than a qualitative way. Money is not treated as a qualitative convention which is *part* of macro-structure, where its value is the outcome of a relativistic interplay between the stock of future real value, which it represents, and the flow of new credit. Equally, the capital stock is not conjoined in a relativistic way with new investment flows, highlighting how, on the one hand, the whole basis of new investment lies in the existence of capital stock while, on the other hand, commitment to it leads to nervousness concerning new ventures. The absence of this stock–flow relativism can be attributed to the adoption of notions of causality which involve the sequential modelling of perception and 'disequilibrium' action rather than treating them simultaneously, as is the case here.

Simultaneity, in orthodox Keynesian modelling, involves something quite different – the flow interactions in fixed structure representable by a system of simultaneous equations. When Keynes accepted Hick's IS–LM representation of his system he departed from perception–action simultaneity to the causality contained in orthodox thought.[19] Not surprisingly, the dynamic simultaneity of perception and action soon disappeared. There was no place in the orthodoxy for Keynes's discussion of expectations in the context of investment behaviour and liquidity preference. Without these Keynesian dynamics were stultified, depending on only the principle of effective demand to provide a connection to historical time.

The income–expenditure diagram that we use to teach students the principle of effective demand is thus confined to the south-west quadrant of Figure 8.5, showing how stabilizing injections of government spending can push structure back to IPIA/ISIF in the event of 'shocks' to structure. Planned expenditure relates to perception and available income to action with all *ex post* outcomes on the 45° diagonal. IPIA/ISIF is 'full employment' maintained with the help of a macro-consciousness development which enables ongoing repairs to be undertaken through 'discretionary' policy and 'maintenance' to be undertaken through 'automatic' stabilizers. The northwest quadrant development of IPIA/ISIF was left to the benign discretion of investors with no clear analysis of what would happen if the government overspent. The analysis of inflation, like investment, was left hanging in an 'inflationary gap'. The crucial stock/flow relativities necessary to analyse these important phenomena were not recognized in orthodox analysis although we see fragmentary acknowledgement of them in the work of Michael Kalecki on investment and Paul Davidson on money in the post-Keynesian tradition. Even Keynes himself, with his 'inward looking' perspective on macro-structure, underestimated the extent to which stabilization policy, in correcting a stock/flow problem, would lead to an extended period of economic development without significant inflation.

In Chapter 3 we argued that Keynesianism was too 'demand side' in emphasis, with little explicit analysis of the supply side. Within our analytical framework here it is clear why the demand/supply labels are inappropriate and misleading. What Keynes really over-emphasized was structural stabilization at the expense of structural development on the evolutionary path of macro-structure. We also saw in Chapter 3 that Keynes had an idealistic notion of how government, at the core of macro-consciousness, would carry out its stabilization responsibilities. He did not address the problem that, in the course of development, stabilization policy would become a vehicle for social restructuring developments and provide a permissive regime for inflation. Keynes was much more concerned with the prospect that, in the long run, falling rates of profitability would stultify investment, forcing the state to intervene increasingly. In all this Keynes remained speculative, for such long-run projections were beyond the compass of his model and of any reasonable logic in an unknown evolutionary future. What was important was that Keynes had managed to influence that future by providing macro-consciousness with a suitable logic which would ensure the active pursuit of stabilizing intervention for the first time in history outside of national emergency conditions.

However, in order that further progress can be made, it must be recognized that Keynes's treatment of the stock–flow relativity is inadequate to analyse properly modern economies half a century later. The principle of effective demand was cast in terms of monetary flows juxtaposed to monetary valued stocks. Although useful in analysing recession and stabilization, it cannot shed light on the forward-looking dimension of co-ordinated behaviour depicted in our *homo creativus* construct. Monetarists have demonstrated forcefully that, in the dynamics of development, monetary flows must be disentangled into price and output effects. Or to put it more generally, monetary valuations cannot be taken as a homogeneous measure of current and future flows of output. Heterogeneity, or qualitative diversity, is the very essence of the expectations, aspirations, new structures and new characteristics which are so central to the *homo creativus* dimension of behaviour. What Keynes merely implied in the *General Theory* must become central to any analysis of evolutionary development.

Conclusion

In this chapter we have begun the task of harnessing *homo creativus* for the purpose of providing an evolutionary approach to macroeconomic analysis. We began by arguing that the notion that a unit of consciousness consisted of internal motional structure and external consciousness could be applied just as much to the whole economy as any other level of aggregation. However, at the level of the economy, the unit of consciousness was perceived as having particular characteristics: it contains an internal structure shared by everyone but an external consciousness dominated by governmental authority. Thus stability is an essential characteristic for creativity in peripheral units of consciousness but, at the same time, introduces the potential for inertia and anti-evolutionary tendencies. However, the symbiotic or conflictual potential of this interplay was not our central concern, but, rather, where the three corners of the macro-debate – the micro-construct of *homo economicus*, the macro-construct of Walrasian equilibrium and the Keynesian theory of effective demand – stood in such an evolutionary setting.

To deal with the first two, our six postulates had to be controlled by four assumptions to get us into a world where a comparison could be made. However, in addition to making explicit the kinds of assumptions that are necessary before we can entertain a neo-classical approach, such simplification had the advantage of providing a more manageable stage upon which to introduce our dynamic dichotomy. The essence of this dichotomy is derived from the discussions of the problems of using a space–time dichotomy in Chapter 6. Dynamics involve motional events recorded in space and time. Each event, in the case of a fourth-level motional structure, involves the interplay of perception and action. If this is 'perfect' then it is essentially motionless – it is structure; if it is imperfect then it is the product of external consciousness, representable as two overlapping dimensions. Purposeful behaviour involves 'converting' external consciousness into structure.

Adopting this notion of dynamics thrusts learning and experience effects, normally tagged on to orthodox economic analysis, to the centre of the stage. Now, although our dynamic dichotomy is clearly an ideal taxonomy within which to discuss the development of *homo creativus*, *homo economicus* looks a highly deterministic individual who, when taken to be in equilibrium, records no motional action at all, even in a world highly cushioned by our four assumptions. Jumping up to that great aggregation of *homi economici*, the Walrasian equilibrium, 'core' macro-consciousness becomes an auctioneer who ensures that the micro-dimensionless points of equilibrium will be matched by a macro-dimensionless point. Timelessness is inescapable, whereas even under the burden of our assumptions *homo creativus* can enjoy learning to be a manager then enjoy being one!

In order to capture the Keynesian theory of effective demand, it was necessary to take two steps towards reality by relaxing two assumptions and allowing entropic decay and mortality to exist. We still have a non-evolutionary world of people learning to be and being managers but, in contrast to neo-classical analysis, we find that the Keynesian theory of effective demand fits into our dichotomy in an elemental way, concerned with structural decay. The static comparison of different income–expenditure flow levels is found to be comprehensible in the context of the introduction of a social innovation in external macro-consciousness in the form of stabilization policy. However, our *homo creativus* dichotomy also reveals the major defect of the Keynesian model: the escape from entropy can only be considered in conjunction with the evolutionary development of new structure; a one shot change, in the form of the introduction of stabilization policy, is not enough. In our dynamic dichotomy, the Keynesian deficiency is not the lack of a supply side story but rather the lack of an evolutionary one. Although it has been acknowledged that macro-consciousness is likely to be predominantly preoccupied with maintenance, of which demand management is surely a component, the evolutionary implications of such a change, and reactions to it, require analysis if we are to understand the development of postwar economies.

In particular, it is clear that forward-looking contracts have a pivotal role to play in understanding evolution. The contract can be of three different types. First, in productive structure it can be viewed as a device to facilitate production planning, like inventories, and this is the way that the contract has been looked on predominantly in the orthodox contractual literature reviewed in Chapter 4. As such, it can be viewed in the same terms as forward versus spot markets, i.e. as a risk reducing, communication enhancing device. The second type of contract is the 'alliance' which is prevalent in conflict zone activity. It is a temporary device in the ever changing environment of conflict.

The third, and most important, type is the creative contract whereby co-ordination is planned in order to achieve some aspiration. In terms of our external consciousness zone, this provides us with a solid empirical basis for analysis. We can observe *ex post* the value of contracts and the length of time ahead that contracts are outstanding. Just as there can be a gap between effective and notional demand, so there can exist a gap between effective and notional creativity due to an insufficiency of 'credit' in the economy. How such a situation can occur in the modern economy will be examined in the ensuing chapters.

Notes

1 Keynes's 'pragmatism', despite its compatibility with an evolutionary approach, has been criticized by many authors as being in conflict with the setting down of general principles. See, for example, the qualified praise of Keynes by Clark: 'Even now we are still standing too close to make a real assessment of Keynes's contributions to economics, how far they represented permanent additions to our methods of analysis, to what extent they were *ad hoc* proposals to put right the tragic and unnecessary unemployment and depression of the 1930s, which would have been valuable if applied at the time but may have become irrelevant or positively misleading later' (Clark, 1970, p. 53). By 1970 the mark Keynes had made could not be ignored, but behind Clark's statement lies the ghost of Samuelson's sharp dismissal of Keynes's contribution a quarter of a century earlier: 'It is remarkable that so active a brain would have failed to make any

contribution to economic theory; and yet except for his discussion of index numbers in Volume I of the *Treatise* and a few remarks concerning 'user cost' [in the *General Theory*], which are novel at best only in terminology and emphasis, he seems to have left no mark on pure theory' (Samuelson, 1946, quoted in Moggeridge, 1976, p. 156).

2 See Olson (1982) which is best read as a sequel to Olson (1965).

3 See Nelson and Winter (1982), Ch. 16, for a discussion of the evolution of public policies.

4 The approach taken by Bausor (1984) is similar in spirit to the analytical framework developed here.

5 Penrose (1959) was one of the first to develop, explicitly, an analysis of the dynamics of firm behaviour linking growth, structure and the consciousness of management.

6 Analogous to 'mass' in physics where we perceive 'symmetry' in relations. In physics, 'symmetry' is the building block of motional analysis of fixed structures. As soon as the physics of sub-atomic particles encounters situations of structural alteration then the symmetry laws are observed not to hold. This is a commonplace situation in 'structurally loose' behaviour in the *U* consciousness zone.

7 More generally, the Bayesian method of capturing adaptive or learning processes, in terms of changes in subjective probability distributions, has offered an approach to empirical work which has tried to develop this 'discrete' approach within conventional models. See Hey (1985) for a good exposition of this approach. See Murphy (1965) for a general review of the possible methodologies that can be adopted to model adaptive processes of this type. Cross (1983) offers an exposition of how adaptive modelling can enrich our depiction of quite orthodox models with neo-classical long-run equilibrium solutions.

8 Typically, a person learning to drive a car experiences initial rapid advance as core expertise is learnt, then enters a zone of learning which is non-hierarchical, involving the learning of several parallel peripheral co-ordinations where a non-linear learning situation prevails. Acknowledgement of this kind of increase in efficiency associated with learning-by-doing has been in 'Verdoorn's Law' in the economic growth literature. See Boulier (1984) for some discussion of the nature of the learning processes underlying this 'law'.

9 Bausor (1983) comes to a similar conclusion as to the very special case status of 'rational' neo-classical models in historical time.

10 See Kay (1979, 1982) for statements of this requirement and its attendant problems.

11 This accords with the position of Latsis (1972) who argues that there is, in fact, no free choice in the 'long-run' equilibrium of *homo economicus*. It is a predetermined position which only needs to be located by a decision-maker.

12 To quote Schotter (1981): 'A social institution is a regularity in social behaviour that . . . specifies behaviour in specific recurrent situations, and is either self-policed or policed by some external authority' (p. 11).

13 This is a reality which frustrated Keynes greatly: 'It may turn out I suppose, that vested interests and personal selfishness may stand in the way. But the main task is producing first the intellectual conviction and then intellectually to devise the means. Insufficiency of cleverness, not goodness is the main trouble. *And even resistance to change as such may have many motives besides selfishness*' (italics added) (Keynes in letter to T. S. Eliot in 1945, quoted in Moggeridge, 1976, p. 39).

14 Political scientists such as Nozick (1970) emphasize that such support has very little to do with actual voting for political parties and much more to do with the degree to which the public co-operate with the 'permanent' bureaucratic dimension of government. It is with the latter that the degree of 'social consensus' in governmental structure and consciousness resides.

15 George Stigler has repeatedly stated such a position.

16 See Dow and Dow (1985).

17 Again, the unit of consciousness we choose will have a bearing on the extent to which we can estimate the probability of the occurrence of conflict. For example, an individual thief has difficulty in calculating in a probabilistic way the outcome of his conflictual action.

18 In the popular mind, conflict is often associated with irrationality, but as soon as we acknowledge that consciousness and structure are changing this need not be so, as we shall see in the next chapter.

19 See Hicks (1979) for further discussion of his own and Keynes's conception of the role of causality in macroeconomics.

9 *Structural Change in the Long Run of Evolutionary Time*

> A characteristic of commitment . . . is the fact that it drives a wedge between personal choice and personal welfare, and much of traditional economic theory relies on the identity of the two.
>
> Amartya Sen (1977)

In the last chapter, four assumptions were made in order to generate a 'fixed consciousness' or evolutionary short-run case of our behavioural postulates. This *homo creativus* idealization encapsulated *homo economicus* as a special case. By the conclusion of the chapter, all but one of these assumptions had been relaxed in order to discuss Keynes's dynamic analysis. It was found, however, that Keynesian analysis, particularly in its orthodox guise, is incapable of fully capturing the forward-looking dynamics contained in economic behaviour. Although it is possible to interpret Keynes's approach in terms of our perception/action dichotomy in conditions of structural decline, it cannot be extended to deal with economic development, because of the limited nature of the stock/flow dichotomy when used in historical time analysis. Since it is a truism that economic development involves change in both structure and consciousness, the structural fixedness of Keynesian stock/flow assumptions must limit their usefulness in the analysis of evolutionary dynamics.

The purpose of this chapter is to relax assumption A2 and allow structure and consciousness to change in historical time. However, it is not intended that we should leave the short-run perspective, in the manner of Joseph Schumpeter, but rather to see how long-run dynamics are likely to affect short-run economic decision-making. Central to the postulates in Chapter 7 is the idea that all decision-making is 'short run' in the sense that 'fixity' will always exist in historical time. The long-run view is something that impinges on consciousness and, in turn, influences short-run behaviour, creating the actuality of the long run in historical time.

In Chapter 3 it was argued that the new Classical method of bringing the long run to the short run through rational expectations was, in principle, correct and in accord with Keynes's own more general emphasis on expectations. Of course, where the two differ is that the former makes strong assumptions about future equilibrium and the latter argues that the equilibrium method cannot be applied to guide expectations concerning the long run, making the structural forces of inertia of much greater importance. The objective here is to argue that our method suggests a relativistic middle course, involving both structure and consciousness, which can be analysed in historical time and is policy relevant. However, that is the subject of Chapters 11 and 12. For the present, let us look more generally at the evolutionary long run from the perspective of our behavioural postulates.

The Historical Constraint

In Chapter 8 an idealization of evolutionary dynamics was developed in Figure 8.5. Structural development proceeds as old structure is discarded and new consciousness opens up new structural opportunities. Keynes pointed out that, in the case of macro-structure, there is nothing automatic or natural about such balanced development. In Boulding's terminology,[1] evolution is characterized by movement into 'dead-ends' as much as 'niches'. However, Keynes was careful not to get involved in any more than limited discussion of the evolution of macro-structure and has been criticized for this by Schumpeter.[2] Once Keynes had introduced 'repair and maintenance' dimensions into macro-consciousness through stabilization policy, macro-structure could proceed on its idealized balanced path.

Structural change, beyond the introduction of this social enlightenment, was not addressed formally by Keynes. In terms of our analysis, assumption A2 held, with mutations of consciousness side-stepped by the introduction of 'animal spirits' and discussion of catastrophic shifts in consciousness and structure avoided. Again, in Chapter 2, it was argued that there were good reasons for this position in the politically polarizing world of the 1930s. However, today, such a position would hardly seem justified. It is true that once we drop A2 we are catapulted into a different world inhabited by names such as

Marx, Schumpeter, Rostow and Weber. It is a world where the divisions between economics, sociology and political philosophy necessarily collapse.[3] However, our interest is not in formulating long-run theories of structural change, Pasinetti-style,[4] but rather in enquiring into the way in which visions of the long run in our consciousness interact with the structural constraints that we always face.

In Chapter 8, when we considered the interplay of creative and conflictional behaviour, it was acknowledged that all consciousnesses operate in power hierarchies, exerting force and having force exerted upon them. The developmental path of structure will depend very much on the configuration of these forces in the interaction of consciousnesses. Most models of evolutionary dynamics tend to posit phases where defined consciousnesses such as, for example, 'capitalists' and 'workers' form a productive power structure where, over time, there is a rise in 'countervailing power' which leads to catastrophic breakdown and the formation of a new power structure.[5] The Marxist model conceives of alienation giving rise to class consciousness and solidarity. Schumpeter, in contrast, preferred to analyse evolution in terms of the rise and fall of monopolist consciousness in the process of technical change. Marcuse closed the circle by arguing that the whole system of monopoly capitalism itself adopted the communication techniques used to preserve monopoly structure in order to prevent the formation of radical class consciousness.

The potential dynamic combinations of even only these three theorists' visions of the interplay of consciousness and structure are very large. Clearly, for our purposes, it is necessary to abstract from them the common dynamic which is relevant to our analysis of short-run behaviour. Marcuse may have been correct that macro-consciousness contains oppressive ideology, yet it can also be argued that macro-consciousness has averted crises by the incorporation of radical ideas. Hirschman has traced the manner in which macro-consciousness seems to oscillate in this regard in different historical epochs.[6] It seems that economic structure can be viewed as 'good' or 'bad' only with regard to the specific historical conditions in question. Thus, no generalizations can be provided as to the optimal structural arrangements in the future without explicit reference to historical conditions in the present. Hirschman's historical analysis is centrally concerned with the relativity of consciousness and structure.

This raises fundamental problems with the static notion of

social welfare.[7] It is not clear whether perfect competition or imperfect competition is preferable without taking explicit account of historical conditions. Dynamic welfare maximization would relate to choosing that evolutionary path which leads to the maximum degree of co-ordination. Now, since we *have* structure and know what it is, the optimal ideology would adjust macro-consciousness in a way that evolution can proceed from that structure. Such an optimum is not wholly abstract, since at any point in time we already have observable commitments of varying degree of firmness into the future and old structure observable in different stages of decline.

The long-standing orthodox position that market competition is a dynamically superior state to imperfect competition relates directly to an understandable aversion to situations where the politics of power dominate motional outcomes. This is the basis of libertarian and neo-Austrian philosophical positions. Much of the popularity of these philosophies derives directly from a concern to provide a macro-consciousness which permits evolution with a sharp dichotomy of 'constitutionalized' laws to facilitate co-ordination, and decentralized 'freedoms' to engage in innovatory activity. Thus, evolution generates structures which have power over, say, nature, but not over other human structures. The latter voluntarily operate within productive hierarchies but are 'free to choose' to do so. Thus, consciousness is simplified into individual consciousness, which can operate independently, and a macro-consciousness which is collectively enforced.[8]

The high value assigned to libertarian thought by, for example, Friedman and Hayek would seem to be fully justified as ideology which facilitates economic development. However, it does not seem particularly insightful in any examination of actual historical development. Their particular visions of *homo creativus* must be tempered by the *actuality of historical commitment*. Evolution alters structure, yielding new ways that power can be used to exploit. Thus, as evolution proceeds, the rules embodied in macro-consciousness must be modified. For example, to have a set of rules to facilitate competition amongst small firms in an economy which has become structurally committed to large firms is likely to increase rather than reduce exploitation. Absence of such 'rule mutations' is likely to plunge macrostructure into inertia and conflict.

Recognition that the reality of historical commitment requires constant rule mutation has, of course, been recognized in common law as well as in much of the consumer protection and factory legislation of the past century.[9] The delicate balance between protection and facilitating new development has always been recognized in the moral philosophy that lies behind the legal structure. However, even though such issues were central to the thought of Adam Smith and other political economists of the past, they receive little attention in modern orthodox economic thought. Qualitative considerations as to how to devise and update rules to facilitate structural development have taken second place to quantitative concerns about the flows of inputs and outputs generated by the power of an assumed fixed economic structure.

Once macroeconomic policy became concerned with the stabilization and development of macro-structure it became artificial to pretend that 'rule mutation' could be ignored by macroeconomists. However, we have seen that, in fact, macroeconomics has clung to fixed structure assumptions, even though, in practice, macroeconomic policy has had to be set in an environment of structural change. It has always been understood, intuitively, by policy-makers that the dynamics of existing structure and forward commitments have to be consistent in a relativistic sense. For example, an 'indicative planning' element in macro-consciousness, such as has been strongly in evidence in Japan but weakly so in the UK, attempts to phase industrial development and decline at similar rates. Such a strategy bonds macro-consciousness to macro-structure in a qualitative sense. Slowness in the phasing out of old structure leads to evolutionary imbalance with non-linear increases in conflictual or entropic activity with a related re-allocation of resources from creative activity. On the other hand, an excessive cut-back in structure can seriously diminish the security upon which creative development is based.

Once we recognize, explicitly, the importance of historical commitment, the way we depict the interplay between power and structural development has to be qualified. No optimal structure exists which is applicable in all epochs of evolutionary time and, equally, anti-evolutionary power effects will be different in each phase of evolutionary development. Thus, what constitutes 'unfairness' will not relate to actual macro-structure but rather its relativity to the ideology and aspirations contained in macro-consciousness. Innovations in macro-consciousness will precipitate virtuous circles where macro-structure develops and reinforces macro-consciousness. Ultimate inertia in macro-structure will tend to coincide with periods where such aspirations have assumed a core place in macro-consciousness, leading to a vicious circle of fragmentation of macro-consciousness and, ultimately, macro-structure itself.

Thus, economic dynamics in historical time are the product of the interplay of the qualitative and the quantitative at all times. Structure, which is qualitative, forms a power base which is quantifiable in terms of inputs and outputs of characteristics of some type. In turn, structure changes through the medium of qualitative consciousness. In Figure 8.5 we rendered dimension-less that which orthodox economists give dimension to, preferring to give qualities, such as efficiency and uncertainty, explicit dimension in terms of structural evolution. Thus, stock and flow are no longer distinct – a stock forms and flows appear, a stock collapses and flows disappear. The evolving macroeconomy appears as a sequence of changes of input and output characteristics over historical time. 'Production' occurs but there is no 'production function' but rather a cumulative progression of new structure, where the core–peripheral relation of structure and consciousness is of central importance.

It has already been stated that it is not our purpose to theorise about long-run evolutionary change, but rather to explore the influence of long-run views on short-run behaviour. We are not interested in specific power interplays between groups or, like Hannah Arendt, in tracing the origins of totalitarianism.[10] We are not interested in how exploitation and alienation occurred in particular conditions but rather the manner in which historical commitment itself can both liberate and enslave, even though we assume that behaviour is rational. It is central to orthodox economics that rational behaviour operates subject to constraints. However, these constraints are generally modelled in a static way. Historical constraints require a different treatment because of the way that they span the future and define the present. The prisoner's dilemma, so popular in political science, is an example of rational behaviour in the presence of historical constraints. The outcome may appear irrational, viewed from a static, full information prospective, but it is not from a dynamic perspective. Conflict is also popularly considered as irrational from the safety of such a historical vacuum, but in conditions of rapidly changing historical constraints in the 'heat of battle' each individual action can be construed as rational and an outcome of the interplay of existing structure and future commitment.[11]

The inability of consciousness to foresee conflict or to even understand why it came about *ex post* is a very common observation. The historical dynamics of structure in conflictual situations is hard to predict and difficult to remember, thus, it is not surprising to find that rational behaviour in such conditions is interpreted as irrational. Such rationality does not fit well with the kind of macro-consciousness necessary for constructive, co-operative evolution of economic structure. In particular, conventional views of risk cease to have general relevance in situations of structural change, whether we are dealing with the rapid case of conflict or the evolving case of development. Before we go on to discuss further the influence of historical commitment on motional events in historical time, it is worth deliberating on the concept of risk a little more.

Co-ordination and Risk

The cotton-wool world of Chapter 8, inhabited by *homo creativus*, does not exist. Many creative motions involve not only risk of failure but risk to existing structure itself. For example, people learning to ski may break a leg or even die. These events have low probabilities of outcome in most circumstances and people will insure against them. However, insurance companies calculate probabilities over large samples of people; for any given individual the probability will depend on the level of aspiration attempted. Novice skiers who launch themselves down 'black runs' are risking existing structure in the conflict zone with the most likely outcome being serious injury. What started out as an attempt at a co-ordinated interaction with the environment, turns into a confrontation with the environment, fired by the forces of gravity. The key to this transformation is the irreversibility of the commitment towards a particular aspiration.

However, there is little doubt that consciousness units derive utility from some risk to existing structure set against some aspiration. Moving towards an aspiration in a methodical manner yields utility from structure formations but, also, taking risk and 'winning' is clearly another source of utility. For example a long-distance runner will achieve utility from cutting his marathon time, which is analytically separate from winning at *any* speed. There exists a complete range of tastes in this regard from Russian roulette players through to the most timid and risk averse. Here we are not interested in the range of possible cases except to acknowledge the coexistence of tastes for conflict in some measure as well as co-ordination. Social psychologists know well the distinction. Winning or domination yields an addictive 'high' in relative contrast to not winning. Steady achievement of creative objectives yields a steady flow of utility. Fromm distinguished these into 'having' and 'being' strategies. Religions and customs have long recognized that creative development involves discouragement of the former and promotion of the latter. The formation of macro-consciousnesses are designed, explicitly, to promote co-ordination.

The fact that macro-consciousnesses exist to facilitate co-ordination necessarily means that they exhibit a high degree of inertia, otherwise they would not constitute a reliable set of rules or conventions. Thus, as we have already argued, macro-consciousness is highly risk averse. Risk-taking is the province of micro-consciousness operating from secure, low risk macro-structure. It follows that when we are dealing with macro-phenomena we observe motional processes which are highly predictable and well structured. Solidified core structure is accompanied by peripheral structure which is fluid. As structural change proceeds, the solid core remains intact and the peripheral change either reinforces or undermines the core foundations. Macro-structure does not mutate smoothly but, rather, alters abruptly in the throes of crisis. This micro–macro interaction, whereby macro-structure remains inert while micro-foundations slowly slip away below, reflects a core–peripheral or hierarchical structural relationship in the economic system. By its very nature, as an integrated system of commitments, irreversible decisions and contracts, it must necessarily operate in this way. Only by ensuring a reliably ordered hierarchical set of consciousnesses can the risks associated with commitments be minimized and proper communication and co-ordination proceed.

We shall return to this theme more forcefully in the next chapter. In the meantime, the objective is to analyse the historical dynamics of such inertia/catastrophe processes for any consciousness unit in order to show that such dynamics are rational given the behavioural postulates set out in Chapter 7. The comparative statics in evolutionary short-run analysis, set out in Chapter 8, are useful to capture the essence of co-ordination behaviour. However, to track, empirically, real processes in historical time it is necessary to deal with actual dynamics. Even in our comparative statics it was acknowledged that developmental choice is heavily directed by precommitment and, indeed, it is this that often gives short-run comparative statics so much predictive power in certain historical phases of evolution. The Keynesian model was a good example, only slowly ground out of history by the forces of inertia.

Catastrophic collapse, frequent as it may be in history, is hard to predict in any instance, such is the complexity of dynamic structure. It is difficult to track the erosion of the underlying checks and balances in the face of external shocks. Yet post-mortems can reveal the logic of demise. It is not prediction of collapse that the evolutionary scientist is interested in but rather the provision of modifications, corrections, etc., which will prevent that unpredictable event and enable further evolution to proceed. The positivist sees macroeconomics as providing predictions to guide policy to keep the economy on its stable path. The evolutionary economist, on the other hand, sees the economy as tending, inevitably, towards ossifying inertia, requiring continual innovation to provide new structural feedbacks which break this inertia before it threatens the core of the system.[12]

The development of creative rules and conventions is an essential part of evolution in the sense that such developments in macro-consciousness translate uncertainty into quantifiable risk. The uncertainty involved in structural fragmentation is avoided and the uncertainty associated with new commitments is given quantifiable dimension. Keynes, in recognition of this, preferred to talk in terms of the 'degree of confidence' rather than risk and uncertainty. If we look on risk and uncertainty as being on a core–peripheral continuum of consciousness, Keynes was clearly more interested in shifts in the relativity between risk and uncertainty perceptions over historical time. The evolving firm wishes to assume investment risks as much through necessity as choice, because of historical commitment to a depreciating structure.[13] To do nothing is, thus, a non-neutral position. Waves of uncertainty reduce confidence, by curtailing the range of risk, while at the same time encouraging an attitude of defensiveness with regard to existing commitments. Thus, within our consciousness/structure relativity, instability of investment intentions would seem to be quite consistent with rational behaviour in the face of historical commitment.

In the discipline of marketing we observe how firms attempt continuously to develop and avoid crises by timely structuring and redevelopment exercises.[14] We also observe in firms the dramatic manner in which illiquidity leads to catastrophe and the high status that accountants hold as a result. In the hands of marketing with its forward perspective and accountants with their caution lie the checks and balances so necessary to a firm's evolution. Conventional neo-classical theory, typically, pays little attention to either the qualitative preoccupations of marketing, preferring to assume homogeneity of product, or of the liquidity fears of accountants, preferring to assume synchronization of payments and receipts, present-value calculations in the face of assessable risk, etc. In a Walrasian world such things are of little importance, but in one where evolution and co-ordination are at the centre of things they are vital. Let us now examine, in general terms, the historical time dynamic phases which are experienced by an evolving structure which adheres to our postulates in Chapter 7.

The Development Phase

In Chapter 7 our postulates depicted a world where a consciousness unit *U* attempts to maximize the degree of co-ordination within a set of constraints and opportunities imposed by 'higher' consciousnesses. All *U*s form commitments to particular structured paths and experience a developmental phase where learning and experience raises efficiency. In Chapter 8 we depicted the evolutionary short-run state without introducing actual historical time dynamics which are characterized by behavioural persistence, inertia and catastrophic abandonment. Although, methodologically we can mimic orthodox theory and envisage *U* operating on the margin, choosing the activity which yields the highest utility, once we are in historical time we must allow for the existence of history and the cumulative and irreversible commitments associated with it.[15]

One of the great truths of economics, which was derived from accountancy and has endured as a logical 'law', is the idea that 'bygones are bygones'. This 'law' was popularized by Alfred Marshall, in thoroughly non-Walrasian fashion, to model the firm's production behaviour in a real world of fluctuating prices and revenue. In textbooks, it is frequently used to demonstrate the marginalist proposition, yet it is a proposition which is much more about fixity, or commitment. Indeed, it is the latter that makes the problem tractible and easy for the student to comprehend. Once we move into the orthodox 'long run', the marginalist propositions become much more difficult to sustain and relate to everyday historical experience. The problem with this 'long run' is that the firm, typically, has to make discrete or lumpy investment decisions in the absence of the kind of information necessary to make the correct marginalist decision.

Clearly, the existence of history severely limits the scope for making substitutions on the strength of marginalist calculations. History itself is the binding constraint. Thus, all marginal decisions on the choice of motional activity should be cast within some defined 'commitment dimension'. In practice, what this means is that costs and benefits should be viewed in terms of sunk costs and cumulative benefits. More specifically, let us select a discrete example of co-ordination behaviour, for example, a construction project.

Any project will have some estimated value on completion EV_p. This estimate will normally be held with some probability in a risky world. Furthermore, the costs of completing the project will also be an estimate. Before embarking on a project, the extent to which accurate assessment of these costs and benefits is undertaken is critical. The more committing and discrete the project the more important this will be for, when the wheels begin to turn, it is difficult to go back. All co-ordination activity is discrete in historical time, what varies is the extent to which the path of project development yields retainable value. For example, a project called 'learning to play golf like Jack Nicklaus' can be abandoned with a retainable value such as a 'six handicap' golfer. On the other hand, a project called building a bridge may have no retainable value until it is complete.

Generally, following Scitovsky, we have depicted utility as deriving from the relativity of the tension of commitment and the aspirational goal. As historical time elapses, U will continue in a particular activity provided the expected completion value is greater than the expected costs to be incurred minus the expected net value involved in switching resources such as time and money to a different project. In Figure 9.1, EV_1 is the expected completion value of a discrete project, EC_1 is the expected costs to be incurred and C is the actual cost already incurred in the project at any point in time. Once the project is embarked upon it becomes increasingly attractive as construction proceeds since the net benefit of completion, $EV_1 - (EC_1 - \Sigma C)$, continually widens. Thus, in the later stages of the project, even if the completion value falls to EV_2, completion

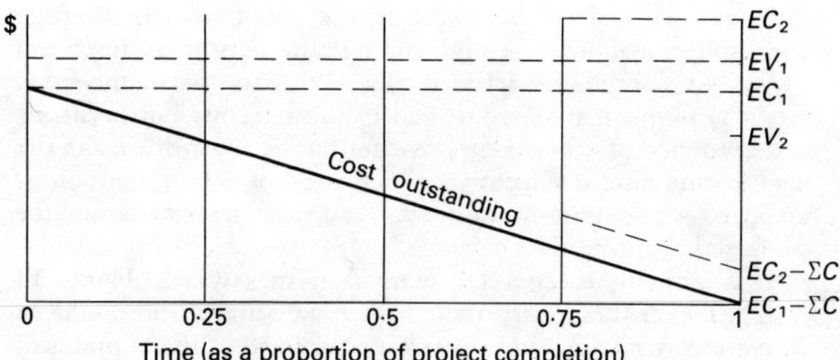

Figure 9.1 The locking in effect of sunk costs in discrete projects

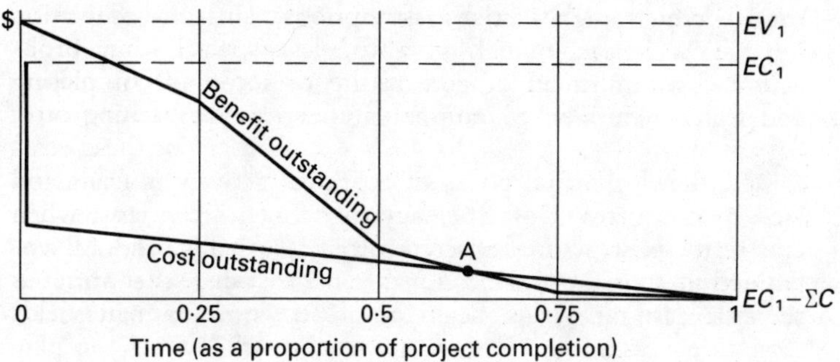

Figure 9.2 The locking in effect of set up costs in continuous projects

will be overwhelmingly worthwhile. Similarly, if costs escalate, say, to EC_2, completion will be rational.

Thus, the existence of commitment has a gravitational effect, concentrating activity by making the marginal decision weigh in a project's favour even when it is a loss-maker. The less discrete a project, of course, the weaker this gravitational effect will be.

In Figure 9.2 we have an aspiration EV_1 and an expected cost of achieving it EC_1, the bulk of which is initial outlay. As time passes, higher levels of achievement are attained leaving diminished EV outstanding. There comes a point A where the expected cost exceeds the expected benefit from continuing. It is important to note that in this case the 'locking in' comes from the existence of a commitment to initial fixed costs.

Bygones are, indeed, bygones but the initial cost ensures that the aspirational level is high enough to permit a significant period of continuous activity. The existence of membership fees has frequently been justified in these terms. Furthermore, the existence of set-up costs in continuous reward activities is also a switching disincentive which promotes the retention of achieved structured motion even when a switch would be preferred.

It is difficult to envisage many activities which do not fit into either of these categories. Either they are of the building-up variety with discrete rewards or they are of the continuous reward variety involving significant set-up commitment. Mixtures of both can, of course, exist but it is hard to envisage many activities where the extreme of no set-up commitment and continuous activity reward exists. Any behavioural model which makes such assumptions, such as the freely flexible Walrasian model, is a timeless special case. In all activity, commitment or contracting of some sort is present and leads, naturally, to rational preferences for continuity of behaviour.

The developmental phase of motional activity is characterized by the growth of efficiency in defined activities and the end result is structure. Discrete projects usually produce well defined material or organizational structure whereas continuous reward learning yields behavioural structure or patterning. Consciousnesses pursue developmental paths which end, in turn, in systematic behaviour accompanied by maintenance activity. Assumption A4 argued that we can envisage a kind of structural equilibrium where there exists a stable power base of structure and where conscious motional activity is concentrated on maintenance. This condition could also be seen as a state of inertia, with overall behaviour operating similarly from one period to another.[16] In historical time, structure should appear empirically stable, inviting equilibrium interpretations and propositions that shocks can be absorbed by the maintenance properties of the system in question, which is able to re-establish equilibrium. However, this empirical picture of stable equilibrium is not general because evolutionary systems which become inert move inexorably toward catastrophic adjustment. It is to the general properties of this phase of evolution in historical time that we now turn.

The Catastrophic Phase

When we are dealing with developed behavioural structures which are stable, again, the distinction between discrete and continuous motional structure has to be made. In general, continuous structures, e.g. riding a bicycle, once formed require little maintenance. In contrast, discrete structures which involve, not imprinted psychological patterns but rather physically constrained organizations of motions, e.g. the bicycle itself, require continuous maintenance. Such discrete structures constitute the summation of the intellectual qualities of their builders, whereas continuous structure involves existing intellectual quality. In general, the more rigid and inflexible the structure the more maintenance it requires. Furthermore, over historical time, maintenance costs will rise. Just as discrete structures do not exist until they are completely built, so they do not fade away, but rather, suddenly cease to exist. A car is created from its core to its periphery. In decline, a car can be maintained on its periphery but will suddenly cease to exist because of core breakdown.

Continuous structure, on the other hand, suffers a much lower incidence of deterioration given its much higher degree of flexibility and its disembodied characteristics. The ability to ride a bicycle can be retained for a lifetime. Ageing results in more cautious riding but this merely reflects peripheral adaptation of the skill to cope with the process of deterioration in physical, discrete structure. This core durability of such skill ensures that structured motion can be applied for long periods in a wide variety of situations and, thus, need not be regarded as inert. It is general skill compared with specific skill, for example. Of course, in the complex economic system, continuous and discrete structure is in continual interface. Discrete projects will be undertaken by firms who employ labour with general skills and, in turn, these general skills accumulate into discrete structures which deteriorate. Breakdown of discrete structures can limit the applicability of continuous structures, particularly when they have become closely bonded. In the structural hierarchy which is the economic system we see a two-way flow between the continuous, flexible periphery and the discrete, rigid core. Evolutionary potential depends on a delicate dialectic whereby change on the periphery only occurs given the security of the core while the necessary slow change in the core depends on feedback from the periphery. This two-way interaction is the essence of any evolutionary change. When core rigidity dominates then the system becomes oppressive and inert, whereas if peripheral flexibility is allowed to dominate then the system becomes chaotic in the absence of reliable information channels through the core.

As in the case of development, we can examine the conditions where inertia of a discrete structure results in catastrophic adjustment. If, for example, we take a familiar example, the family car, we observe that, typically, cars are owned for several years. Once the decision to purchase has been made on the rational expectation that the summation of use-value exceeds the price in some notional way, then bygones are bygones and we would expect the owner to continue to make the car part of his 'living structure' until the point was reached where the future expected depreciation (value + psychic) plus expected maintenance cost exceeded the same on a new car of some type. A 'catastrophic' switch would then occur even though the car provided exactly the same service as the day it was purchased.

A car is a structure bought and sold on well defined markets and all these micro-catastrophes can be aggregated into smooth demand curves. As exogenous factors lengthen and shorten the time of car holding so this is reflected in demand fluctuations. However, there exist discrete structures which are much more difficult to replace. For example, acquired economic power involves, not maintenance, but rather explicit defence. The absence of alternatives yields catastrophic results of the involuntary variety, as structure is breached by external events. Schumpeter laid great stress on such a process in his theory of creative destruction, depicting the rise and collapse of monopoly structures.[17] Indeed, the organizational structure we call the firm would seem to contain inherent inflexibilities which are quite marked. Once again, survival and evolution is very much the outcome of the two-way core–peripheral interaction discussed earlier. More recently, Bienkowski has also discussed the process in the context of bureaucratic power in planned economies.[18]

The example of the 'car catastrophe' emphasizes that the existence of a well organized co-ordinating system of prices, contracts, insurance and finance facilitates adjustment and prevents involuntary catastrophes. The evolution of discrete structures at all levels depends on the provision of such communicatory devices and on the ability of such devices, for example, in the form of law and custom, to alter over time. To take a trivial example, there is a rather poor resale market in pop-up toasters, despite their universal use in households. Consequently, the normal behavioural pattern is to await an involuntary catastrophe before replacing the toaster with a new one. Relative prices will play no role except in a post-catastrophe context.

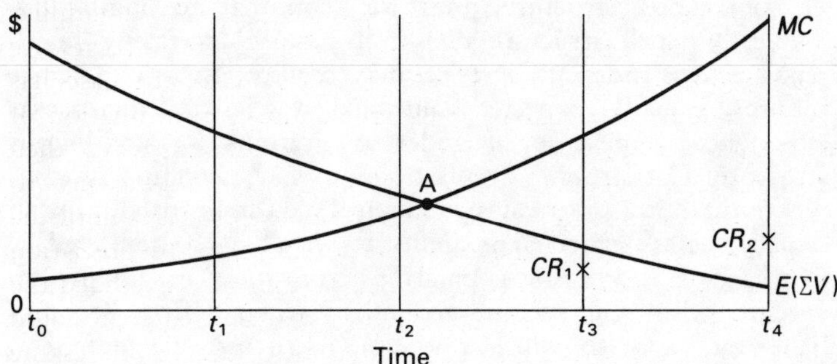

Figure 9.3 The rational basis of inertia and catastrophe in the history of discrete structure

In Figure 9.3 we have depicted a case of a discrete structure with no resale value, although such an assumption is unnecessary. After it is acquired, bygones are bygones and the structure will be used as long as it provides positive value. Maintenance costs *MC* are presumed to rise as the structure ages, and the flow of value to fall, so that the expected flow of value $E(\Sigma V)$ also falls. Clearly, the latter need not fall if full maintenance is undertaken. However, full maintenance costs would be sharply non-linear over time so the tendency is to restrict maintenance to critical areas to an increasing extent. For example, repairs to minor peripheral damage will not be undertaken, lowering maintenance costs but simultaneously reducing the flow of value. Eventually, the cut off point 'A' will be reached beyond which maintenance cost cannot be justified in terms of the expected remaining value of the structure and a 'repair strategy' is adopted. At t_3 the cost of a repair CR_1, is less than $E(\Sigma V)$ and it is undertaken. At t_4, CR_2 is greater than $E(\Sigma V)$ and the structure is scrapped.

What is noticeable about this inertia/catastrophe process is that although a structure performs its function one day and not the next there will be many sub-structural clues as to impending disaster. In well organized markets this qualitative information is reflected in rates of depreciation and other information about sub-characteristics of structures. In more specific structures other pressure gauges can always be found. In the case of the macro-system there exists a multitude of social and economic indicators to provide clues as to the health of macro-structure.

Continuous structure does not conform to Figure 9.3. Typically, such structure does not require increasing maintenance over time but, instead, may require less as experience mounts. Equally, expected value may not fall but increase as experience suggests even wider applications for continuous structure. Catastrophic events occur to such structure in cases where there is a prior catastrophe in the discrete structure with which it is associated. The ability to walk will be removed if, in an accident, a person is paralysed from the waist down. Job specific skills will become redundant when a firm becomes bankrupt, and so on. Continuous structure is peripheral structure, continually forming bonds which yield discrete structure in flexible ways. It is qualitative and operates subject to the rules set out by the core of the structure.

The intimacy of core and periphery, of discrete and continuous structure, is no better illustrated than in the case of the firm simply because these interactions have become central to accountancy practice. The firm contains a discrete core in the form of fixed costs and a continuous periphery which involves the particular skills of the firm in producing revenue. Some revenue flows into the core to sustain it and, in turn, the core provides the framework to produce further revenue on the periphery. The bankruptcy catastrophe occurs, not because the firm is not functioning as it did in the past, but because it has become illiquid. Financial claims cannot be met without selling the discrete core itself. The firm does not run down but ceases trading in dramatic fashion. It is commitment to discrete structure, combined with an imbalance in the essential two-way core–periphery flows, which ensures structural collapse through financial starvation. It is frequently the case that bankruptcy occurs not because the firm is unsuccessful but merely because of this imbalance, which is continually monitored through gearing ratios etc. Fortunately, the existence of contractualized financial resources, close monitoring of financial indicators and the existence of bankruptcy laws themselves minimize the extent of involuntary catastrophe. Take-overs, mergers, redundancies, plant closures, all offer soft options in many cases. Above all, the existence of a system of contracts enables proper liquidity flow planning in the face of illiquid commitments.

Hierarchies and History

The historical process that has been discussed has been concerned with the fact that the structure that we observe has two dimensions. At a point in time it will be hierarchically ordered to some degree and, over time, structure will exhibit enough continuity to constitute 'history'. U_1 and U_2, two consciousness units which rationally perceive advantage from co-ordinated motion, will form a bonded core while retaining different peripheral characteristics. The aspiration pursued draws asymmetrical commitment as development proceeds. The process of decline, on the other hand, involves inertia which derives directly from the asymmetrical nature of commitment. The structure remains but energy is diverted on the periphery in other directions. Structure is not dismantled, but rather, becomes redundant. The cumulative growth of structure driven on by aspirations or 'optimism' is replaced by the cumulative growth of discord driven by protectionism or 'pessimism'.

The co-operation of U_1 and U_2 cannot be analysed over historical time as simply the operation of self-interest, even though self-interest may have been the initiating force. As co-operation proceeds there comes into being a new consciousness U_1U_2 which has its own interests which, in the beginning, are so compatible with the separate interests of U_1 and U_2 as to make little difference. The process of decline is one where the interests of U_1U_2 become incompatible with the interests of U_1 and/or U_2. Instead of being the province of co-operation the U_1U_2 structure becomes subject to alien forces of U_1 and U_2 self-interest. This ensures a process of structural ossification and eventual fragmentation unless the source of the incompatibility of individual and group aspiration is removed by some kind of structural innovation. As history moves into internal conflict and towards ultimate structural catastrophe, we can observe the breakdown of the hierarchy that was established in U_1U_2.[19]

As has been discussed, there are many examples of these general dynamics of structures in the history of commercial enterprises, as analysed by authors such as Nelson and Winter,

Earl and Kay.[20] Clearly, particular histories will be contingent on the unique configuration of co-ordinations involved. At the macroeconomic level, such processes can be dealt with at a higher level of abstraction, since we are dealing with a core-consciousness shared by millions of personalities and a hierarchical structure which is necessarily rigid. However, the same maxims apply. Marcusian macro-consciousnesses form in their own right leading frequently to schizophrenic splits between an individual's 'own' interest and that of his macro-consciousness. The historical macro-dynamics in such situations tend to span long periods of time and lead to significant upheavals in society. Although such history is portrayed in political terms, the primary structural evolution involved is often economic. Economic power structures persist but non-economic power structures tend to be transient and are manifest in periods of crisis.[21]

The development of macroeconomics over the past half-century has made it much more explicit that macro-consciousness is primarily economic, binding the governmental core to the performance of macro-system indicators. In turn, governments have pursued innovations which could improve such performance. However, macro-economics itself has not reflected the evolutionary process of which it is a part. Evidence of discord on the periphery of macro-structure in the form of, for example, inflation has not been looked on as such. Instead of being viewed as the natural concomitant of evolutionary inertia it has been viewed, instead, as some kind of exogenous disease which, if cured, would reinstate some 'idealized' macro-structure. Clearly, the methodology of macroeconomics will have to change if economic evolution is to be properly understood.

Conclusion

In this chapter the assumptions imposed in Chapter 8 have all been relaxed allowing full rein to all the postulates in Chapter 7. The character of the evolutionary long run was discussed in a necessarily qualitative way for this long run cannot be predictable in any quantifiable sense; it is quantifiable only in the post-mortems of historians. However, it is possible to identify the kinds of qualitative interactions that give rise to this history. Co-ordinated motion extends from the power of existing structure, fuelling evolutionary development if it is flexible but precipitating conflict and oppression if it becomes rigid. The essence of evolutionary dynamics concerns the interplay of these phases of co-ordinated development and conflictual stagnation.

In the case of macro-structure this interplay extends over very long periods of time and, in order to illustrate these evolutionary dynamics, most of the examples taken in the chapter were of micro-consciousness situations where events occur much more quickly. The main message of these examples was the central role of commitment in determining much of short-run behaviour. All motional events proceed from discrete core-structure, which yields power, combined with continuous peripheral structure. How the relativity of the two varies over time will dictate the developmental or conflictual tendency of motional events. What we regard as a catastrophic event will depend greatly on the level of aggregation we choose and the time-scale over which such catastrophes are viewed.

It was also illustrated that, in a world of commitment, what is crucial for creativity and innovation in the short run is the extent to which macro-structure provides security in the evolutionary long run in terms of consistent rules and support systems. Thus, when we are dealing with a macro-economic system in evolutionary short runs that can be measured in decades rather than years, we know that commitments will render a significant degree of predictability to events. At the same time, we know that, if core macro-structure does not evolve enough, predictability will diminish. If it is allowed to change too drastically, once again, predictability will diminish. Sustaining macroeconomic evolution is something of a 'knife-edge' problem, yet events proceed slowly enough that it is quite feasible to identify a slide in one direction or another and correct it, provided there is a general political consensus to do so.

We discussed in Chapter 8 how Keynesian theory enabled governments to become good at preventing slides in one direction, by providing security to those taking on long-run commitments. However, Keynesian theory was insufficiently explicit about how governments would ultimately cope with slippage in the other direction when commitment formation slowed due to the natural onset of inertia in the evolving economic system. Instead of considered alterations of security and incentive systems so that they were directed at new areas of creativity and innovation, macroeconomic policy initiated discretionary rule changes that increased commitment-reducing instability. It is to this era of macroeconomic mismanagement that we now turn, applying our evolutionary perspective to shed light on how macroeconomic theory and policy must change before another phase of macroeconomic development can proceed.

Notes

1 See Boulding (1981).
2 See Schumpeter (1954) for his views on Keynes's model, taken from the perspective of a theorist unconstrained by the need to worry about actual policy-making in the short run.
3 See Simon (1984) for emphasis of this point.
4 See Pasinetti (1981) for an excellent example of a post-Keynesian model of structural change which has a thoroughly Keynesian short run.
5 The author of the term 'countervailing power', Galbraith (1952), in fact, provides an account of the evolution of consciousness and structure as well, placing him far ahead of the time that he wrote.
6 See Hirshman (1982).
7 See Sen (1977, 1982).
8 The Austrian view has been most closely associated with F. A. Von Hayek. See, for example, Hayek (1960, 1972). Barry (1979) provides a good overview of Hayek's philosophy. Kirzner (1979) and Littlechild (1978) provide a clear overview of the Austrian position. Hutchinson (1981) compares the Austrian approach to that of Keynesians and Marxists. It has a great deal in common with the views of Shackle (1972) in the area of expectations and the rejection of the quantifiability of uncertainty.
9 The evolutionary development of ethical and legal arrangements is discussed in Cooter and Kornhauser (1980) who focus, particularly, on the development of the common law.
10 See Arendt (1951).
11 The systematic nature of the onset of catastrophic situations has now become recognized in the applied mathematical modelling of 'catastrophe theory'. See Isnard and Zeeman (1976) for a review.
12 Some of the most original and vivid discussions of these historical processes is in Myrdal (1976) in the context of developing countries and their structural change.
13 To quote Simon: 'Inaction is the state that prevails when no positive action is being undertaken, and it is qualitatively different from action' (Simon, 1984, p. 53).
14 See Earl (1984) for an extended discussion of these processes in firms.

15 See Salter (1966) for an analysis of rationality in the face of commitment to particular technologies.
16 See Day (1984) for a discussion of Schumpeter's vision of equilibrium as a state of inertia. See Wagener and Drukker (1985) for signs of revival of interest in Schumpeter's method.
17 See Schumpeter (1934, 1950) for the development of his theory of creative destruction. Freeman (1982) discusses Schumpeterian and other theories of 'long' cycles.
18 See Bienkowski (1981).
19 See Berger and Piore (1980) for a good example of a segmentation method which builds explicitly on core–peripheral hierarchy and its dynamics. See also Piore (1979) for a more general statement of the structuralist/institutional view.
20 See Nelson and Winter (1982), Earl (1984) and Kay (1984).
21 Williamson (1975, 1979) sees the economic benefits of hierarchical organization in terms of transaction costs and related informational benefits. Most objections to hierarchical organizations arise when they become the vehicle of power rather than co-ordination and the suggestions of alternatives by, for example, Herbst (1976) amount to no more than improvements in periphery–periphery communications which rely less on the kind of core–periphery hierarchy which concentrates economic power. The theory of hierarchical systems has been developed most extensively in Mesarovic, Macko and Takahara (1970).

10 *An Evolutionary Framework for Macroeconomic Analysis*

> If one is a true simplifier and not just sloppy and lazy then one must be able to claim to arrive at essentials which are also to be found in what one regards as complicated.
>
> Frank Hahn (1983)

In the last three chapters an attempt has been made to outline a perspective on economic behaviour which is explicitly dynamic in contrast to that contained in the *homo economicus*/Walrasian vision of the economic system. This perspective was drawn from a wide variety of standpoints, within and beyond the limits of the economics discipline, and expressed in a set of postulates in Chapter 7. The behavioural characterization contained in these postulates is one of a consciousness which is 'individual' in the sense that there exist unique configurations of identifications with 'greater' consciousnesses. Such consciousnesses were conceived of as being hierarchical in nature with, for example, identification with the 'nation' or the 'economy' being a macro-consciousness shared by millions of people, or identification with the 'firm' constituting a micro-consciousness. Although 'firm' consciousnesses may be competitive, provided both are associated with a common macro-consciousness then such competitiveness is limited to certain agreed areas.

This representation of a hierarchy of consciousness implies that any kind of individual choice, such as economic choice, is simultaneously facilitated and restricted by 'higher' consciousness. Both security and freedom are derived from macro-consciousness. It follows, of course, that a symbiotic relationship exists between micro and macro. If a micro-consciousness becomes disassociated with a macro-consciousness then the latter will begin to lose its strength. In Chapter 8 the power hierarchy of consciousness was held constant in order to examine how visions of consciousness contained in Keynesian and neo-classical macroeconomics could be classified. It was concluded that both strands of macroeconomic thought contained static, non-hierarchical representations which were inappropriate for the analysis of historical time dynamics.

Although Keynes made a significant advance over the neo-classical abstractions of his time, his use of perception–action motional dynamics was restricted to situations of system correction. His adoption of the idea of macro-consciousness was confined to the belief that public servants could be trusted to act in the best interests of society and that an expectation could exist as a consensus or group phenomenon which was irreducibly macroeconomic in nature. Keynes argued most strongly the view that there was a macro-structure which displayed interdependencies which implied that it could not be dismantled smoothly. However, without some analysis of the determinants of macro-consciousness it was neither possible to explain why this macro-structure came to be or how it could change. This deficiency was widely pointed to in the postwar period not only by monetarists but also by, for example, James Tobin in his classic piece on the demand for money.[1]

Perhaps a more endemic flaw, in the sense that it still persists in the IS–LM textbooks of today, lies in Keynes's neglect of Dennis Robertson's point that net investment results in both a change in capacity and structure of the economy. Paradoxically, this 'flaw' remains, not because of blind loyalty to Keynes but because, in a Walrasian IS–LM model, which is a flow model, it is comparatively easy to 'dynamize' it into a Wicksellian-style expectational model which, in turn, fits well with a neo-classical growth model. In Chapter 3 we discussed how such developments have led to the demise of the principle of effective demand, which, in the context of the analysis here, represents the truly dynamic constituent of the Keynesian model.

In avoiding the evolutionary implications of investment, Keynes closed the door on the analysis of how consciousness solidifies into structure and laid himself open to subsequent charges by neo-classical economists that, in their terms, the Keynesian model lacked a 'supply side'. Neo-classical economists were quite justified in viewing the Keynesian model in terms of aggregate supply and demand for, as we have discussed, Keynes adopted the Marshallian habit of fixing supply to define the short run. In order to examine the dynamics of quantity demanded, prices were fixed so that income effects became the medium through which macroeconomic co-ordination is achieved. No wonder neo-classical economists dismissed such price-fixity as unreasonable in such a neo-classical framework and, furthermore, dismissed Keynes's claims that the future beyond the short run was intractible. Given the kind of stock–flow dichotomy adopted by Keynes it was simply not possible to extend his dynamic analysis beyond the short-run question of stabilizing existing economic structure. Investment involves a stock–flow overlap which cannot be grasped by an aggregate production function relating input flows to output flows through a fixed productive structure.

It has been argued in the last three chapters that evolution involves structural change which is a qualitative process. Analysis which takes structure as fixed cannot, by definition, deal with structural change. Relationships between inputs and outputs, summarized by production functions, cannot be stable in historical time as the productive structures that they caricature are created, move up experience curves, metamorphose into new structures or simply die. In translating consciousness into structure, *homo creativus* is, indeed, confronted by fixity *determined by historical commitment*, as discussed in Chapter 9, but such fixity is not constancy in the sense we would conceive of it in, say, physics because it demands *activity* to maintain it in the face of entropy. Thus it cannot be isolated from the creative process of structural change. The decisive feature of structural fixity is that it ensures that maintenance of existing structure and the creation of new structure will bear a relativistic relation to each other.

The purpose of this chapter is to build up the beginnings of an analytical framework which can augment Keynes's principle of effective demand, not by introducing a meaningless 'supply side', but rather by taking explicit account of the evolutionary dimension of the short-run macroeconomy. It is worth re-emphasizing that what we mean by the 'short run' is the evolutionary one defined in Chapter 8 where *consciousness* rather than structure is assumed to be fixed. The Marshallian definitions of short run and long run are of little use in a structurally changing economy, particularly when consciousnesses are not only aware that such change is going on but actively pursue it.

Levels of Consciousness

Keynes conducted his analysis at the level of the national economy, dividing flows of income and expenditure into convenient consciousnesses with individuals assuming, simultaneously, the roles of consumers, investors, savers, moneyholders, etc. The Keynesian problem was that communication problems between these consciousnesses arose resulting in underutilization of productive structure. As we have seen, Keynes's solution was to introduce a new macroeconomic consciousness, the stabilizing government, exercising discretion in its fiscal and monetary actions. The government was no longer to be a 'parental authority' only passing laws to protect citizens, to facilitate enterprise and to provide public goods through taxation. Representing the core of macroconsciousness in the economy it has the power to inject money into the economy, not simply by altering the money supply, a policy action which could be offset or distorted by the financial system, but rather through public works with a broad, decentralized effect on disposable incomes.

We are all familiar with the circular flow model which Keynes used to trace multiplier interactions in the real economy, and his delineation of consciousnesses is still universally accepted in macroeconomics. However, what is not widely recognized is that the action of each consciousness has a qualitatively different impact on productive structure. The standard IS–LM model homogenizes all multiplier impacts into a common monetary-valued impact so that it becomes a matter of indifference whether a fiscal or a monetary action is selected to stabilize the economy. Furthermore, divisions between, say, consumption expenditure and investment expenditure become arbitrary – the division between induced and autonomous expenditure comes to be viewed as a functionally more appropriate division. On the monetary side the same kind of argument has been applied – why distinguish moneyholding into different categories consistent with different consciousnesses?[2]

We saw in Chapter 3 how the distinctive structural features of Keynes's model were systematically broken down in the postwar period and, indeed, there was insufficient in his justifications to prevent this from happening. Keynes's reluctance to acknowledge Dennis Robertson's point that investment was, qualitatively, very different from consumption and his acceptance of Hicks's interpretation of the *General Theory* certainly did not help either. The structuralist perspective, far from becoming mainstream, was swept into the backwaters of economics. For a while it resided in the zone we could label long-run macroeconomics – in the work of, for example, Harrod, Kaldor and Kalecki – but, eventually, when interest in growth economics waned in the 1970s, the approach was banished to the special case subject of development economics where it came to be formalized by, for example, Taylor.[3]

It is paradoxical that economists agree, as they must, that structural change has taken place in past developmental history and will take place in future development, but isolating what the appropriate structure is for current theoretical analysis receives little attention. There is an illusion that, because the institutional structure we are confronted with seems to be fairly stable, we can ignore structural change. What is forgotten is that, over short periods, consciousness can alter significantly, contributing to either structural continuity or discontinuous structural change. In economic theory which, correctly, attempts to abstract from the morass of history, and is, therefore, primarily concerned with consciousness rather than structure, fixity of behavioural assumptions is almost universal.

Keynes carved up economic structure into pieces which corresponded to the key consciousnesses as he saw them in his time. It was a very crude breakdown, sufficient for the purpose of expositing the mechanics of stabilization policy. Today, the configuration of consciousnesses is different and so are the problems that economic structure confronts. Once again, in order to avert future crises in economic structure we must try to get the breakdown right.

We can begin by viewing Keynes's breakdown from a different perspective – from the perspective of the hierarchy of consciousness. In his *Treatise on Money*, Keynes made the interaction of the financial sector and the industrial sector central to his analysis of macroeconomic instability. The casino-like behaviour of the former was seen as inducing industrial firms to rely less on raising capital through extending share ownership and more through retention of profits and borrowing from the banking system which lay at the conservative end of the financial system. The traditional hierarchal relationship between ownership and control was breaking down. Speculation, instead of performing a stabilizing role, was increasingly prone to cause destabilization. Furthermore, with a lack of new issues, investors were turning their attention to speculation in government stock. Increasingly, there was slippage in the system where new money formed the basis of lending not to industry but to speculators, causing asset prices to spiral away from the levels consistent with the state of the real economy. The foolhardy could raise loans to buy from the wise in such spirals, with the latter reaping economic rents from their superior knowledge and the former inducing chains of bankruptcies in the wake of financial crashes.

After the Great Crash of 1929 the Anglo-American economic system entered a period of conservatism. Industry relied on self-financing and only short-term borrowing from the banks. Capital was available but the demand for loans could not match the flow of savings into 'safe assets'.[4] The schism between finance and industry resulted in conditions of depression which, Keynes argued in the *General Theory*, could be rectified by the government, uniquely placed at the top of the consciousness hierarchy, ensuring that national income be stabilized. The core of the economic structure would interact with the periphery – consuming wage labour – to provide macro-structural stability. Attempts to stimulate and control by acting through the financial sector would be abandoned. Deficit financing would ensure that real multiplier effects would occur and that there would be sufficient money available to meet liquidity needs. In the new industrial system, where income was vital for consumption and investment, the government could perform the stabilizing and informational function that the financial system could not.

The old system, where the economic structure was characterized by a core–peripheral set-up of finance–industry–labour, had faded. It was no longer the case that large firms were private, with ownership prior to management, that finance was dominated by *rentier* capital and that workers did not save. Savings flowed into the banking end of finance, and industry was increasing its demand for liquidity support in the banking sector while retaining profits for re-investment. The introduction of stabilizing government at the core of macro-consciousness had several effects. First, it stabilized the impact of expenditure fluctuations in the industrial sector, with reassuring repercussions on industrial consciousness. Second, increased borrowing from the financial market provided the stability that it needed to attract the new flows of worker savings through the emerging pension funds, insurance companies, etc. Speculation became more about anticipating open-market operations than what was going on in the real sector of the economy, which in turn was guided more by the stance of fiscal policy than anything else. The financial sector, with its increased emphasis on a borrowing rather than an ownership link with industry, became a partner which could raise borrowed money for large projects within both the private and public sectors. The existence of large financial institutions provided the backing for major industrial innovations.

Thus, the social innovation of government stabilization spawned the development of a sequence of major industrial innovations in the postwar period. The climate of macroeconomic stability, the availability of liquidity and large-scale lending from the savings institutions generated virtuous circles which raised the standard of living consistently. The core consciousness of government was a consensus, fitting well with the consciousness of finance and industry. Support on the periphery of the macro-system was also strong so long as the standard of living rose as promised. Political dispute tended to be confined to issues as to whether the public or private sectors were better suited to managing innovation and, of course, how the rising real income should be distributed.

By rearranging the Keynesian system into a hierarchy of consciousness we can see more clearly the way in which the macro-system has developed since the 1930s. The conventional Keynesian treatment of the macro-system as a flow of funds system cannot distinguish the levels of consciousness which are critical to the formation of economic structure. *Homo creativus* will engage in creative co-operation, for example, working for an organization, if there are identification links with such a structure. The organization will, in turn, identify with its industry and the industry with government and the economy. These lines of consciousness stretching from the core to the periphery of the economy are critical for economic co-ordination, providing commonly held beliefs which both inform and offer the security within which micro-consciousness can function effectively. Breakdowns in these hierarchical lines of consciousness herald the breakdown of the macro-system itself as micro-consciousnesses become alienated and form either neutral or conflictual relations with the, now oppressive, macro-consciousness.

We have identified, at the core of the complex macro-structure which exists, a macro-consciousness managed by the government. We have already argued that, being the 'highest' consciousness upon which the rest of the system depends, it is necessarily conservative and cautious. It resists the political whims of successive governments and has its heart in the civil service not in Parliament. Politicians will legislate and tinker around with policy modifications but, in general, the policy apparatus and the vision of the economy which accompanies it remains intact for long periods. However, it is not necessary to appeal, as Keynes tended to do, to public spiritedness to explain why the custodians of macro-consciousness uphold it so zealously. In return for their maintenance of this core power they receive economic rent, just as the police do as custodians of the law or the military as defenders of the nation. However, they are not idle recipients, engaging as they do in reinforcing bureaucratic rituals and overseeing the fiscal procedures that ensure the harvest of economic rent they are due.

In the Keynesian era, the public bureaucrat donned the mantle of stabilizer, in place of the financial market speculator of an earlier era. Each epoch has a class of non-earners who perform the task of reinforcing the belief system upon which the rest of the system depends. In feudal times it was the clerics, in the capitalist era the financial *rentiers* and in the Keynesian economy, the public bureaucrats. The important point to note is that, even though, as a group, they receive economic rent from their power, in a macro-sense their existence can raise the productivity of the whole system through the cohesion and certainty of belief that they foster. In this sense they are no different from the upper-stratum of management in a large corporation which is also engaged in seemingly esoteric activities for much of the time in exchange for large economic rents.

As we move from the periphery to the core of economic structures, the link between actual productivity and remuneration becomes more and more indirect. We move from productivity which is quantitative to that which is qualitative. Hierarchical lines of consciousness break down when micro-consciousnesses perceive management as using their power to extract economic rent at their expense. Most of the protests concerning the inefficiency of government in the economy reflect this kind of discontent, and it is no different in kind to the protests of serfs in the Middle Ages that feudal lords did not deserve their tithes or protests of workers in the nineteenth century that the owners of capital were expropriating surplus value. These core–peripheral crises in the hierarchy of consciousness affect all types of economic structures at all times and are instrumental in structural change.

Levels of Structure

In the second part of Chapter 4 a 'sketch' was made of the contractual economy to provide a broad basis for the analysis which followed. In the second part of Chapter 8, the principle of effective demand, which had constituted the intellectual basis for a social innovation in the earlier sketch, was deemed to be an incomplete vehicle for macroeconomic analysis further down the evolutionary path, in the 1980s. From the 'vague' and the 'incomplete' we will now attempt to provide a more concrete basis for macroeconomic analysis.

As macroeconomists we are interested in the behaviour of measurable economic aggregates. In practice, this involves the summation of monetary flows over defined periods or the summation of money-valued stocks at a point in time. In neoclassical macroeconomic equilibrium it is not necessary to make this distinction because the flows are structured in a manner that relates them intimately to stocks of, say, productive assets. However, in the real world of historical time, the dichotomy of stocks and flows has real meaning even though the margin between such concepts is distinctly fuzzy. Stocks relate to the core of macro-structure and flows to the periphery. In the Keynesian short run the core is rigid and quantifiable and the periphery involves flows of characteristics which are qualitatively diverse but aggregative through a common quality measure such as money-value.

The stock–flow dichotomy was made explicit by Keynes because he perceived that, in historical time, there are episodes where stocks are underutilized as flows diminish. Keynes perceived that the core–peripheral interdependence, discussed in Chapter 9, meant that the health and development of core productive structure, i.e. the capital stock, depended on peripheral buoyancy, i.e. in consumer expenditure. At the same time, he perceived that the latter could only remain buoyant in the security of stable development of the former. Thus, the principle of effective demand centres on this core–peripheral macro-interdependence with Keynes advocating stabilization policy to provide the necessary link between the two.

Keynes saw that the economic system had entered a period of pre-catastrophe inertia in the 1930s, with sub-macro catastrophes, such as the Great Crash and sequences of bankruptcies, providing evidence to support such a conclusion. The macro-core innovation suggested, although intended to rectify this evolutionary situation, did not spell out the manner in which the process of fresh evolutionary development would proceed. It was not a 'supply side' that was lacking but rather an evolutionary perspective beyond the immediate concern of avoiding crisis. The future was left, precariously, in the hands of the 'animal spirits' of investors.

The dynamic precariousness induced by investor behaviour was attributed to the fact that large amounts of investment expenditure is in the hands of a small number of economic agents, just as in the political arena entry into national conflict can be precipitated by a powerful political minority. The precariousness of such a situation was emphasized very early after Keynes's *General Theory*, in Roy Harrod's 'knife-edge' growth model.[5] However, the latter model is too narrow in its focus to capture the full set of checks and balances provided in the macro-system. In contrast, Hicks has argued that the fix-price sector of the economy, where most investment expenditure occurs, is rather stable relative to the flex-price sector.[6] In the dynamics of history the important message of Chapter 9 is that *both* situations can prevail in different phases of the evolutionary process.

There is a necessary relativity between the degree of commitment ahead through past investment and nervousness on the margin as to future investment decisions. The fix-price sector offers both stability and instability. 'Locking in' by commitment must be accompanied by serious conflictual tendencies when structure is threatened. This is a rational process which must operate in the core of any decision-making structure. Being rational we can suppose that it must be tractible in some sense, particularly at the highly aggregated macro-level. Post-Keynesian theorists such as Kalecki have approached the question of investment behaviour from the standpoint of a hierarchy which is characterized by imperfect competition or 'degrees of monopoly' and examined dynamic models associating investment with profitability.[7] However, such a hierarchical division is necessarily a spatial representation at a point in time, thus disqualifying the analysis from entering historical time in any predictable manner, unless changes in the 'degree of monopoly' can be tracked over time. Although Kalecki's dynamic analysis is superior to the comparative steady-state growth model proposed by Kaldor,[8] it continues to exhibit a general lack of dynamic predictiveness, so typical of cyclical models.

Although we can identify the methodology contained in the

post-Keynesian Kaldor-Kalecki (KK) approach as an acknowledgement of hierarchical arrangements within the macroeconomic system, this identification is not explicit. The KK approach links both to a Keynesian evolutionary short run and a neo-Marxist evolutionary long run, but is insufficiently general to provide the basis for a broader evolutionary approach within which various schools of evolutionary thought could debate from a consensus foundation. The principle of effective demand proved to be applicable to the analysis of several competing schools of macroeconomic thought, thus establishing its generality as a feature of the macro-system. The neo-Marxist long run, however, proved to be a narrow and deterministic path not accepted widely as a consensual starting point for dynamic analysis.

The principle of commitment in historical time, so central to Keynes's principle of effective demand, is lacking in KK models. Structured commitments do exist in the capitalist/worker distinction made, but in terms of assumptions imposed on the analysis. Full group commitment is assumed with no marginal slippage from one group to another or to a new group rising up from the evolutionary process. Once such dimension is provided, then an adjustment process through income distribution is proposed. Thus, the economic process is conceived of as the product of conflictual tension between the core (capitalists) and the periphery (workers). Commitment exists only in the 'static' sense of group allegiance in the income distribution struggle. No commitment between capitalist and worker exists to engage in productive activity.

Of course, in the real world of historical time, capitalists and workers enter into contractual arrangements to co-operate into the future. More often than not the 'industrial muscle' of the workers evolves, not from their prior solidarity, but rather from the commitment incurred by capitalists, in terms of capital goods and contractual commitments to provide goods. Equally, the 'exploitation' indulged in by capitalists need not be associated with any pre-meditated plan, but rather from the voluntary actions of workers contractualizing themselves into specific locations and specific skills. It is this process of historical commitment, through contractualization, that KK analysis lacks, yet is the source of prior creative economic behaviour.

At the cutting edge of time what we have are a stock of unexpired contracts and a flow of new contracts into the future. The stock can manifest itself in many forms. It can be discrete in the form of, say, capital goods, or it can be continuous in the form of agreement to provide flows of services of, say, labour. The postulates in Chapter 7 provide the basis for this continual ebb and flow of contractual activity in the general behavioural urge to match perception and action in ever higher degrees of co-ordination. Contractual overlaps between consciousnesses create new joint consciousnesses which are hierarchically prior to the originals. In turn, this prior consciousness can generate outputs of characteristics not possible before.

The macroeconomy that we attempt to measure in money values is the summation of all these flows of characteristics at the periphery of the macrosystem. As we travel inwards towards the macro-core we move from complex combinations of consciousnesses to simpler ones higher up the hierarchy. The consciousnesses we perceive are less 'individual' and more 'social'. As we make this progression, the contractual time scale becomes much longer and less explicitly defined but more rigid in construction. Thus, our massively complex macroeconomy pivots on a few fundamental structures embodied in the core of group consciousness. These revolve around laws, customs and ethics which, if destroyed, cause drastic reverberations in the quantifiable macroeconomy but, if extended, enable economic development to proceed.

It has been emphasized that consciousness and structure are relativistic in nature. The latter is merely the former when it becomes durable. In turn, what we mean by durable will depend very much at what level of aggregation we look at the economy. At the micro-level we can observe structures with macro-consciousness links which are in no sense rigid. If we then move to the macro-level we observe that macro-consciousness and structure are very discrete with the aggregation of peripheral micro-structures amounting to a flexible summation of consciousness which is ever-changing. From a hierarchical perspective, what is structure and what is consciousness depends greatly on whether we are looking upwards or downwards. Furthermore, the time-scale is also critical in the sense that time translates consciousness into structure – slowly at the macro-level but with great rapidity at the micro-level.

When we aggregate the valuations of quantifiable outputs of goods and services in the economy, qualitative dimensions tend to be missed. Activities in the realm of consciousness rather than 'productive' structure can receive zero valuation; for example, education and training is frequently viewed as a 'cost' which will yield future benefits, yet there is no attempt to assign a part of current output valuation to the credit of institutions of education and training. This view of a sector producing cumulations of quality tends to breed a related view that the sector is being supported on expropriated economic rents. In the case of more concrete capital investment, the measurement of output is restricted to expenditure on material, equipment and labour inputs. There is no attempt to impute value from the cumulation of qualitative structure. Once the project is complete and output flows, only then will the value of the structure register. Macroeconomic valuation does not coincide with the notions of productivity that project backers have. The *true* valuation of the investment project, in the construction phase, is the summation of surplus value over the life of the created structure. Of course, qualitative potential is difficult to measure but it is worse to omit it completely.

The other serious bias in macroeconomic productivity measures works in the opposite direction. There is no attempt to disentangle, from the valuation of output, real productivity versus the receipt of economic rents from the exercise of power. As we have emphasized, as Schumpeter did, that structure is created to yield economic rents, so those rents are not part of current productivity. Again disentanglement of economic rent from productivity valuation is difficult, particularly in an economy where rents accrue to power structures formed a long time ago, often through non-economic means.

The upshot of these two qualitative omissions from macromeasurement is underemphasis of the productivity of the creative in the unstructured zone of consciousness and the overemphasis of productivity in existing productive structure. Obsession with the measurable can lead to situations where a shift away from creativity towards the levying of 'unjustifiable' economic rents by one part of economic structure on another will not show up clearly in quantitative trend measures of productivity. Furthermore, it is precisely the economically unstructured who bear the brunt of attempts by economically structured groups to expropriate economic rent. The relative fortunes of coalminers and teachers in the German hyperinflation of 1920–3 provided a graphic illustration of such a process.[9] The process of inflation is, of course, a macroeconomic indicator which betrays the existence of struggles for economic rent just as growing unemployment reflects the pressures that result from lack of creative activity.

When we are considering what we mean by the creative

sector of the macroeconomy it is necessary to be somewhat arbitrary, for the economy is an organic whole with separable consciousness and structure in all parts of it. However, for the purposes of presenting a tractible analytical framework which could be of some policy relevance we can isolate two sectors where creativity is central. The first is in the capital goods industries which produce the innovative structures for the capital-intensive (or mass) production process. We can include a portion of education in this sector. This sector is all about the innovative skill of labour working outside or within productive organizations, including the mass producers themselves. Its quantitative counterpart is, of course, fixed investment. The second creative sector is in the labour-intensive service sector. This sector is not attempting to produce large quantities of homogeneous product but rather a vast array of heterogeneous services. Ingenuity is required to bring together materials, many provided by the mass-production process, and continuous skills to provide services which are predominantly short-lived, although some may attain mass-market status. Permanent structure is not much in evidence, as activities come and go. It is activity that may go unrecorded, like housewife services, because there is no transaction, or it may be in the 'black economy', partially or wholly. Education, again, must be included in this sector, providing many of the general skills upon which this sector depends.

Between these two creative sectors lies the mass-production sector in its highly structured form. Measured in terms of value of productivity, this sector completely dominates the others. It is composed of a highly specialized group engaged in production with wage labour at one end and management at the other. Traditionally, in economics, management and workers in productive structures have been depicted as adversaries. In the modern large corporation, which is largely independent of its owners in the traditional sense and very powerful, these groups have tended to form alliances to some degree or other. As Kenneth Galbraith and many others have emphasized, the sheer power of these organizations comes from their ability to mass produce at low unit cost and sell to a heavily conditioned public.[10] This type of organization has prospered and developed with great rapidity in the Keynesian era to such an extent that we now live not in a planned economy but rather in a few planned economies.

Marcuse, as we saw in Chapter 6, argued strongly that this sector projected materialist propaganda with such intensity that people became 'one-dimensional' in their consciousness, living in a world of rampant consumerism and working in low-creativity environments. Of course, the corollary is that the mass-production sector sucks in disposable income, leaving little for the traditional creative service sector. The latter declined, proportionately, in the Keynesian era. There remained of course, creative services to provide to the managerial minority who were immune from the compulsion to consume the mass-product. However, a great deal of surplus was channelled into investment in the creative capital sector to devise more sophisticated capital equipment to produce more output. Revolutionary product development was rarely the primary goal, merely replacement machines to produce more faster or to repackage and restyle the product more easily.

The provision of durables in the home, in agriculture, in distribution, and of processed foods not only raised productivity but it also hit the creative service sector hard.[11] One kind of employment was declining as another type, in mass products, in public services or in creative peripherals of mass-production, was increasing. Through the 1950s and the 1960s the structure of the economic system underwent a massive evolutionary change and, as structure changed, so did consciousness, as alertly perceived by Hirsch, Scitovsky, Fromm, *et al.* The consolidation of materialist consciousness in production and consumption was, of course, accompanied by its antithesis, not only in the writings of the popular philosophers, but also in the restructuring efforts of those wishing to provide an alternative consciousness. Ecologistic, anti-materialist consciousness, formed in the late 1960s, became pockets of alter-consciousness in the 1970s.

This economically enriching trend was hardly recognized as such by the orthodox materialist consciousness running through society. To 'opt out' was a loss of production and consumption potential. The enriched diversity of lifestyles, of handmade products and the regeneration of ecological disaster areas received no weight in macro-measures. At best, only the craft sales of the more commercially inclined, rather than self-help structures, have been picked up. Just as much of the economic growth of the postwar era constituted the progressive 'commercialization' of services which had gone unmeasured in the past, so the re-emergence of a consciously directed, non-materialist, service economy has been increasingly ignored by the data we have. Our indicators are very good at tracking inflation of prices but very poor in reflecting structural change.

The materialist consciousness has, at its centre, the idea that the 'wealth that matters' is that generated by the mass-production sector. Although this was challenged a long time ago in, for example, Vance Packard's *The Wastemakers* and in Kenneth Galbraith's *The Affluent Society*, it has persisted through the influence of the economic measures that we equate with economic well-being. As the size of manufacturing employment has shrunk relative to that in services, the implications of this measurement error has become more and more serious. Furthermore, the qualitative shift which has accompanied this change is not recorded, namely, the increasing production of mass-produced equipment specifically designed to aid the increasingly complex service sector. Microcomputers, high-tech tools and pre-processed materials all offer flexible inputs into this new type of labour-intensive activity.

The idea that the mass-productive sector is the source of true wealth is a static vision, for the ongoing increase in productivity is attributable to the creative design of new productive equipment which saves labour, energy and raises productive potential. At any point in time it seems that productive structure is all important yet it is the creative consciousness of the capital goods industries that dictates the future. Furthermore, advances in information and communications enable the creative industries to market directly to the new service sector.

Confronting these changes in macroeconomics demands a breakdown of aggregates which delineates clearly the creative sectors of the economy. To do so involves explicit acknowledgement of the evolutionary dynamics of human structure in Figure 7.4 in Chapter 7, suitably modified to relate to existing aggregates in Keynesian macroeconomics.

An Evolutionary Taxonomy of the Macroeconomy

We have argued that Keynes offered a 'fixed structure' model and any attempt to 'evolutionize' his model must logically begin with investment, which reflects the creativity input into manufacturing industry and, to a lesser extent, service industries. Not all investment is necessarily creative; some falls into the category of maintenance. For example, investment in inventories is a maintenance activity and payment for repairs and replacement parts is also in that category. Furthermore, a portion of investment can be classified as 'defensive' in order to protect economic quasi-rents. Product re-designs, packaging and new advertising expenditure can also fall into such a category. The closer we get to the production line the more investment expenditure tends to be maintenance. The further away we go, the more we are in the 'end-zone' of consciousness, in 'pure' research and in the innovations of small firms outside the mainstream of manufacturing. There has been a great deal of contention throughout the history of industrial economics about where such lines should be drawn. There is no doubt that it is true that there have been examples of large firms buying up or simply squashing small-firm innovators, and there have also been studies that suggest that large-firm research departments are often engaged in resistance to disruptive innovations.[12]

It is an impossible task to assess just how much investment falls into the creative and maintenance categories but, in a qualitative sense, we can accept the distinction. Wherever we turn, pitfalls exist in attempting to associate a particular set of data with a certain type of dynamic behaviour. However, a good guide to whether or not creative investing is going on in manufacturing industry is the rate of increase in productivity. If this is slowing while investment expenditure is rising we can be sure that much of it is being channelled into maintenance or 'protectionist' activity and little into fundamental innovation. We do not observe, in the modern economy, large monopolistic firms restricting output to maximize profits. What we do observe is massive expenditure on activity intended to preserve or increase 'market share'.

Productivity is not increased significantly either by replacing obsolete products with the updated models, i.e. through qualitative change, or through the rapid replacement of old equipment with new equipment to produce the same product, i.e. through quantitative change. Although such maintenance activity generates employment in managerial functions, the rate at which the assembly line worker is liberated from repetitive tasks is slowed, as is the rate of flow of genuinely new goods and services to the consumer. The maintenance-conscious large firm induces not an actual excess capacity but rather an underutilization of creative potential in the innovative sector of producer services.

Although it is natural for the economist to identify creativity with investment in the macroeconomy, there is a tendency to ignore creativity in the consumption component of aggregate expenditure. The provision of goods and services on the periphery of the macroeconomy is popularly viewed as a labour-intensive area which has exhibited low productivity growth.[13] However, this is a serious misunderstanding borne of a homogeneous view of products. Typically, the service sector does not seek to invest in capital goods to reduce labour, but rather to extend the quality and range of service offered. For example, 'fast food' tends to be relatively capital intensive but has increased employment because of increased demand for the product as a substitute for home-produced food. Increased diversity of services is a form of productivity growth which can easily escape our conventional methods of assessing productivity. Furthermore, as the service sector induces switches away from domestic, non-monetized activity such as food processing, so the availability of time for other activities increases. The ability of the consumer to engage in more leisure, creativity and social interaction is, once again, a form of productivity growth not adequately captured in money valued measures.

In order to clarify the distinctions we have been making, a breakdown of the macroeconomy can be presented which, in a simple way, captures the essence of the argument. In Figure 10.1 we have a circular flow diagram where income and expenditure have been divided into three categories: production, maintenance and creativity. The income of consciousnesses grouped in each category will depend on expenditure which, in turn, flows from total income. Creativity depends on saving to provide the protection necessary to generate new structure. Maintenance of existing structure relies on 'tithes'. These need not necessarily be taxes in the conventional sense but rather a whole range of expenses and insurances that are paid by all structures.

All the conventional aggregates in Keynesian expenditure definitions contain all three of these types, furthermore there is a vast range of non-monetized activities which will flow unmeasured through this taxonomy. In common with the Keynesian definitions, consciousness is not aligned with individuals. Typically all individuals will have all three. In a hierarchical sense, dividing consciousnesses in this way provides a more coherent micro–macro binding. Innovations in macro-creativity will tend to have 'knock-on' effects on micro-creativity – confidence and optimism feed from the core to the

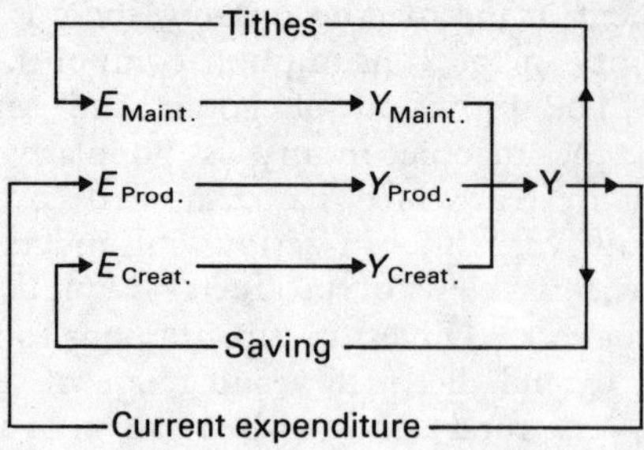

Figure 10.1 The circular flow of income from an evolutionary perspective

periphery of the macro-system. Equally, a tendency for over-protectionism to exist in the macro-conciousness will soon lead to a similar attitude on the periphery. The core–peripheral interactions of consciousnesses are relativistic. For example, the social creativity embodied in stabilization policy sparked off a sustained period of micro-creativity in the postwar period, but when 'state paternalism' became over-maintenance, it began to reverse these micro-creativity trends.

The taxonomy in Figure 10.1 constitutes a specific expression of the dynamic perception–action framework in Figure 8.5 in Chapter 8. Expenditure and income flows involving production in Figure 10.1 constitute the pivotal point in Figure 8.5 which captures existing structure. Income and expenditure on creativity reflects activity in the *PA* zone of Figure 8.5 and maintenance involves defensive activity in the *SF* zone of Figure 8.5. The economic structure which yields product is continually subject to entropy, mitigated by maintenance and sidestepped by creativity. The balance of consciousness between creativity and maintenance is critical for the ongoing evolution of economic structure. Too much expenditure on maintenance diminishes flows into creativity so that an ageing economic structure has to bear the increasing demands of managerial activity. Equally, too much expenditure on creativity is likely to disrupt production, while management is neglected, resulting in chaos and confusion in the macro-system.

It is to examine such dynamics that the taxonomy in Figure 10.1 has been devised. However, in order to do so we shall have to set the flows more firmly in the context of historical time. Both creativity and maintenance can be long term or short term with regard to the length of commitment involved. At the core of the macro-system they tend to be long term and, on the periphery, short term. It is to such considerations that we shall turn in the next chapter.

Conclusion

In this chapter we have attempted to provide a vision of the macroeconomy which is evolutionary in character. Although it is well known that investment expenditure is the focus of the developmental tendencies of the macroeconomy, the stock–flow dichotomization contained in the short-run Keynesian model precludes a proper integration of a development dimension. In order to capture this dynamic dimension it has been argued that the conventional method of disaggregating expenditure flows requires revision. The natural taxonomy, suitable for macroeconomic analysis in an evolutionary context, is a split into creative, productive and maintenance components. It is the interplay of these three types of activity which determine evolutionary tendencies and, even a crude disaggregation into such categories, would be more enlightening. Furthermore, the theory of effective demand can be exposited just as much in these categories as in the conventional Keynesian categories.

Another critical change required in any evolutionary evaluation of the macroeconomy is in the manner in which qualitative output is measured. The tendency to undervalue creative activity by not imputing future returns, in the form of quasi-rents, understates the contribution of creativity and overstates the contribution of production and maintenance activity. Also, the tendency to ignore increases in qualitative diversity as a form of productivity growth, particularly in the service sector, is an omission of growing importance as the service sector grows relative to manufacturing. Furthermore, the increasing popularity of 'do-it-yourself' services, not adequately recorded in transactions, requires attention in an economy which is becoming increasingly decentralized because of advances in information technology. Once again, there is a danger that the productivity contribution of such developments will be seriously understated.

Thus, the Keynesian income–expenditure method of valuing economic activity has become obsolete in a spatial sense – increasingly overstating goods and understating services –

and in a temporal sense – increasingly unable to capture the evolutionary development of the modern economy. The problem with such a conclusion is that it means that the data that we have militate against solving the evolutionary conundrums of the postwar era. However, in the next chapter, which looks back over this era, it will be argued that things are not so hopeless as they seem.

Notes

1 See Tobin (1958).
2 This homogenizing process was, as we have already noted, advanced speedily by the monetarists in the Keynesian era. It was convenient in an empirical sense to do so. Simon rejects strongly their empirical approach to macroeconomic behaviour: 'As Leontief and Orcutt, among others, have pointed out, the idea of validating economic theories with aggregative data is a will-o'-the-wisp that has led econometrics down the garden path of ever more sophisticated statistical methodologies' (Simon, 1984, p. 40).
3 See Harrod (1948), Kaldor (1955), Kalecki (1937) and Taylor (1983).
4 See Moss (1984) for a development of the finance versus industrial capital approach updated by a modern theory of the firm and connected to macroeconomic issues. See, also, Minsky (1980, 1982) for another approach in this tradition.
5 See Harrod (1948, 1973).
6 See Hicks (1974).
7 See Sawyer (1982) for further discussion of Kalecki's model.
8 See Kaldor (1955) for his seminal piece and see Blatt (1983) for discussion of its potential for tracking historical time dynamics.
9 See Besciani-Turroni (1937).
10 See Galbraith (1972).
11 See Gershuny and Miles (1983) for an extended discussion of the changing nature of the service sector in the postwar period.
12 See Earl (1984) for examples.
13 See Gershuny and Miles (1983) for an example.

11 *The Evolution of the Mixed Economy*

> Public policies may reflect not changes in objective conditions but shifts in values, or understandings.
>
> Richard Nelson and Sidney Winter (1982)

The productive structure that we perceive at any point in historical time has a commitment dimension into the future. This is observable in the expected life of economic structures and in the contracts made beyond the present. The value of money, for example, depends critically on this commitment to the future since money is no more than IOUs which stand or fall on belief as to ability to repay. In a technical sense, contracts are not essential to productive activity since it is possible to conceive of continuous auction markets doing the same job. However, auction markets can make production planning more difficult, making it rational to use contracts to ensure continuity, with stocks taking up unanticipated shocks. Much of the conventional contractual literature reviewed in Chapter 4 dealt with situations where contracts are justified in this sense.

However, the area where contracts are essential is in creative activity. Creating structure requires loans and other support to see the project through, as discussed in Chapter 9. Although the auction market can cope with the future in the case of homogeneous commodities, it is not possible in the case of brand new economic structures producing a heterogeneous variety of new goods and services. In the Keynesian model, flows of savings finance creative investment, but the current nature of the model does not capture the reality that flows of saving must be guaranteed into the future before they are of use for a substantial investment project. Short-term saving, such as liquid bank deposits, can be lent long term because of the aggregate characteristics of deposit holding but, none the less, offer a qualitatively different kind of loan to that financed by long-term savings. The key criteria in bank-lending is the availability of a tangible asset as security, thus, much of bank-lending is 'conservative', financing liquidity and the purchase of existing assets. By its very nature, bank-lending will often finance maintenance rather than creativity.

The purpose of this chapter is to use the taxonomy developed in Chapter 10 to provide an analytical framework within which the evolutionary dynamics of the macroeconomy can be discussed. With this logic, the implications for the interrelationships of the conventional macro-variables that we observe will be outlined. In the second part of the chapter the implications for empirical methodology will be explored in a preliminary manner.

Macro-innovation – The Virtuous Circle

The Great Depression was a period of idle capacity. It was also an era of 'protectionism'. In terms of our taxonomy, the emphasis was on defensive maintenance and the absence of creative risk-taking. Entropy gradually eliminated obsolete economic structure, leaving an economy with a large excess capacity of labour. Whether stabilization policy alone could have rectified this situation very quickly remains a moot point because macro-consciousness and macro-structure were transformed by the onset of a war economy. Important innovations in the chemical and electrical industries occurred and the macroeconomies of all the advanced nations emerged from the war on an entirely different footing to that which had existed before. We have already noted that Keynes himself underestimated the success of stabilization policy, but he was looking at a 1930s economy which had an idle capital stock which was also, to a worrying extent, an obsolete capital stock. The postwar economy, which Keynes had barely time to glimpse, was so different not so much in structure but in consciousness that all things were possible.[1] This climate ensured that technological advances in the war could be harnessed into creative developments. Furthermore, in the years following the war, even though state intervention in the economy was controversial, there was no doubt in any investor's mind that the state would be a supportive and stabilizing influence.

Thus, this implicit contract that the state formed with the rest of the economy forged a new macro-consciousness which resulted in contractual confidence and the gradual development, from core to periphery, of creative activity. Labour released by this process was absorbed by the public service sector and the administrative functions of large firms to such an extent that there was an excess demand for labour even into the early 1960s. Productivity growth in the rapidly concentrating mass-production sector yielded enough surplus to meet this increased maintenance burden. The macroeconomy was moving up an experience curve which involved increased large-scale management and planning in the public and private sectors, accompanied by productivity growth in the form of new products and services and more capital-intensive production techniques. Furthermore, this process did not require the pre-existence of savings. The authorities could meet liquidity and credit needs by creating new money – IOUs which held their value because of a general belief that stimulation was associated with economic growth. Monetary policy was 'accommodating'.

In terms of Figure 10.1 in Chapter 10, bureaucratization of the macroeconomy yielded levels of creative expenditure which could generate sufficient income to absorb production, as well as support maintenance activities. Such was the esteem of the new bureaucrats, planning at the centre of things, that they themselves secured long-term contracts to maintain the continuity of planning. There was a sociological revolution where, for example, the social services took over what the family had previously provided and the small-scale retail sector was swept away in favour of supermarkets. Individuals were less and less dealing with each other on the periphery of the economy and more and more with the large bureaucracies and their products. The social and ecological minuses in this development were, however, not set against the rate of economic growth.[2] The macro-consciousness vision of 'progress' was held almost universally.

The virtuous circle, at least in strictly economic terms, has been described as one of reaping the benefits of bureaucratization, planning and stabilization in the corporate sector and the public sector. It is seen as a system of economic management which, for the economy as a whole, enabled progress to occur up an experience curve for a long time. But how can we capture, simply, these dynamics in terms of money valued flows in our Figure 10.1 taxonomy? To do so we must give these flows both a monetary and a time dimension.

Figure 10.1 depicted the following in any period t:

$$Y_p = E_p \tag{1}$$

$$Y_m = E_m \tag{2}$$

$$Y_c = E_c \tag{3}$$

$$Y_p + Y_m + Y_c = Y \tag{4}$$

$$Y = S + T + E_p \tag{5}$$

$$Y_c = S \tag{6}$$

$$Y_m = T \tag{7}$$

where:

p = production,
m = maintenance,
c = creativity.

If we let X_p denote real current output of all goods and services which constitute current consumption and all the variables in our identities are also defined in real terms, then:

$$Y_{pt} = X_{pt} = E_{pt} \tag{8}$$

Furthermore, in the absence of maintenance or creative development $X_p = \bar{X}_p$ and $\bar{X}_p$ would be subject to systematic degeneration over time:

$$\bar{X}_{pt} = a\bar{X}^{b}{}_{pt-1} \tag{9}$$

where $0<a<1$ and $0<b<1$.

This process releases resources to provide the foundation of creative development. In the macroeconomy this constitutes unemployed variable inputs, such as labour, second-hand equipment and scrap materials. These are not, however, used without the support of creative activity.[3] Creative activity does not add to *current* production but to *future* production so that in any time period productivity rises due to *past* creative activity. Thus, there will be long 'innovation lags'. Furthermore, the existence of experience curves will mean that productivity growth will be spread over several periods so that there will be a distributed-lag relationship between ΔX_{pt}, the flow of 'new productivity' and E_c:

$$\Delta X_{pt} = f(E_{ct-1}, E_{ct-2}, \ldots, E_{ct-n}) \tag{10}$$

However, this relationship will only hold provided that there is adequate effective demand, i.e. E_{pt}, to cover $\bar{X}_{pt} + \Delta X_{pt}$. If it is inadequate then there will be idle new capacity and/or an increase in the rate of entropy in old capacity. Despite the fact that inadequate demand generates unemployment, naive, Thatcher-style economics welcomes the destruction of old capacity and the release of resources for more productive activity. However, the blunt instrument of expenditure cuts is not so discriminating, affecting new capacity and the will to create new capacity in ways that can ensure that many idle resources will not be taken up.

The availability of resources to support creative activity and, therefore, future productivity growth comes from saving. Resources released by entropic degeneration, in the form of previous production and maintenance expenditure, may vanish from productive structure with matching cuts in income. No additional financial resources are available and they may even be reduced. In such circumstances, as Keynes emphasized, the brakes are applied to creative development through postponement of new projects, etc., to try to offset the flow of new capacity in the pipeline of contractual obligations. This commitment is relatively large, compared with the 'theoretical' end of the creative process, so the cuts borne by the latter can be very severe. Thus we have the paradox, widely observed in Thatcher's Britain, of an increased rate of entropic decay in old structure being associated with cutbacks in several areas of creative development of new structure.

As the flows of E_{ct} in eq. 10 diminish, then so does productivity growth in the future. The necessity of maintaining effective demand to facilitate creative development and a rate of entropic decay which is slow enough to, in some crude sense, match this development is as important as ever. However, we know that this task is more difficult than it was in the past, and in order to see why, we must consider the role of maintenance in our income–expenditure flows.

What maintenance does, whether at the macro-level, in stabilization policy, or at the micro-level of the individual, is to slow down the entropy rate. Its ability to do so tends to be non-linearly related to expenditure (E_{m}):

$$a^{\star} - a = dE_{\mathrm{m}}^{c} \qquad (11)$$

where $a^{\star}$ is the improved rate of entropic degeneration, with an upper limit of unity and with $0<e<1$. The inter-temporal problem which arises is that maintenance expenditure draws expenditure away from creativity when it is practised to an excessive degree. Although it may be possible to compensate for past deficiencies in creativity, this can only be done at the expense of current creativity. The choice of a maintenance-led rather than a creativity-led strategy will be made by consciousness units that have established power which they seek to reinforce in the face of insecurity concerning any kind of strong commitment to risky, creative ventures. Fear concerning the future state of aggregate demand will be an important factor in generating such a strategy, leading to increased use of resources for maintenance by the powerful, and welfare losses amongst both the highly creative, and those employed in unprotected, decaying productive structure.

The Great Depression can be looked on as such an era, with lack of macro-security resulting in a maintenance consciousness, leading to high unemployment and a lack of creative investment. There was no shortage of saving relative to creative demands, but the bulk of it was channelled into low risk and short-term investments. In order to see this clearly it is necessary to recognize, explicitly, the importance of contractual length when flows of expenditure are directed into creative activity. Short-term saving is highly liquid and held mainly in the banking system for maintenance rather than creative purposes. This saving is normally termed 'money' to distinguish its relative liquidity. However, the banking system, relying on the aggregate characteristics of deposits, is able to lend longer term provided that there is tangible security to back the loan. What this means is that high-risk creative activity is not supported to any significant extent. Liquidity support and loans for the purchase of existing assets are the main focus of banking business.

Similarly, borrowers can be divided into long term and short term. Once again, what constitutes short term is not so much the nature of the asset, but its *marketability*. So, a house-purchaser is a short-term borrower in the sense that it is fairly easy to liquidate and pay off a loan. Of course, there is always a fallacy of composition in such definitions as, for example, banks have discovered when there has been a serious 'run' on their deposits. Long-term borrowing occurs when market value remains well below the borrowed amount for significant periods of time. Contracts of this type involve risk but not the fallacy of composition problem, since what is created is a new and unique structure which is not widely held. The resultant structure may turn out to have no economic value because there is no demand for the output flows generated, but that is not due to a fallacy of composition but rather a misperception of future co-ordination possibilities.

As Keynes argued, the problem in the Great Depression was liquidity preference – the preference for short term and safe, over long term and risky. Thus, it is necessary to divide saving into two categories:

$$S = E_c + E_{ms} \qquad (12)$$

E_{ms} constitutes saving used to stabilize against fluctuations, to pay for repairs and to maintain and strengthen existing structure. Unlike T, which is transfer income, E_{ms} generates contractual claims but, unlike E_c, relies on increased valuation of *existing* structure to cover repayment. The Great Depression was an era where macro-consciousness precluded very much creative initiative, either on the side of investment or saving. There was no significant mismatch between the two, which would have been reflected in the path of variables such as interest rates. This was no more clearly in evidence than in the case of business savings which were carefully channelled into safe rather than risky projects.

The postwar Keynesian era was very different, with deficit finance channelling savings into public-sector developments of a long-term nature with increases in the money stock generating IOUs which could provide the necessary finance of liquidity by the banking system. Income was generated to stimulate production and funds were made available for creative developments. Provided stabilization policy could extend the level of creative activity into the future, then anticipations of productivity growth would ensure that monetary expansion would not be inflationary. The social innovation of stabilization policy introduced a dimension of macro-consciousness which involved an implicit contract whereby the government could issue *unbacked* debt, i.e. money, in return for the creative act of providing stabilizing cover for macro-structure. Of course, such an arrangement could never be formalized and relied on a system of belief embedded in macro-consciousness. However, the principle is the same as in any act of creativity: IOUs are issued on the promise that repayments are made when structure is created. Thus, the government could erase its budget deficits from enhanced tax revenue from a more productive economic structure.

An essential prerequisite of the success of such monetary expansion was the parallel intervention of government in the creative process – supporting education, aiding private investment and developing infrastructure. In this sense, monetary expansion was truly accommodating and quite different to the attempts at 'monetary policy only' stabilization that had been criticized so much in the past by quantity theorists. It is in this context that the Radcliffe view has been so badly misunderstood. None the less, in the early postwar period, when rising creativity had not yet shown itself in productivity growth, there was, indeed, a danger of inflation. The rationing regime which persisted until the mid 1950s and resulted in forced saving was, undoubtedly, a factor which prevented inflationary pressure and permitted productivity growth to 'catch up' with creativity. However, the rates of productivity growth experienced by both the UK and the US settled down to lower levels than in those countries with a more explicit industrial policy.

The value of money has been depicted as depending on the state of macro-consciousness about the contractual future of macro-structure. Money itself is held for maintenance purposes to provide a cushion against unanticipated liquidity fluctuations. It is essential that productivity growth and creativity are not handicapped by shortages of liquidity. However, if macro-consciousness is, instead, preoccupied by protective maintenance, money will be used to increase or hold power. It will be used to finance speculations in existing structure in ways that have varied throughout evolutionary history: to facilitate stock price speculation, to finance property speculation or to increase the power of a particular political or economic group. There is no unique process whereby money changes from the indicator of strength in economic structure to the vehicle on which its weaknesses are accentuated. However, it remains the key indicator of the ongoing state of macro-consciousness.

Upward movements in prices offer a clear indication of increased maintenance activity in the economic system and to the onset of economic decline. In the Great Depression prices did not rise but, instead, fell slowly. However, we cannot separate the experience of the 1930s from that of the 1920s. The latter decade was characterized by a wide variety of price rises, indicating a widespread maintenance consciousness which inhibited creativity. The productive potential in the 1930s was lowered and economic conditions were generated where the rate of entropy was so high and the availability of 'loose' credit so restricted that maintaining power through price movements was no longer feasible.

Inflationary conditions generally signal the end of an expansionary period and are less in evidence once decline and depression has set in. The game of musical chairs that inflation reflects is over and the power mould is set until more serious, non-economic struggles begin. In the postwar era, these processes have been more protracted and we have seen inflation and unemployment overlap in a manner almost unprecedented in historical experience. It is to that qualitatively different era that we now turn.[4]

Macro-maintenance – The Invisible Plateau

The notion that maintenance activity can divert resources away from creative activity is, of course, a familiar idea and has appeared in many guises: the Treasury View of the 1930s, the Bacon and Eltis thesis and the crowding-out hypothesis. Here, however, the divisions that we have chosen are not the familiar ones in macroeconomics. On the contrary, government spending has been identified, in part, with some fundamental creative developments and private investment expenditure has been seen as frequently concerned with maintenance rather than creativity. Furthermore, a distinction has been made between saving for maintenance purposes and saving for creativity, i.e. money and credit have been divided qualitatively rather than quantitatively. The monetary sector of the macroeconomy is viewed as very much about consciousness rather than structure, rendering attempts to classify, say, Keynesianism and monetarism in terms of the degree of verticality of an LM or an IS curve unenlightening.

Money derives its value from the structure which it represents. If macro-consciousness perceives that economic structure will generate output flows into the future then the monetary assets which represent that structure will have value. However, if it is perceived that lack of creativity and over-maintenance exists then the value of money will fall. The quantity theory of money may not hold at full employment, yet it could do so below full employment – it all depends on the state of macro-consciousness. An economy which exhibits a contractual profile which suggests future increases in productivity growth will not be much concerned with controlling monetary growth. On the other hand, an economy which has become 'static', with a shortening contractual profile, will be one where monetary expansion will be perceived as fuelling positional maintenance and generating inflation. There is no reason why structural unemployment should not exist in such an economy. It is interesting to consider the 'classic' episode of hyperinflation of 1920–3 in the Weimar Republic.[5] Inflation ruled out any possibility of long contracts to facilitate creative activity so that there existed a 'boom' period of production and maintenance, quickly followed, at monetary reform, by high unemployment. No serious monetarist has claimed that monetary control could have had such a rapid and large impact within a conventional quantity theory model. However, if we, instead, view it as an economy concerned with positional maintenance rather than creativity, fuelled by monetary expansion, we can see why post-hyperinflationary unemployment was so serious.

The possibility that increases in maintenance at the expense of creativity can both raise productivity and employment, albeit in an unsustainable evolutionary sense, is attractive for a politically desperate government. It has the monetary means to stimulate and to permit a redistributive process in favour of a preferred group. Furthermore, it can ride on the back of any past creative activity yielding current productivity growth. The clearest depictions of such processes have been drawn from Latin American modern history when the ravages of political expediency have been both rapid and dramatic. However, such processes are much less easy to track in advanced economies such as the US and the UK. Political business cycles and electorally convenient stop–go episodes have been identified in the Keynesian era, but only on the margin of the Keynesian consensus.

The Keynesian consensus represented the core of macro-consciousness and it is the erosion of that which is of interest in an evolutionary sense. Already, in the early chapters of this book, the rise and decline of the Keynesian consensus was tracked. However, such changes are much more difficult to discern in the history of economic structure itself than in the history of ideas. The way in which we have chosen to record macro-data makes it very difficult to observe structural slippage. What we have is a set of macro-aggregates which ill-fit the kinds of maintenance-production-creativity divisions that we have made here while, at the same time, there are some measures that offer limited insights into the changes taking place. Inflation and unemployment rates are obvious examples of the latter. With such poorly defined data, only long retrospective views are capable of identifying evolutionary trends leading up to abrupt and clearly observed catastrophic changes in the economy. The history of ideas offers clues but, again, only in the negative sense of 'growing disquiet' rather than anything concrete, given the ever-present data problem.

It is difficult to say precisely when in the 1960s the benefits of the macro-innovation of stabilization policy began to run out in the UK and the US. As we have emphasized, it would have been impossible to say at the time, for nothing would seem to have changed. It would be easy to point to the incoming Labour government of 1965 with its substantial expansion of spending on public services and infrastructural projects or, in the US, to the free-spending Kennedy–Johnston administration's similar policy. Shifts away from emphasis on creativity towards maintenance were undoubtedly reflected in these political events, but they were certainly not viewed in these terms at the time and it wasn't until well into the 1970s before Bacon and Eltis pointed to the 'burden' of public service expansion. Furthermore, as we have emphasized, the productivity effects of such shifts are both very slow and complex.

At some point, over-maintenance began to exist in the economy, hidden behind the macro-data. It could not be detected in aggregate employment data, for jobs had altered qualitatively not quantitatively. There were more jobs in maintenance and less in creativity, but the shift didn't much affect measures of value-added. Thus, money-valued economic growth did not indicate much change in this trend. The ongoing debate was not one about over-maintenance and under-creativity but rather one about the merits of private sector versus the public sector. By the end of the 1960s the invisible plateau that the macro-economy was on began to be betrayed by statistics on inflation, unemployment and the balance of payments, although they were not looked on as such at the time.

The shifts of employment into maintenance activity, primarily in the public sector, played havoc with relativities, thus initiating an inflationary process where the large manufacturing sector had the power to award productivity-related wage increases and pass on any other 'positional' increases in the form of price rises. In the public sector, maintenance and creative workers had to negotiate comparable increases through strenuous collective bargaining. In general, those engaged in maintenance could defend their relative incomes because of their disruptive potential, while the creative sector suffered because of lack of political leverage. From the late 1960s onwards, these tendencies became more marked, resulting in inflationary spirals backed by monetary expansion. The latter gradually became less about accommodation of productivity growth and more about accommodation of power struggles.

The availability of liquidity to facilitate the inflationary process meant that it was still possible to have savings going into creative activity, unlike the inter-war years. There was no shortage of savings on offer, often at very attractive negative real rates of interest. Neither could there be the old fears concerning aggregate demand, which the government was always anxious to control.[6] Bureaucratization, both in the public and private sectors, began to stifle rather than facilitate evolution. The exercise of power was increasingly preferred to innovation in order to enhance and protect relative status. British management became infamous for its reluctance to be innovative, the trade union movement, with its bureaucratic rule-books, became known for its resistance to change and, of course, the public sector bureaucracy was as weighed down with 'red-tape' as any other in the world. The 'centralism' around which the Keynesian consensus was built began to obstruct creative development. The successful use of power to obtain material gains began to sap the morale of the productive, on the periphery of the macro-system and, of course, reduced emphasis on creative activity closed up previously available mobility hierarchies.

The sharpness which had characterized the shift from the 1920s maintenance economy to the 1930s depression economy was not present in the postwar economy. The invisible plateau contained an overlap of inflation, yielded by power struggles, and unemployment, due to the entropy process. Productivity rose, but not by enough to provide the economic surplus necessary to generate enough new employment. Powerful bureaucracies did very well but the unskilled and the creative did not prosper.

The 1970s witnessed a curtailment of creativity which was even more drastic than productivity growth figures suggest. Domestic capital goods industries were in severe decline with large manufacturers as well as consumers switching to imported durables. Before the flow of North Sea oil in the UK case, this trend resulted in increasing balance of trade deficits. Thus, capital–labour substitution could proceed in manufacturing industry, releasing labour with nowhere to go once the flow towards maintenance activity had stopped in the public and private sectors. Gradually, from the beginning of the 1970s, began a secular rise in unemployment due to a mixture of rising capital intensity and entropy in manufacturing. Of course, unemployment itself involves an automatic maintenance burden on the macroeconomy which necessarily begins to debilitate the public sector's ability to promote creativity.[7] Rising public sector deficits in a sluggish economy lead naturally to 'housekeeping' policies which establish a vicious circle of creativity loss.

Even though 'deindustrialization' had led to dramatic declines in creativity in the provision of producer services to and by the capital goods industries over the past twenty years, the service sector as a whole has continued to expand. As long as durable goods could be imported, expansion of consumer services could proceed on the periphery of the macroeconomy, thus employment loss has been mitigated particularly in 'female' occupations. The capital intensity revolution in the provision of household services has proceeded rapidly as well as in the leisure service industry (video recorders, home micros, etc.). Also, the diversity of consumer services offered has increased, although to a lesser extent in the UK than the US. Increasingly, the UK has taken on the character of a primary resource country such as Australia with the benefits of resources being spread directly through the consumer service sector. Oil and the ownership of international financial capital constitute the dominant 'resources' in modern Britain.[8]

The success of the service sector as an employer in the UK and the US has encouraged some to look to the service sector for future development.[9] And, as we have seen, this emphasis is, indeed, correct but with one qualification: consumer services alone are not enough. The ongoing creative development of productivity enhancing producer services to manufacturing, suitably translated into durable goods and services, is essential to balanced development. If we look at economies which lack the latter, we see that their fortunes change sharply in the wake of resource demand fluctuations. New Zealand and Australia come to mind as examples of resource-based locations with well developed consumer services. Both have gone through periods of fast economic growth, by conventional measures, only to find that it could not be sustained.

The UK macroeconomy has been on an invisible plateau with increasing resources being switched to maintenance of power structures, generating both inflation and unemployment. The money backed power struggles of the early 1970s gave way to a shift in government policy in favour of financial capital with monetary control, cuts in public sector creativity, and high real rates of return on financial assets. Structural unemployment began to rise much more sharply, as did income inequality between the centres of bureaucratic power and the less powerful. Beneath an illusion of economic growth, the structure of the macroeconomy became ever more intense and vulnerable to catastrophic events in oil and international financial markets. Although many elements of Keynesian stabilization policy continued to operate, macro-consciousness had, rationally, come to espouse the belief that crude Keynesian expansionism would do little more than fuel yet another inflationary power struggle.

All these evolutionary shifts cannot be captured in conventional measures of economic growth.[10] High levels of maintenance, supported by oil and financial power, count as productivity along with peripheral and ephemeral consumer services, while fundamental creative producer services have disappeared without adequate measurement. In a high maintenance economy, managers and bureaucrats of all types hold increasing power as the links between creativity and rewards are broken. The economic rents that they earn from their informational and communications monopoly are not counted as such. Our macroeconomic statistics cannot capture the creativity and productivity sapping effect of such shifts in power.

If it was possible, even roughly, to separate expenditure and income into the maintenance, production and creativity divisions suggested in our income/expenditure equations, then we could track this evolutionary process much better. Furthermore, if we could relate the degree of forward contracting to future increases in productivity growth then we could have some predictive basis for assessing the progress of 'aggregate supply'. In other words, we could forge a link between consciousness and structure and explore the nature of perception and action fusions that have been most successful and, thus, to be encouraged by macroeconomic policy. Beneath the quantitative study of the interactions of our three types of expenditure and their relationship to the constraints of past commitment and future plans, a considerable amount of qualitative evaluation of structural change is necessary to 'fix' quantitative analysis in the unique context of a particular historical epoch.

Evolutionary Modelling

It has been argued up to this point that current presentations of macroeconomic data do not provide a very useful way of tracking the evolution of economic structure or the manner in which economic consciousness, in the form of contract formation, translates into structure. The proposition that we do not know about the evolution of the macroeconomy could be countered by the defence that there exist macroeconometric models of great complexity which are very good at predicting the macroeconomy. The underlying methodology of such models and their constituent equations is termed as 'disequilibrium dynamic'. In other words, they contain long-run equilibrium solutions and, when shocks are imposed, there is a disequilibrium adjustment process towards a new equilibrium.[11]

Since the development of rational expectations in macroeconomics, this approach has come under something of an attack, both in terms of how these models are constructed and how policy impacts are viewed as working through them. In essence, critics argue that if there is some degree of rationality, which need not be 'complete' in any sense, then prior views about where a variable will settle down at a new equilibrium will hasten the adjustment of the variable to its future value. In the context of policy shocks, such views are capable of nullifying the intention of a policy almost immediately.[12] This has led to the view that using fixed parameters plus disequilibrium modelling is inappropriate and that an equilibrium scheme with varying parameters is a preferred starting point for modelling in an information-rich, expectation forming macroeconomy.[13] The problem with this approach is, however, that it encounters as much difficulty in modelling expectational processes as the Keynesian approach has in modelling disequilibrium dynamics.[14] Invariably, rational expectation modellers have resorted to the same methodology as Keynesian disequilibrium modellers – they have used statistically-based modelling procedures in the absence of any economic knowledge concerning expectation formation.[15]

As was emphasized in Chapter 4, the forward-looking dimension of the rational expectations approach has to be applauded, but in terms of our vision of the macroeconomy here, little advance has been made. If Keynesian modelling took an 'over-structured', unconscious view, then rational expectational modelling has taken too rigid a view of consciousness with too little cognizance of structure.[16] However, given the kind of macroeconomic aggregates that modellers have had to deal with, there has been little choice but to take the approaches that they did. Equally, the three-sector model discussed here cannot be made to match the aggregate data. However, is there anything that we can do, within the confines of existing data, to offer a methodology which could get us closer to our evolutionary ideal?

First of all, the separation of expectations and adjustments that forms the basis of many of the differences between empirical schools should be recognized for what it is: an unacceptable causal division of consciousness into a perception/action sequence which results in, and depends upon, fixity of economic structure. In its place we must have a non-equilibrium vision of consciousness forming into structure through the accumulation of perceptional knowledge and the acquisition of active skills.[17] In many ways, this process is already reflected in the macroeconometric models that we have but is not recognized as such.

If we set expectational and adjustment rationalizations aside, we observe that macroeconometric models are driven, not by their economic relations but by their autoregressive structure. This structure is widely regarded as something to 'remove' to get to hidden long-run parameters. However, our analysis here suggests that the existence of an evolving structure and contractual consciousness implies that this autoregressiveness is, in fact, the most important confirmation of economic behaviour.[18] All structure will necessarily have a future flow of commitments which will guarantee that, say, 90% of activity tomorrow will be the same as today. Furthermore, at any point in time there will exist a contractual structure in historical time. Suppose that the average contractual period is five years, then in any year we know that 80% of activity is precommitted. For example, strong autoregressive properties have been observed in the case of investment, with its necessarily long contractual horizons. Equally, of course, this autoregressive pattern has not been particularly stable. This is to be expected when the interplay of structural commitment and confidence results in rapid fluctuations in the formation of investment contracts as projects are deferred and shorter projects suddenly preferred to longer ones.[19]

We do not tend to observe such instability in productive structure itself because, once in place, there is every incentive to be as productive as possible. Consequently, what we should see in productive structure is experience curve effects operating when structure is expanding and accelerating rates of decay when structure is contracting.[20] So, once again, we should not observe a constant autoregressive relationship over time when we are investigating macro-variables such as GDP. However, we would expect to observe systematic parametric shifts over time. What kind of empirical methodology can we use to capture the proximate effects of evolutionary processes at work in the macroeconomy?

We can provide a simple framework within which such processes could be more easily discussed. Suppose

$$X_t = X_{t-1} - Z_{t-1} + W_t \tag{13}$$

where:

X_t = the output of characteristics flow from X-structure in period t;
Z_{t-1} = that part of X_t which is lost because of entropy or ephemeral effects;
W_t = that part of X-structure which is new because of creativity or, again, emphemeral effects (this was ΔX_t in earlier equations).

We can assume that emphemeral effects are random so that:

$$Z_{t-1} = \bar{Z}_{t-1} + z \tag{14}$$

$$W_t = \bar{W}_t + w \tag{15}$$

$$\mathrm{X_t} = X_{t-1} - \bar{Z}_{t-1} + \bar{W}_t + (z + w) \tag{16}$$

We have argued that $\bar{Z}_{t-1}$ will be dependent on the 'life' of productive structure at any point in time. As the mean residual life of productive structure shortens, because of a lack of creative development, then $\bar{Z}_{t-1}$ will rise as a proportion of X_t, as expressed in eq. 16. We have also argued that $\bar{Z}_{t-1}$ can be lessened by increased maintenance expenditure at the expense of $\bar{W}$ in the future. $\bar{W}_t$ is productivity growth, which is the fruits of past creativity and resultant experience or learning effects over historical time. Its relationship with the past will depend on the mean length of contracts. It will be stable in a situation of long contracts but, as mean contractual length shortens, it will tend towards current expenditure on creativity, which is a volatile variable.

It is not our purpose here to develop formally the dynamics

of the creativity/maintenance interaction, but to explore what the possibility of such dynamics imply for the kinds of macro-relationships we conventionally deal with. In a period of innovatory activity we should observe $X_t > X_{t-1}$, i.e. sustained productivity growth due to the spread of innovative benefits. The mobilization of labour and materials will be such that this productivity growth will be difficult to explain solely by conventional inputs into an aggregate production function. This phenomenon was widely observed in studies of economic growth in the 1950s and 1960s.[21] However, in 'short-run' Keynesian studies this empirical observation was viewed differently. Typically, we observe the following construction in the literature:

$$X_t = aX_{t-1}^{b} + f(\ldots\ldots) + (\text{error}) \tag{17}$$

X_{t-1} is related to X_t non-linearly for the 'disequilibrium' or 'expectational' reasons. In terms of eq. 16, it is predominantly $\bar{Z}_{t-1}$ effects that are being picked up. On the other hand, f(. . . . .) contains vectors of prices, etc. This time it is $\bar{W}_t$ effects which are being approximated. Another procedure favoured in structural equations is:

$$X_t = f(\ldots\ldots, Y_t) + (\text{error}) \tag{18}$$

A lagged dependent variable is not included but rather a 'higher' variable such as real income (Y_t) entered non-linearly. Up until the early 1970s such specifications did very well in US and UK studies, such was the structural harmony prevailing in these macro-systems. Afterwards, it became increasingly necessary to introduce X_{t-1} in some '*ad hoc*' way to generate any kind of 'meaningful' result.

By the 1970s the days of harmonious economic development and virtuous circles was over. Productivity growth was slowing down and over-maintenance was being reflected in indicators such as inflation and interest rates.[22] Both these variables betrayed a shift in macro-consciousness towards maintenance of structure. And, much more steadily, lack of creativity was ageing productive structure, allowing entropy to operate in a manner which was raising unemployment and worsening the balance of trade. Of course, none of this could be picked up in conventional specifications, due to the omission of $\bar{Z}_{t-1}$ and the misunderstanding of $\bar{W}_t$ with its contractualized bond with future productivity. The plateau that the macro-economy was on was not recognized, with macroeconometric modellers preferring merely to complicate lag structures to fit time-series data, regularly revising these for forecasting purposes. The crucial shift away from creativity to maintenance which was evidenced in inflation rates, interest rates, unemployment rates and exchange rates was not captured by these macro-modellers.

We have argued that one of the main reasons that macro-modellers have found it so difficult to deal with structural change is the way they choose to split up the macro-system for analysis. In a Keynesian model, maintenance expenditure is recorded as part of production just as much as creative expenditure. Unemployment is viewed as about *generalized* excess supply, not the decay of productive structure, and inflation is seen as about *generalized* excess demand, not about over-maintenance and positional behaviour.[23] Furthermore, when the specific cause of the supply problem has been addressed, a particular group has been seen as the source of the problem, e.g. poor investment by businessmen or monopolistic practices amongst trade unions. The same applies to specific studies of excess demand: too much profit-taking by large firms or excessive push by trade unions. Thus, such studies are necessarily fragmented from the main thrust of macro-analysis in a way that treating such problems as problems in macro-consciousness cannot be.[24]

However, this does lead to the conclusion that it is difficult to make very much progress using conventional macro-econometrics. A first step might be the adoption of the new evolutionary modelling methodologies which deal with systematic parametric shift, but, without a fundamental regrouping of the macro-data dealt with, it is likely that this approach can be informative only to a limited extent. In economics, technique is prone to run ahead of data development. For example, it would appear much more informative and useful to develop data concerning the contractual patterns that exist, say, in investment expenditure, so that the degree of commitment could be predicted, than to apply a battery of varying parameter tests to the 'horizonless' data that we already have.

Providing a contractual dimension to economic data would help us to chart the manner in which the macro-system solidifies in expansion and fragments in stagnation. The lengthening of contractual periods in the core of the macro-system leads to co-ordination towards the periphery and, equally, shortening leads to fragmentation of co-ordination. The variation of contractual length and the association with inflation,[25] requires data which can be used to test hypothesis concerning the core–peripheral processes of structural formation and breakdown.

However, it takes many years to develop new types of data and even more years to generate enough observations for scientific enquiry. Economic policy cannot wait that long and must rely, as Keynes did, on the application of systems logic.[26] The dynamic logic that has been presented here does point to structural deficiencies which could be rectified by economic policy. It is with possible rectifications that the next chapter is concerned.

Conclusion

This chapter has been concerned with presenting an analytical framework of the macroeconomy which could be usefully employed to capture evolutionary dynamics. No attempt has been made to formalize the interactive dynamics discussed, only the main dynamic principle has been emphasized. It is an evolutionary principle which applies to the macro-system as much as any other ecological system. An essential balance between creativity and maintenance must exist otherwise the macro-system will become so 'petrified' that it will suffer catastrophic change. We have attempted to set out a few simple equations which, if clothed with appropriate data, could help us to track these structural changes and, hopefully, provide us with an understanding that would enable us to avert catastrophes.

Even in the absence of quantification of our evolutionary scheme, it has been argued that the evolutionary approach taken provides a new interpretation of the nature of the macroeconomist's two favourite variables: inflation and unemployment. Both are manifestations of evolutionary changes in the heart of macro-structure. Their coincidence in the 1970s reflects the tendency for maintenance to be prior to creativity, slowing productivity growth and raising unemployment. This overlap contrasts with the past, particularly the sequence of inflation, then unemployment, in the 1920s and 1930s when there existed no forces of Keynesian stabilization to provide a 'validation' route for the tithes of those involved in maintenance. However, it is clear that this validation process, and the resultant overlap of inflation and unemployment, avoided the sharpness of the shift from growth to depression experienced in that earlier period.

In the 1980s, people came to view monetary growth and excessive government spending growth with suspicion, a point emphasized by monetarists and new Classical economists. Yet it is misleading for the latter to suggest that only foolishness or lack of anticipation could result in people believing that monetary and fiscal policy could have real effects. The evolutionary approach argues that it will depend on the evolutionary stage of the economic system. In the 1950s and 1960s people had an optimistic view of monetary and fiscal expansion which was justified by economic events, just as the pessimism of the 1970s and 1980s is justified by changed evolutionary circumstances. *Homo creativus* places his rationality in an evolutionary context whereas *homo economicus* has a static rationality. Furthermore, there is no sleight of hand in the way that we get from individual rationality to the macroeconomic level with *homo creativus*. It is the formation of commonly held macro-consciousness and how it shifts in waves of optimism and pessimism that dictates the macroeconomic results.

This view of the economic system tends to turn the way we view macroeconomics upside down. Instead of building up from micro-foundations, macro-economic behaviour is seen as, in part, the outcome of shared macro-consciousness. What we observe at the macroeconomic level is synchronized behaviour down through a hierarchy of complementary macro- and micro-consciousnesses. As macro-consciousness and related macro-structure become obsolete this hierarchy fragments into non-co-operative cells which concentrate on maintenance rather than creativity. This is reflected in the breakdown in the pattern of macroeconomic indicators that were previously synchronous in their movement. Thus creativity withers from core to periphery and can only be revived by a radical shift in macro-consciousness. However, proper characterizations of such interplays and how they are reflected in the breakdown of econometric relationships require a great deal of further study, as well as the development of more appropriate empirical methods and data disaggregations to understand such evolutionary processes.

In the latter part of the chapter, the inadequacies of conventional macroeconometrics for this purpose was discussed briefly. Given the distance of what is being suggested here from empirical reality, no more than a speculative few words about current empirical methods seemed necessary. Although the possibilities of obtaining appropriate data are real, the thrust of the evolutionary argument is one of logic rather than empirical verification. Structural change in an evolutionary process will never be strictly verifiable by the kinds of statistical techniques that we have. It follows that policy prescriptions for facilitating evolution will have to depend more on the application of logic than hypothesis testing, logic not just of why the evolutionary patterns of the past existed but also logic as to how *homo creativus*, in his macro and micro dimensions, will respond to new innovations in macro-economic policy.

Notes

1 See Carabelli (1985) for a view of Keynes's thought which emphasizes consciousness and the possibilities of converting consciousness into new structure.

2 It wasn't until the late 1960s that the costs of economic growth became widely discussed. See, in particular, Mishan's (1969) challenge to orthodox views of progress at that time.

3 It is important to emphasize the hierarchical nature of these substitutions. An unemployed labourer will not be able to become a designer of computerized information systems. The essence of the process is one of sequential promotions towards creative functions which opens up vacancies at the bottom of the hierarchy. The high status of creative activity and upward mobility towards it was normal in the 1950s and 1960s boom.

4 See Glyn (1982) for a Marxist view of postwar economic development and slow-down which builds on Mandel's (1975) classic work and contrasts with the analysis here.

5 See Bresciani-Turroni (1937).

6 See the Wilson Committee Report (1980).

7 Kregel (1983) argues, convincingly, that postwar Keynesian policy laid too much emphasis on the provision of security-enhancing maintenance and too little on the promotion of investment in both the public and private sectors. Thus, public sector deficits are seen as an inevitable consequence.

8 It is these two factors which largely determine international expectations concerning the value of sterling in the mid 1980s.

9 See Gershuny and Miles (1983) and Bauer and Sammelson (1981).

10 See Giersch and Wolter (1983) for a discussion of some of the problems involved in modelling acceleration–deceleration explanations of postwar economic development. For a long-run perspective on shifts in productivity growth, see Maddison (1979).

11 In recent times the Cambridge Economic Policy Group have been the only macroeconometric modellers who have tried to escape

from this approach (see Lawson, 1982). Paradoxically, they lost their Social Science Research Council funding on the grounds that their work was methodologically unsound!

12 See Lucas (1976) for the classic exposition of this critique.

13 See Lucas and Sargent (1981).

14 See Leamer (1983) and Sims (1980) for some discussion of these difficulties.

15 To quote Simon: 'The ponderousness of contemporary econometric techniques simply crushes the fragile data to which they are applied' (Simon, 1984, p. 40).

16 Hahn puts it a little more strongly. New Classical 'empirical' economists, such as Barro, who use rational expectations . . . 'have become advocates of a Panglossian view of the world which in its silliness has not often been surpassed in our subject. They have decided that no state of the economy can be in equilibrium unless it is Pareto-efficient. Since the economy is in equilibrium more or less all the time, a syllogism has been completed. We are asked to share their naive glee at this confusion' (Hahn, 1983, p. 11).

17 See Day and Groves (1975) for a wide range of approaches which attempt to offer ways of dealing, in a quantitative way, with these processes.

18 This realization has come to influence modelling, particularly in the US where vector autoregressive models (VAR) have been proposed in place of traditional methodologies. See Gordon and King (1982) and Nelson and Plosser (1982).

19 See, for example, Bishoff's (1971) comparisons of different investment models.

20 It has not been common to look for experience curves in short-run macroeconomic studies. Experience curves have been confined to long-run models. For example, Kaldor and Mirrlees (1962) work on technical progress using a modified version of Verdoorn's Law. At the microeconomic level, see Schmookler (1966). For a more historical approach see David's (1974) study which echoes the theoretical propositions of Arrow (1962). Klein (1977) attempts to generalize the approach in a similar spirit to that here.

21 See Solow (1970).

22 See Foster (1979) for analysis of the manner in which the relationship between these indicators broke down in the 1970s in the UK. Froyen and Waud (1984) analyse the underlying shift in the relationship between price and output changes. Layard and Nickell (1985) provide a thorough analysis of the rising unemployment trend.

23 Monetarists such as Laidler and Parkin (1975) have emphasized difficulty in driving an analytical wedge between cost-push and demand-pull inflation since the former will also result in increases in demand. The problem with such simplification is that it takes

us further away rather than closer to the causes of inflation despite the enhanced 'operational' quality of the resultant hypothesis. See Hudson (1982).

24 Laidler and Parkin (1975) correctly identify this problem but prefer to argue for a fixed macro-structure methodology rather than try to argue that the macro-expectations, which they see as so important, are influenced by, and in turn, influence macro-structure.

25 See, for example, Parkin (1986).

26 It is well known that Keynes attacked the econometric methods developed by Tinbergen, largely on Popperian grounds (see Pheby, 1985). Keynes's answer was to rely on systems logic, thus shifting away from the issues in the Popperian debate about hypothesis testing to drawing conclusions from descriptive information about the economic system. Keynes was interested in the *patterns* of structure and what is being suggested here is that we can observe how patterns evolve, not to predict but to track systematic *tendencies* and, thus, enable us to understand the structural modifications necessary for further evolution.

12 *Curing Stagflation: An Evolutionary Approach*

> I would be morally outraged by a local ordinance designed to promote fire prevention by prohibiting the fire department from responding to any alarms for a month. There is a strong analogy to attempting to prevent inflation by committing the government not to deal with recession no matter how deep it becomes. A democratic society must have better cooperative ways to instil such socially desirable efforts than by threat and fear.
>
> Arthur Okun (1981)

In the last two chapters we have presented a macroeconomic approach designed to capture the evolutionary dynamics at work in the macro-system. In the absence of an appropriate division of aggregate flow data and suitable measures of commitment and contractual horizons, the proposed analytical framework can only be viewed as preliminary, as a beginning of a logic which could form the basis of a new macro-consciousness. The 'evidence' for the existence of such an evolutionary picture of the macro-system is qualitative, 'romantic quality' in Pirsig's terms, without any precise quantitative measurements to verify the propositions made. Pirsig notes the frequency with which scientific advances have been qualitative events receiving only quantitative verification at a later date. Poincaré wrote at length about this phenomenon[1] and, indeed, the discoveries of Einstein and, more recently, Ferber in physics have come into this category. Economics is qualitatively different in its nature to physics. If physics can be described as a study of the motional properties of solids then economics can be described as a study of the solidification of motion. In economics, Smith, Marx and Keynes, the three best known economists in history, developed qualitative visions of the dynamics of economic structure unsupported by quantitative evidence of the 'hypothesis testing' type. Each prescribed policies or strategies prior to the formalization and flow of quantitative evidence presented in support at a later date.[2] Each was a representative of a radical consciousness challenging the prevailing macro-consciousness and, in turn, each moulded macro-consciousness, influencing the evolution of economic structure in fundamental ways.

Today, it is unfashionable, or even unprofessional, in economics to prognosticate on policy without in-depth empirical work to yield 'predictions' useful for policy formulation. Yet that does not seem to be the way that policy development has occurred in the past. Today, we are trapped by the inadequacies of empiricism which cannot provide a secure base for policy formulation. All we have is an ability to short-term forecast a limited range of economic variables because of the inherent continuity of economic structure. The position that has been taken here is to argue that the primary business of the macroeconomist is not to tinker with shocks to a fixed structure but to devise new structures compatible with evolutionary development. Although the scope to formalize, quantify and impress everyone with scientism is much reduced and the probability of obscurity very high, this creative task of the macroeconomist is of central importance. To carry over our dynamic distinction into economics itself, much of conventional macroeconomics is maintenance activity, maintenance of the beliefs that hold prevailing macro-consciousness together, at the expense of creative activity.[3]

Evolution of structure is usually viewed as a slow, long-run process, but it is punctuated by sharp phases of catastrophic events. Beneath this pattern lies a macro-consciousness which is capable of shifting with great rapidity under the dual tensions of conservatism (maintenance) and radicalism (creativity). Evolutionary progress requires new structure which can encompass both in some proximate manner. We have emphasized what an outstanding job Keynes did in this regard, whatever misgivings we might have about the economic system that Keynesian consciousness ultimately spawned. In this chapter, the purpose is to propose a policy innovation which is directed towards the avoidance of simultaneous inflation and unemployment in economies which are, structurally, quite different to those that Keynes had in mind.

The policy innovation suggested will, like that of Keynes, be crude in construction, requiring fine tuning to the particular institutional and cultural characteristics of a selected economy. However, it will be directed mainly to the particular pattern of structural change that has occurred in the UK, with great rapidity, and the US, at a slower rate, in recent times. However, in constructing the policy proposal, the general evolutionary principles that we have discussed will be central. These apply whatever the institutional and cultural characteristics of a particular economy. However, it is inevitable that what is being suggested is open to criticism from many directions. It must be borne in mind that we are looking for no more than a starting point, an illustration of the advantages of the evolutionary approach, which can provide the basis for discussion, debate and development of something more pragmatic and operational. Furthermore, in searching for the basis of a new consensus in macro-consciousness, what is being suggested is *both* outside the prevailing economic orthodoxy *and* transcends existing political divisions, so we can expect strong criticism from every quarter.[4]

Policy Priorities

The main thesis in this book has been the importance of creativity, accompanied by a willingness to discard the obsolete, not only to facilitate economic development but also to maximize the utility of individual agents in the economy. Furthermore, we have been careful to define productivity growth in the broadest possible terms to include qualitative enrichment in even the most trivial of services provided on the periphery of the economic system.

The central problem in the economic system has always been one of communication, of how the creativity or productivity of one group can be discovered by another. As Simon has emphasized, the evolution of large productive organizations has been based largely on an informational advantage derived from organizing production on fixed hierarchical lines.[5] The modern problem that we have been dealing with here is one where the domination of these powerful organizations over communication has tended to reduce peripheral interchange of services in favour of the products and employment offered by these large productive organizations. At the other end of the creativity range, these organizations have tended to make it difficult for the producer services sector to be truly innovative in a way that is a challenge to large firm interests.

The communicative power of the large productive organization can be so strong that it not only has repercussions on the ability of peripheral social and economic agencies in forming bonds, but it can also serve to separate human beings from their natural environment. The ecological implications on the environment are often not visible to the urban consumer – the inconsistency of a taste for high levels of consumption and a high quality environment are simply not perceived. Thus, environmental 'services' or the benefits of ecological co-operation are lost in favour of mass production. However, once information is provided on such matters people tend to alter their perception in fundamental ways.

Often, in the face of this power, the initial instinct is to attack these mass-production organizations, and the bureaucracies which maintain them, with anarchistic fury. Yet, it is undoubtedly true that the economic benefits that they provide are invaluable and that no advanced economy could be viable without them. There is also evidence that their 'socialization' through nationalization, for example, does little to alter their character. The bureaucratic grip merely becomes tighter and creativity diminishes or becomes directed into areas which are more controversial than in privately-run organizations. The large organization also comes under criticism for increasing capital intensity in production and shedding labour, yet productivity growth in manufacturing relieves labour from boring work, provides the basis for service sector development, generates demand for the creative skills of the producer services sector in designing new equipment and creates interesting new 'servicing' jobs to keep the capital stock functioning.

There is clear confusion in the popular mind between the social benefits of complex development in productive structure and the social costs incurred by the influence of these structures on macro-consciousness. Perhaps what is more important is the fact that, as their productivity has risen, both in terms of output-per-man and diversity of good or service produced, so social and ecological priorities have begun to establish themselves. The mass production of durable goods and sophisticated tools has permitted the expansion of diverse service production and the re-establishment of widespread peripheral social and economic interaction. In particular, the provision of information technology has enabled new dimensions in peripheral communication to be created. The rise in environmental interaction through an increased ability to 'consume' leisure in non-urban locations has bred a new concern for environmental protection.[6]

In an evolutionary sense, the mass production sector has moved beyond the taste-confining, job-confining phase of development. It is the anchor of the modern economy and we depend on its productivity growth to provide the basis for more complex activity on the periphery in producer and consumer services. However, we are unaccustomed to thinking in terms of productivity growth and labour shedding as the route to better employment. The wage-labour economy is clung to, paradoxically, by the wage-labourers themselves. Furthermore, the framework we use for economic policy analysis cannot cope with this change either.[7] When we are thinking in terms of designing a new kind of macroeconomic policy, the priority is to get maintenance down and creativity up.

Getting maintenance down is a question of breaking the power that is in existing structure to engage in protective strategies. This power in the modern economy is primarily vested in bureaucracy although the benefits may be spread to other types of activity. For example, a large firm which engages in restrictive practices is likely to benefit its workers as well as managers and owners. Protective strategies in the macro-system manifest themselves in inflationary processes, thus anti-inflation policy amounts to the same thing as the curbing of bureaucratic power. Now, we know that all anti-inflation strategies have been plagued with problems, almost all of them stemming from the absence of a 'getting creativity up' dimension to policy. Paradoxically, the worst example in this regard has been the Thatcher one which has been dedicated ostensibly to 'stimulating the supply side'. Indiscriminate deflationary policy has destroyed productive capacity before its time and depressed the flow of new creativity, resulting in a failure to eradicate over-maintenance from the economy. Growing dependence in an entropic economy merely enhances the power of bureaucracy, so that, instead of inflation, the distribution of income is skewed away from both the creative and those released by the entropic forces.

Productivity growth is borne of past creativity, so 'getting creativity up' involves stimulating productivity growth. In the policy proposal that is outlined below it will be demonstrated that this is possible in the mass productive sector of the economy in a scheme which also prevents inflation and stabilizes the economy. As has been emphasized, macroeconomic policy is crude and what is proposed is no exception. The character of the policy mix that surrounds such a policy proposal remains open to debate since it deals with a complex economy. For example, indicative planning may be the way to stimulate 'producer services' creativity and productivity, but decisions also have to be made on how best to generate the kind of education and training required in producer services. In consumer services, strategies to facilitate flexible interaction might be of help while the view might be taken that 'laissez-faire' is the best position. Liberalization of restrictive practices and the espousal of market principles might be preferred. In the proposal that follows no judgement is made on these matters. Policy is only directed at three macroeconomic requirements of the economic system: first, to provide a stimulus to productivity growth in the large-scale productive sector; second, to provide curbs on the capacity of power structures to indulge in over-maintenance resulting in inflation; and third, to ensure a stable flow of income in the peripheral zone of the economy to facilitate qualitative innovation and development in producer and consumer services to avoid rising unemployment.

The dynamics of inflation and unemployment are of central concern in modern economies because they are social indicators of an evolutionary crisis involving catastrophic potential beyond the domain of economics. The centrality of concern for these indicators is reflected in the policy priority given to them by governments. Politicians, using instinct more than the guidance of economic theory, appreciate the social dangers inherent in inflation and unemployment. We have seen how orthodox economic theories cannot help because of their reliance on 'fixed structure' assumption. Many clever economic theories of inflation and unemployment have been developed but none provide an adequate policy apparatus necessary to get to grips with the underlying evolutionary problem. Our purpose here has not been to provide yet another 'explanation' of inflation and unemployment, which can be subject to econometric test, but rather to provide guidance in the formulation of the required structure altering policy apparatus necessary to remove the underlying cause of these macroeconomic symptoms.

The Proposal

If we examine the modern macroeconomy in a static sense within the context of Hicks's (1974) taxonomy, we observe that postwar industrial concentration has generated a fix-price sector which dominates the macroeconomy. Not only is this sector dominant in a quantitative sense but also in qualitative terms since it encompasses the most complex and sophisticated productive activity and is supported by an intricate structure of interconnecting contractual obligations. Economic development has come to rely heavily on the innovative capacity and productivity growth of this sector. Consequently, when economists refer to the 'supply side problem' they are referring, in the main, to the fix-price sector. Although the small business/flex-price sector has made an enormous contribution to employment growth, largely through the rapid increase in the provision of services, it can be argued that it has been endogenously determined by productivity growth in the fix-price sector, with the fruits of such progress spread through the application of demand management.[8]

Thus, the slowing of productivity growth which has occurred in the UK and the US is concentrated, largely, in the fix-price sector. Also, it is in this sector that the exercise of power has resulted in inflation. There has been a tendency to argue that it is the public sector side of the fix-price sector that has been the primary initiator of inflation. However, the experience of the first half of the 1980s in the UK, when public sector price and income increases were tightly controlled by government and trade union power seriously curbed by legislation, suggests that inflationary impetus from the private side of the fix-price sector is significant. It follows that any policy devised to stimulate productivity growth and curb inflation should be concentrated in the fix-price sector, in both its public and private sub-sectors.

How does our evolutionary macroeconomic analysis help us in this task? First of all, we know that creative development and entropy go hand in hand. Attempts to introduce schemes to encourage firms to become more labour-intensive will militate against our evolutionary objective. A scheme to raise productivity growth in the fix-price sector is, in the first instance, one that provides incentives which may well result in the substitution of labour with capital. However, we have argued that there is no reason to suppose that overall unemployment need rise because of such substitution.[9] It depends on the maintenance of aggregate demand and the rapidity of service sector development. Up until now the only significant incentives offered have been selective investment aids, designed to increase the quantity and quality of the capital stock and to encourage industry into particular regions.

However, the links between overall productivity growth and these incentives have proved to be tenuous and indirect due to 'moral hazard' and the misguided nature of government priorities.[10]

In designing an incentive structure it is necessary to keep *homo creativus* firmly in mind. There is plenty of evidence to suggest that he is as agile at taking full advantage of slackly designed incentive systems as he is in finding loopholes in disincentive systems, such as statutory prices and incomes policies. However, *homo creativus* is always keen to co-operate with incentive systems which are 'fair' and result in mutual benefit. It is only when he is given a hand-out with no clear guidelines as to what he has to do in return, or when curbs are imposed on him without any compensating advantage, that we can expect non-co-operation.

First of all, we must understand the configuration of key overlapping consciousnesses that we face. There is management consciousness (*M*), labour consciousness (*L*), firm consciousness (*M-L*), management-government consciousness (*M-G*) and labour-government (*L-G*) consciousness. The relative importance of these unities of consciousness will vary but we know that certain configurations recur. Strong *M*, strong *L* and weak *M-L* is bad for productivity and prone to lead to industrial conflict. We also know that inflation uncertainty increases *M-L* divisiveness in settling wage contracts. We know that *M-G* and *L-G* will be influenced by which political party is in government. Thus, we must devise a scheme which has three priorities. First, inflation uncertainty must be reduced; second, incentives must be devised to bring workers and management closer together; and third, there must be an incentive to co-operate with the social objectives of government.

The first priority could be addressed by the introduction of an indexation scheme to protect wage settlements from inflation. However, such arrangements have not been prevalent because of the uncertainty of management as to the course of the firm's product price relative to prices in general. Also, trade unionists have feared that indexation could remove their ability to negotiate for unanticipated profits. The second priority has been widely recognized, but increased worker participation is something which is difficult to legislate. Even with such a change, there would still remain the third priority, of consolidating the link between government and firm. There already exist harmonious *M-L* firms who pass on 'mark-up' price increases which stem from wage and salary rises.

It is this third priority which most intimately connects government and firm, and is the one with which government has had most difficulty in the past. Prices and incomes policies have weakened, rather than strengthened, *M-G* and *L-G* consciousness bonding. Appeals by government for restraint and responsibility have had little effect. The ineffectiveness of both voluntary and compulsory prices and incomes policies have led to their virtual abandonment as viable policy options. While governments have preferred to pursue recessionary policies to curb inflation, the notion that a prices and incomes policy might work through a tax incentive structure has begun to be discussed widely.

Although there are many variants of these kinds of tax-based incomes (TIP) policies, they all have the characteristic of offering a voluntary, decentralized tax penalty and/or tax credit scheme depending on whether a firm and/or a union allows wage and/or price inflation to be above (penalty) or below (credit) some defined norm.[11] Would such a scheme induce *homo creativus* to co-operate with the anti-inflation intentions of government? As Okun (1981) pointed out, schemes that penalize through levying taxes are unlikely to help. *Homo creativus* takes great delight in devising ways to avoid paying taxes, particularly those deemed to be 'unfair' in some sense. However, Okun felt that a scheme which did not penalize anyone but rather provided tax rewards to non-generators of inflation might well appeal to the co-operative spirit of *homo creativus*.

Is there any evidence to support such a contention? In the rather sad history of prices and incomes policy experimentation there does exist one piece of evidence which, at least, points in Okun's direction. In the UK the 'Social Contract', or voluntary policy which survived in varying forms from 1975 to 1979, founded on strong *L-G* connections between the Labour government and the trade unions, has been found by subsequent researchers to have had a significant effect on inflation. One of the novel characteristics of this policy was that it was negotiated on the promise of a tax cut, providing some indirect evidence that such reciprocation may well have helped to provide enhanced *L-G* bonding. However, the other lesson we learn is that the Social Contract perished because it lacked any way of dealing with differential productivity growth resulting in the 1978–9 'Winter of Discontent', clearly breaching our second priority.

Once we begin to entertain the possibility of providing tax rebates for the non-generation of inflation, which are received by specific economic agents rather than everyone in general, the question arises as to other possible effects of such rebates. First, there is the simple Keynesian point that any tax cut will be expansionary and will raise the budget deficit. Second, there is the 'supply-siders' point that the tax cut might induce the economic agent to become more productive even though it had already been 'earned' for good behaviour.[12] However, should that happen, it might mean more growth, thus raising tax revenue to help erase the budget deficit while the fiscal stimulus would have helped to increase demand in line with the extra supply. Clearly, many dynamic paths can be envisaged and some of them could generate the kind of symbiosis that we are searching for.[13] What is required is a scheme with a set of rules which ensure a symbiotic result.

The Policy Channel One of the advantages of Keynesian demand management was that it could be operated in a centralized and largely anonymous manner, without invoking the kind of legislative intervention so typical of prices and incomes policies. In this sense statutory prices and incomes policies are not in the true spirit of Keynesian stabilization but more reminiscent of controls in Eastern European countries. Influencing productivity growth would, necessarily, have to be decentralized in operation. However, we are fortunate that the modern economy has a reliable policy channel, from core to periphery, ideally suited for transmitting such a policy, namely the taxation system. Governments have been reluctant to juggle around with the taxation system too much in the past for the understandable reasons that stability and certainty of tax structure reduces administrative costs.[14] However, transmitting tax rebates through a stable structure is another matter entirely. At the end of the fiscal year it is common practice to pay tax rebates under existing fiscal arrangements.

The most convenient policy channel is clearly the income tax system through which our scheme would transmit tax rebates, at the end of the fiscal year, to employees of selected firms. The rebate structure is designed to encourage productivity growth, ensure adequate expansion of effective demand and discourage inflation generation. The rebates would represent a tax cut, specifically directed towards these priorities and, to ensure that stabilization policy would remain separate from the spending aspirations of government, demand management would be confined to automatic and discretionary responses through the income tax system's rebate structure. The scheme would provide three primary and two secondary instruments through which discretionary intervention could occur, to augment the automatic characteristics of the scheme, depending on the different political and economic standpoints of different governments.

Recognizing that the wage contract is fundamental to all successful economic activity and that disputes concerning inflation protection and rewards for productivity growth constitute destructive influences on contractual harmony, the scheme attempts to conjoin the interests of workers and management. Rewards for overall firm performance would be received by all employees of a firm through rebates on income taxation. Thus, a bond of common interest is created while, at the same time, the interests of the state are supported, not by moral suasion, but by financial incentives to everyone involved. In a sense, the scheme attempts to simulate the conditions prevailing in the fix-price sector of the Japanese economy, i.e. enhanced contractual security, strong firm loyalty, worker/management co-operation and close liaison between the state and business in terms of evolutionary priorities.[15]

If it is the case that macro-system evolution has meant that 'the market' no longer has any operational meaning, then broadly based supply side tax-cuts, deregulation and welfare reductions merely induce redistribution and enhance misery and conflict. The scheme to be suggested offers an alternative which demands no radical reform and penalizes no one, irrespective of the presumed 'justice' of their current position. In a highly sensitive, interdependent system of production and consumption, questions of justice and fairness in the distributions of economic power that exists cannot be answered by economists; they are simply part and parcel of 'the system'. In particular, economists can only be 'positive' by looking ahead from the current position and attempting to devise methods and policies which will facilitate welfare improvements for all. This is what the scheme attempts to do.

Coverage The fix-price sector of the economy is an abstraction. Inevitably, any real-world division of the economy into fix-price and flex-price sectors involves a large intermediate or 'fuzzy' area. However, it is almost certainly the case that inclusion of the 1000 largest employers in the scheme in the

UK case would cover most of this sector and, even if some important firms remained uncovered, they would be heavily influenced by decisions taken in the covered sector. In the US, coverage would have to be greater. However, exact coverage remains something to be discussed and debated – it has no effect on the scheme's structure.

Information Attempts to provide decentralized incentive structures through the income tax system are rare from the standpoint of macroeconomic policy. However, the system of allowances contained in all income tax systems means that such connections already exist for other purposes. Proposals to introduce, for example, tax-based incomes policies have been dogged by criticisms that they are administratively costly to operate and monitor.[16] Much depends on whether a proposal introduces new channels or simply relies on modifications of old ones. The scheme here relies on the existing system of income tax and, in particular, the system of 'pay-as-you-earn' between firms and the income taxation authority. The following two pieces of information are already available from an income tax authority:

E_{jt}: the total earning of all employees of firm j in year t;
T_{jt}: the total pay-as-you-earn income tax payments of all employees of firm j in year t.

The new information required to administer the scheme is readily available to all large firms with developed accountancy and marketing functions:

Y_{jt}: the total turnover of firm j in year t;
G_{jt}: the total domestic turnover of firm j in year t;
F_{jt}: a weighted average of the domestic prices charged for all products sold by firm j over year t.

In the past, attempts to implement price controls, which required information akin to F_{jt}, tended to be criticized because of problems of quality variation, discounts and the introduction of new products. However, the scheme here is not price control. Price information is only required to establish employee eligibility for tax rebates. Firms remain free to adjust prices in any way they wish. However, problems concerning new products and quality change would continue to arise. These will be discussed later. The required formula for computing F_{jt} would be as follows:

$$F_{jt} \equiv \sum_{i=0}^{i=n} \left[\frac{G_{ijt}}{G_{jt}} \cdot F_{ijt} \right]$$

where:

G_{ijt} = domestic turnover of product i in firm j in period t;
F_{ijt} = actual price of product i domestic sales in firm j in period t;
n = number of different products sold on the domestic market.

This formula ensures that prices are appropriately weighted relative to their importance in total turnover.[17] The onus would be on notified firms to present this information by a prescribed deadline. Since the scheme would be restricted to large and responsible organizations with efficient information systems it is unlikely that any information provision problem would arise.

The Computed Variables With the information provided by the income tax authority and the covered firms, rebates would be computed as follows:

(1) P_t = average domestic product price in the covered sector

$$= \sum_{j=1}^{j=m} \left[\frac{G_{jt}}{\sum_{j=1}^{j=m} G_{jt}} \cdot F_{jt} \right]$$

where:

m = number of firms in the covered sector;

and:

$$p_t = \frac{P_t - P_{t-1}}{P_{t-1}}$$

(2) $$y_{jt} = \frac{Y_{jt} - Y_{jt-1}}{Y_{jt-1}}$$

or $Y_{jt} = Y_{jt-1}(1 + y_{jt})$

where:

y_{jt} = rate of increase of total turnover of firm j in year t.

$$(3) \quad f_{jt} = \frac{F_{jt}-F_{jt-1}}{F_{jt-1}}$$

$$\text{or} \quad F_{jt} = F_{jt-1}\,(1+f_{jt})$$

where:

f_{jt} = rate of increase of firm j's average prices in year t.

(4) x_t = average rate of productivity growth in the covered sector in year t

where:

$$x_t = \frac{\Sigma Y_{jt}-\Sigma Y_{jt-1}}{\Sigma Y_{jt-1}} - p_t$$

This definition merely states that average productivity growth will be a weighted average of individual firm productivity growth. However, the information specified does not relate to the actual productivity of the firm but only to real turnover growth. In order to preserve simplicity and to avoid the danger of over accumulation of stocks of finished goods the scheme only acknowledges 'effective' productivity, i.e. relating to output of goods and services actually sold. If we were to assume that product quality remains unchanged over time, then we could compute a firm's productivity growth from the following identity:[18]

$$x_{jt} = y_{jt} - f_{jt}$$

Now, although much of conventional economics makes homogeneity assumptions of this type, in historical time the range of products produced by a firm tends to change, with new products replacing obsolete ones. As product quality changes, a new product may absorb more or less costs than the previous one. Thus, quality changes will be reflected in price changes. So when quality improves through the introduction of a more sophisticated product, price could rise and sales fall. In such a case our simple formula would record negative productivity growth. Clearly, where productivity growth manifests itself in quality improvement, y_{jt} could represent a better measure than $(y_{jt}-f_{jt})$. The other side of the quality coin arises in cases where a reduction in quality is used as an alternative to an inflationary price increase. In this case our formula would yield productivity growth equal to turnover growth and, thus, overstate the true position.

Although the problem of productivity growth manifesting itself in quantity and quality change has been considered in microeconomic studies,[19] it has only been possible to do so when quality change can be translated into measurable specification revision. In an imperfectly competitive environment, where pricing practices and product life-cycle strategies vary widely, the degree to which price changes can be attributed to quality changes is strictly limited. Deaton and Muellbauer (1980) make the general observation that the 'supply of quality' has been largely neglected in consumer economics in much the same way as 'technical progress' in the economic growth literature.

Taking the quality question to its logical limit, it could be argued that all price increases represent quality increases for, when a firm agrees to a large wage increase which is passed on in price increases, we have a situation where, in terms of the perceived value of money over the relevant contract period, the quality of the product is deemed to have increased in money terms. The extent to which consumers continue to purchase the same amount of the product merely confirms this quality increase.[20] Difficulties in distinguishing quantity and quality arise in all types of economic policy. In the scheme proposed here, the central preoccupation is in discouraging qualitative re-evaluations of existing products and services which result in a generalized tendency for prices to rise. Thus, *ex ante* the presumption has to be made that all price rises are of this type for the purpose of awarding rebates for the non-generation of inflation and productivity growth. However, if *ex post* it is discovered that aggregate p_t is approximately zero, then it can be safely assumed that all price changes were relative and that y_{jt} measures productivity growth. To extend the rule of thumb further than that would be difficult. However, as we shall see in the next section, since we are not dealing with a system of price control but rather a criterion for setting rebates, the potential for distortion is not great.

The Rebate Formula Using the data computed from firms' returns, the following formula would be used to determine the tax rebate paid to all employees of a firm. Whether this lump-sum rebate would be distributed in equal amounts or in proportion to individual income tax paid would be determined in the political process. For example, a rightist government might insist on the latter and a leftist on the former, while a centrist administration might prefer it be left to each firm to decide.

$$R_{jt} = [a_t + b_t\,(\frac{x_{jt}}{x_t})]\,[1-c_t f_{jt}]\,E_{jt} + (E_{jt}-T_{jt})(p_t-f_{jt})$$

where a_t, b_t and c_t are policy instruments set in a discretionary way as part of Budgetary policy prior to each fiscal year:

a_t = the non-inflation rebate rate paid to a firm which records zero productivity growth;
b_t = a coefficient which translates productivity deviations from the average, x_t, into rebate rates;
c_t = a coefficient which determines the rate at which productivity rebates are scaled down as a firm inflates its prices;

and:

$$\text{if } P_t > 0,\ x_{jt} = y_{jt} - f_{jt}$$
$$\text{if } P_t = 0,\ x_{jt} = y_{jt} \text{ and } c_t f_{jt} \text{ is set at } 0$$

The first part of the R_{jt} formula relates to productivity growth and inflation generation. Provided a firm holds its prices steady, earnings will be supplemented by a productivity rebate irrespective of how fast earnings growth is. The instruments a_t and b_t will determine the degree to which productivity growth is rewarded relative to non-inflation generation, and c_t will determine how rapidly an inflation-generating firm phases itself out of the scheme.

These three instruments would be determined by the political process. For example, a rightist government might wish to keep a_t 'low' and b_t 'high' to channel productivity benefits in the covered sector to those most deserving, thus providing strong productivity incentives. A leftist government might prefer a 'high' a_t and a 'low' b_t to ensure that the global benefits of productivity growth would be spread to those employed in organizations where the potential for productivity growth is limited. The drawback of emphasizing productivity incentives is that it would encourage employees of firms exhibiting low productive growth to attempt to inflate, having little to lose from doing so, in order to narrow the widening differential between themselves and the high productive growers. The rightist government, in order to counter such behaviour, would, inevitably, have to choose a 'high' c_t which could easily result in negative rebates for unproductive inflators. In other words, our carrot could be modified into a stick. The 'leftist' strategy would probably not suffer from this problem and, therefore, a 'low' c_t could be chosen. However, the reduced emphasis on rewards for high productivity growth might well result in a lowering of overall x_t, thus lessening the size of the cake to be shared.

Governments would have different views on the most effective combination for a_t, b_t and c_t. Furthermore, a given government would almost certainly modify them depending on economic conditions and also depending on the other constituents of their policy package over time. In this regard, macroeconomic forecasting and simulation of different policy regimes would continue to be very important prior to Budgetary decisions on these instruments.

The second part of R_{jt} constitutes a form of partial indexation. It ensures that, if inflation is generated in the covered sector, the earnings of employees of a firm which holds its prices stable will be protected. However, any increase in a firm's price would be deducted from the general inflation index. Although this part of the scheme offers some inflation protection to earners it is not intended to offer full protection. Price increases emanating from the uncovered domestic sector and the foreign sector which exceed covered sector inflation are not fully compensated. The scheme treats them as relative rather than absolute price increases which have to be absorbed. The objective is not to cushion earners from all inflation but only to provide them with some assurance that they need not follow any wage inflation surge in some sub-sector of the covered sector. The limited nature of this provision is based on the belief, which dates back to Keynes, that relative earnings are more important than absolute earnings in a contractual context. However, Keynes abstracted from dynamic considerations of real wage differentials due to different rates of productivity growth. The scheme proposed here allows relative earnings flexibility and focuses only on attempts to increase wage share by inflation generating tactics. Of course, should the scheme be successful in lowering p_t to zero, then the necessary funding of this quasi-indexation would also fall to zero.

Again, the strength of this quasi-indexation dimension of the scheme could be debated in the political arena. If, in rebate calculations, values of $(p_t - f_{jt})$ were permitted to assume negative values, then the indexation could be self-financing with the over-inflators compensating the under-inflators, so long as p_t was greater than zero. Such an arrangement would have some attractions for a rightist administration which might be concerned with the budget deficit implications of the scheme. Also, such an arrangement would be consistent with allowing $(1 - c_t f_{jt})$ to become negative as discussed earlier in the productivity component of the rebate formula. A leftist administration would probably allow both $(1 - c_t f_{jt})$ and $(p_t - f_{jt})$ to take minimum values of zero on the grounds that the increasing deficit effect of the latter could be offset by reductions in rebates as p_t increased in the former. Furthermore, in as much as such an administration opted for a 'high' a_t and a 'low' b_t to spread the benefits of productivity growth, a penal dimension to indexation might be viewed as unnecessary. Once again, the outlook of a given administration could vary over time. For example, the self-financing indexation system could be introduced when the economy began to overheat, but in a recession a government financing scheme could be used when the competitive pressure generated by productivity growth differentials is low and when an injection need not be inflationary.

What the scheme outlined attempts to do is to introduce a relatively simple policy framework which contains five new instruments, if we include the two options as to whether to allow rebates to assume negative values. Thus, the scheme provides ample scope for governmental discretionary decision-making and modification, depending on political preference. Despite differing views as to the appropriate values of these instruments, the policy could embody a fundamental consensus with regard to the policy framework for the promotion and reward of productivity growth and non-generation of inflation. Clearly a political trade-off would tend to exist with, on the one hand, over-zealous reward of productivity growth being bought at the price of rendering the scheme penal to deter inflationary pressure, and, on the other hand, over-equitable spreading of social productivity growth leading to a self-defeating slowing of that growth due to lack of incentive. The latter state of affairs might also result in inflation as the high productive growers attempted to recoup their losses through substantial wage claims. In practice, political aspirations to set extreme values of instruments would be curbed by politicians' instincts to avoid crisis and instability. The discretionary flexibility which the scheme provides could only exist if there was political consensus to work within the scheme. Selection of extreme instrument values would be tantamount to abandonment of the scheme for something quite different, beyond the consensus, and would involve the usual political risks attendant on radical changes.

Exactly where do these limits lie and how would the scheme fit with other dimensions of macroeconomic policy, for example demand management and external balance considerations? How would intermediate objectives, such as control of the budget deficit and the money supply, be viewed if such a scheme existed? If high values of a_t and b_t were necessary to make the policy work, what sacrifices would have to be made with regard to public sector expenditure growth? Given the crudeness of the policy, what political flashpoints or administrative loopholes would be likely to undermine the effectiveness of the policy in the long run? All these questions constitute major studies in themselves and, therefore, are unlikely to be answered in any formal way within the confines of this chapter. However, it is possible to deal with these questions in enough detail to demonstrate the feasibility of the policy and to provide a basis for further discussion of the questions raised.

Taxation and Public Expenditure If the proposed scheme was introduced, to be effective (a_t+b_t) would have to be large enough to provide sufficient incentive to dissuade firms' employees from making wage claims financed by price increases. Essentially, this involves the selection of (a_t+b_t) at a level which would mean that wage inflaters would have to increase prices excessively to compensate for rebate losses. In an oligopolistic pricing structure, where falling out of line on prices is undesired in any case, uncertainty as to competitors' productivity growth and consequent wage–price strategy would be increased by the existence of the scheme. In the scheme, it is always the firm with the lowest productivity growth which has least to lose in sanctioning wage rises through price rises. However, in an oligopolistic context, such a firm is likely to be one which has been losing a share of the market and, therefore, one which fears raising prices most.

Exactly what (a_t+b_t) would be necessary over time would have to be decided by political decision-makers, weighing the advantages of a high (a_t+b_t) against the accompanying sacrifices. There is little doubt that (a_t+b_t) represents a selective tax cut which would have to be covered by borrowing, monetary growth, tax increases or expenditure cuts. As the scheme is constructed, (a_t+b_t) represents a deduction in the average rate of income taxation paid by a sub-sector of key income earners in the economy. If real tax revenue is growing in line with real earnings growth which, in turn, is driven by productivity growth, the introduction of the scheme would involve a transitional shift, after which real tax revenue would continue to grow at the same rate as real earnings.

A rightist government might wish to take a cost-benefit approach to the scheme in setting (a_t+b_t):

$$\text{Cost} = E_t(a_t+b_t)$$
$$\text{Benefit} = E_t t - E_0 t$$

where E_0 = that level of real earnings which would have prevailed in the absence of the scheme;
and: t = marginal rate of income tax.

(a_t+b_t) would be set where:

$$\Delta E_t(a_t+b_t) = \Delta[t(E_t-E_0)]$$

In other words (a_t+b_t) would be determined by the difference between productivity growth with and without the scheme. However, as is often the case with this kind of cost-benefit approach, there may not be a positive (a_t+b_t) which yields marginal benefit greater than marginal cost because of the narrow definition of benefit in terms of tax revenue. First, productivity growth in the covered sector may spread to the uncovered sector yielding further increases in tax receipts. Second, tax cuts represent injections which can have multiplier effects which, in turn, stimulate tax revenue. This has been recognized in the past when governments have stimulated a recessionary economy and the argument continues to have force in a fully employed economy where there is an expansion of demand which is accompanied by productivity growth. Third, there are intangible benefits from the removal of inflation.

In sum, the tax system exists to perform social functions, thus, costs and benefits can only be viewed in social terms, a position clearly held by Keynes with regard to deficit finance. A leftist government would probably be unconcerned with a cost-benefit approach and would be inclined to accept the shift in the rate of income tax necessary to make the policy effective. The likely preference of a leftist government for 'high' *a*/'low' *b* combinations would ensure that it was a stronger inflation dampener rather than productivity growth stimulator in any case. A leftist government might also feel less inhibited in raising the economy-wide standard rate of income tax, as well as increasing the progressivity of the tax system, to cover the preferential rate in the covered sector. A centrist government, on the other hand, might prefer to sweep away the various haphazard tax subsidies which currently exist, e.g. mortgage interest relief, to finance the scheme or even introduce wealth taxes as a logical adjunct to the scheme, i.e. increased taxes on economic rent to provide incentives for income yielded by productive effort. However, in making the transition to the scheme it would seem unwise for any government to take any kind of politically motivated reformist action which would disturb the status quo simply because the losers would associate their misfortune with the introduction of the scheme.

As a social innovation anticipated to yield future benefits, finance by borrowing and monetary expansion would seem logical, particularly if the economy is in recession in any case. In such conditions it is vital to provide a demand side stimulus to productivity growth as well as a supply side one. The larger the size of (a_t+b_t), the greater the demand stimulus will be and the stronger the anti-inflation property of the scheme in the covered sector. The old problem of just how much demand stimulation to initiate will, of course, remain. A leftist government which pursued, simultaneously, substantial public spending would, in all probability, destroy the scheme and have to resort to a centrally controlled prices and incomes policy. A rightist government, on the other hand, obsessed with balancing the budget, by insisting that rebates be financed by expenditure cuts, would fail to reap the 'Keynesian expansion' benefits that the scheme is designed to offer. The scheme demands a commitment to the view that, provided stabilization operates through tax changes rather than public expenditure charges, 'demand side' advantages of tax cuts can be enjoyed alongside the 'supply side' advantages in terms of productivity growth.

These advantages are not restricted to an under-fully employed economy since, at full employment, the scheme permits demand stimulation only in the presence of supply increase and the absence of price inflation. Clearly, since the scheme covers only a part of total employment in the economy, the net effect of the scheme on total tax revenue position can only be understood when more is known about the reaction of the uncovered sector. The usual principles of modelling, forecasting and demand management would come into play in this context. In terms of implementing the scheme in an economy which is below full employment, perhaps the best strategy is one whereby the transition to the scheme is financed by some combination of borrowing and money growth followed later by slow adjustments of the fiscal structure to accommodate the scheme. Provided that all demand management was directed through the taxation system, the amount and composition of government spending would be a political matter. Such spending, once freed from the demands of stabilization policy, could be kept on a stable growth path over time. Growth in expenditure on public administration could be tied to growth of tax revenue which, in turn, would depend on overall economic growth. The specific rules adopted, once again, would be subject to political debate.

The Open Economy If we look at all Anglo-American schools of macroeconomic thought we see that there is unanimity on one issue: the rising marginal propensity to import has been a major factor in diminishing the effectiveness of demand management on the domestic economy and increasing the tendency for balance of payments deficits to be generated. As constituted, the scheme does not provide any controls with regard to imports but it does offer certain properties which could arrest the deterioration of the external situation.

First, the tax rebates provide a stimulus to domestic firms which would enhance their international competitiveness. The rebate is superior to an export subsidy because it is related to growth in productivity which is translated into actual sales and it accrues to employees, not to the owners of firms. The latter feature has the advantage that the benefit is spread to labour and not just profit, as is often the case with government subsidies. Second, the scheme is designed so that any increase in prices charged in foreign markets does not reduce rebates and may, in fact, increase them. Large firms in the fix-price sector of the domestic economy are presumed to be in flex-price international markets. So, if they can drive up their foreign prices through, say, quality improvements or innovation then rewards will be provided through the scheme. This feature of the scheme would gradually work against the existing state of affairs where some firms, for example, car manufacturers, charge high domestic prices, trading on customer loyalty, and low international prices for their products.

There is little doubt that the forces set in motion by the scheme are of the medium-term variety and that, initially implementation of the scheme, accompanied by demand expansion, would lead to a worsening of the balance of payments. However, this would seem to be a situation where devaluation should be permitted for two reasons. First, devaluation is ineffectual when it is undermined by the marking-up of import prices into domestic prices. The scheme would tend to make devaluation more effective because it would discourage the passing-on of such increases. If firms allow import prices to drive up their selling prices, their employees lose rebates. In this context, the scheme is designed to stiffen the position of purchasing executives and encourage them to engage in expenditure switching towards domestically produced goods. Also, the quasi-indexation arrangements do not include uncovered sector prices, so employees would be unprotected from rises of retail prices emanating from increased prices of imported goods. This too would set up expenditure switching forces which would assist devaluation. Second, devaluation is only a fruitless policy when it is attempted on a path of secular decline where that decline is unaffected by the temporary advantage to exporters of a lower exchange rate. In as much as the scheme could induce a productivity turnaround on the supply side then devaluation would provide the ideal stimulus, in parallel with domestic demand expansion, to encourage firms to increase productivity growth as quickly as possible.

Intermediate Objectives: Budget Deficit and Money Supply In recent times the budget deficit and money supply have become important intermediate objectives within a strategy directed at the final objective of inflation control. The price paid has been the abandonment of unemployment as a final objective. The proposed scheme provides a set of intermediate instruments and objectives which are directed simultaneously at productivity stimulation and inflation control and, therefore, the importance of the budget deficit and the money supply are reduced considerably. Although there is little doubt that a massive increase in the budget deficit, financed by money growth, could lead to inflation in the uncovered and, ultimately, the covered sector, the scheme does permit tax rebate induced budget deficit increases and money supply increases to take place, given the guarantee of non-inflation generation and productivity growth. Since the value of increased turnover is always in excess of increased covered sector earnings plus rebates, it is only after multiplier expansions of covered sector earnings into uncovered sector income that increased turnover would be matched fully by effective demand. In the absence of excess liquidity, some monetary growth would seem essential to facilitate this process.

Whether or not the uncovered sector would simply generate inflation under such circumstances is an open question. As a flex-price sector, to do so there would have to be excess demand which, in turn, would imply that the sector was at full capacity. With excessive unemployment, it is unlikely that this is the case. A large component of the flex-price sector is the service sector and small business sector, both of which involve low set up costs and a tendency to grow rapidly, largely through employment in labour intensive activities, encouraged by general expenditure growth. By its very nature, i.e. large numbers of small producers providing differentiated goods and services, prices will not rise quickly and a quantity response is more likely.[21] The uncovered sector would not be badly approximated by an IS–LM model below full employment where output is as much about qualities as quantities, i.e. there is always 'excess capacity' in the uncovered sector in the sense that increases in levels of expenditure bring forth new activities and new services which currently exist only as potential within the skill and intellectual capacity limits of the population. Evidence from the United States suggests that the response of the service sector, in terms of providing the primary source of employment growth, is massive and that it is not a sector characterized by tendencies to generate inflation.[22]

The Quality Problem It would not be wholly inaccurate to say that much of modern economics has been obsessed with quantity at the expense of quality. Although the importance of quality has been emphasized here, the scheme suggested does not take full account of quality change. This is mainly due to the near impossibility of direct measurement of quality. As it stands, the scheme is 'quality fixed' so that any increase in a firm's average price is interpreted as inflationary. However, there are a number of ways in which the scheme does allow for quality change.

First, a firm can alter the structure of its product prices without altering its average product price by, for example, selling off obsolete lines at cut prices while charging a high price for new products. Second, a firm can allow quality change to go into increased quantity of sales rather than price rises, as is often the case in the fast-moving domestic appliance and audio-visual product markets. In as much as dramatic economies of scale or steep experience curves exist, the scheme merely encourages the spread of such benefits to consumers. Third, a firm which makes a strategic decision to move into products which are significantly more expensive would have to negotiate with their employees, persuading them that the rebates forfeited in the current year would be more than compensated for in high turnover in subsequent years. As such, the scheme introduces a 'tax' on quality change which would ensure that quality changes based on, for example, short-term advertising campaigns would not be used to raise prices but be confined to their traditional role of winning larger market share at a fixed price. Fourth, the scheme permits all price increases to be counted as productivity increases in the event that the average rate of inflation in the covered sector turns out to be approximately zero, thus a firm which is convinced that the price increase that they initiate is non-inflationary may well find at the end of the day that such a conviction is vindicated.

The fact that the scheme necessarily deals with quality change only in a proximate way could be regarded as the price paid, in productivity terms, for the assurance that zero inflation will prevail. The loss of rebate suffered by genuine quality promoters would be due to those who caused prices to increase simply to take advantage of some monopoly power which enabled them to mark up profits or earnings, despite the incentives not to do so. There would also be those firms who reduce the quality of products, e.g. reducing the size of chocolate bars, to keep prices constant, taking advantage of some product illusion or brand loyalty to keep up turnover. However, the overall objective of keeping inflation at zero would be maintained and, in a world of only relative price differentials, it is very likely that consumers would perceive such a quality reduction, resulting in a rapid loss of market share. Whether or not the policy would be subject to rapid 'slippage' as chocolate bars shrank and cars were stripped of accessories, is something which could only be determined after implementation. The costs of reorganization, the threat of consumer switches to uncovered sector products and the uncertainty of competitors' strategies would all be a deterrant to financing wage increases in this manner.

One of the obvious advantages of effective inflation control is the improvement in the quality of information concerning relative prices. As such the scheme would tend to enhance competition in oligopolistic markets, eradicating any short-term monopoly profits emanating from inferior consumer information. The other way in which such competition is enhanced is through the device of measuring productivity by adjusted turnover. Any firm which gained a larger market share from others would be rewarded for doing so.

Conclusion

In this chapter we have moved, perhaps in undue haste, into the field of economic policy. The objective has been to provide an example of policy design which takes explicit account of the vision of the macroeconomy contained in this book. The proposal focuses on the central malaise of the UK economy, and, to a lesser extent, the US economy. However, in all probability, the US will experience the same problem to an increasing extent in the future. It is the conjunction of inflation and low productivity growth, inducing effects such as increasing unemployment and a range of other social problems, which is at the centre of our attention.

The policy suggested makes no attempt to break up what would be seen by some as monopoly power, but, instead, introduces incentives which build on the contractual co-operation that exists between management and workers, providing a mutual reward for the non-generation of inflation. The scheme proposed has similarities to suggestions labelled as tax-based incomes policies in the past but differs in the sense that reliance is on rewards rather than penalties. Also, TIP schemes have been criticized for interfering with productivity growth, whereas the scheme proposed here provides incentives to encourage productivity growth and, as such, our evolutionary scheme is a 'supply side' policy in orthodox terminology. The rewards offered for non-inflation plus productivity growth represent tax cuts, as advocated by many 'supply siders', which accrue to those who are actually capable of significant supply increases. The scheme also contrasts with the proposals of Marston and Turnovsky (1985) concerning indexation. The adoption of a non-evolutionary, orthodox view of the labour market leads them to advocate that those with above average productivity growth should subsidize the indexation of those with below average productivity growth through a tax payment/rebate system. In other words, the incentive structure is reversed with damaging consequences in our evolutionary frame of reference.

The policy also differs from that of Layard (1982), Vines *et al.* (1983) and Weitzman (1983) in that encouragement of employment, either through explicit subsidies as in the Layard case, through the design of the fiscal system in the Vines *et al.* case, or through the establishment of a 'share economy' in the Weitzman case, is not a part of the scheme. In fact, the scheme proposed is likely to discourage employment in the fix-price sector. Employment expansion is regarded as a goal which should be pursued in the flex-price sector, particularly in the labour-intensive service sector. In order to ensure that demand management and supply side policy are unified, it is proposed that all attempts to undertake stabilization policy should operate through the taxation system, leaving questions concerning government spending growth to be decided through the political process. The scheme is constructed in a way that would ensure that demand management would become semi-automatic since increases in aggregate supply at stable prices would result in automatic demand stimulation through resultant tax rebates. Conversely, widespread attempts to wage inflate would result in a deflationary impact as tax rebates shrank towards zero.

The proposal is extremely simple to implement, given the existing level of information availability, and would involve a much smaller amount of administrative effort than, for example, the Vines *et al.* proposals. The policy is truly decentralized with no firm debarred from making any pricing or wage-setting choice that it wishes and, perhaps more importantly, the scheme permits a wide diversity of political opinion to be reflected in the choice of instrumental parameters, offering a good chance of a new policy consensus. There is no pre-commitment to any political line in the scheme, only a belief that the promotion of contractual harmony overrides political issues and that economists can contribute in suggesting social institutions to that end. Undoubtedly, the crudeness of the scheme would render it obsolete in time, as evolution of the economic system proceeds. However, even if it were half as successful as Keynes's social innovation, its implementation would be highly worthwhile.

The scheme is simple, some would say naive, but it is no more so than Keynesian stabilization policy. If we look on economic policy as being primarily about communication and consciousness formation, there are distinct advantages in simplicity. These advantages could lead to evolutionary gains which could postpone the inevitable obsolescence of the policy much further into the future than the sceptic might suggest. However, one of the main intentions of the proposal is to stimulate debate in the hope that a more practical version can emerge. Even the proposal as it stands could benefit from various simulation exercises to track the impacts on other macroeconomic variables and fiscal magnitudes. Also, the scheme could be subject to game-theoretic simulation to check whether or not the incentive structure is stable as it stands.[23]

The proposal may well come as something of a disappointment to the ecological, anti-materialist school of thought, given that it seems to promote the interests of the mass production section which they abhor. In this regard, the words of Pirsig, again, come to mind:

> The way to solve the conflict between human values and technological needs is not to run away from technology. That's impossible. The way to solve the conflict is to break down the barriers of dualistic thought that prevent a real understanding of what technology is – not an exploitation of nature, but a fusion of nature and the human spirits into a new kind of creation which transcends both. (Pirsig, 1974, p. 284)

The kinds of changes that the ecological school wishes to see can only come on the flexible periphery of an economic system with a healthy productive core. Productive structure is on the verge of providing the technology, in mass produced form, which can facilitate decentralized activity. It must be encouraged to evolve in this direction, through strengthened contractual security and incentives to use economic power as a base for creativity, not protectionism. The proposal attempts to encourage all these things, as well as reducing the obstructive potential of both public and private sector bureaucracies.

By its very nature, macroeconomic policy can only deal with a limited range of economic problems in the core of macro-structure and macro-consciousness. As such it can be no more than a way of *facilitating* evolution. The precise nature of the evolution that results depends on yet to be discovered 'fusions of nature and the human spirit'.

Notes

1 See Poincaré (1905).

2 Even in physics, the logical propositions concerning relativity were not verified empirically until a later date when it was possible to conduct experiments using equipment and techniques unavailable to Einstein.

3 Carl Sagan, in his lectures about the dangers of normative influences in astronomy, often tells the story of Lovell's observation of 'canals' on Mars and how a highly developed scientific literature grew up identifying the details of this non-existent irrigation system. Poor observational data permitted human idealizations about higher level civilization to be inferred widely. The parallels are strong with economists 'seeing' an underlying Walrasian market system through the 'fog' of econometric analysis and providing idealizations about the existence of a superior free market social organization.

4 See Scitovsky (1976) for discussion of the difficulties involved in presenting analysis outside the frames of reference of different schools of thought.

5 See Simon (1984).

6 These trends have led futurologists, such as Toffler (1981), to predict fundamental decentralization of production and reversals of the bureaucratic-centralist tendencies of the past half-century.

7 Recent proposals by, for example, Layard (1982) and Vines *et al.* (1983) to provide incentives for firms to increase their employment reflect this short-term perspective.

8 See Gershuny and Miles (1983) for an extended discussion of this difference between manufacturing and services in the US and UK.

9 It is clear that many Keynesians have come to regard productivity growth and employment growth as incompatible. This is understandable within a short-run framework but once we consider the long-run dynamic context this incompatibility need not exist. This has been well understood in the Harrod-Domar tradition in the past. Proposals to introduce employment subsidies contained in Layard (1982) and Vines *et al.* (1983) reflect a contemporary view that in a stagnating economy this incompatibility must exist. However, it is inevitable that the implementation of such policies will tend to raise employment in the short run at the expense of higher rates of job creation in the long run. Any policy which lowers productivity growth and hence

aggregate supply offers no durable solution for the stagnating economy.

10 See Sumner (1981) for some analysis of the problems that are confronted in providing investment incentives.

11 For a review of the tax-based anti-inflation policy literature see Bosanquet (1983), Colander (1979) and Seidman (1978). The seminal pieces were by Scott (1961) in the UK and Wallich and Weintraub (1971) in the US. There are two dominating features of this literature: first, that tax penalties are used to 'stiffen' or 'strengthen' management resistance to wage inflation and, second, that the approach is not founded in any particular school of thought. In Foster (1984) it is argued that this general lack of theoretical foundations is both a strength and a weakness and that the Okun tax rebate approach is much better founded in a distinctive evolutionary approach to the macroeconomic system. Thus, the Okun approach is in a different tradition to the rest of the literature, as is the proposal to be set down here.

12 See Canto, Joines and Laffer (1983) for a good exposition of 'supply side economics' and Minford (1983) for the more analytical new Classical approach.

13 See Perkins (1982) for a discussion of the symbiotic possibilities of tax cuts plus a listing of the advantages of a switch in emphasis to taxation variation in stabilization policy.

14 See Vines *et al.* (1983) for recent proposals which do involve varying tax rates on an ongoing basis in order to stabilize employment.

15 The Japanese system relies on unique cultural traditions which may, ultimately, prove ephemeral in the face of Western values which emphasize individualism. Sinha (1982) provides an interesting analysis of the interaction of Japanese culture and the functioning of the economy. In the Euro-American countries, after a protracted period of high material aspirations, cultural and moral suasions have become inappropriate and explicit material incentives seem to be essential in the design of a 'supply side' policy. Hirsch (1977) presents the best known analysis of this cultural shift and its socioeconomic effects.

16 See Dildine and Sunley (1978) for a discussion of these problems.

17 This formula is not necessarily optimal. The issue of index number bias is left aside to be resolved in the implementation phase.

18 Since x_{jt} is computed only on domestic products, inflation in the price of goods sold abroad would be included in y_{jt}. All increases in foreign turnover are regarded as a productivity increase for the purposes of the scheme.

19 See Deaton and Muellbauer (1980) who point out that the 'supply of quality' has been largely neglected in economics (p. 270). Such difficulties in disentangling the 'quality improvement' component of price increases is analogous to the difficulty in measuring the

contribution of technical progress to the economic growth process. Attempts have been made to construct 'quality corrected' price indices but only in cases where specification changes are quantifiable (see, for example, Cubbin, 1975, and Ohta, 1975).

20 This view that inflation is merely an indication of the declining quality of money has been central to the monetarist tradition and has reached its logical limit in new Classical models, where monetary growth instantly lowers its quality and raises prices. The scheme here attempts to break this 'monetary pessimism' offering rewards and compensations to those who do not make such a response.

21 Sinha (1981) also provides a picture of the 'subcontracting' sector of the Japanese economy which exhibits this type of rapid quantity/quality responsiveness.

22 In the postwar period a substantial proportion of service sector employment growth occurred in the public sector which, Bacon and Eltis (1978) argue, changed from an endogenous phenomenon in the early years to an exogenous force, which 'crowded out' private sector activity in the later years. However, evidence for the United States suggests that the private service sector has accounted for a substantial amount of endogenous employment growth. Sinha (1982) also argues that the small business/subcontracting sector in the Japanese economy is endogenously affected by the fortunes of the large business sector, simultaneously exhibiting a higher rate of employment growth while experiencing more fluctuations as macroeconomic shocks are absorbed.

23 See, for example, Maital and Lipnowski (1985) who subject tax-based incomes policy schemes to game-theoretic simulation.

13 *Conclusion*

> In short, neither the crushing powers of the centralised state nor the teachings of mutual hatred and pitiless struggle which come, adorned with the attributes of science, from obliging philosophers and sociologists, could weed out the feeling of human solidarity, deeply lodged in men's understanding and heart, because it has been nurtured in all previous evolution.
>
> Peter Kropotkin (1902)

Any reader thumbing hurriedly through this book might well come to the conclusion that what is being proposed is yet another interdisciplinary approach to our economic problems. It is worth emphasizing that this is not the case. Attempts to blend specialized disciplines can never offer a set of simple guidelines, only complexity and potential confusion. What we have tried to do here is to alter the basic non-economic premisses upon which economic analysis is built to take account of evolutionary changes in the economic system. Other disciplines, such as management science, sociology, social psychology and political science, were investigated because they are better equipped to perceive such changes. The end result is a perspective which is thoroughly economic in character and needs to be defended as such in times when the subject is coming under attack from so many quarters.

This defence of the economic perspective is not induced by chauvinism or a desire to protect vested interests, but because economics is, and always has been, a subject which has promoted co-ordination, co-operation and creativity as the highest ideals in the province of human behaviour. Infusion of political forces, for example, into economic analysis signals a loss of idealism, an acceptance of the power of interest groups formed by history. When the ideals that economists strive towards are not being achieved, economics fragments and pessimism becomes the order of the day. The presence of crisis in the economy, on the one hand, merely strengthens the conflictual view of economic relations while, on the other hand, the difficulties faced by economic policy-makers encourage the view that intervention is ineffectual.

It has been argued that the dynamic perspective embodied in *homo creativus* offers a behavioural foundation which enhances the distinctiveness of the economic approach. The contract, a universal device observed in the real world, constitutes the institutional arrangement which replaces the auction market as the mechanism that generates forward-looking co-ordination in the macroeconomy. The contract can promote structural change in the future, whereas the auction market is the great conciliator of past decisions. Furthermore, the contract makes explicit the process whereby economic consciousness interfaces with economic structure in a way that emphasizes the importance of qualitative factors. There has been a tendency in economics to focus attention on the quantifiable while underplaying the qualitative by holding consciousness and structure constant.

In macroeconomics, this quantification goal has been seriously undermined by developments over the past decade. First, the development of the vector-autoregressive approach to forecasting has demonstrated the significant inertial quality of economic structure. Second, the rational expectations approach has demonstrated, in a logical way, the ability of economic consciousness to adapt to economic change in a way that makes quantification difficult. It is clear that the qualitative forces which bind together consciousness and structure can no longer be assumed away in macroeconomic analysis. However, once we recognize, explicitly, the role of qualitative factors, there are profound methodological implications for macroeconomics.

The notion that 'hypothesis testing' is possible in macroeconomics is untenable once we admit qualitative factors and remove the kind of disequilibrium/equilibrium divisions adopted in orthodox econometric modelling. Not only is secondary source macroeconomic data unsuitable for such physics-style experiments, but it is also the case that the ever-changing interface of consciousness and structure depicted in our dynamic behavioural construct cannot be tested in this way in any case. However, the abandonment of a 'hypothesis testing' methodology does not mean the end of quantification in economics. On the contrary, once this restrictive view is removed, the quantitative potential is increased.

It is often argued that the vector-autoregressive approach to econometric modelling and forecasting is 'atheoretical', yet, in elemental form, the fact that much of what happens in the future is determinable in the past *is* a theory. It is a qualitative theory of structural continuity. Once we recognize this for what it is, there is unlimited potential for quantitative forecasting in economics. Macroeconometric modellers need no longer feel guilty about the eclecticism and theoretical non-identifiability of their 'dynamic' specifications. Not only do we always need good *ceteris paribus* forecasts but we also need the information provided by such models as to the logical structure of the economic system. Econometric models tell us a great deal about the co-variation of key macroeconomic variables and, more interestingly, show us how and when particular variables begin to assume deviant paths. To those interested in the evolutionary development of the economy, information concerning the slowing down and fragmentation of a development phase is of great value.

We know that in the face of certain kinds of shocks, involving shifts in consciousness or structure, econometric forecasts are unreliable, based, as they must be, on the past. However, it is this very unreliability which opens the door to another form of quantification. The only way we can begin to understand the effects of such qualitative shocks is to examine logically how the economic system, particularly on the side of consciousness, is likely to respond given the general logic of structure as it exists. Not only are such logical exercises of great value in conditioning econometric forecasts in the wake of such shocks but they are also of value in exploring the possible effects of various policy initiatives. To date, rational expectations theorists have preferred to conduct such exercises on a limited range of policies fed through a logical model which is abstract in construction rather than one which is an up-to-date depiction of the economy. In an evolutionary context, the logic of game theory seems much more relevant in gaining an understanding of expectational interaction as developed by, for example, Robert Axelrod (1984).

Once we abandon the false scientism concerned with providing empirical support for hypotheses, macroeconomics can re-establish its credibility. Short-term forecasts can be provided along with logical exercises which, in order to be continually relevant, must be evolutionary in character. Much empirical work has to be done by economists to detect, in past data, evolutionary trends upon which logical propositions can be based and data must be disaggregated with evolutionary shifts very much in mind. In a world of rapidly developing information technology there is no reason to suppose that such a task cannot be achieved. Furthermore, in addition to disaggregation of data collected over comparable time periods, the analysis of contractual data, with varying time dimension, offers empirical opportunities to understand forward-looking behaviour in ways entirely new in the subject.

In an evolutionary context, macroeconomists are not limited to modelling, for example, monetary and fiscal shocks through a fixed-parameter model but have a much more important role as systems analysts and designers. In this sense they are analogous to control engineers or organic chemists rather than experimental physicists. Optimal structural alteration is the concern of the evolutionary macroeconomist rather than flow variations through structural fixity. Or, to put the point in a much older context, macroeconomists should be more concerned with the ongoing design and redesign of automatic stabilizers than the calculation of the size of discretionary intervention. For many years, Milton Friedman and others in the monetarist and new Classical tradition have argued for the same thing, but from a much narrower, static, market clearing vision of the macroeconomy. Thus, much of the discussion has centred on limited questions such as the introduction of constitutionalized monetary rules.

Once we broaden our vision of the macroeconomy to a system subject to continual evolutionary change, we must accept that rules become obsolete, encouraging government to resort to discretionary intervention. This perpetual tendency towards obsolescence ensures that it is not possible to constitutionalize automatic stabilizers for all time. The role of the evolutionary macroeconomist is to ensure that such systems are continually updated and improved upon to meet new situations. It is in this area that Keynesian policy has been most obviously deficient. Thus, there are few Keynesian counterparts to the 'supply side' proposals of new Classical economists to alter the structure of incentives faced by, for example, entrepreneurs and the unemployed.

As economists we must, of course, be aware of the fact that loss of discretion is unpopular amongst politicians who prefer to be seen to be 'doing something' for their supporters rather than to be presiding over a well oiled, automatic policy apparatus. However, we saw in the Keynesian era that consensus on the structure of economic policy is possible and that, in such circumstances, the contribution of the economist is highly regarded. A new emphasis on policy design would, in all probability, enhance the status of economists in the eyes of the public and relieve politicians of decision-making in areas that they are ill-equipped to deal with.

It is in the area of persuasion that logical presentation is so important. Policy design can only be defended by appealing to the logic of evolutionary development. In order to communicate to a wide audience this must be done in a simple way against a solid empirical background of econometric forecasts. It is in these pedagogic exercises in logic that the contractual approach is so important since it is capable of encapsulating different schools of thought in macroeconomics, creating the theoretical consensus which forms an essential counterpart to any policy consensus. The typical method of modelling economic behaviour has been in terms of portfolio or demand/supply substitutions, in the face of price differentials of various types. The contractual approach to modelling begins from a different perspective: the degree of complementarity of plans into the future.

In the past, it has been recognized that the income effect complicates the substitution effect in orthodox demand theory. Keynes, in ignoring price effects, produced a theory of effective demand solely concerned with income effects. In evolutionary macroeconomics, the association with demand theory is severed with ongoing contracting generating income flows and substitution comprising a force which can range from minor marginal adjustment through to catastrophic shifts. Changing the conventional mode of thinking amongst economists to such an evolutionary perspective represents the greatest challenge facing macroeconomics. Although the Keynesian orthodoxy, stylized in the IS–LM model, shifted macroeconomics away from the simple demand/supply dichotomy, we saw how macroeconomists could never quite shed this central dichotomy from their thinking. The reason for this is understandable: a coherent alternative did not exist.

Critics of Keynesian justifications of 'rigidities' such as Robert Lucas and Thomas Sargent have always argued that the weakness of such analysis is that it is not derived from economic theory. We have seen how attempts to graft on optimal contracts to market clearing analysis has not been very successful in rebutting such claims. However, what has been regarded as economic theory is very narrow. It is *homo economicus* engaged in substitution behaviour in the context of clearing markets. Once we extend economic theory to include *homo creativus* in historical time, forming contracts which are fulfilled, we have an equally valid non-*ad hoc* alternative to begin to understand the rigidities and continuities that are so commonly observed in the real world.

Throughout this book a plea has been made to include, explicitly, qualitative factors in economic analysis, using quantitative analysis to detect when qualitative shifts are of importance and taking full account of the qualitative potential of economic consciousness when designing policy. Attempts to avoid confronting structural quality effects by, for example, resorting to 'dynamic specification' in short-run macroeconomics, or by pretending that consciousness quality effects are described by 'technical progress residuals' in long-run macroeconomics, cannot be sustained any longer. However, this is not to say that the old quantitative approach is redundant. In true evolutionary spirit, the approach will still have a place in the scheme of things.

This is particularly true in the emerging field of open economy, or international, macroeconomics. As the world economy has become increasingly integrated in the postwar period, particularly in terms of the growth of international production, so the international dimension of macroeconomics has received increasing emphasis. The notion that international questions should be left as the province of international economists has weakened as more powerful multiplier effects and monetary connections have been observed in the international economy. It is no longer accurate to describe the world economy as a collection of individual economies trading with each other. Nearly half of world production now comes from multinational firms operating across the world economy.

There is little doubt that this evolutionary development of the world economy was facilitated by the Keynesian expansionism of individual countries, particularly the United States, in the postwar period. However, the 1970s were characterized by a growth of protectionism in the face of this expansion of multinational production given its implications for the independence of government in particular countries. This growth in protectionism has been accompanied by a tendency towards recessionary policies as individual countries have attempted to solve unilaterally their domestic inflation and balance of payments problems. In turn, of course, this slackening of demand has induced a slowing down of multinational investment.

The plight of the world economy in the 1980s is not dissimilar to that of advanced economies, such as the United States, in the 1930s. By that time the US economy was characterized by large, imperfectly competitive firms whose business spanned the whole North American continent. These firms were faced by large labour unions, which negotiated wages and conditions of employment, some strong and some very weak. Typically the 'protectionism' of strong firms and unions, combined with a non-interventionist stance by government, resulted in unemployment of the weak, excess capacity and slow economic growth.

In the modern international economy it is not labour unions but countries which behave in a protectionist manner. Once again it is the strong who gain and the weak who suffer excess capacity and unemployment. The prescription for the international economy is the same as that for the US economy in the 1930s. It suffers a Keynesian lack of effective demand, requiring expansion through international policy co-ordination in order to provide a stable environment once again for multinational investment and growth. In order to analyse this condition, all we require is traditional quantitative analysis of monetary and fiscal shocks which are necessarily discretionary given the impossibility of designing automatic stabilizers across many countries.

A major feature of the current literature on international macroeconomics, which we are not reviewing here, is that it is predominantly 'demand side', not 'supply side'. It is quite proper that this should be the case given that the international economy has an effective demand problem. To tackle supply side problems requires specific analyses of individual countries with unique evolutionary paths. It is no use saying that international interactions are all important and, thus, resigning ourselves to observing secular decline relative to other countries. Neither is it helpful to the international economy to take a protectionist position in such a situation. A supply side, or, in our terms, an evolutionary perspective on individual countries, is entirely compatible with a demand side, or, in our terms, non-evolutionary, perspective on the international economy.

In the end, how much demand expansion, either internally or externally generated, can occur in any economy will depend critically on the rate of productivity growth achieved. In this sense demand management in advanced economies has to be set more firmly in the medium-run context of evolutionary policy design. Crude short-run Keynesianism is only relevant in the international economy with its large excess capacity in the raw material, primary commodity, basic manufacturing sectors predominantly in LDCs. As was the case with labour supply in the 1930s, real income cuts are inappropriate. Only by stimulating spending power can the effective demand gap be closed.

Exactly how this is done and how compromises are made with regard to ecological and cultural effects of further development in LDCs is beyond the scope of this book. Here we have been concerned with post-industrial economies and their quest to move towards a new epoch of evolution which will strike a new balance betweeen technology intensive activity and cultural and ecological priorities. The problems of the post-industrial economy and the less developed economy are starkly different. The former requires decentralization, minimizing the discretionary interference of political interest groups involved in government. The latter requires the formation of a centralized international agency with discretionary power to co-ordinate the expansionary policy they require so badly.

However, these different requirements are not unrelated for, in as much as advanced countries evolve towards technology intensive, high productivity growth, environmentally balanced economies, so it will be easier for less developed countries to achieve their goals further down the path of evolution. Successful, strong economies tend to rely less on the exercise of power to maintain real standards of living than those on a path of secular stagnation. We can only hope that the evolutionary perspective in this book can offer a beginning in reaching towards new macroeconomic policies to facilitate such progress. Perhaps, once again, economists can be permitted to make a central contribution to the process of economic evolution, overcoming the same political forces which Keynes saw in his own time:

> Is the fulfilment of these ideas a visionary hope? Have they insufficient roots in the motives which govern the evolution of political society? Are the interests which they will thwart stronger and more obvious than those which they will serve?
>
> John Maynard Keynes (1936) p. 383.

Bibliography

Ackoff, R. L. and Emery, F. E. (1972), *On Purposeful Systems* (London: Tavistock).

Addison, P. (1977), *The Road to 1945* (London: Quartet).

Akerlof, G. (1979), 'The case against conservative macro-economics', *Economica*, vol. 46, pp. 219–38.

Akerlof, G. (1984), *An Economic Theorist's Book of Tales: Essays that Entertain the Consequences of New Assumptions in Economic Theory* (Cambridge: Cambridge University Press).

Alchian, A. A. (1950), 'Uncertainty, evolution and economic theory', *Journal of Political Economy*, vol. 58, pp. 211–22.

Allais, M. (1966), 'A restatement of the Quantity Theory of Money', *American Economic Review*, vol. 56, pp. 1123–57.

Allport, K. H. (1955), *Theories of Perception and the Concept of Structure* (New York: Wiley).

Ando, A. and Modigliani, F. (1963), 'The life-cycle hypothesis of saving: aggregate implications and tests', *American Economic Review*, vol. 53, pp. 55–84.

Andrews, P. W. (1964), *On Competition and Economic Theory* (London: Macmillan).

Angyal, A. (1969), 'A logic of systems' in F. E. Emery (ed.), *Systems Thinking, Vol. 1* (London: Penguin), pp. 17–29.

Angyal, A. (1981), 'Personality as a hierarchy system' in F. E. Emery, *Systems Thinking*, pp. 125–37.

Archibald, G. C. (1979) Review article of *Appraisal in Economics*, in S. Latsis (ed.), *Journal of the Philosophy of Social Science*, pp. 304–25.

Arendt, H. (1951), *The Origins of Totalitarianism* (New York: Harcourt).

Arestis, P. and Skouras, T. (eds) (1985), *Post-Keynesian Economic Theory* (Brighton: Wheatsheaf).

Arrow, K. (1962), 'The economic implications of learning by doing', *Review of Economic Studies*, vol. 29, pp. 155–73.

Artis, M. J., Bladen-Hovell, R., Karakitsos, E. and Dwolatzky, B. (1984), 'The effects of economic policy: 1979–82', *National Institute Economic Review*, no. 108, pp. 54–67.

Ashby, W. R. (1967), 'The set theory of mechanism and homeostatis' in D. J. Stewart (ed.), *Automation Theory and Learning Systems* (Washington, D.C.: Thompson Book Co), pp. 23–51.

Averitt, R. T. (1975), 'Time's structure, man's strategy: the American experience' in H. F. Williamson (ed.), *Evolution of International Management Structures* (Newark: University of Delaware Press), pp. 13–39.

Axelrod, R. (1984), *The Evolution of Co-operation* (New York: Basic Books).

Azariadis, C. (1975), 'Implicit contracts and underemployment equilibria', *Journal of Political Economy*, vol. 83, pp. 1183–201.

Azariadis, C. and Stiglitz, J. (1983), 'Implicit contracts and fixed-price equilibria', *Quarterly Journal of Economics*, vol. 93, pp. 1–22.

Bacon, R. and Eltis, W. (1976), *Britain's Economic Problems: Too Few Producers* (London: Macmillan).

Baily, M. N. (1974), 'Wages and employment under uncertain demand', *Review of Economic Studies*, vol. 41, pp. 37–50.

Balogh, T. (1982), *The Irrelevance of Conventional Economics* (London: Weidenfeld & Nicolson).

Barro, R. J. (1979), 'Second thoughts on Keynesian economics', *American Economic Review, Papers and Proceedings*, vol. 69, pp. 54–68.

Barro, R. J. and Grossman, H. I. (1971), 'A general disequilibrium model of income and employment', *American Economic Review*, vol. 61, pp. 82–93.

Barry, N. P. (1979), *Hayek's Social and Economic Philosophy* (London: Macmillan).

Bauer, W. and Sammelson, L. (1981), 'Towards a service-oriented growth strategy', *World Development*, vol. 9, pp. 499–514.

Bausor, R. (1982–83), 'Time and the structure of economic analysis', *Journal of Post-Keynesian Economics*, vol. 5, pp. 163–79.

Bausor, R. (1983), 'The rational expectation hypothesis and the epistemics of time', *Cambridge Journal of Economics*, vol. 7, pp. 1–10.

Bausor, R. (1984), 'Towards a historically dynamic economics: examples and illustrations', *Journal of Post-Keynesian Economics*, vol. 6, pp. 360–76.

Becker, G. (1976), *The Economic Approach to Human Behaviour* (Chicago: Chicago University Press).

Begg, D. (1982), *The Rational Expectations Revolution in Macroeconomics* (Oxford: Philip Allan).

Bell, D. and Kristol, I. (1981), *The Crisis in Economic Theory* (New York: Basic Books).

Benassy, J. P. (1975), 'Neo-Keynesian disequilibrium theory in a monetary economy', *Review of Economic Studies*, vol. 42, pp. 503–23.

Berger, S. and Piore, M. J. (1980), *Dualism and Discontinuity in Industrial Societies* (Cambridge: Cambridge University Press).

Beveridge, W. H. (1944), *Full-Employment in a Free Society* (London: Allen & Unwin).

Bienkowski, W. (1981), *Theory and Reality: the Development of Social Systems* (London: Allison & Busby).

Bischoff, C. W. (1971), 'Business investment in the 1970s: a comparison of models', *Brookings Papers on Economic Activity*, no. 1, pp. 13–58.

Blatt, J. M. (1983), *Dynamic Economic Systems* (New York: M. E. Sharpe).

Bleaney, M. F. (1985), *The Rise and Fall of Keynesian Economics* (London: Macmillan).

Blondel, J. (1981), *The Discipline of Politics* (London: Butterworths).

Boland, L. A. (1982), *The Foundations of Economic Method* (London: Allen & Unwin).

Boland, L. A. (1985), 'The foundations of Keynes' methodology: *The General Theory*' in T. Lawson and M. H. Pesaran (eds), *Keynes' Economics: Methodological Issues* (London: Croom Helm), pp. 181–94.

Bosanquet, N. (1983), 'Tax-based incomes policy', *Oxford Bulletin of Economics and Statistics*, pp. 33–49.

Bosworth, B. P. (1983), 'Comment on R. J. Gordon' in J. Tobin (ed.), *Macroeconomics, Prices and Quantities* (Oxford: Blackwell).

Boulding, K. E. (1981), *Evolutionary Economics* (London: Sage Publications).

Boulier, B. (1984), 'What lies behind Verdoorn's Law?', *Oxford Economic Papers*, vol. 36, pp. 259–67.

Breit, W. and Ransom, R. L. (1971), *The Academic Scribblers: American Economists in Collision* (New York: Rinehart & Winston).

Brennan, H. G. and Buchanan, J. M. (1981), *Monopoly in Money and Inflation (Hobar Paper 88)* (London: Institute for Economic Affairs).

Bresciani-Turroni, C. (1937), *The Economics of Inflation* (London: Allen & Unwin).

Brittan, S. (1983), *The Role and Limits of Government* (London: Temple Smith).

Buchanan, J. and Tullock, G. (1962), *The Calculus of Consent* (Anne Arbor: University of Michigan Press).

Buchanan, J. M. and Wagner, R. E. (1977), *Democracy in Deficit: The Political Legacy of Lord Keynes* (New York: Academic Press).

Buchanan, J. M., Wagner, R. E. and Burton, J. (1978), *The Consequences of Mr Keynes* (London, IEA Hobert Paper No. 78).

Buiter, W. H. and Miller, M. H. (1983), 'Changing the rules: economic consequences of the Thatcher regime', *Brookings Papers in Economic Activity*, no. 2, pp. 305–80.

Cagan, P. (1956), 'The monetary dynamics of hyperinflation' in M. Friedman (ed.), *Studies in the Quantity Theory of Money* (Chicago: University of Chicago Press), pp. 25–117.

Cairncross, A. (1985), *Years of Recovery of British Economic Policy 1945–51* (New York: Methuen).

Caldwell, B. J. (1982), *Beyond Positivism: Economic Methodology in the Twentieth Century* (London: Allen & Unwin).

Cannon, W. B. (1963), *The Wisdom of the Body* (New York: Norton).

Canto, V. A., Joines, D. H. and Laffer, A. B. (1983), *Foundations of Supply Side Economics: Theory and Evidence* (New York: Academic Press).

Carabelli, A. (1985), 'Keynes on cause, chance and possibility' in T. Lawson and M. H. Pesaran (eds), *Keynes' Economics: Method-*

ological Issues (London: Croom Helm), pp. 151–80.

Carter, M. and Maddock, R. (1984), *Rational Expectations: Macroeconomics for the 1980s?* London: Macmillan).

Casson, M. (1981), *Unemployment: A Disequilibrium Approach* (Oxford: Martin Robertson).

Cencini, A. (1984), *Time and the Macroeconomic Analysis of Income* (London: Pinter).

Chamberlin, E. (1934), *The Theory of Monopolistic Competition* (Cambridge, Mass.: Harvard University Press).

Chandler, A. (1962), *Strategy and Structure* (Cambridge, Mass.: MIT Press).

Chandler, A. (1977), *The Visible Hand: The Managerial Revolution in American Business* (Cambridge, Mass.: Harvard University Press).

Chick, V. (1973), *The Theory of Monetary Policy*, 2nd edn (Oxford: Blackwell).

Chick, V. (1983), *Macroeconomics after Keynes: A Reconsideration of the General Theory* (Oxford: Philip Allan).

Clark, C. (1970), *Taxmanship*, 2nd edn (London: Institute of Economic Affairs).

Clower, R. W. (1965), 'The Keynesian counter-revolution: a theoretical appraisal' in R. W. Clower, *Monetary Theory: Selected Readings* (Harmondsworth: Penguin), pp. 270–97.

Colander, D. (1979), 'Incomes policies: MIP, WIPP and TIP', *Journal of Post-Keynesian Economics*, vol. 1, pp. 91–100.

Collard, D. (1978), *Altruism and Economy: A Study in Non-Selfish Economics* (Oxford: Blackwell).

Commons, J. R. (1961), *Institutional Economics* (Madison: University of Wisconsin Press).

Cooter, R. and Kornhauser, L. (1980), 'Can litigation improve the law without the help of judges?', *Journal of Legal Studies*, vol. 9, pp. 139–63.

Courakis, A. S. (1978), 'Serial correlation and a Bank of England study of the demand for money: an exercise in measurement without theory', *Economic Journal*, vol. 88, pp. 537–48.

Cross, J. G. (1983), *A Theory of Adaptive Economic Behaviour* (Cambridge: Cambridge University Press).

Cross, R. (1982), 'The Dunheim-Quine Thesis, Lakatos and the appraisal of theories in macroeconomics', *Economic Journal*, vol. 92, pp. 320–40.

Crotty, J. R. (1980), 'Post-Keynesian economic theory: an overview and evaluation', *American Economic Review, Papers and Proceedings*, vol. 70, pp. 20–5.

Cubbin, J. (1975), 'Quality change and pricing behaviour in the UK car industry 1956–1968', *Economica*, vol. 42, pp. 43–58.

Darwin, C. (1929), *The Origin of the Species by Means of Natural Selection* (London: Watts).

David, P. A. (1974), *Technical Change, Innovation and Economic Growth* (London: Cambridge University Press).

Davidson, P. (1972; 1978), *Money and the Real World* (London: Macmillan).

Dawkins, R. (1976), *The Selfish Gene* (Oxford: Oxford University Press).

Day, R. H. (1967), 'Profits, learning and the convergence of satisficing to marginalism', *Quarterly Journal of Economics*, vol. 81, pp. 302–11.

Day, R. H. (1984), 'Disequilibrium economic dynamics: a post-Schumpeterian contribution', *Journal of Economic Behaviour and Organisation*, vol. 5, pp. 56–76.

Day, R. H. and Groves, J. (eds) (1975), *Adaptive Economic Models* (New York: Academic Press).

Dean, J. W. (1981), 'The dissolution of the Keynesian consensus' in D. Bell and I. Kristol, *The Crisis in Economic Theory* (New York: Basic Books), pp. 19–34.

Deaton, A. and Muellbauer, J. (1980), *Economics and Consumer Behaviour* (Cambridge: Cambridge University Press).

Denison, E. F. (1962), *The Sources of Economic Growth in the United States and Alternatives Before Us* (New York: Committee for Economic Development).

Dildine, L. L. and Sunley, E. M. (1978), 'Administrative problems of tax-based incomes policies' in A. M. Okun and G. L. Perry (eds), *Curing Chronic Inflation* (Washington, Brookings), pp. 363–89.

Dornbush, R. (1980), *Open Economy Macroeconomics* (New York: Basic Books).

Dornbush, R. and Simonsen, M. H. (1983), *Inflation, Debt and Indexation* (Cambridge, Mass.: MIT Press).

Dow, A. C. and Dow, S. (1985), 'Animal spirits and rationality' in T. Lawson and M. H. Pesaran (eds), *Keynes' Economics: Methodological Issues* (London: Croom Helm), pp. 46–65.

Dow, S. C. (1985), *Macroeconomic Thought: A Methodological Approach* (Oxford: Blackwell).

Downs, A. (1957), *An Economic Theory of Democracy* (New York: Harper & Row).

Dreze, J. H. (1975), 'Existence of an equilibrium under price rigidity and quantity rationing', *International Economic Review*, vol. 16, pp. 301–20.

Duesenberry, J. (1949), *Income, Saving and the Theory of Consumer Behaviour* (Cambridge, Mass.: Harvard University Press).

Earl, P. E. (1983), *The Economic Imagination: Towards a Behavioural Theory of Choice* (Brighton: Wheatsheaf).

Earl, P. E. (1984), *The Corporate Imagination: How Big Companies Make Mistakes* (Brighton: Wheatsheaf).

Eatwell, J. and Milgate, M. (eds) (1983), *Keynes's Economics and the Theory of Value and Distribution* (London: Duckworth).

Eichner, A. S. (ed.) (1979), *A Guide to Post-Keynesian Economics* (White Plains: M. E. Sharpe).

Eichner, A. S. and Kregel, J. A. (1975), 'An essay on post-Keynesian theory: a new paradigm in economics', *Journal of Economic

Literature, vol. 13, pp. 1293–314.
Eldredge, N. (1985), *Time Frames: the Rethinking of Darwinian Evolution and the Theory of Punctuated Equilibria* (New York: Simon & Schuster).
Emery, F. E. (ed.) (1969), *Systems Thinking*, Vol. 1 (London: Penguin).
Emery, F. E. (ed.) (1981), *Systems Thinking*, Vol. 2 (London: Penguin).
Emery, F. E. (1981), 'The emergence of ideal-seeking systems' in F. E. Emery (ed.), *Systems Thinking*, Vol. 2 (London: Penguin), pp. 431–58.
Fisher, I. (1911; 1963), *The Purchasing Power of Money* (New York: Augustus Kelley).
Foster, J. (1976), 'The redistributive effects of inflation – questions and answers', *Scottish Journal of Political Economy*, vol. 23, pp. 73–98.
Foster, J. (1979), 'Interest rates and inflation expectations: The British experience', *Oxford Bulletin of Economics and Statistics*, vol. 41 (May), pp. 145–64.
Foster, J. (1981), 'The political economy of Mrs Thatcher's monetarism', *Quarterly Economic Commentary*, vol. 6, pp. 44–60.
Foster, J. (1984), 'Tax-based anti-inflation policies: in search of theoretical foundations' (University of Glasgow: Discussion Paper).
Freeman, C. (ed.) (1982), *Long Waves in the World Economy* (Guildford: Butterworth).
Friedman, M. (1953), 'The methodology of positive economics' in *Essays in Positive Economics* (Chicago: University of Chicago Press), pp. 3–43.
Friedman, M. (1956), 'The Quantity Theory of Money: A restatement' in M. Friedman, *Studies in the Quantity Theory of Money* (Chicago: Chicago University Press), pp. 3–21.
Friedman, M. (1957), *A Theory of the Consumption Function* (Princeton: Princeton University Press).
Friedman, M. (1971), 'A monetary theory of nominal income', *Journal of Political Economy*, vol. 78, pp. 323–37.
Friedman, M. (1980), 'Memorandum to the Treasury and Civil Service Committee', *Memoranda on Monetary Policy*, Session 1979–80 (HMSO, HC 720).
Friedman, M. and Meiselman, D. (1963), 'The relative stability of monetary velocity and the investment multiplier in the United States, 1898–1958' C.M.C. *Stabilisation Policies* (Englewood Cliffs, New Jersey: Prentice-Hall).
Friedman, M. and Schwartz, A. (1963), *A Monetary History of the United States: 1867–1960* (Princeton: Princeton University Press for NBER).
Friedman, M. and Schwartz, A. (1982), *Monetary Trends in the United States and the United Kingdom: Their Relationship to Income, Prices and Interest Rates, 1867–1975* (Chicago: University of Chicago Press for NBER).

Fromm, E. (1941), *Escape from Freedom* (New York: Rinehart & Winston).

Fromm, E. (1956), *The Sane Society* (London: Routledge & Kegan Paul).

Fromm, E. (1978), *To Have or to Be?* (London, Cape).

Froyen, R. T. and Waud, R. N. (1984), 'The changing relationship, between aggregate price and output: the British case', *Economica*, February, vol. 51, pp. 53–67.

Furnam, A. and Lewis, A. (1986), *The Economic Mind* (Brighton: Wheatsheaf).

Galbraith, J. K. (1952), *American Capitalism: the Concept of Countervailing Power* (Boston: Houghton Mifflin).

Galbraith, J. K. (1972), *New Industrial State*, 2nd edn (London: Penguin).

Galbraith, J. K. (1976), *The Affluent Society*, 3rd edn (Boston: Houghton Mifflin).

Georgescu-Roegen, N. (1971), *The Entropy Law and the Economic Process* (Cambridge, Mass.: Harvard University Press).

Gershuny, J. and Miles, I. (1983), *The New Service Sector Economy* (London: Pinter).

Giersch, H. and Wolter, F. (1983), 'Towards an explanation of the productivity slowdown: an acceleration-deceleration hypothesis', *Economic Journal*, vol. 93, pp. 35–55.

Glyn, A. (1982), 'The productivity slowdown: a Marxist view' in R. C. O. Matthews (ed.), *Slower Growth in the Western World* (London: Heinemann), pp. 148–65.

Gordon, W. C. (1980), *Institutional Economics: the Changing System* (Austin: University of Texas Press).

Gordon, R. J. and King, S. R. (1982), 'The output costs of disinflation in traditional and vector autoregressive models', *Brookings Papers on Economic Activity*, no. 1, pp. 205–44.

Green, H. A. J. (1977), 'Aggregation problems in macroeconomics' in G. C. Harcourt (ed.), *The Microeconomic Foundations of Macroeconomics* (London: Macmillan), pp. 179–94.

Grossman, S. J. and Stiglitz, J. E. (1980), 'On the impossibility of informationally efficient markets', *American Economic Review*, vol. 70, pp. 393–408.

Guha, A. S. (1981), *An Evolutionary View of Economic Growth* (Oxford: Clarendon Press).

Haavelmo, T. (1954), *A Study in the Theory of Economic Evolution* (Amsterdam: North Holland).

Hahn, F. H. (1977), 'Keynesian economics and general equilibrium theory: reflections on some current debates' in G. C. Harcourt (ed.), *The Microfoundations of Macroeconomics* (London: Macmillan), pp. 25–40.

Hahn, F. H. (1980), 'Monetarism and economic theory', *Economica*, vol. 47, pp. 1–17.

Hahn, F. (1983), 'Some Keynesian reflections on monetarism' in

F. Vicarelli, *Keynes's Relevance Today* (London: Macmillan), pp. 1–20.

Handy, C. B. (1981), *Understanding Organisations* (Harmondsworth: Penguin).

Hansen, A. H. (1953), *A Guide to Keynes* (New York: McGraw-Hill).

Harris, M. (1975), *Cows, Pigs, Wars and Witches* (London: Hutchinson).

Harrod, R. F. (1939), 'An essay in dynamic theory', *Economic Journal*, vol. 49, pp. 14–33.

Harrod, R. F. (1948), *Towards a Dynamic Economics* (New York: Macmillan).

Harrod, R. F. (1973), *Economic Dynamics* (London: Macmillan).

Hart, O. D. (1983), 'Optimal labour contracts under asymmetric information: an introduction', *Review of Economic Studies*, vol. 50, pp. 3–35.

Hayek, F. A. (1960), *The Constitution of Liberty* (London: Routledge & Kegan Paul).

Hayek, F. A. (1972), *A Tiger by the Tail: The Keynesian Legacy of Inflation* (London: Institute of Economic Affairs).

Heiner, R. A. (1983), 'The origin of predictable behaviour', *American Economic Review*, vol. 73 (September), pp. 560–95.

Henderson, H. (1979), *Creating Alternative Futures* (Berkley: Berkley Publishing Corp.).

Hendry, D. F. (1980) 'Econometrics – alchemy or science?', *Economica*, vol. 47, pp. 387–406.

Hendry, D. F. and Ericsson, N. R. (1983), 'Assertion without empirical basis: an econometric appraisal of Friedman and Schwartz' Monetary Trends in the UK' in Bank of England Panel of Academic Consultants, *Panel Paper*, no. 22 (October), pp. 45–101.

Herbst, P. G. (1976), *Alternatives to Hierarchies* (Leiden: Martinus Nijhoff).

Hey, J. D. (1983), *Data in Doubt* (Oxford: Blackwell).

Hicks, J. R. (1932), *The Theory of Wages* (New York: Macmillan).

Hicks, J. R. (1937), 'Mr Keynes and the Classics: A suggested interpretation', *Econometrica*, vol. 5, pp. 147–59.

Hicks, J. R. (1973), 'Recollections and documents', *Economica*, February, vol. 33, pp. 2–11.

Hicks, J. R. (1974), *The Crisis in Keynesian Economics* (Oxford: Basil Blackwell).

Hicks, J. R. (1977), *Economic Perspectives* (Oxford: Oxford University Press).

Hicks, J. R. (1979), *Causality in Economics* (Oxford: Blackwell).

Hirsch, F. (1977), *The Social Limits to Growth* (London: Routledge & Kegan Paul).

Hirsheifer, J. (1977), 'Economics from a biological viewpoint', *Journal of Law and Economics*, vol. 20, pp. 1–52.

Hirschman, A. O. (1982), 'Rival interpretations of market society:

civilising, destructive or feeble?', *Journal of Economic Literature*, vol. 20, pp. 1463–84.

Hodgson, G. (1985), 'Persuasian, expectations and the limit to Keynes' in T. Lawson and H. Pesaran (eds), *Keynes' Economics: Methodological Issues* (London: Croom Helm), pp. 10–45.

Hollis, M. and Nell, E. J. (1975), *Rational Economic Man: A Philosophical Critique of Neo-Classical Economics* (Cambridge: Cambridge University Press).

Hoover, K. (1984), 'Two types of monetarism', *Journal of Economic Literature*, vol. 22, pp. 58–76.

Hudson, J. (1982), *Inflation: A Theoretical Survey and Synthesis* (London: Allen & Unwin).

Hume, D. (1939), *A Treatise of Human Nature*, in D. D. Raphael (1969), *British Moralists: 1650–1800* (Oxford: Clarendon), pp. 3–58.

Hume, D. (1752; 1955), 'Of money' in E. Rotwein (ed.), *D. Hume: Writings on Economics* (Edinburgh: Nelson).

Hutchison, T. W. (1978), *On Revolutions and Progress in Economic Knowledge* (Cambridge: Cambridge University Press).

Hutchison, T. W. (1981), *The Politics and Philosophy of Economics: Marxians, Keynesians and Austrians* (Oxford: Basil Blackwell).

Ischboldin, B. (1958), *Economic Synthesis* (New Delhi).

Isnard, C. A. and Zeeman, E. C. (1976), 'Some models from catastrophe theory in the social sciences' in L. Collins (ed.), *Use of Models in the Social Sciences* (London: Tavistock), pp. 44–100.

Johnson, H. G. (1971), 'The Keynesian revolution and the monetarist counter-revolution', *American Economic Review*, vol. 61, pp. 1–14.

Jones, S. R. G. (1984), *The Economics of Conformism* (Oxford: Blackwell).

Jordan, N. (1981), 'Some thinking about "system"' in F. E. Emery, *Systems Thinking*, Vol. 2 (London: Penguin), pp. 15–39.

Kaldor, N. (1955), 'Alternative theories of distribution', *Review of Economic Studies*, vol. 23, pp. 83–100.

Kaldor, N. (1970), 'The new monetarism', *Lloyds Bank Review* (July), pp. 1–18.

Kaldor, N. (1972), 'The irrelevance of equilibrium economics', *Economic Journal*, vol. 82, pp. 1237–55.

Kaldor, N. (1982), *The Scourge of Monetarism* (Oxford: Oxford University Press).

Kaldor, N. (1986), *Economics Without Equilibrium* (Cardiff: University College Cardiff Press).

Kaldor, N. and Mirrlees, J. A. (1962), 'A new model of economic growth', *Review of Economic Studies*, vol. 29, pp. 174–92.

Katona, G. (1975), *Psychological Economics* (New York: Elsevier).

Katouzian, H. (1980), *Ideology and Method in Economics* (London: Macmillan).

Katz, D. and Kahn, R. L. (1960), *The Social Psychology of Organisations* (New York: Wiley).

Kay, N. M. (1979), *The Innovating Firm* (London: Macmillan).

Kay, N. M. (1982), *The Evolving Firm* (London: Macmillan).

Kay, N. M. (1984), *The Emergent Firm* (London: Macmillan).

Kelly, G. A. (1963), *A Theory of Personality: The Psychology of Personal Constructs* (New York: Norton).

Keynes, J. M. (1923; 1971), *A Tract on Monetary Reform. Collected Writings, IV* (London: Macmillan).

Keynes, J. M. (1930; 1971), *A Treatise on Money. Collected Writings, V, VI* (London: Macmillan).

Keynes, J. M. (1936), *The General Theory of Employment, Interest and Money* (London: Macmillan).

Keynes, J. M. (1937), 'The general theory of employment', *Quarterly Journal of Economics*, vol. 51, pp. 209–23.

Keynes, J. M. (1940), *How to Pay for the War* (London: Macmillan).

Keynes, J. M. (1930; 1971), *A Treatise on Probability. Collected Writings, VIII* (London: Macmillan for the Royal Economic Society).

Kirzner, I. M. (1979), *Perception, Opportunity and Profit* (Chicago: University of Chicago Press).

Klein, B. (1977), *Dynamic Economics* (Cambridge, Mass.: Harvard University Press).

Klein, L. (1970), *The Keynesian Revolution* (London: Macmillan).

Klein, L. (1983), *The Economics of Supply and Demand* (Oxford: Blackwell).

Koestler, A. (1964), *The Act of Creation* (London: Hutchinson).

Koestler, A. (1975), *The Ghost in the Machine* (London: Pan Books).

Koestler, A. (1978), *Janus: a Summing Up* (London: Hutchinson).

Kornai, J. (1971), *Anti-equilibrium: An Economic Systems Theory and the Tasks of Research* (Amsterdam: North Holland).

Kregel, J. A. (1973), *The Reconstruction of Political Economy: An Introduction to Post-Keynesian Economics*, 2nd edn (London: Macmillan).

Kregel, J. A. (1976), 'Economic methodology in the face of uncertainty', *Economic Journal*, vol. 86, pp. 209–25.

Kregel, J. A. (1980), 'Markets and institutions as features of a capitalistic production system', *Journal of Post-Keynesian Economics*, vol. 3, pp. 32–48.

Kregel, J. A. (1983), 'Budget deficits, stabilisation policy and liquidity preference: Keynes's post-war policy proposals' in F. Vicarelli, *Keynes's Relevance Today* (London: Macmillan), pp. 28–50.

Kropotkin, P. (1902), *Mutual Aid: A Factor in Evolution* (New York: Doubleday).

Kuhn, T. S. (1962; 1970), *The Structure of Scientific Revolutions* (Chicago: Chicago University Press).

Kuhn, T. S. (1977), *The Essential Tension* (Chicago: Chicago University Press).

Lachmann, L. M. (1976), 'Towards a critique of macroeconomics' in E. G. Dolan (ed.), *The Foundations of Modern Austrian Economics* (Kansas City: Sheed and Ward), pp. 152–9.

Laffont, J. J. (1975), 'Macroeconomic constraints, economic efficiency and ethics: an introduction to Kantian economics', *Economica*, vol. 42, pp. 430–7.

Laidler, D. E. W. (1981), 'Monetarism: An interpretation and assessment', *Economic Journal*, vol. 91 (March), pp. 1–28.

Laidler, D. (1982), 'Did macroeconomics need a rational expectations revolution?', *Working paper No. 8215C* (University of Western Ontario: Department of Economics).

Laidler, D. (1982a), *Monetarist Perspectives* (Oxford: P. Allen).

Laidler, D. E. W. and Parkin, J. M. (1975), 'Inflation: a survey', *Economic Journal*, vol. 85, pp. 741–809.

Lakatos, I. (1970), 'Falsification and the methodology of scientific research programmes' in I. Lakatos and A. Musgrave (eds), *Criticism and the Growth of Knowledge* (Cambridge: Cambridge University Press).

Lancaster, K. (1966), 'A new approach to consumer theory', *Journal of Political Economy*, vol. 74, pp. 132–57.

Latsis, S. (1972), 'Situational determinism in economics', *British Journal for the Philosophy of Science*, vol. 23, pp. 207–45.

Lawson, T. (1982), 'Keynesian model building and the rational expectations critique', *Cambridge Journal of Economics*, vol. 3, pp. 32–48.

Lawson, T. (1983), 'Different approaches to economic modelling', *Cambridge Journal of Economics*, vol. 7 (March), pp. 77–84.

Lawson, T. (1985), 'Keynes, predictions and econometrics' in T. Lawson and M. H. Pesaran (eds), *Keynes' Economics: Methodological Issues* (London: Croom Helm), pp. 116–33.

Layard, P. R. G. (1982), *More Jobs, Less Inflation* (London: Grant McIntyre).

Layard, P. R. G. and Nickell, S. (1980), 'The case for subsidising extra jobs', *Economic Journal*, vol. 90, pp. 51–73.

Layard, R. and Nickell, S. (1985), 'The causes of British unemployment', *National Institute Economic Review*, no. 111, pp. 62–85.

Leamer, E. E. (1983), 'Lets take the con out of econometrics', *American Economic Review*, vol. 73, pp. 31–43.

Leijonhufvud, A. (1968), *On Keynesian Economics and the Economics of Keynes* (Oxford: Oxford University Press).

Leijonhufvud, A. (1981), *Information and Co-ordination: Essays in Macroeconomic Theory* (Oxford: Oxford University Press).

Leibenstein, H. (1950), 'Bandwagon, snob and Veblen effects in the theory of consumers' demand', *Quarterly Journal of Economics*, vol. 64, pp. 183–207.

Leibenstein, H. (1976), *Beyond Economic Man* (Cambridge, Mass.: Harvard University Press).

Lipsey, R. (1966), *An Introduction to Positive Economics*, 2nd edn (London: Weidenfeld and Nicolson).

Littlechild, S. C. (1978), *The Fallacy of the Mixed Economy: An*

'Austrian' Critique of Economic Thinking and Policy (London: Institute of Economic Affairs).

Loasby, B. J. (1976), *Choice, Complexity and Ignorance* (Cambridge: Cambridge University Press).

Lucas, R. E. Jr (1975), 'An equilibrium model of the business cycle', *Journal of Political Economy*, vol. 83, pp. 1113–44.

Lucas, R. E. (1976), 'Econometric policy evaluation: a critique' in K. Brunner and A. H. Meltzer (eds), *The Phillips Curve and Labour Markets* (Amsterdam: North-Holland), pp. 19–46.

Lucas, R. E. Jr (1977), 'Understanding business cycles' in K. Brunner and A. H. Meltzer (eds), *Stabilisation of Domestic and International Economy* (Amsterdam: North Holland), pp. 7–29.

Lucas, R. E. Jr and Sargent, T. J. (1981), 'After Keynesian macroeconomics' in R. E. Lucas Jr and T. J. Sargent (eds), *Rational Expectations and Econometric Practice* (London: Allen & Unwin), pp. 295–319).

Macfie, A. L. (1955), 'The Scottish tradition in economic thought', *Scottish Journal of Political Economy*, vol. 2 (June), pp. 81–103.

McCloskey, D. N. (1983), 'The rhetoric of economics', *Journal of Economic Literature*, vol. 21, pp. 481–517.

MacIntyre, A. (1970), *Marcuse* (Glasgow: Collins Modern Masters).

McMahon, C. (1981), 'Morality and the invisible hand', *Philosophy and Public Affairs*, vol. 10, pp. 247–77.

Maddison, A. (1979), 'Long-run dynamics of productivity growth', *Banca Nazionale del Lavoro Quarterly Review*, vol. 33, pp. 247–90.

Maital, S. and Lipnowski, I. (1985), *Macroeconomic Conflict and Social Institutions* (Cambridge, Mass.: Ballinger).

Malinvaud, E. (1977), *The Theory of Unemployment Reconsidered* (Oxford: Blackwell).

Mandel, E. (1975), *Late Capitalism* (London: New Left Books).

Marcuse, H. (1964), *One-dimensional Man* (London: Routledge & Kegan Paul).

Margolis, H. (1982), *Selfishness, Altruism and Rationality* (Cambridge: Cambridge University Press).

Marshak, J. (1968), 'Decision-making: economic aspects' in *International Encyclopedia of the Social Sciences* (New York: Free Press), pp. 42–55.

Marshall, A. (1890), *Principles of Economics* (London: Macmillan).

Marshall, A. (1923), *Money, Credit and Commerce* (London: Macmillan).

Marston, R. C. and Turnovsky, S. J. (1985), 'Macroeconomic stabilisation through taxation and indexation: the use of firm-specific information', *Journal of Monetary Economics*, vol. 16, pp. 375–96.

Marx, K. (1867:1879) (1965–66), *Capital*, 3 Vols (Moscow: Progress Publishers).

Maslow, A. (1954), *Motivation and Personality* (New York: Harper & Row).

Masters, R. (1981), 'The value – and limits – of sociobiology' in E. White (ed.), *Sociobiology and Human Values* (New York: Lexington Books).

Matthews, R. C. O. (1954), *The Trade Cycle* (Cambridge: Cambridge University Press).

Mayer, T. (1978), *The Structure of Monetarism* (New York: Norton).

Maynard-Smith, J. (1976), 'Evolution and the theory of games', *American Scientist*, vol. 64, pp. 41–5.

Meade, J. E. (1982), *Wage-fixing* (London: Allen & Unwin).

Mesarovic, M. D., Macko, D., and Takahara, Y. (1970), *Theory of Hierarchical Multilevel Systems* (New York: Academic Press).

Minford, P. (1983), *Unemployment: Cause and Cure* (Oxford: Mainstream).

Minsky, H. P. (1976), *John Maynard Keynes* (London: Macmillan).

Minsky, H. P. (1980), 'Money, financial markets and the coherence of a market economy', *Journal of Post-Keynesian Economics*, vol. 3 (Fall), pp. 21–31.

Minsky, H. P. (1982), *Inflation, Recession and Economic Policy* (Brighton: Wheatsheaf).

Mises, L. (1949), *Human Action* (New Haven: Yale University Press).

Mishan, E. J. (1969), *The Costs of Economic Growth* (Harmondsworth: Penguin).

Modigliani, F. (1977), 'The monetarist controversy or should we forsake stabilisation policy?', *American Economic Review*, vol. 67, pp. 1–19.

Modigliani, F. and Brumberg, F. (1954), 'Utility analysis and the consumption function: and interpretation of cross-section data' in K. Kurihara (ed.), *Post-Keynesian Economics* (New Jersey: Rutgers University Press), pp. 388–436.

Moggridge, D. E. (1976), *Keynes* (London: Macmillan).

Mosley, P. (1984), *The Making of Economic Policy: Theory and Evidence from Britain and the US since 1945* (Brighton: Wheatsheaf).

Murphy, R. E. (1965), *Adaptive Processes in Economic Systems* (London: Academic Press).

Moss, S. (1984), *Markets and Macroeconomics* (Oxford: Blackwell).

Muth, J. F. (1961), 'Rational expectations and the theory of price movements', *Econometrica*, vol. 29, pp. 315–35.

Myrdal, G. (1976), 'The meaning and validity of institutional economics' in K. Dopfer (ed.), *Economics in the Future: Towards a New Paradigm* (London: Macmillan), pp. 56–93.

Nagatani, K. (1981), *Macroeconomic Dynamics* (Cambridge: Cambridge University Press).

Neary, D. and Stiglitz, J. E. (1982), 'Towards a reconstruction of Keynesian economics: expectations and constrained equilibria', *Quarterly Journal of Economics*, vol. 98 (supplement), pp. 199–228.

Negishi, T. (1979), *Microeconomic Foundations of Keynesian Macroeconomics* (Amsterdam: North Holland).

Nelson, C. R. and Plosser, C. I. (1982), 'Trends and random walks in macroeconomic time series', *Journal of Monetary Economics*, vol. 10, pp. 139–62.

Nelson, R. R. and Winter, S. G. (1982), *An Evolutionary Theory of Economic Change* (Cambridge, Mass.: Belknap Press of Harvard University Press).

Nordhaus, W. D. (1983), 'Macroconfusion: the dilemmas of economic policy' in J. Tobin (ed.), *Macroeconomics. Prices and Quantities* (Oxford: Blackwell), pp. 247–84.

Nozick, R. (1970), *Anarchy, State and Utopia* (New York: Basic Books).

Okun, A. M. and Perry, G. L. (eds) (1978), *Curing Chronic Inflation* (Washington, D.C.: Brookings).

Okun, A. M. (1981), *Prices and Quantities: A Macroeconomic Analysis* (Washington, D.C.: Brookings).

Olson, M. Jr (1965), *The Logic of Collective Action* (Cambridge, Mass.: Harvard University Press).

Olson, M. Jr (1982), *The Rise and Decline of Nations: Economic Growth, Stagflation and Social Rigidities* (New Haven: Yale University Press).

Ohta, M. (1975), 'Production technologies of the US boiler and turbo generator industries and hedonic price indexes for their products: a cost function approach', *Journal of Political Economy*, vol. 83, pp. 1–26.

Packard, V. (1960), *The Waste Makers* (London: Longman).

Parkin, M. (1986), 'The output-inflation trade-off when prices are costly to change', *Journal of Political Economy*, vol. 94, pp. 200–24.

Patinkin, D. (1956; 1965), *Money, Interest and Prices* (New York: Harper & Row).

Patinkin, D. (1976), *Keynes' Monetary Thought* (Durham, N. Carolina: Duke University Press).

Pasinetti, L. L. (1974), *Growth and Income Distribution* (Cambridge: Cambridge University Press).

Pasinetti, L. L. (1981), *Structural Change and Economic Growth* (Cambridge: Cambridge University Press).

Penrose, E. T. (1952), 'Biological analogies in the theory of the firm', *American Economic Review*, vol. 42, pp. 809–19.

Penrose, E. T. (1959), *The Theory of Growth of the Firm* (New York: Wiley).

Perkins, J. O. N. (1982), *Unemployment, Inflation and New Macroeconomic Policy* (London: Macmillan).

Pesaran, M. H. and Smith, R. (1985), 'Keynes on econometrics' in T. Lawson and M. H. Pesaran (eds), *Keynes' Economics: Methodological Issues* (London: Croom Helm), pp. 134–50.

Pheby, J. (1985), 'Are Popperian criticisms of Keynes' methodology justified?' in T. Lawson and M. H. Pesaran (eds), *Keynes' Economics: Methodological Issues* (London: Croom Helm), pp. 99–115.

Phelps, E. S. (ed.) (1970), *Microeconomic Foundations of Employment and Inflation Theory* (New York: Norton).

Piore, M. J. (1979), *Unemployment and Inflation: Institutional and Structural Views* (White Plains, Ill.: M. E. Sharpe).

Pirsig, R. M. (1974; 1976), *Zen and the Art of Motor Cycle Maintenance* (London: Corgi).

Poincaré, H. (1905; 1952), *Science and Hypothesis* (New York: Dover).

Polanyi, M. (1967), *The Tacit Dimension* (Gordon City, N.Y.: Doubleday Anchor).

Poole, W. (1976), 'Rational expectations in the macro-model', *Brookings Papers on Economic Activity*, no. 2, pp. 463–505.

Popper, K. (1944; 1961), *Poverty of Historicism* (New York: Harper & Row).

Presley, J. R. (1979), *Robertsonian Economics: An Examination of the Work of Sir D. H. Robertson on Industrial Fluctuation* (New York: Holmes & Meier).

Radcliffe, Lord (1959), *The Committee on the Working of the Monetary System: Report*, Cmnd. 827 (London: HMSO).

Rawls, J. (1971), *A Theory of Justice* (London: Oxford University Press).

Rifkin, J. (1980), *Entropy: A New World View* (New York: Viking Press).

Robbins, L. (1934), *The Great Depression* (London: Macmillan).

Robertson, D. H. (1940), *Essays in Monetary Theory* (London: King).

Robinson, J. (1933), *The Economics of Imperfect Competition* (London: Macmillan).

Robinson, J. (1952; 1980), *The Generalisation of the General Theory and Other Essays* (London: Macmillan).

Robinson, J. (1962), *Economic Philosophy* (London: Franklin Watts).

Robinson, J. (1965), 'The General Theory after twenty-five years' in *Collected Economic Papers*, Vol. 3 (Oxford: Basil Blackwell), pp. 100–3.

Robinson, J. (1971), 'The second crisis of economic theory', *American Economic Review*, vol. 62 (papers and proceedings), pp. 1–9.

Robinson, J. (1973), 'What has become of the Keynesian revolution?' in *After Keynes* (1973) (Oxford: Blackwell), pp. 1–10.

Robinson, J. (1977), 'What are the questions?', *Journal of Economic Literature*, vol. 15 (December), pp. 1318–39.

Robinson, J. (1978), *Contributions to Modern Economics* (Oxford: Blackwell).

Robinson, J. (1978a), 'History versus equilibrium' in J. Robinson, *Contributions to Modern Economics* (Oxford: Basil Blackwell), pp. 126–36.

Robinson, J. (1980), *Further Contributions to Modern Economics* (Oxford: Blackwell).

Robinson, J. (1980a), 'Time in economic theory', *Kyklos*, vol. 33. Reprinted in J. Robinson, *Further Contributions to Modern Economics* (Oxford: Blackwell), pp. 88–95.

Robinson, J. and Eatwell, J. (1977), *An Introduction to Modern Economics*

(Maidenhead: McGraw-Hill).
Rosen, S. (1985), 'Implicit contracts', *Journal of Economic Literature*, vol. 23, pp. 1144–75.
Rostow, W. W. (1960), *The Stages of Economic Growth* (Cambridge: Cambridge University Press).
Rostow, W. W. (1979), *Getting From Here to There* (London: Macmillan).
Rotwein, E. (ed.) (1955), *D. Hume: Writings on Economics* (Edinburgh: Nelson).
Rowthorn, R. E. (1977), 'Conflict, inflation and money', *Cambridge Journal of Economics*, vol. 1, pp. 215–40.
Rowthorn, R. E. (1980), *Capitalism, Conflict and Inflation* (London: New Left Books).
Sachs, W. M. (1976), 'Toward formal foundations of teleological systems science' in F. E. Emery, *Systems Thinking*, Vol. 1 (London: Penguin), pp. 399–421.
Salter, W. E. G. (1966), *Productivity and Technical Change* (Cambridge: Cambridge University Press).
Samuelson, P. A. (1939), 'Interactions between the acceleration principle and the multiplier', *Review of Economic Statistics*, vol. 21, pp. 75–8.
Samuelson, P. (1947), *Foundations of Economic Analysis* (New York: Atheneum).
Samuelson, P. (1963), 'Problems of methodology: discussion', *American Economic Review, Papers and Proceedings*, vol. 53, pp. 231–6.
Santomero, A. M. and Seater, J. J. (1978), 'The inflation-unemployment trade-off: a critique of the literature', *Journal of Economic Literature*, vol. 16, pp. 499–544.
Sargent, T. J. (1976), 'Testing for neutrality and rationality' in *A Prescription for Monetary Policy* (Federal Research Bank of Minneapolis).
Sargent, T. J. (1984), 'Autoregressions, expectations and advice', *American Economic Review, Papers and Proceedings*, vol. 74, pp. 408–14.
Sargent, T. J. and Wallace, N. (1976), 'Rational expectations and the theory of economic policy', *Journal of Monetary Economics*, vol. 2, pp. 169–84.
Sawyer, M. (1982), *Macro-economics in Question: the Keynesian-monetarist Orthodoxies and the Kaleakian alternative* (Brighton: Wheatsheaf).
Schmookler, J. (1966), *Invention and Economic Growth* (Cambridge, Mass.: Harvard University Press).
Schneider, H. K. (1974), *Economic Man: The Anthropology of Economics* (New York: Free Press).
Schotter, A. (1981), *The Economic Theory of Social Institutions* (New York: Cambridge University Press).

Schumacher, E. F. (1973), *Small is Beautiful: Economics as if People Mattered* (New York: Harper & Row).

Schumacher, E. F. (1977), *A Guide for the Perplexed* (London: Cape).

Schumpeter, J. A. (1934), *The Theory of Economic Development* (Cambridge, Mass.: Harvard University Press).

Schumpeter, J. A. (1950), *Capitalism, Socialism and Democracy*, 3rd edn (New York: Harper).

Schumpeter, J. A. (1974), *History of Economic Analysis* (London: Allen & Unwin).

Scitovsky, T. (1976), *The Joyless Economy* (Oxford: Oxford University Press).

Scott, M. F. G. (1961), 'A tax on price increases?', *Economic Journal*, vol. 71, pp. 351–66.

Seckler, D. (1975), *Thorstein Veblen and the Institutionalists* (London: Macmillan).

Seidman, L. S. (1978), 'Tax-based incomes policy' in A. M. Okun and G. L. Perry (eds), *Curing Chronic Inflation* (Washington: Brookings), pp. 301–62.

Sen, A. (1970), *Collective Choice and Social Welfare* (Edinburgh and San Francisco: Holden-Day).

Sen, A. K. (1977), 'Rational fools: a critique of the behavioural foundations of economic theory', *Philosophy and Public Affairs*, vol. 6, pp. 317–44.

Sen, A. K. (1982), *Choice, Welfare and Measurement* (Oxford: Basil Blackwell).

Shackle, G. L. S. (1972), *Epistemics and Economics* (Cambridge: Cambridge University Press).

Shackle, G. L. S. (1973), 'Keynes and today's establishment in economic theory: a view', *Journal of Economic Literature*, vol. 11, pp. 516–19.

Shackle, G. L. S. (1974), *Keynesian Kaleidics* (Edinburgh: Edinburgh University Press).

Sharpe, J. A. (1974), 'Economic synthesis: a review of the work of Boris Ischboldin', *Review of Social Economy*, vol. 32, no. 2, pp. 85–112.

Sheffrin, S. M. (1983), *Rational Expectations* (Cambridge: Cambridge University Press).

Sidelsky, R. (1977), *The End of the Keynesian Era* (London: Macmillan).

Simon, H. (1955), 'A behavioural theory of rational choice', *Quarterly Journal of Economics*, vol. 69 (February), pp. 99–118.

Simon, H. (1976), 'From substantive to procedural rationality' in S. J. Latsis (ed.), *Method and Appraisal in Economics* (Cambridge: Cambridge University Press), pp. 120–39.

Simon, H. A. (1984), 'On the behavioural and rational foundations of economic dynamics', *Journal of Economic Behaviour and Organisation*, vol. 5, pp. 35–55.

Sims, C. A. (1980), 'Macroeconomics and reality', *Econometrica*,

vol. 48, pp. 1–48.
Sinha, R. P. (1983), *Japan's Options for the 1980s* (London: Croom Helm).
Smith, A. (1749; 1976), *The Theory of Moral Sentiments* (Oxford: Clarendon). Edited by D. D. Raphael and A. L. Macfie (Glasgow edition).
Smith, A. (1776; 1976), *An Inquiry into the Nature and Causes of the Wealth of Nations* (Oxford: Clarendon). Edited by R. H. Campbell and A. S. Skinner (Glasgow edition).
Solow, R. M. (1970), *Growth Theory: An Exposition* (New York: Oxford University Press).
Solow, R. M. (1979), 'Alternative approaches to macroeconomic theory: a partial view', *Canadian Journal of Economics*, vol. 12, pp. 339–54.
Sraffa, P. (1960), *Production of Commodities by Means of Commodities* (Cambridge: Cambridge University Press).
Stein, J. L. (1982), *Monetarist, Keynesian and New Classical Economics* (Oxford: Blackwell).
Strom, S. and Thalborg, B. (1979), *The Theoretical Contributions of Knut Wicksell* (London: Macmillan).
Sumner, M. (1981), 'Investment grants', in D. Currie *et al.* (eds), *Macroeconomic Analysis* (London: Croom Helm), pp. 123–51.
Taylor, J. B. (1980), 'Aggregate dynamics and staggered contracts', *Journal of Political Economy*, vol. 88, pp. 1–23.
Taylor, J. B. (1983), 'Rational expectations and the invisible handshake' in J. Tobin (ed.), *Macroeconomics. Prices and Quantities* (Oxford: Blackwell), pp. 63–84.
Taylor, L. (1983), *Structuralist Macroeconomics* (New York: Basic Books).
Taylor, L. (1984), 'Social choice theory and the world in which we live' a review of A. Sen (1982), *Choice, Welfare and Measurement* (Oxford: Blackwell), *Cambridge Journal of Economics*, vol. 8, pp. 189–96.
Tinbergen, J. (1937), *An Econometric Approach to Business Cycle Problems* (Paris: Mermann).
Tinbergen, J. (1939), *A Method and its Application to Business Cycle Problems* (Paris: Herman and Cie, Editeurs).
Tobin, J. (1958), 'I iquidity preference as behaviour towards risk', *Review of Economic Studies*, vol. 25 (February), pp. 65–86.
Tobin, J. (1959), 'Towards a general Kaldorian theory of distribution', *Review of Economic Studies*, vol. 27, pp. 119–20.
Tobin, J. (1970), 'Money and income: post hoc ergo propter hoc?', *Quarterly Journal of Economics*, vol. 84, pp. 301–17.
Tobin, J. (1980), 'Stabilisation policy ten years after', *Brookings Papers on Economic Activity*, vol. 1, pp. 19–71.
Tobin, J. (ed.) (1983), *Macroeconomics. Prices and Quantities* (Oxford: Blackwell).
Toffler, A. (1981), *The Third Wave* (London: Pan Books).

Trevithick, J. A. (1975), 'Keynes, inflation and money illusions', *Economic Journal*, vol. 85, pp. 101–13.

Trivers, R. L. (1971), 'The evolution of reciprocal altruism', *Quarterly Review of Biology*, vol. 41, pp. 35–57.

Tylecote, A. (1981), *The Causes of the Present Inflation* (London: Macmillan).

Veblen, T. B. (1898; 1900), 'Why economics is not an evolutionary science', *Quarterly Journal of Economics*, vol. 12, pp. 373–426; vol. 14, pp. 240–69.

Vicarelli, F. (1983; 1985), *Keynes's Relevance Today* (London: Macmillan).

Vines, D., Maciejowski, J., and Meade, J. E. (1983), *Stagflation Volume 2: Demand Management* (London: Allen & Unwin).

Wagener, H. J. and Drukker, W. (1985), *The Economic Law of Motion of Modern Society – a Marx-Keynes-Schumpeter Centennial* (London: Cambridge University Press).

Wallich, H. C. and Weintraub, S. (1971), 'A tax-based incomes policy', *Journal of Economic Issues*, vol. 5, pp. 1–17.

Ward, B. (1972), *What's Wrong with Economics?* (London: Macmillan).

Weintraub, E. R. (1979), *Microfoundations: The Compatibility of Microeconomics and Macroeconomics* (Cambridge: Cambridge University Press).

Weisskopf, W. (1979), 'The method is the ideology: from a Newtonian to a Heisenbergian paradigm in economics', *Journal of Economic Issues*, vol. 13, pp. 869–84.

Weitzman, M. L. (1983), 'Some macroeconomic implications of alternative compensation systems', *Economic Journal*, vol. 93, pp. 763–83.

Wicksell, K. (1936; 1965), *Interest and Prices*, translated by R. F. Kahn (New York: Augustus M. Kelly).

Williamson, H. F. (ed.) (1985), *Evolution of International Management Structures* (Newark: University of Delaware Press).

Williamson, O. E. (1975), *Markets and Hierarchies: Analysis and Antitrust Implications* (New York: Free Press).

Williamson, O. E. (1979), 'Transaction-cost economics; the governance of contractual relations', *Journal of Law and Economics*, vol. 22, pp. 233–61.

Williamson, O. E. (1985), *The Economic Institutions of Capitalism* (New York: The Free Press).

Wilson, E. O. (1975), *Sociobiology: The New Synthesis* (Cambridge, Mass.: Harvard University Press).

Wilson Report (1980), 'Committee to review the functioning of financial institutions, *Report*, Cmnd. 7937 (London: HMSO).

Wilson, T. (1980), 'Robertson, money and monetarism', *Journal of Economic Literature*, vol. 28, pp. 1522–38.

Wong, S. (1973), 'The "F-twist" and the methodology of Paul Samuelson', *American Economic Review*, vol. 63 (June), pp. 312–25.

Wong, S. (1978), *The Foundations of Paul Samuelson's Revealed*

Preference Theory (London: Routledge & Kegan Paul).

Worster, D. (1977), *Nature's Economy: A History of Ecological Ideas* (Cambridge: Cambridge University Press).

Younes, Y. (1975), 'On the role of money in the process of exchange and the existence of non-Walrasian equilibrium', *Review of Economic Studies*, vol. 42, pp. 489–501.

Zarnowitz, V. (1985), 'Recent work on business cycles in historical perspective: a review of theories and evidence', *Journal of Economic Literature*, vol. 23, pp. 523–80.

Index